The Political Economies of Media

The Political Economies of Media

The Transformation of the Global Media Industries

Dwayne Winseck

Dal Yong Jin

BLOOMSBURY ACADEMIC

First published in 2011 by

Bloomsbury Academic
an imprint of Bloomsbury Publishing Plc
36 Soho Square, London W1D 3QY, UK
and
175 Fifth Avenue, New York, NY 10010, USA

CIP records for this book are available from the British Library and the Library of Congress

ISBN 978-1-84966-353-3 (hardback)
ISBN 978-1-84966-420-2 (ebook)

This book is produced using paper that is made from wood grown in managed, sustainable
forests. It is natural, renewable and recyclable. The logging and manufacturing processes
conform to the environmental regulations of the country of origin.

Printed and bound in Great Britain by the MPG Books Group, Bodmin, Cornwall

Cover design: Sharon Cluett
Cover image: © Eric Fischer

Contents

Figures

Tables

Contributors

Amelia Arsenault serves as the George Gerbner Fellow at the University of Pennsylvania, Annenberg School. She is also a Visiting Scholar at the Center for Global Communication Studies at the University of Pennsylvania and a Research Associate at the USC Center on Public Diplomacy at the Annenberg School. Her research focuses on communication and power, media and information and communication technology (ICT) ownership, media and ICT for development, and public diplomacy. Her scholarly publications have appeared in the *ANNALS of the American Academy of Political and Social Science; International Sociology, Information, Communication, and Society*; and the *International Journal of Communication*. She earned her PhD in Communication from the University of Southern California, Annenberg School for Communication; an MSc in Global Media and Communication from the London School of Economics and Political Science; and a BA in Film and History from Dartmouth College. Prior to beginning her postgraduate studies, she spent several years living in Harare, Zimbabwe, where she served as the film coordinator for Zimbabwe International Film Festival Trust.

Martín Becerra is a Full Professor at the Communication School, National University of Quilmes and the University of Buenos Aires, Argentina. He is also a member of CONICET (Consejo Nacional de Investigaciones Científicas y Tecnológicas). He obtained his PhD in Communication Sciences, Autonomous University of Barcelona (Spain). He is the author of *Information Society: Project, Convergence, Divergence* (Universidad Nacional de Quilmes, 2007), *Research Journalism in Argentina* (Universidad Nacional de Quilmes, 2007) with Alfredo Alfonso, *Journalists and Tycoons* (Periodistas y Magnates, Prometeo, 2006) with Guillermo Mastrini, and *The Speech Owners* (Los dueños de la Palabra, Prometeo, 2009), also with Guillermo Mastrini.

Susan Christopherson is a J. Thomas Clark Professor in the Department of City and Regional Planning at Cornell University. She is an economic geographer (PhD, University of California, Berkeley) whose research and teaching focus on (1) economic development, (2) urban labor markets, and (3) the media industries. Her international research includes studies in Canada, Mexico, China, Germany, and Jordan as well as multicountry studies. In the past 3 years, she has completed studies on (1) production trends affecting media industries in New York City, (2) advanced manufacturing in New York's Southern Tier, (3) the photonics industry in Rochester, and (4) the role of universities and colleges in revitalizing the upstate New York economy. Her book, *Remaking Regional Economies: Power, Labor, and Firm Strategies in the Knowledge Economy*

(Routledge, 2007) focuses on barriers to regional economic development in the US economy. She has written numerous articles for academic journals on subjects ranging from labor standards to the competition between US and Canadian regions for film and television production. Her work in the field of economic development has concentrated primarily on strategies for revitalizing the economy of upstate New York.

Aeron Davis is a Reader in Political Communications at Goldsmiths College, University of London. He is the Director of MA in Political Communications and an active participant in the Leverhulme-sponsored Spaces of the News project and Centre for the Study of Global Media and Democracy. He has conducted research on communications at the UK Parliament, the London Stock Exchange, among major political parties, and across the trade union movement. He has published some 30 articles and book chapters on these topics and is the author of *Public Relations Democracy* (MUP, 2002), *The Mediation of Power* (Routledge, 2007), and *Political Communication and Social Theory* (Routledge, 2010).

Terry Flew is a Professor of Media and Communications in the Creative Industries Faculty at the Queensland University of Technology, Brisbane, Australia. He has been an author of two books, six research monographs, 26 book chapters, 38 refereed academic journal articles, and an editor of five special issues of academic journals. He is the author of Australia's leading new media textbook, *New Media: An Introduction. New Media* was first published by Oxford University Press in December 2002; the third edition was published in January 2008. His second book, *Understanding Global Media*, was published by Palgrave in March 2007. He has also contributed chapters to leading international edited collections and has published in first-tier scholarly international academic journals such as *International Journal of Cultural Policy, Television and New Media, Communication and Critical/Cultural Studies*, and *International Journal of Cultural Studies*.

Christian Fuchs is the Chair for Media and Communication Studies at Uppsala University, Sweden. He is also a board member of the Unified Theory of Information Group in Vienna, Austria, and editor of the journal *TripleC (cognition, communication, co-operation): Open Access Journal for a Global Sustainable Information Society*. His fields of research are critical theory, information society studies, media and society, ICTs and society, and critical media studies. He has published more than 120 academic works, including the books *Internet and Society: Social Theory in the Information Age* (Routledge, 2008) and *Foundations of Critical Media and Information Studies* (Routledge, 2011). He is the coordinator of the research project "Social Networking Sites in the Surveillance Society" (2010–13) that is funded by the Austrian Science Fund.

Dal Yong Jin is an Assistant Professor at Simon Fraser University, Canada. He finished his PhD degree from the Institute of Communications Research at the University of Illinois at Urbana Champaign in 2004. His major research and teaching interests are media industries, new media and convergence, globalization and media, transnational cultural studies, telecommunications policy, and the political economy of media and culture. He is the author of two forthcoming books entitled *Hands On/Hands Off: The Korean State and the Market Liberalization of the Communication Industry* and *Online Game Empire*. His work has been published in several scholarly journals, including *Media, Culture and Society; Games and Culture; Telecommunications Policy; Television and New Media; Information Communication and Society*; and *Javnost—The Public*.

Guillermo Mastrini is a Full Professor at the Communication School, University of Buenos Aires, Argentina. He is the past president of the Argentine Federation of Social Communication Schools. He is in charge of the courses "Communication Planning and Policies" and "Information Economy" at the University of Buenos Aires. His book-length publications include *Globalization and Monopolies in Latin America's Media* (*Globalización y monopolios en la comunicación en América Latina*, Biblos, 1999), *Much Ado About Laws: Economy and Politics of Communication in Argentina* (*Mucho ruido, pocas leyes. Economía y políticas de comunicación en la Argentina*, La Crujía, 2005), and *Journalists and Tycoons* (*Periodistas y Magnates*, Prometeo, 2006).

Bernand Miège is a Professor Emeritus of Communication Studies at the University Stendhal of Grenoble (France), where he teaches communication theory, the industrialization of culture and information, and the development of ICTs and new media. He has written 16 books, including (in English) *The Capitalization of Cultural Production* (International General, New York, 1989). Several of these publications have been translated into various languages.

Marc-André Pigeon is Director, Financial Sector Policy, Credit Union Central of Canada. He is also a sessional lecturer at Carleton University, Ottawa, Canada. He recently completed his doctoral dissertation on media's role in the evolution of fiscal and monetary policy in Canada. Prior to joining the Task Force, Marc-André worked as lead researcher for the Standing Senate Committee on Banking, Trade and Commerce and the House of Commons Standing Committee on Finance. He also worked as a researcher at the Levy Economics Institute in New York, a think tank specializing in finance-related issues as well as a financial journalist at Bloomberg Business News in Toronto.

Peter A. Thompson is a Senior Lecturer in the School of English, Film, Theatre and Media Studies, University of Wellington, Victoria, New Zealand. He has published extensively on the NZ public broadcasting reforms since 1999, and has conducted research into public broadcasting funding mechanisms in the Organisation for Economic Co-Operation and Development (for the Ministry for Culture and Heritage) and approaches to measuring broadcasting quality (for the NZ Broadcasting Commission). He also chaired the working party that reviewed public submissions on the redrafted TVNZ Charter and helped revise the Charter document. Peter's other main area of research concerns communication processes in financial markets.

Elizabeth Van Couvering is a Lecturer of Media and Communications at Leicester University. A UK internet pioneer, prior to beginning her academic studies, Dr Van Couvering worked at Cyberia, United Kingdom's first cybercafe, in 1994; at one of its first domestic Internet Service Providers, Easynet; at one of the first UK web agencies, Webmedia; and afterward at a range of internet marketing companies in the United Kingdom, including Webmedia, Excite, Jupiter Research, and Organic Online. This career gave her a front-row view of the internet boom and bust of the late 1990s and its aftermath. During her studies, she continued to consult on online website and traffic measurement methodologies with clients such as Nielsen Online and the IAB Europe. In addition to her PhD from the London School of Economics and Political Science, Dr Van Couvering holds an MBA from the Open University and a BA in Cultural Anthropology from Bryn Mawr College.

Dwayne Winseck is a Professor at the School of Journalism and Communication, with a cross-appointment to the Institute of Political Economy, Carleton University, Ottawa, Canada. He obtained his PhD from the University of Oregon in 1993 and has lived and taught in Britain, the People's Republic of China, the Turkish Republic of Northern Cyprus as well as the United States. His research examines the political economies of communication, media history, new media, surveillance and national security, and theories of democracy and globalization. He has published widely in leading scholarly journals and has recently become a regular contributor to the online edition of *The Globe and Mail*, Canada's leading daily newspaper. His latest book (coauthored with Robert M. Pike), *Communication and Empire: Media, Markets and Globalization, 1860–1930* (Duke University, 2007), won the Canadian Communication Association's G.G. Robinson Award for book of the year in 2008.

Preface

Media and information and communication technologies (ICTs) industries have been some of the most dynamic and fast-growing sectors of economies, within countries and globally, during the past two decades. Conversely, they have also borne the brunt of significant new trends, notably the financialization of the global economy, and the fallout of these unstable processes, primarily in the form of the repeated downturns in the global economy since the late 1990s. These crosscutting trends, at least initially, were driven by the neoliberal form of globalization and a steep rise of capital investment in all sectors of the media and ICT industries. The rapid development of digital technologies, including the internet, mobile, and social networking sites (SNSs), have also propelled the rapid growth of these industries, while government policies have promoted the convergence of new and old media through the, by and large, permissive stance they have taken toward mergers and acquisitions (M&As). The upshot has been, at least until the economic crisis since 2007/8, the rapid development of the media and ICTs industries and a shift from the framework of national industrial capitalism to global information capitalism.

The rise of enormous media conglomerates during the latter 1990s also signified the trajectory of development, although, as this volume emphasizes, this does not mean that we should see such entities as unshakeable edifices. Indeed, several bastions of the old order—AT&T, Time Warner, Bertelsmann, ITV, Vivendi, and Canwest, to name a few—are being restructured and, in some cases, dismantled. Some media firms have crashed altogether, or stand on the precipice of financial ruin, largely due to the crushing weight of debt incurred during the waves of M&As from the mid-1990s to, roughly, 2007. As a result, a chorus of voices now claims that the "media are in crisis." In contrast, several SNSs, search engines, and online digital media services (Facebook, Google, Apple, etc.) are flourishing, although even these entities have not been immune to the economic slowdown that has engulfed many areas of the world since 2008. The cumulative outcome of these processes—that is, increased intensity of capital investment, consolidation, permissive government policies, unstable models of corporate organization, economic instability, digitization, the rapid pace of developments in technology and media use, and so on—mean that all aspects of the "network media" industries now exist in a heightened state of flux. Understanding these conditions is no easy task, but such is the aim of this collection of original and thought-provoking chapters.

All of the contributors to this volume are well aware that political economies of the media as a form of critical inquiry continue to evolve in relation to developments in their objects of analysis—media institutions, technologies, markets, and society—and to changes in scholarship. They are, furthermore, sensitive to the fact that with so much changing all around us we must be more open than ever to theoretical revision. The collection does not claim that political economies of the media should be placed at the top of the intellectual pecking order in communication and media studies at the expense of other approaches. However, we do insist that they should be absolutely central to the field. The volume is also underpinned by the conviction that the media industries must be taken as serious objects of analysis in their own right.

The volume's 12 chapters are organized into four sections. The introductory essay begins by introducing the concept of the "network media industries," a composite of the 10 largest media industries ranked according to worldwide revenues: television, internet access, newspapers, books, film, magazines, music, radio, internet advertising, and video games. The concept helps to establish the parameters of this volume, and the detailed empirical portrait of these industries that ensues serves as a common referent point for the chapters that follow. The introductory essay also offers a critical "theoretical mapping" of four influential schools of thought or political economies of the media: neoclassical economics, radical media political economy, Schumpeterian institutional political economy, and the cultural industries school.

To be sure, neither all of the contributors to this volume nor communication and media studies as a whole can be so neatly labeled. However, these schools, and their various offshoots, do offer a reasonably comprehensive view of the field and function as useful foils against which other schools can be understood. Reviewing these different schools also helps to frame several important questions that are central to this volume and to the field of communication and media studies as a whole:

- Do digital media technologies, especially the internet, pose fundamental threats to traditional media players or create more opportunities for the latter to expand into new markets?

- Are media markets becoming more or less concentrated over time, and how do we know one way or another?

- Are the traditional media—journalism, press, and music industries especially—"in crisis"?

- Are the media industries truly global, mainly national, or something else entirely?

- Does the emerging network media environment constitute a vastly enlarged space of commodification or a zone of "autonomous mass self-expression" that has the potential to improve the conditions of people's lives and further democratize culture, especially when measured against the standards set by the "industrial media" since the mid-nineteenth century?

The chapters that follow the introductory essay are organized into three parts. Part Two includes four chapters that plumb the key theoretical schools in political economies of the media deeper than the initial pass offered in the Introduction, while also engaging with important debates in the field (Miège, Flew, Mastrini and Becerra, Arsenault). In the first chapter of this section, Bernand Miège outlines some of the principal elements of the cultural industries school and sets out the major elements that define the terrain of the network media and cultural industries in the twenty-first century. In Chapter 2, Guillermo Mastrini and Martín Becerra then address the main theoretical approaches in relationship to protracted questions of media ownership and concentration in South America. In Chapter 3, Terry Flew offers a valuable appraisal of the monopoly capital school, before covering some of the major aspects of neoclassical economics, economic geography, and industrial organization theory en route to applying creative industries theory to the global media. Lastly, in Chapter 4, Amelia Arsenault rounds out the chapters in Part Two by drawing out some of the ties that link the ideas of Austrian institutional political economist Joseph Schumpeter to an emergent approach that we can label the network political economy approach, which is closely associated with the work of, among many others, Manuel Castells and Yochai Benkler. She then uses this approach to map the global networks of the communication, information, and media business.

The five chapters in Part Three examine several key processes and trends that now define the digital, networked media: (1) the processes of consolidation and fragmentation in the US-based television and film industries and their impact on media and cultural workers (Susan Christopherson); (2) persistent claims that the "traditional media" are being decimated by the relentless onslaught of the internet, declining advertising revenues, and the global financial crisis (2007–) (Dwayne Winseck); (3) the dismantling of some of the major media conglomerates that were assembled in the late 1990s but have since fallen into disarray (e.g. AOL–Time Warner, Vivendi–Universal) (Dal Yong Jin); as well as (4) the historical evolution of the internet, several common economic characteristics of capitalist media development that appear to apply to "old" and "new" media alike as well as the significant new commodities that characterize "Web 2.0" social media (Elizabeth Van Couvering, Christian Fuchs).

The five chapters in this section engage with specific elements or sectors of the network media industries, while identifying the theoretical and methodological premises at the heart of each author's approach. In Chapter 5, Susan Christopherson, for instance, revisits debates over the nature of work in the television and film industries that have been given new life by the creative industries approach. However, she is skeptical of how that school continues to downplay the industrial restructuring and greater concentration that have occurred in some areas of the television and film industries since the 1990s, a stance informed by economic geography, interviews with people in these industries, and years of fieldwork. Chapter 6 by Dwayne Winseck critically assesses the "media in crisis" claims as they relate to Canada. In Chapter 7, Dal Yong Jin examines the dismantling and restructuring of major media conglomerates during the first decade of the twenty-first century, a process that he calls "de-convergence." In Chapter 8, Elizabeth Van Couvering offers a valuable historical overview of the internet and the rise of a new commodity— "traffic"—at the heart of what she calls navigational media. Christian Fuchs, in Chapter 9, rounds out the section by combining aspects of a Marxian analysis with ideas from Herbert Marcuse, C.B. MacPherson as well as Carole Pateman to build a radical critique of social media or Web 2.0. The key feature of the argument that he develops is that, in their basic economic form (corporate ownership, advertising funding, private ownership of content), such media fit snugly within the framework of capitalist media development and thus are unlikely to supersede the stunted forms of "elite" or "limited" democracy that Joseph Schumpeter and others have always believed are the most suitable for complex capitalist societies.

Three chapters in Part Four complete the volume. They do so by examining the formation and circulation of economic and policy "conventions" and discourses. In Chapter 10, Peter A. Thompson examines the uncertain future of public service media in a digital age using two case studies of the BBC and TVNZ (New Zealand). His case studies show how the BBC and TVNZ are being challenged and circumscribed in their digital media activities by a combination of commercial media interests, embedded institutional policy trajectories, and "fiscally constrained" Treasuries that often work at cross-purposes with other state institutions involved in media and cultural policy.

In Chapter 11, Aeron Davis charts the parallel rise of specialized financial and business news outlets and the development of financialization within Anglo-Saxon-style, free-market economies. The former cannot simply be seen as the handmaidens of the latter, but as his interviews with financial market players, policy-makers, and journalists over several years show, they function as crucial circuits in the formation of "elite consensus" around certain economic conventions that anchor the worldviews of financial traders, economists, central bankers, and other key policy-makers. In Chapter 12, Marc-André Pigeon takes a similar tact, but with a focus on Canada and drawing heavily on critical discourse analysis, to highlight how the highly technical language of fiscal policy *and* financial markets are fused together into certain "economic conventions" through policy discourses and media narratives about the economy. Davis and Pigeon both observe that these "conventions" simultaneously serve to delineate the range of public discourse about the economy while helping to bind economic reality to the actions of economic players through a common language, perceptions, and beliefs. In turn, these discourses are integral to attempts to "rationally manage" modern capitalist economies, but as contemporary events illustrate so vividly, in this they have singularly failed, given the recurring bouts of instability that continue to buffet our world, with costs and consequences that have yet to be fully comprehended.

Ultimately, this collection aims to open up a discussion about political economies of media, both in terms of the status of such approaches as forms of inquiry and "objects of analysis." For too long, the treatment of such approaches in the singular has served to obscure the diversity within these schools of thought and as an easy target for critics. The contributors to this collection aim to inspire and equip readers to do their own critical analyses of the media industries, and their place in the world, with a sense of the importance and joy of it all.

Dwayne Winseck

February 24, 2011
Dal Yong Jin

Acknowledgments

Throughout this project, I have been fortunate enough to share ideas with many colleagues, especially those who I meet each year at the International Association of Media and Communication Researcher (IAMCR): Wayne Hope, Peter Golding, Graham Murdock, Helena Sousa, among others. Indeed, it was at an IAMCR conference in Paris in 2006 that I first talked about putting together this collection. Since then, Emily Salz at Bloomsbury, the publisher Frances Pinter, and their colleagues have helped bring this idea to fruition. Three anonymous reviewers assessed the project both in its initial proposal stage and once it was finished. Their commentary helped immensely in the development of a well-crafted volume that I hope will leave an impact on how one thinks about the political economies of media.

This book also marks the long-term influence of a number of other people. Janet Wasko especially has been a wonderful inspiration and friend since my days at the University of Oregon in the 1990s. Peter Thompson has been a good friend and fantastic intellectual sparring partner since the mid-1990s. Likewise, Oliver Boyd-Barrett has always given me his time and shared ideas generously with me. I am fortunate as well to have personable colleagues at the School of Journalism and Communication, Carleton University: Ira Wagman, Chris Russill, Sheryl Hamilton, Michael Dorland, Miranda Brady, Joshua Greenberg, Melissa Aroncyzk, Eileen Saunders, and Nancy Peden.

Robert M. Pike continues to be a great friend and a wise advisor. In the past two years, I was also fortunate enough to be invited to participate in an outstanding research project. The International Media Concentration Research Project is spearheaded by Eli Noam, Professor of Finance and Economics at Columbia University in New York, and I would like to thank him for involving me in such an ambitious project and for expanding my horizons.

This volume has also been beset by the loss of University of Pennsylvania Law School Professor C. Edwin Baker, who passed away on December 8, 2009. Ed had intended to pen a chapter for this book and had sent along some sketches as to what it might look like. Regrettably, he was not able to complete the chapter, and we are the lesser for it. This is doubly tragic because Ed's publication of *Media Concentration and Democracy: Why Ownership Matters* (Cambridge University, 2007) had transformed him into a key participant in Anglo-European debates about the impact of the internet on journalism and the concentration of media ownership and markets after many years of toiling diligently on such themes in relative obscurity.

Finally, two of the most important people in the world to me are my daughter, Forest, and my partner, Kristina. Forest has continuously inspired me and made it easy to know what it means to love your children. She and her circle of friends have taught me that the kids are, for the most part, alright. I am doubly fortunate to have married a wonderful, smart, quirky, warm, and (com-)passionate woman, Kristina Ropke. I am lucky to have her at my side as my champion and my muse.

Dwayne Winseck

I would like to acknowledge the School of Communication at Simon Fraser University and the School of Humanities and Social Sciences at KAIST for offering me extremely supportive intellectual environments between Fall 2009 and Spring 2011. I have been fortunate to work in both institutions during the period. My greatest debt is to my family, wife Kyung Won Na and two daughters, Yu Sun and Yu Young, for all their support.

Dal Yong Jin

PART ONE

Introductory Essay

The Political Economies of Media and the Transformation of the Global Media Industries

Dwayne Winseck

Carleton University

Setting the scene: baseline considerations

In this introductory chapter, I want to set the scene for this book and to paint a broad portrait of a certain view of communication and media studies, and the role of different political economies of the media in the field. Communication and media studies often labor under the illusion that political economy comes in one flavor, but here I suggest that we can identify at least four perspectives that have considerable currency in the field. They are (1) conservative and liberal neoclassical economics; (2) radical media political economy, with two main versions, the monopoly capital and digital capitalism schools; (3) Schumpeterian institutional political economy and two recent offshoots, the creative industries and network political economy schools; and lastly (4) the cultural industries school. Of course, neither all of this volume's authors nor communication and media studies as a field can be placed so neatly in these categories, but other approaches can be thought of as derivatives of them (e.g. cultural economy, neo-Marxian political economy, critical cultural political economy, and economic geography).

To begin, we need to clearly specify our "object of analysis." To that end, I focus on the "network media industries," a composite of the 10 largest media and internet industries, ranked by total worldwide revenues: television, internet access, newspapers, books, films, magazines, music, radio, internet advertising, and video games. These industries do not exist all on their own but are surrounded by the "social ecology of information" and flanked, on one side, by the telecoms industries and, on the other, by the information, communication, and technology (ICT) sector. I use the concept of the network media industries in a way that follows Yochai Benkler (2006). The construct refers to the core and emergent public communications media that migrate around various distribution networks and media platforms and devices. It is not convergence, per se, but a network of media tied together through strategies, capital investment, ownership, technologies, uses, alliances, rights regimes, and so on. Methodologically and empirically, the concept is an important tool because it establishes what is included and excluded from analysis.

The network media concept also reflects judgments about how far digitally mediated communication has been subsumed by the processes of commercialization and capital accumulation (McChesney 2008; Mosco 2009a; Schiller 1999a). I follow the cultural industries' claim that understanding the capitalization of the communication and media industries is essential but that the process itself is never complete (Miège 1989). In other words, digital network media are immersed within the market, but they also enable and depend upon forms of expression that are not market driven. These ideas line up well with Benkler's concept of the "social production of information" and what others call "gift culture," the "digital commons," and "mass self-expression" (Andrejevic 2007; Castells 2009)—an amalgamation of which I call the "social *ecology* of information" (see below). These ideas also fit well with the cultural industries school's emphasis on how the uncertainty and habits of people's lives and patterns of media use erect strong barriers to the complete commodification of media and culture.

Political economies of media take it as axiomatic that the media must be studied in relation to their place within the broader economic and social context. This context is undeniably one where capitalist economies have expanded greatly over the past quarter of a century, albeit at a relatively slow pace in most of the Euro-American "advanced capitalist economies" since the post-1973 "long downturn." After expanding across the planet, however, the global economy has staggered badly from one crisis after another in recent years, starting with the Asian Financial Crisis of 1997, followed by the collapse of the dot-com bubble (late 2000–3), and the global financial crisis that erupted in 2007–8. The impact of these events on all aspects of the network media has been substantial in the Euro-American countries. Elsewhere, however, almost all media, from newspapers to the internet, are growing at a fast clip, as is the case in, for example, Brazil, China, India, Indonesia, Russia, and Turkey (Organisation for Economic Co-operation and Development (OECD) 2010: 7; PriceWaterhouseCoopers (PWC) 2010: 29).

The fact that the global financial crisis (2008) fell so fast on the heels of the collapse of the telecoms–media–technology (TMT), or dot-com bubble, should certainly disabuse us of the notion that improved communications will create "perfect information" and therefore "perfect market," the mainstream economists holy grail. During the dot-com bubble years (1996–2000), the media, telecoms, and internet industries served as objects of massive financial investment and speculation (Brenner 2002; "The Great Telecom Crash" 2002). Some scholars also argue that the fast paced growth of business media, such as *Business Week*, CNBC, and *The Economist*, especially in India and China, have essentially served as the "handmaidens" of Wall Street and "the City" (London) (Shiller 2001; Chakravarty and Schiller 2010). Things are likely more complicated than that, however, as the chapters by Aeron Davis and

Marc-André Pigeon in this book explain, but can essentially be boiled down to the idea that elite business-oriented newspapers (e.g. *Financial Times, The Wall Street Journal, The Economist*), television channels (CNNfn, CNBC), and specialized news services (e.g. Bloomberg, Dow Jones, Thomson Reuters) help to circulate and crystallize certain key economic "conventions" among financial market traders, central bankers, policymakers, politicians, and journalists. The public is well aware of the financial world and its impact on people's lives, but most people are neither all that interested in nor the primary subjects of these "convention-making conversations."

Many observers argue that some segments of the media, journalism and music especially, that were already staggering from the steady rise of the internet and falling advertising revenues have been tipped headlong into the abyss by the global financial crisis of 2007–8. The financial crisis, however, has also spurred many governments to invest substantial sums of stimulus money into next generation networks (NGNs), basically 100 Mbps fiber-to-the-home networks. In Australia, Korea, France, the United Kingdom, the United States, and at least a dozen other countries, more than US$71 billion has been pledged to develop universally accessible fiber and/or wireless-based NGNs over the next few years. The most ambitious of these projects, in Australia, will bring 100 Mbps fiber networks to over 90 percent of homes in the next 5 years through a new government-created company, the National Broadband Network Company (NBN Co.). In Sweden and Holland, municipal governments and cooperatives are doing the same thing (Benkler, Faris, Gasser, Miyakawa, and Schultze 2010: 162–4; Middleton and Givens 2010). These are the digital public works projects of the twenty-first century. Some wonder if they mark the renationalization of telecoms after 30 years of privatization and neoliberalism (IDATE 2009: 16).

In reference to the United States, Robert McChesney and John Nichols (2010) argue that the crisis now facing journalism will only be turned around if new forms of journalism and public media, including universal, affordable, and open broadband internet services, are well-financed by these stimulus projects. The range of such initiatives suggests that we live in unconventional times, and in such times the boundaries of what is possible expand. Of the nonconventional media options now on offer, Benkler (2010), Benkler *et al.* 2010), McChesney and Nichols (2010: 96–7), and Eli Noam (2009: 15–16) identify the following "ideal types": public service media (e.g. BBC), employee or co-op ownership, effective nonprofit media (Wikipedia), municipal broadband networks, community media, small commercial media (Talking Points Memo, Huffington Post, GlobalPost), and volunteer partisan media (Indymedia). This is truly an impressive display of structural diversity. It is significant and should not be underplayed. But is it revolutionary? As we will see, that depends on whether you ask followers of Joseph Schumpeter or Karl Marx.

Perhaps, however, this is just another wave of "creative destruction" that happens every so often to wipe away the old, and usher in the new, as Joseph Schumpeter (1943/1996: 83) put it in his classic, *Capitalism, Socialism and Democracy*. This, I believe, would not adequately capture the essence of the situation either. There is scant evidence to support the view that traditional media are going the way of the dinosaur, although many of the media conglomerates cobbled together near the end of the twentieth century have since been restructured, dismantled, or fallen into financial disarray, as Chapters 6 and 7 in this book show. For the most part, however, the traditional media are not in crisis. Among the top 10 internet companies worldwide, 3 are well-known media conglomerates, and another is a nonprofit entity: Google, Microsoft, Yahoo!, Facebook, Wikipedia, AOL, Ask.com, CBS, Apple, News Corporation (News Corp.)—ranked by monthly users (Comscore 2010a). Internet-centric firms have obviously carved out an influential role for themselves, and this is even more apparent among second-tier firms, all of which are internet centric, with five Chinese firms figuring prominently among them: Glam Media (14th), Tencent (16th), Baidu (17th), NetShelter Technology (19th), and Alibaba (20th) (Comscore 2010a: s.03). Nonetheless, when we turn our gaze to the traditional media, the "big 10 global media conglomerates" are not, give or take a few additions and deletions, all that different from the end of the 1990s: Disney, Comcast, News Corp., Viacom–CBS, Time Warner, Bertelsmann, Sony, NBC-Universal, Thomson Reuters, and Pearson, ranked in that order on the basis of revenues (2009).

Of course, such rank-ordered lists assume that paying attention to the top 10 global media companies and top 10 to 20 internet companies is a wise thing to do. I believe that it is. Figure I.1 gives a sense of the scale of the telecoms, ICT, and network media sectors and the social ecology of information, respectively, and a portrait of how all the pieces fit together. Table I.1 introduces the biggest 10 players in the traditional media, internet, telecoms, and ICT sectors, respectively. Table I.2 then shows the revenues for the "network media industries" (the 10 largest media and internet sectors) from 1998 to 2010. The goal in each case is to establish some common empirical referent points for the discussion that follows. Each of the authors in the book also presents key elements of their own approach, essentially offering a guide on how to do political economy of media research. Creating a set of common empirical reference points also helps guard against what Terry Flew (2007) calls the "fallacy of big numbers," that is, big numbers that come with no proper sense of scale. He implies that this is primarily a problem of critical media political economy, but it is far wider than that, as we will see.

Gathering information on the media industries, even in countries that are relatively open by global standards, is not easy (Noam 2009). In Canada, for instance, as my experience with the International Media Concentration Research Project (IMCRP)[1] shows, and in the United States, as other researchers

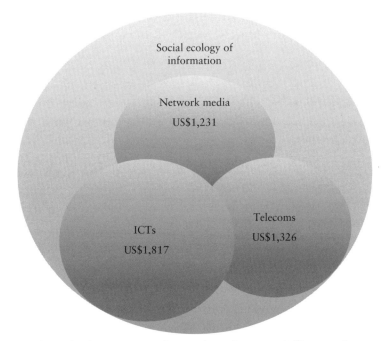

Figure I.1 The multiple economies of network media, 2009 (billions, US$)
Sources: PWC (2010: 36), IDATE (2009: 24), Canadian Radio-television and Telecommunications
Commission (CRTC) (2010), OECD (2007b: 163).

state, regulated companies' claims that the data they provide to policy-makers
are "trade secrets" are often accepted and thus excluded from the public record.
As a result, crucial data that are needed to properly examine the media
industries are off-limits (Frieden 2008). Matters are worse in (ex-)authoritarian
countries, as Guillermo Mastrini and Martín Becerra note in their study of the
media and telecoms industries in South America in this book, because the topic
has been a forbidden area of public discussion and academic research until
relatively recently. Consequently, there is no systematic data collection on the
subject, and much baseline research needs to be done.

Public corporate documents, such as Annual Reports, Financial Statements,
and so forth, are essential reading for political economists. The 2009 Annual
Report of Baidu—the world's 17th largest internet company,[2] and China's
equivalent to Google—for example, offers important insights into its ownership,
business models, and so on. It also offers an exquisitely detailed discussion of
the difficulties of operating one of the world's largest internet firms in a country
where that is strictly supervised by an all-powerful Ministry of Industry and
Information Technology (Baidu Inc. 2010: 21–8). Consultants' reports can also
be excellent sources of information but are often inconsistent over time, tied too
closely to clients' needs, and prohibitively expensive. The *Global Entertainment*

Table I.1 The "big 10" in the media, internet, ICT, and telecoms industries (2009) (billions, US$)

Firm	Ownership	Base	Capitalization	Revenue	International revenue US$ (%)
"Big 10 global media companies" by capitalization and revenue					
Disney	Diversified	United States	49.5	36.1	24
Comcast	Roberts	United States	57.1	35.8	0
News Corp.	Murdoch and others	United States/Australia	26.5	28.0	45
Viacom–CBS	Redstone	United States	27.6	27.2	28
Time Warner	Diversified	United States	33.7	25.8	30
Sony	Diversified	Japan	20.2	21.7	27
Bertelsmann	Bertelsmann/Mohn	Germany	Private	21.4	65
NBC Universal	Diversified/GE	United States	161.3	15.4	25
Thomson Reuters	Thomson Family	Canada/United Kingdom	26.7	13.0	94
Pearson	Diversified	United Kingdom	11.4	8.8	87
"Big 10 internet companies" by capitalization and revenue					
Google	Brin/Page/Schmidt	United States	197.0	23.7	43
Yahoo!	Yang	United States	23.6	6.5	27
Apple Inc.	Steve Jobs	United States	164.1	4.0	55
AOL	Diversified	United States	2.5	3.3	12
Microsoft	Gates/Ballmer	United States	211.0	3.1	43
News Corp.	Murdoch and others	United States/Australia	26.5	2.4	45
IAC (Ask)	Diller/Liberty Media (Malone)	United States	2.5	1.4	15
CBS	Redstone	United States	27.6	0.6	14
Facebook*	Zuckerberg	United States	15.0**	0.15	NA
Wikipedia	Jimmy Wales Volunteer Foundation	?		Patron	?

"Big 10 telecoms companies" by capitalization and revenue

AT&T	Diversified	United States	165.4	123.0	0
Verizon	Diversified	United States	94.0	107.8	0
NTT	Diversified	Japan	49.7	104.1	0
Deutsche Tel	Diversified	Germany	64.3	90.1	56
Telefonica	Diversified	Spain	127.5	79.1	65
Vodafone	Diversified	United Kingdom	92.1	70.5	87
France Tel	France	France government (27%)	66.1	64.1	56
Tel. Italia	Diversified	Italy	30.0	37.9	20
BT	Diversified	United Kingdom	8.7	36.8	22
Sprint Nextel	Diversified	United States	10.9	32.3	0

"Big 10 ICT companies" by capitalization and revenue

Nokia	Diversified	Finland	47.4	57.1	57
Microsoft	Gates/Ballmer	United States	211.7	43.5	43
Apple	Steve Jobs	United States	164.1	32.5	55
Cisco	John Chambers	United States	130.4	36.1	46
Oracle	Larry Ellison	United States	98.0	23.2	56
SAP	Diversified	Germany	58.0	14.9	80
Ericsson	Diversified	Sweden	29.4	27.2	98
Sony	Diversified	Japan	20.2	57.0	75
Motorola	Diversified	United States	17.9	22.0	46
Alcatel-Luc.	Diversified	France	7.7	21.1	91

Note: Revenues for cross-listed firms were allocated by sector. ICT list compiled to include firms most relevant to media and internet advertising. *Facebook is a private firm; **estimate based on Microsoft investment of US$240 million for 1.6 percent share.

Sources: Compiled using OECD (2008, 2009), Comscore (2010a), and Corporate *Annual Reports* and Bloomberg (2010), for each company.

Table I.2 The "big 10 network media, entertainment, and internet industries," 1998–2010 (global revenues, millions, US$)

	1998	2000	2004	2008	2009	2010 (estimate)	% change
Television	202,893	243,322	279,971	342,509	334,461	351,300	+73
Internet access	15,556	35,483	110,370	210,788	228,060	247,453	+1,490
Newspapers	142,794	156,641	174,395	174,723	154,887	149,317	+4.6
Books	94,442	97,340	103,407	109,485	108,201	108,516	+15
Film	46,484	52,803	82,834	82,619	85,137	87,385	+88
Magazines	69,814	76,972	75,817	79,931	71,475	69,548	−0.4
Music	51,201	54,000	62,955	66,802	68,436	71,410	+40
Radio	38,289	45,658	67,696	75,243	67,269	68,298	+93
Internet advertising	953	6,533	17,922	58,068	60,568	66,176	+6,844
Video games	15,968	17,738	27,807	51,390	52,507	58,168	+264
Total	678,394	786,490	1,003,174	1,251,558	1,231,001	1,277,571	+88

Note: I have taken the internet out of the telecoms sector and put it into the "network media." Revenue for ICTs was extrapolated from figures for 2008 based on 4.5 percent per annum growth rate identified by IDATE (2009).

Sources: PWC (2003, 2009), PWC (2010: 33) for all segments, and IDATE (2009).

and Media Outlook by PWC that I use heavily in this introduction, for example, is US$1,500 per edition for a single user or US$6,000 for a library license. Online information sources such as Alexa.com, Comscore, Experien Hitwise, and Internet Stats World also offer timely data on internet use, some of which are free.

All approaches to the political economy of media take it as axiomatic that the media industries—the structure of the markets they operate in, their patterns of ownership, the strategies of key players, trajectory of development, and so on—are important objects of analysis. As Figure I.1 shows, ICTs are the biggest of the three sectors, with revenues of US$1,817 billion in 2009 versus US$1,326 billion for telecoms (excluding internet access)[3] and US$1,231 billion for all 10 segments of the network media industries *combined*. In total, the network media industries, telecoms, and ICTs had worldwide revenues of US$4,374 billion, or about 6.5 percent of global GDP, in 2009 (IDATE 2009: 24). The social ecology of information is, by definition, "priceless" and is valued by different criteria (see below). Table I.1 identifies some basic descriptive characteristics of the "big 10" firms in each of the network media, telecoms, internet, and ICT industries: that is, capitalization, ownership, total revenues, global receipts, and national base. One other point that can be quickly sketched here is the rapid growth of the internet from about 200 million users worldwide in 1998 to 2 billion in 2010. The tectonic shift in the center of gravity of internet use to Asia, notably China, from the United States and Europe over this period also stands out (International Telecommunications Union (ITU) 2010: 201; see Figure I.5).

Two other features in Table I.2 are important for the discussion that follows. First, the network media industries nearly doubled in size between 1998 and 2010. The steady upward trajectory was interrupted in 2009 in the wake of the global financial crisis, but this was followed by the expectation that total revenues will clamber back to new heights in 2010 (PWC 2010; IDATE 2009). Otherwise, *every* segment of the media industries has grown, except for newspapers and magazines, which seem to have peaked in 2004, stayed steady afterward until 2008, before falling in the 2 years since. This trend strongly challenges claims that the traditional media are "in crisis." Matters are not as clear-cut with respect to newspapers, however, with some arguing that the industry is in demise (McChesney and Nichols 2010; Goldstein 2009; Scherer 2010), while others claim that the fate of the newspaper business has always closely tracked the ups and downs of the economy, thus suggesting that the current state of the press reflects long-term trends rather than a crisis, per se (Garnham 1990; Picard 2009; OECD 2010: 6). I return to a detailed examination of these questions below.

The last word for now on Tables I.1 and I.2 and Figure I.1 relates to the concept of the "social ecology of information," an idea that I appropriate mainly from Yochai Benkler's (2006) account of the expanding diversity of media and informational forms that are created for reasons other than money and profit. The "social ecology of information" has no direct, measurable economic value but instead should be seen as sitting in the background of the network media, ICTs, and telecoms domains as well as straddling both the market and nonmarket areas of life.

The "social ecology of information" concept is novel, but it is not new because all societies possess deep "stocks of knowledge" (Melody 1987; Polanyi 1944/1957). These "stocks of knowledge" are typically taken for granted but appear to be gaining greater visibility by being dis-embedded from their ordinary contexts and re-embedded in the flows of communication enabled by digital technologies.[4] The fact that the internet pushes the ability to create and share information, by design, outward to the edges of the network and into the hands of more speakers extends and deepens such processes. This, of course, allows the market to penetrate into more and more domains of life, as many critical political economists argue (Mosco 2009a; Schiller 1999a), but it has also breathed new life into the social ecology of information as well (Benkler 2006; Lessig 1999).

The online encyclopedia, Wikipedia, is the poster child for these ideas, given that it relies on volunteer contributors, does not accept advertising, and is based on an alternative model of property, that is, the GNU Free Documentation License. Wikipedia is also the fifth most visited website in the world, another indication that the social production of information is not peripheral to either the internet or to digital media economies but is central to them (see Table I.2). The social ecology of information concept also reflects the fact that, historically, many foundational features of the internet—the WWW, Mozilla, Netscape, Yahoo!, Lycos, Google, TCP/IP, Linux, the hyperlink structure, and so forth—emerged from the public domain or "digital commons" (Lessig 2004).

The social ecology of information also retrieves an idea advanced by Aristotle more than two millennia ago, who observed that people devote some of their labor to meeting their own needs (i.e. *self-production*), the needs of others with whom they share a social bond (i.e. *the community*), and commerce (i.e. *the market*) (Swedberg 2005). These "multiple economies" are present in all societies and represent one more reason for using the plural "economies" in the title of this book. Lastly, the social ecology of information concept highlights another feature of *all* theories of media political economy: the understanding that information and communication are "strange commodities" or, in the language of neoclassical economics, public goods. As communication scholars grasp, communication uses peculiar symbolic expressions (language, symbols, images, gestures, thoughts) that do not conform to conventional definitions of products. Communication, and the media of communication, provides the "stuff" from which we build our sense of self-identity, our perceptions of the world, and social ties with others; it is a source of pleasure and conviviality and the basis upon which societies are organized. In other words, both the social ecology of information and a broad view of our domain offer a more expansive view of communication than the conventional concept of "public goods" in neoclassical economics. As Robert Babe (1995) provocatively concludes, taking all of these ideas into account would lead to a fundamental transformation of economics into the political economy of communication.

Big sweeping trends, critical details, and political economies of the media

Political economies of the media evolve in relation to developments in their objects of analysis—media institutions, technologies, markets, and society—and to changes in scholarship. The fact that so much is changing around us means that we must be open to theoretical revision more than ever. People who embrace political economy do not just sit back passively on the receiving end of these changes but try to influence them by, among other things, doing policy-relevant research and fostering knowledge that can be used by social and media reform and activist movements. Just how closely scholarship should be tied to political ends, however, is a hotly contested issue, as we will see.

In the latter half of the 1990s, it seemed easier to speak confidently about globalization, particularly in its Anglo-American or neoliberal version, the consolidation of national and global media conglomerates as well as the wholesale triumph of the commercial media model of development that had first been staked out in the United States and subsequently exported around the world. However, it was the techno-enthusiasts who seemed to crow loudest, predicting the imminent demise of television (Gilder 1994), the music business (Barfe 2003), the press (Negroponte 1995), radio, and in short, the "old media regime" entirely due to the rapid growth of the internet (Thierer and Ekselsen 2008: 31).

Many critical media political economists responded to such triumphalism by taking an opposing tack, arguing that the "enormous market power of the media giants" gave them the capacity to "colonize the internet" (McChesney 2000: xxii). The unprecedented US$350 billion amalgamation of AOL–Time Warner in 2000 appeared to confirm just such prospects (Bagdikian 2004: ix). The fact that AOL immediately abandoned its role as an outspoken advocate of the need for all internet service providers (ISPs) to have open and nondiscriminatory access to cable and telecoms networks to deliver their services to customers did not bode well either. This was especially true in light of the fact that AOL had played a lead role funding open access movements in the United States and Canada in the late 1990s, chalking up significant victories along the way. Once AOL–Time Warner was in place, however, vertical integration, synergy, cross-promotion, and portals designed as "walled gardens" became the "new norm."

AT&T's resurrection as a dominant player across telecoms, media, and internet in 1998 also fueled concerns that the open, end-to-end internet was being sacrificed on the altar of corporate consolidation and convergence. The company's Internet Services CEO, Daniel Somers, further stoked the flames by exclaiming, "AT&T didn't spend $56 billion to get into the cable business to have the blood sucked out of our veins" (quoted in Lessig 2000: 995). Legal decisions at the time giving AT&T the First Amendment right to program, edit, and control its network as it saw fit also seemed to bless the corporate takeover of the internet (*Comcast Cablevision v. Broward County* 1999). Telefonica's (Spain) purchase of Dutch television producer Endomol (e.g. "Big Brother," "Fear Factor," "Deal or No Deal") and the ISP Terra Lycos as well as the French utility and telecoms provider Vivendi's acquisition of Universal Film Studios indicated that these trends were global. As Peter Curwen (2008) observed in 1999, in the first of an annual series of articles published over the following decade, "the era of the telecoms, or perhaps more appropriately simply 'coms,' dinosaurs bestriding the world is upon us" (Curwen 2008: 3). Or was it?

The above examples were part of a bigger, global trend. Indeed, as Figure I.2 depicts, two powerful waves of consolidation, the first from the mid-1990s to 2000, followed by a more modest surge from 2003 to 2007, fundamentally restructured the network media industries. The first wave of mergers and acquisitions began in the United States in *anticipation* of the Telecommunications Act of 1996 and rippled outward as one country after another opened their markets. The 1997 World Trade Organization's *Basic Telecommunications*

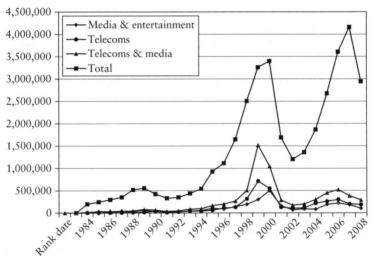

Figure I.2 Worldwide mergers and acquisitions in the media and telecoms industries, 1984–2008 (millions, US$)
Source: Thomson Reuters (2009).

Agreement consolidated these trends on a global scale. In the final 3 years of the 1990s alone, the capacity of global telecom networks multiplied 100 fold because of massive levels of investment and rapid development of the internet (Brenner 2002; Federal Communications Commission (FCC) 2000). These trends did not add up to deregulation, however, as the number of telecom and media regulators worldwide skyrocketed from just 14 in 1990 to 100 in 2000, to 150 today (ITU/UNCTAD 2007: 66). The mandate of these agencies, however, is not primarily to serve as a check on unbridled market forces but to deepen and extend them.

These dynamics fueled the rise of massive communication and media conglomerates that, at least for a time, stood at the apex of a rapidly converging communication environment. In the United States, vertical integration between all the Hollywood film and major US television networks reached unmatched levels, with Rupert Murdoch's News Corp. leading the way by combining Twentieth Century Fox film studios with the launch of Fox television (1985/86), Sony's acquisition of Columbia (1989), Time and Warner's merger in 1989 and launch of the WB network (1995), Disney's takeover of ABC (1995), Viacom's merger with CBS (1999), and later in the game, as General Electric–NBC purchased Universal Studios in 2004 (Winseck 2008). Elsewhere, particularly in midsize media economies such as Latin America and Canada, as Chapters 2 and 6 in this book show, family-owned media businesses morphed into huge media conglomerates, with some taking advantage of globalization to expand abroad and diversify (especially Televisa, Cisneros, Globo, and Canwest).

At the same time, however, and especially in Latin America, these large media groups remain at a crossroads, with ample opportunities to expand but their options hemmed in by the potential for powerful telecoms-based rivals to enter their domains, on one side, and by the more assertive regulators, on the other. In Latin America, media reform is now on the agenda in ways that would have been unthinkable a decade ago. Elsewhere, governments in Australia, Britain, Canada, the European Union, and the United States, among others, have conducted more examinations of media concentration in the past decade than the previous quarter of a century combined, and there is mounting public and scholarly interest in the issue (Baker 2007; Canada 2006; McChesney 2008; Noam 2009; Rice 2008; United Kingdom, House of Lords, Select Committee on Communications 2008). All in all, these are additional signs indicating that we may be witnessing the "return of the state" and standing on the cusp of a post-neoliberal era.

By the end of 2000, the TMT bubble had burst and with it many of the earlier prophesied scenarios failed to materialize. A decade after his 1999 article, Peter Curwen (2008) reached a very different conclusion, stating that rather than a handful of "coms dinosaurs" straddling the earth, "a settled structure" for the telecoms, media, and technology sector "remains a mirage" (Curwen 2008: 3). In fact, several bastions of the "old order"—Time Warner, AT&T, Bertelsmann,

Vivendi, and ITV, among others—have been restructured or dismantled since the turn of the century. Others have crashed entirely (Kirch Media, Adelphia, Canwest, Knight Ridder, etc.) or now stand on the brink of financial ruin (e.g. the Prisa Media Group). In 2005, Telefonica sold its stake in Endomol to Mediaset, the giant media group owned by Italian Prime Minister Silvio Berlusconi. Some elements of the media, the press in particular, appear to be in grave trouble, as venerable titles such as *The New York Times, Le Monde*, the *Guardian, Chicago Tribune*, and *LA Times* struggle to attract new benefactors, hive off parts of their operations, and lay off media workers in droves. By 2009, the severity of the situation led the Conservative Government in France to bail out the daily press at a cost of US$800 million. In the meantime, websites such as papercuts.org and newspaperdeathwatch.com chronicle the carnage. As the Project for Excellence in Journalism (2009: 2) stated, this is one of the "bleakest" moments in history for journalism and the press in the United States (cf. Almiron 2010; McChesney and Nichols 2010; OECD 2010; Picard 2009; Scherer 2010; Starr 2009).

Which media political economy?

Making sense of this dynamically shifting terrain turns on the theoretical views and methods that we adopt. As indicated earlier, there is a tendency to see the political economies of media as constituting a single field (McChesney 2008; Mosco 2009a; Hartley 2009; Holt and Perren 2009). David Hesmondhalgh (2007, 2009a) offers an important exception in this regard by distinguishing between the McChesney–Schiller model and the cultural industries school, but even this framework strains to contain the diversity of views on offer. Here I broaden the lens to include the following: (1) conservative and liberal neoclassical economics, (2) radical media political economies (the monopoly capital and digital capitalism schools), (3) Schumpeterian institutional political economy and two of its contemporary progeny, the creative industries and network political economy schools, and (4) the cultural industries school.

Neoclassical political economy

The neoclassical approach is probably the most well-known school, instantly recognized by its stress on the "marketplace of ideas" in democratic societies. The heritage of John Milton's *Areopagitica* (1644) through to John Stuart Mill's *On Liberty* (1859) and the views of US legal jurist Oliver Wendall Holmes Jr in the early twentieth century, among others, offer a treasure trove of liberal ideas about free markets and free speech that have been retrospectively fused together into the concept of the "marketplace of ideas"—a neat and tidy bit of phraseology that has lent the neoclassical cannon much rhetorical appeal ever since (Peters 2004: 79).

The two main wings of the neoclassical school—conservatives and liberals—are mainly divided over how each sees the potential for market failure and the role of governments. The latter are more open to the idea that markets sometimes fail and that governments will occasionally need to step in to set things right. However, in both cases, State intervention should be minimized to providing meritorious public goods (e.g. museums, libraries, and "high art and culture"), bringing a small number of essential services to areas not served by private business (e.g. broadband internet to rural communities), and striking a balance between the public good qualities of information versus protecting its status as valuable property. Conservative economists are likely to stress the need for strong government intervention to protect private property rights in information, while their liberal counterparts are more inclined to promote the idea that the wider the information is spread the more valuable it is. Information is a public good because after the high cost of producing the first copy of information is absorbed, the subsequent cost of reproducing, transmitting, and storing it declines quickly to zero—qualities that have been amplified greatly by digital communication technologies. Furthermore, when I consume information, it is still available for others to enjoy (i.e. it is non-rivalrous). For these reasons, the cost of excluding people from information is socially and economically inefficient, a conclusion that leads many economists to oppose strict copyright rules (e.g. Atkinson 2010: 13; Hayek 1945: 519; Pool 1990).

For neoclassicists, especially on the conservative and libertarian side, any notion that information is scarce is a delusion. As Adam Thierer and Grant Eskelsen (2008) of the US Progress and Freedom Foundation exclaim, *"to the extent there was ever a 'golden age' of media in America, we are living in it today"* (Thierer and Eskelsen 2008: 11, italics in original). In this view, the enormous growth of television networks and cable and satellite channels—MTV, HBO, ESPN, al Arabiya, Al-Jazeera, Canal1, to name just a few—has created a cornucopia of choice. Throw into this mix the internet, with its endless well of web pages, news sites, social media, music and video downloading services, and the freewheeling commentary of millions of blogs, and any concerns with media concentration are obsolete. Indeed, media markets have been utterly transformed by the proliferation of new technologies. Goldstein (2007) depicts the magnitude of these changes by comparing the state of the television universe in the 1970s versus today, as shown in Figures I.3 and I.4.

The above-mentioned authors argue that all of the layers in the media system—(1) media content, (2) media distributors, (3) media reception

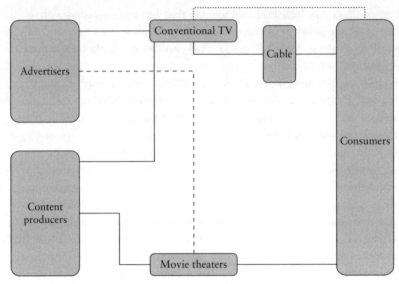

Figure I.3 Television in the video continuum value chain, *circa* 1975

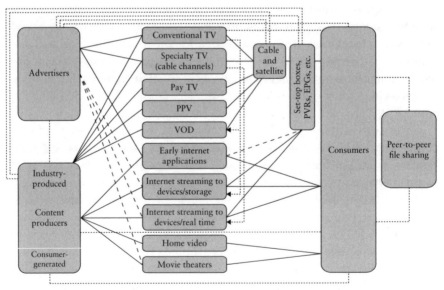

Figure I.4 Television in the video continuum value chain, *circa* 2007–12
Source: Goldstein (2007: 15–16).

and display devices, and (4) personal storage options—have become more fragmented and competitive than ever (Thierer and Eskelsen 2008: 13; Goldstein 2007: 17). Digitization and convergence are drawing different players from the media, telecoms, internet, and ICT industries into a common field of competition. The portrait that emerges is of a complex media ecology organized as so many Lego building blocks that can be snapped together in an endless array of personal choices. If there is a problem, it is not media concentration but that fragmentation is eroding any sense of a common culture (Goldstein 2007; Sunstein 2007).

Of course, not all dimensions of the media conform to the textbook ideals of competitive markets. The existence of potential rivals, for example, to broadband internet networks providers—cable systems, telecom operators, satellite systems, IPTV, wireless cable, public utilities, VOIP, and so on—reveals a contestable market. In contestable markets, incumbent players do have opportunities to abuse their dominant position, but they are constrained by the prospect that rivals on the horizon could become real competitors in practice (Atkinson 2010: 8). Attempts by regulators to correct even limited cases of market failure, it is argued, will make matters worse. For instance, retaining limits on media ownership confers enormous advantages on new rivals such as Apple, Microsoft, Google, Facebook, and Yahoo!, which tend to have capitalization levels greater than traditional media firms and are almost completely unregulated (Thierer and Eskelsen 2008: 20–5). To take another example, attempts to regulate broadband networks are see as interfering with the property rights of network owners, discouraging investment, and short-circuiting market forces in setting private companies' "business models" (Yoo 2008). In the United States, such claims underpin the telecoms and cable companies' opposition to municipal broadband networks and their successful efforts to have many state legislatures pass laws that prohibit such initiatives—despite evidence from other countries that such initiatives have played a vital role in extending broadband internet services faster than would otherwise have been the case (Benkler *et al.* 2010).

Taking these ideas altogether, MIT economics professor Benjamin Compaine (2001) argues that the "marketplace of ideas ... may be flawed, but it is ... getting better, not worse." As he states, looking at the information industries as a whole, even the largest firms are but tiny specks in the competitive universe. In response to critics who argue otherwise, Compaine offers a terse, one-word retort: *internet*. And if a lack of internet access is a problem, its rapid spread will solve the problem soon enough (Compaine 2005: 574).

Columbia University professor of finance and economics, and author of the authoritative *Media Ownership and Concentration in America* (Noam 2009), Eli Noam is another well-known neoclassical economist, but his approach and the conclusions he reaches set him apart from those just addressed. Noam argues that objective economic analysis of the media industries is essential. However, he laments the fact that such studies are rare because ideology tends to color the analysis of most observers, critics tend to overburden the media with all of societies' ills, and most analysts do not clearly specify what elements of the media they are studying (also see Hesmondhalgh 2009a: 249). Noam singles out the work of Ben Compaine and Ben Bagdikian with respect to this latter point. Compaine's overly broad conception of the "information industries," he says, dilutes any potential for concentration to be found. In contrast, Bagdikian's specification of the media is so vague that it is all but impossible to meaningfully assess his dire claim that the number of giant media corporations controlling the bulk of the US media plunged from 50 to 5 between 1984 and 2004 (Noam 2009: 3–22).

Noam (2009) responds to these problems by developing a broad definition of the information industries that covers 100 sectors and divides these into four groups: electronic mass media, telecoms, internet, and ICTs (Noam 2009: 4). He assesses the changes in market structure from 1984 to 2005 in the United States for each sector, then combines them at successively higher stages of abstraction to portray trends over time for each group, and then for the "information industries" as a whole. Several important results emerge: First, a "U-shaped" pattern can generally be seen for each level of analysis, with concentration declining in the 1980s (under Republican administrations), rising steeply in the 1990s (during the Clinton administrations), before plateauing in the 2000s (under Bush II). Overall, concentration in the media, telecoms, ICTs, and internet is more serious than Compaine suggests but not as catastrophic as Bagdikian alleges. In the mass media, the top firm in each sector typically accounts for just under a quarter of the market, followed by three others with 10 percent market share each, and many small players rounding out the rest. Companies in one sector, however, "are not necessarily the same firms across the various industries" (Noam 2009: 5). For the mass media as a whole, the top five companies' share of the market doubled from 13 percent in 1984 to 26 percent in 2005—half the level cited by Bagdikian but substantial all the same (Noam 2009: 5). Lastly, Noam demonstrates that the internet is neither an antidote to media concentration nor immune to such outcomes. In fact, many dimensions of the internet exhibit high, and growing, concentration: search engines, ISPs, broadband internet, web browsers, and media players, among others (Noam 2009: 290–3).

Noam offers several valuable lessons. First, his findings are historically informed and reflect a liberal temperament, where an open mind and systematic research are deployed to discover answers to meaningful questions. Second, he shows that consolidation is not foreign to the media industries but endemic to them. Third, he argues that digitization is creating stronger economies of scale, lower barriers to entry, and digital convergence. In the end, Noam concludes that a two-tier media system is crystallizing around a few "large integrator firms" (e.g. Apple, Google, and traditional media conglomerates), surrounded by numerous smaller, specialist firms (Noam 2009: 33–9). Ultimately, whether the future of the media is bright or bleak will largely turn on us and politics.

Radical media political economies: the monopoly capital and digital capitalism schools

Radical media political economies have a long and diverse set of influences that have shaped their development. One thing held in common, however, is that the neoclassical claim to being a "value-free" science is seen as being neither tenable nor desirable (Babe 1995; Murdock and Golding 2005; Mosco 2009a).

I want to initially focus on the scholarship of Robert McChesney because he has been a key figure in the monopoly capital school for over a decade. Many critics claim that the monopoly capital school, and McChesney's work specifically, is thin on theory; weak on history, method, and evidence; and that it rests on the dubious media effects tradition (Hartley 2009; Hesmondhalgh 2009a; Holt and Perren 2009). Some of these claims hit their mark, but many critics misconstrue the monopoly capital school, and McChesney's work specifically, and thus are wide off their target.

McChesney takes the media industries as serious objects of analysis, both in the United States and globally, and places greater emphasis on the "public good" characteristics of journalism and media goods than neoclassical economists. This is not because he is prone to wishful thinking but because information and media goods are "public goods," as we saw earlier. Seen in the light of free press principles and theories of democracy, we all benefit from living in a society where quality journalism and a rich media environment exist, whether we directly consume these "goods" or not. Indeed, it is hard to argue with the idea that it is better to live in a society of knowledgeable and tolerant citizens rather than ignorant and parochial ones (cf. Baker 2007).

The problem, however, is that news and information goods that lack effective commercial demand will be underproduced in the media marketplace—*unless* they are subsidized by advertising or some other form of subsidy (e.g. public license fees for the BBC, access to spectrum and public rights-of-way, copyright). The advertising-for-journalism *quid pro quo* has always been the bastard child of free press theories because it expects commercial media to take on responsibilities that they are ill-equipped, and often unwilling, to do, not least because *by law*, if not just by the laws of capitalism, they must maximize shareholder profits (Baker 2007: 100–21; Curran and Seaton 2003: 345–62; McChesney 2008). McChesney and Nichols (2010) argue that the advertising-for-journalism model, while always a thin reed to begin with, is on the verge of collapse as internet companies such as Google, Yahoo!, Craigslist, and so on pick apart advertising functions from news and journalism functions. The migration of advertising revenue to the internet, coupled with the fact that companies such as Google and Yahoo! create little original content of their own, means that the engine of journalism in the United States is being gutted with no adequate replacement in sight. Add to this the unfolding of the global financial crisis since 2007–8, and these blows could be fatal (cf. Davis 2009; OECD 2010; Scherer 2010; United Kingdom, House of Lords, Select Committee on Communications 2008 for related concerns in Europe and the United Kingdom).

In contrast to critics' charges, McChesney's analysis relies on a fairly extensive body of historical material, especially relative to the standards of the field. I disagree with him on three important points of media history—that is, the "struggle for control model of global media history" that he and Herman use in *The Global Media*, the claim that the definitive historical moments in the early politics of radio in the United States fell between 1927 and 1934 (rather than 1918 to 1926), and a reading of the 1996 US Telecommunications Act that leads him to conclude that it was a complete capitulation to the incumbent telecom and media players negotiated outside of public view (McChesney 2008). That said, however, McChesney has "rediscovered" the history of radical media and media criticism in the United States; his account of radio history makes extensive use of archival material, and his recent book *The Death and Life of American Journalism* (2010) (with John Nichols), uses some of the best scholarships available on the history of the press, post office, and journalism in the United States. Indeed, the bibliography is as impressive as it is long, and the belief that the First Amendment bars the government from implementing policies to help foster high-quality journalism and a good media system is convincingly discredited.

Behind the regularly updated ranking of the small number of mega-conglomerates that McChesney sees as controlling the media industries, he uses a respectable and straightforward "three-tier" model of national and global media systems. In this theoretical model, the first tier consists of 6 to 10 major media conglomerates that dominate film, television, music, radio, cable and satellite, publishing, and internet, followed by another 15 to 20 firms in the United States, and about three dozen worldwide, that makeup the second tier. The actions of the latter, in turn, are constrained by the contexts set by large global media conglomerates, a grouping that most analysts would probably agree includes some variation of the following list: Disney, Comcast, News Corp., Viacom–CBS, Time Warner, Bertelsmann, Sony, NBC-Universal, Thomson Reuters, and Pearson. Finally, the third tier consists of thousands of tiny voices that "fill the nooks and crannies of the media system" (McChesney 2004: 183; Herman and McChesney 1997: 70–1; McChesney and Schiller 2003: 13; Castells 2009; Noam 2009). Ultimately, the whole of the media system is stitched together by strategic alliances that blunt the sharp edge of competition. In sum, the conditions of monopoly capitalism replace those of competitive capitalism, leaving the *liberal ideals* of the "free press" and democracy in tatters as a result (McChesney 2008: 13–14).

Ultimately, McChesney's is not only an academic argument but also a political one designed to inspire people to challenge the prevailing state of affairs.

And if that is a key measure of success, then by all indications McChesney has been hugely successful. He has put media political economy on the map in an unprecedented way, and the media reform group, *Free Press*, that he created (December 2002) with Josh Silver and John Nichols has had a major influence on media politics. Finally, there are limits to his method, as there are with *any* method, but as Noam (2009: 21) states, "one can quibble with some of McChesney's data," but it is not bad.

The main weakness of the monopoly capital school is its view of the media industries as a giant pyramid, with power concentrated at the top and not enough attention paid to the details of key players, markets, and the dynamics and diversity that exist among all the elements that makeup the media. Even a friendly critic like Vincent Mosco (2009a) is at pains to take his distance from the monopoly capital school on the grounds that its focus on big media behemoths embodies a static view of the world that blots out issues of class, race, gender, and other standpoints of resistance, especially labor (see Mosco 2009a: 27, 113, 133). In contrast to hostile critics, however, Mosco (2009a) seeks to establish a dynamic view of the political economy of communication, which he defines as being the "*study of the social relations, particularly the power relations, that mutually constitute the production, distribution, and consumption of resources*"; more broadly, it is "*the study of control and survival in social life*" (Mosco 2009a: 24–5, italics in original). He also identifies four characteristics—history and social change, social totality, moral philosophy, and praxis—of this approach that anchor communication studies in a dynamic Marxian ontology, or in other words, a view of the world that is constantly in motion, with the play of its parts all set amidst a broader set of dynamic processes and forces (Mosco 2009a: 26; Murdock and Golding 2005: 61; Chapter 9 in this book). This is the core of the digital capitalism view.

In contrast to Daniel Bell's (1973) idea of a "postindustrial society" or Manuel Castells' (2009) recent claim that networks have become the axial principle of social organization in the "network society," the digital capitalism approach, as Dan Schiller (1999a) states, views "networks as directly generalizing the social and cultural range of the capitalist economy" (Schiller 1999a: xiv). Rather than emphasizing the *differences* between "industrial societies" of the past and "information societies" of today, the digital capitalism school stresses the underlying *continuity* of capitalist principles of exchange and social organization within both periods. In this view, the media in capitalist societies have always been important businesses in their own right and served to deepen the processes of commodification. Initially, this was done *indirectly* because commercial media relied on advertising for their financial base, instead of direct payments from consumers. Now, however, *direct commodification* is playing a greater role because digital media make it easier, more efficient, and effective than ever to monitor, measure, and monetize the value of content, audiences, and information. Thus, far from constituting a rupture with the past, *the* "central tendency" of digitalization "is to deepen and expand the capitalist market system" (Mosco 2009a: 120).

There is no doubt that a dynamic ontology needs to be at the heart of political economy of *any* kind, but Mosco's effort to shift the focus from *institutional structures* to *dynamic processes*, by and large, abandons the terrain of the media industries as serious objects of analysis. Second, the effort substitutes overly unified *processes* of capitalist integration for a unified *structural* view of the media. Overall, neither version of radical media political economy pays sufficient attention to the complexity of the media industries, the reasons for this diversity, and the pervasive role of uncertainty across all levels of the media (Bustamante 2004: 805; Garnham 1990: 38; Garnham 2005: 18). Writing nearly a quarter of a century ago, Bernard Miège (1989) crystallized the gist of these criticisms in a slim but extremely valuable volume, *The Capitalization of Cultural Production*.[5] Those criticisms are probably even more relevant today than when they were first expressed. They are as follows:

- First, the line between culture and commerce is artificial and ignores the fact that culture has developed *within* industrial capitalism for the past 150 years. The "distrust of technology and artistic innovation" implied by such views is excessive and unnecessary (Miège 1989: 10).

- Second, referring to the industry or "system" "in the singular misleads one into thinking that we are faced with a unified field, where the various elements function within a single process ... The cultural industries are complex, and an analysis must bring out the reasons for this diversity" (Miège 1989: 10).

- Third, "new communication technologies ... contribute to tightening the hold of capitalist production over culture as well as communication, [but] this does not mean that the capitalist industrialization of culture has been fully realized" (Miège 1989: 11)

In other words, the monopoly capital school overemphasizes the tendency toward market concentration, while the digital capitalism school (or Frankfurt school before it) overplays the ineluctable colonization of the lifeworld by market forces and the one-dimensional commodification of all cultural forms, even oppositional ones.[6] These criticisms have been dealt with in several different quarters ever since. In Britain, some neo-Marxian political economists such as Nicholas Garnham, Graham Murdock, Peter Golding, Colin Sparks, and James Curran have responded through a series of (not always friendly) historical encounters with the cultural studies of Raymond Williams, William Hoggart, E.P. Thompson, and the Birmingham school (especially Stuart Hall) (see the chapters by these authors, for example, in Calabrese and Sparks 2004).

They have also paid far greater attention to the coevolution of communication and modernity (Murdock 1993), and been more sensitive to arguments from popular cultural theory about audience autonomy. Several dimensions of this "sensibility" are shared with the cultural industries school as well. Therefore, instead of covering the well-trodden and disputatious terrain between neo-Marxian political economy and cultural studies, the bulk of these points can be addressed by a discussion of the cultural industries school. Doing this will also help to avoid bringing in a bevy of additional writers to whom justice cannot possibly be done and which would not do much to advance the core elements of this introduction anyway. Yet, before turning to the cultural industries school, I want to discuss what I will refer to as Schumpeterian institutional political economy and two of its contemporary progeny, the creative industries and network political economy schools. This is vitally important because Schumpeterian-derived approaches to institutional political economy have long played a pivotal role in scholarship and policy-oriented research, although more outside the field of communication and media studies than from within, and because, as we will see, the cultural industries school itself has developed in crucial ways through ongoing critical conversations with one or another version of this approach.

Creative destruction: Schumpeterian institutional political economy, the creative industries school, and network political economy

The ideas of Joseph Schumpeter are the pillars of the network political economy and creative industries schools. His views also underpin a wide range of other approaches, from information economics to the monopoly capital school (Foster and Magdoff 2009; Freeman and Louca 2001; Pool 1990; Garnham 2000). William Melody (2007a) captures some of the essence of this broad appeal when he observes that "the 'creative destruction' associated with the ICT revolution has introduced obsolescence not only for many older technologies, business models, industry structures, government policies and regulations, but for a significant portion of the conventional wisdom and mainstream thinking across all the social sciences" (Melody 2007a: 70).

The Schumpeterian view differs from neoclassical and radical views in four substantial ways. First, technological innovation is the motor of competition in capitalist economies, not price and markets, as neoclassical economists hold. Second, competition through technological innovation creates temporary monopolies and superprofits, but these are likely to be short lived because "superprofits" attract new rivals. Third, Schumpeter (1943/1996) makes the process of "creative destruction" a central fixture in his view of capitalism, which he outlines as follows:

> The opening up of new markets, foreign or domestic, and the organizational development from the craft shop and factory ... illustrate the same process of industrial mutation ... that incessantly revolutionizes the economic structure *from within*, incessantly destroying the old one, incessantly creating a new one. This process of Creative Destruction is ... what capitalism consists in and what every capitalist concern has got to live in. (Schumpeter 1943/1996: 83, italics in original)

The emphasis on creative destruction as a function of technological and economic forces contrasts with the emphasis on *equilibrium* in the neoclassical view and the Marxist idea that it is people's interaction with the material world (labor) and class conflict that drives socioeconomic change. Fourth, the privileging of technology and economics as "agents" of change over people and social forces embodies Schumpeter's disdain for classical liberal views of democracy and the notion that people have the capacity to govern in complex societies. If radicals and some liberals believe in "strong democracy," Schumpeter held a weak view of "elite democracy." Curiously, a cone of silence has been placed around this aspect in the current revival of Schumpeterian ideas (see Schumpeter 1943/1996: 250–96).

The information economist Ronald Coase (1937) added to these ideas by suggesting that changes in the information environment lead to changes in the organizational structure of firms and markets. Information that is scarce and costly creates bureaucratic hierarchies. This is why the "industrial mass media" of the past were ruled by enormous bureaucratic firms. Conversely, when information costs less to acquire, produce, store, transmit, and consume, markets emerge and hierarchies recede. This idea is central to claims that the steep drop in information costs enabled by digital technologies is tilting the structure, not just of the communication and media industries but society as a whole, toward a much larger role for markets and dispersed forms of socioeconomic organization. A recent OECD (2007a) report expresses this view as follows:

> New digital content innovations seem to be more based on decentralized creativity, organizational innovation and new value-added models, which favour new entrants, and less on traditional scale advantages and large start-up investments. ... [U]ser created content has become a significant force for how content is created and consumed and for traditional content suppliers. (OECD 2007a: 5)

The creative industries approach harnesses these ideas to a broad research agenda that examines the disintegration of media work from the confines of the towering hierarchies of media conglomerates and stresses the need for mid- and micro-range studies of media organizations, media work, the participatory web, and other forms of creative expression that have been enabled by the open innovation ecology (Born 2004; Caldwell 2008; Flew 2007, Chapter 3 in this book; Holt and Perren 2009; Pratt and Jeffcutt 2009). These studies also recast an enduring debate in a new light over whether the creation of cultural goods is best viewed as dominated by global media conglomerates or as a mix of large and small firms that depend on specialized markets, flexible networks of production, unique skills, and social relationships. In several studies in the 1980s and 1990s, Susan Christopherson and Michael Storper (1989) developed and applied an early version of the latter view to an analysis of the film industry. However, in a manner highly relevant to debates today, Asu Aksoy and Kevin Robins (1992) criticized their approach as follows: "Their interest is almost exclusively in examining changes in the film *production* process, and they fail to address the key areas of *film distribution, exhibition and finance*" (Aksoy and Robins 1992: 7, italics added). Variations on this debate continue to be replayed but mainly between creative industries and monopoly capitalism school scholars (e.g. Flew 2007; Miller, Govil, McMurria, Wang, and Maxwell 2005; Moran and Keane 2006; Tinic 2005; see Chapters 3, 4, and 5 in this book).

Terry Flew makes an exceptional contribution to the creative industries approach because he consistently strives to foreground both the centripetal and centrifugal forces at play in the media industries. As Susan Christopherson states in her chapter, however, the bulk of such studies adopt a romantic view of creative workers, even if sometimes battered and bruised by their work, with little sense of how some key elements of the media industries have become more concentrated over time. Also underplayed is the fact that many of these same entities retain control over distribution channels/platforms and the "finance for content property rights" regime that most media professionals labor under to begin with (see Lash and Urry 1994: 113; Garnham 1990, 2000). Three other problems beset the creative industries view. First, by critiquing radical media political economists' focus on big media, but without doing much comparable research of their own, there is a tendency, ironically, to reify political economy as an unified intellectual approach while relying on the very same sources they criticize to ground their own writing (Grossberg 2006: 20). Second, the approach implies a simplistic distinction between people who work with their heads versus those who toil with their hands. Third, it is vague, leading to some pretty big numbers being tossed around, but with little sense of scale (e.g. Hartley 2009: 236).

In the network political economy school, Manuel Castells and Yochai Benkler extend Schumpeter's ideas in a different direction. First, instead of seeing changes in the techno-economic and information environment as only affecting the balance of hierarchies and markets, they stress the *role of the state* and also attach much significance to the "social ecology of information," which they see as growing *alongside* the information marketplace, rather than being subsumed by it, in contrast to radical political economies of media.

Benkler's (2003, 2006) self-described approach to the political economy of information puts technology, individuals, markets, and social justice, in roughly that order, at the center of attention (Benkler 2006: 12–13). He is skeptical of grandiose political philosophical goals but tolerant of State intervention to break up monopolies, expand networks where capital investment is slow on the uptake, and highly critical of the ability of incumbents in the telecom and media industries to bend policy to their own interests. He is keen on the "digital commons," the social production of information, creativity, pleasure, and the potential of the network media to make valuable contributions to many aspects of life, without being naïve. Benkler (2006) describes the network political economy approach as a way of

> framing ... the institutional ecology of the digital environment ... in ways that are more complex than usually considered in economic models. [Institutions] interact with the technological state, the cultural conceptions of behaviors, and with incumbent and emerging social practices that may be motivated not only by self-maximizing behavior, but also by a range of other social and psychological motivations. In this complex ecology, institutions ... coevolve with technology and with social and market behavior. This coevolution leads to periods of relative stability, punctuated by periods of disequilibrium ... caused by external shocks or internally generated phase shifts. (Benkler 2006: 381)

Benkler sees strategic, often incumbent, interests from the telecoms, ICT, and media content industries as being locked in a battle over the future of the information ecology, but not of one mind when it comes to these struggles. Pressures to "flip" the internet from an open network into a more closed system have been a strong, persistent, and sometimes successful part of these efforts (Andrejevic 2007; Benkler 2006; Lessig 1999, 2004; Vaidhyanathan 2004). However, telecom and ICT industries are also sometimes aligned with fans, hackers, and activists in terms of the need to curb the media content industries' copyright maximalist position. At other times, though, they are deeply at odds with the same groups over issues of network neutrality, open source code, privacy, and so forth. These cleavages were revealed during recent hearings on a US Senate bill that aims to give new powers to the Department of Justice, a move that the CEO of the Computer and Communications Industry Association, Ed Black, condemned as follows:

> If legislation like this goes through, we start to break the internet ... . Nobody is arguing that copyright infringement doesn't exist. But Lady Gaga isn't going to go broke tomorrow. We should try to solve the copyright issue in as an unobtrusive and thoughtful way as possible and not creating anti–First Amendment laws. (quoted in Sandoval 2010a, np)

Open internet, copyright, and free speech constitute the "holy trinity" of contemporary media politics, with such issues arising in one country after another. Typically, the push is to have ISPs and ICT firms assume more legal responsibility for protecting copyrighted information. And on each occasion the lineup on each side of the debate is similar. ICT, internet, and telecom firms, along with consumer and freedom-of-expression groups, stand opposed, while the media industries plead that their future hangs in the balance (European Commission 2010; Mansell 2010; United Kingdom 2010). In each case, however, network media politics is conducted strategically. Drawing on Bob Jessop (2008), this means that we need to adopt a conjunctural frame of analysis to understand the nature of such events, rather than a strictly structural or pluralistic approach to politics and policy (Jessop 2008: 34–7).

Ultimately, not all mediated communicative activities are owned, generated, or controlled from within the core of the network media system. Mass self-expression (Castells 2009) and the social production of information (Benkler 2006) have put the power of creative expression into the hands of more people than ever and elevated the logic of the "social ecology of information" in the media as a whole. For Schumpeter's followers, this *is* a revolution *within* capitalism; for those who follow Marx, however, the prospects of that happening have only been slightly brightened by digital media, if at all (Dyer-Witheford 1999; Chapter 9 in this book; Terranova 2004).

Mutations: the cultural industries school

Since its inception in the late 1970s, the cultural industries school[7] has always drawn judiciously from different strands of political economy and systematically engaged the different versions of Schumpeterian institutional political economy that have emerged over the years. This can be seen, for example, in the role now played by the concept of "mutations" among the adherents of this approach (see Chapter 1), a concept critically appropriated directly from the passages in Schumpeter's *Capitalism, Socialism and Democracy* that set out the concept of "creative destruction" (see above). It is also in the foreground of the work of Nicholas Garnham, a leading figure in this school, who also functions somewhat as a bridge between this approach's European roots and British neo-Marxist political economy of communication. As Garnham (2005) explains, the cultural industries school has always taken "the term 'industries' seriously and attempted to apply both a more detailed and nuanced Marxist economic analysis and the more mainstream industrial and information economics to the analysis of the production, distribution and consumption of symbolic forms" (Garnham 2005: 18). In contrast to the "very general model of the capitalist economy" found within *some* mainstream and radical versions of political economy, the emphasis of the cultural industries school is on the unique and specific attributes of the media economy *and* the persistent *barriers* that impede the wholesale commodification of culture (Garnham 2005: 18; Garnham 1990: 37–40).

The cultural industries school has always advanced the idea that different sectors of the cultural industries cannot be treated as one and the same thing because of the crucial organizational differences that exist between what they called the "publishing" (e.g. books, music, film), "flow" (e.g. broadcasting), and "editorial" (e.g. the press) models. Since that time, and based on the ideas of French Canadian scholars Jean-Guy Lacroix and Gaetan Tremblay (1997), the editorial model has been gradually discarded in favor of a "club" model to reflect the growing centrality of the telecoms, cable, and internet sectors in the production, distribution, display, and consumption of media and cultural products. While the media content industries have *always* developed in close proximity to the communication hardware and equipment industries, Bernard Miège observes in Chapter 1 in this book that the dominance of the TiC sectors over the media content and cultural industries is growing over time, with TiC being the acronym for the telecoms, information, and communication sectors.

The dominant cultural industries model in the twentieth century was the "flow" model, based on the central role of television, radio, and in some respects, film (especially during the Hollywood Studio era). The "flow" model is defined by advertising-supported and public service broadcasting, where the demand for a steady flow of programs/content is met by a handful of gigantic, hierarchically organized firms and large steadily employed media workforces that operate under tight, but not complete, administrative and management structures. Programs/content in the flow model is mostly immaterial and, consequently, is neither possessed nor paid for directly by consumers. Instead, advertisers and government funds subsidize media consumption (i.e. *indirect commodification*).

The publishing model, in contrast, is based on creating a "*catalog of content*" that can be sold directly to consumers in as many ways as possible. It is based mostly on material goods that people can touch and pay for *directly* or rent access to: books, music, video, and film. For these goods, the logic of *direct commodification* prevails. The publishing model is also typified by a core group of companies that commission, finance, package, and distribute content, and own the intellectual property rights to their "catalogs." Rather than directly creating content, "publisher firms" depend on independently sourced programming and a "flexible" pool of cultural workers who are paid from royalties and employed from one project to another. Originally, this model played a modest role in the overall scheme of things. Since then, however, it has moved closer to the center of the media, first through policy initiatives, such as the creation of Channel 4 in the United Kingdom in 1982, and subsequently as the template for neoliberal capitalism writ large (Lash and Urry 1994).

The "club" model is a hybrid of elements from the publishing and flow models as well as some new characteristics unique to digital media. The gradual shift from the "flow" to the "publishing" and "club" models reflects the cumulative changes since the 1980s due to the growing centrality of digitization and communication networks (cable, telecoms, DTH, internet, wireless, etc.), corporate consolidation, restructuring and the rise of new players (e.g. Apple and Google), and the proliferation of content receiving and storage devices (Lacroix and Tremblay 1997). These models are being extended through the direct pay model of television and subscription services based on large catalogs of content rather than the scheduled *flow* of programs. Content integrators/ aggregators (Noam) exemplify the "publishing" and "club" models, but they simultaneously continue to cultivate audiences' expectations that content is free. The free culture norm, in turn, does not reflect new expectations, however, but the enduring "sociocultural fact" that information and cultural products are public goods as well as more than a century of socialization by the flow model where most of the costs of media consumption were paid by someone else (Bustamante 2004: 811). The three models of the cultural industries are summarized in Table I.3.

The change from a commercial media model based on *indirect commodification* to one based on *direct commodification* captures an essential feature of these changes. However, this is just a part, albeit an important one, of broader changes that cannot be reduced to a single thing or process, whether technology, market forces, commodification, or corporate consolidation. Instead, they embody a series of mutations, as Miège calls them, that are unraveling the organizational, economic, and technological props that have underpinned the media historically, while reassembling them, with the addition of new elements, into a yet-to-be completed "new digital media order."

The more intense capitalization of the network media industries that coincided with the two waves of media consolidation from the mid-1990s to, roughly, 2007 is also highly significant in relation to these developments. This is not primarily because they fostered even more media concentration in the media industries (although they did, e.g. see Noam 2009; McChesney 2008) but because they signaled that the telecoms, media, and internet sectors had become ensnared in the *financialization* of capitalist economies. In fact, they were at the forefront of the process, accounting for a far greater proportion of all mergers and acquisitions than their weight in the economy dictated. As the TMT frenzy peaked at the end of the 1990s, firms in these sectors were absorbing upward of three-quarters of *all* venture capital investment (Picard 2002: 175; Brenner 2002). As media, telecom, and internet firms became inserted more tightly into the circuits of capital accumulation, they were no longer just competing with one another but with *all* other firms for capital.

Financial investors prefer enormous, vertically integrated media conglomerates (Picard 2002), but the financialization process also reconceives of the corporation as a "portfolio of assets." Consequently, each division, for instance, within Time Warner, News Corp., Disney, Bertelsmann, and so forth—television, cable,

Table I.3 General economic and organizational models of the media industries

	Flow	Publishing	Club
Sector	Broadcast TV & radio	Books, Music, & Film	Digital network media
Content	Continuous flow & immaterial Huge uncertainty, large amount of commercial failures	Durable and fixed in individual copies Huge uncertainty, large amount of commercial failures	All content types Huge uncertainty, large amount of commercial failures
Central function	Programmer & scheduling	Publisher & catalog creation	Publisher & aggregator
Commodification	Indirect—advertising & government subsidies	Direct purchase	Mixture of direct & indirect financing
Industrial structure	Quasi-industrial, vertical integration, & central planning Managerial control of all elements in the value chain	Hub & spoke model—few large companies, shared infrastructure (printing, studios, etc.), project-based networks and small firms	Large infrastructure providers and layers of application, service, & content providers, which may or may not be under common ownership
Market structure	Tight oligopoly, vertical integration	Oligopolistic core surrounded by small firms	Oligopolistic core surrounded by small firms
Creative workers	Steady employment: broadcast workers, technicians, journalists, hosts, etc.	Small core workforce flanked by large pool of writers, directors, composers, artists, etc.	Mix of steady and contract-based labor plus freelance writers, web designers, hosts, etc.

Source: Adapted from Lacroix and Tremblay (1997: 56–65).

DTH, film, books, internet, and so on—must compete against one another, and other firms generally, based on prevailing norms of return on capital investment. Thus, and with no shortage of irony, as *convergence* becomes more feasible, financialization has been regearing the internal operations of media conglomerates in a way that pits one division against another *inside* these companies. This, in turn, reinforces the distinctions between media sectors along the lines identified by the cultural industries school. Consequently, instead of creating well-oiled corporate structures founded on tangible assets, economies of scale, synergy, and expertize, the financialization of the media spawned bloated, debt-laden corporate behemoths governed by the pursuit of unsustainably high levels of capital return, crosscutting objectives and inchoate incentives—perched atop the delusion that all this could, essentially, go on forever. In sum, the logic of financialization and the "bundle of assets" image of the corporation are at cross-purposes with digitalization, economies of scale, synergy, promotional government policies, and so on, which should make convergence more feasible than ever. None of this, however, even touches on the "rational" development of democratic media, the quality of life for media workers, or long-term technological and cultural innovation (Almiron 2010; Bouquillion 2008; Duménil and Lévy 2005; Fitzgerald 2011; Melody 2007b).

"All that is solid melts into air" (Karl Marx): the global transformation of the network media industries

By any account, television, film, music, and the press constituted the core of the mass media during the twentieth century, but as I indicated earlier, there is a great deal of debate over how they have fared as the internet and digital media move closer to the center of the network media universe. The last section of this introductory essay examines this question in light of the theoretical perspectives just discussed.

Despite early widespread rumors about the impending death of television (Gilder 1994), it is thriving, *everywhere* (Miller 2009). At the beginning of the 1980s, there were a handful of television channels in the "advanced capitalist economies" of the OECD. By the end of the twentieth century, there were 600. Now there are roughly 1,200 (OECD 2007b: 175). A total of 200 television channels are available to two-thirds of households in India that pay for cable and satellite television service. In China, 40 percent of households subscribe to such services. The "total television universe" has become more complex and encompasses cable and satellite distribution networks, pay television services, video-on-demand, Internet Protocol Television (IPTV), streaming internet video (Hulu, Daily Motion, YouTube), digital download services (Apple iTunes,

Netflix, BBC's iPlayer), and mobile phones. Watching television is no longer tied to a single device or place but a series of television screens, computers, and portable devices. Television viewing is not shrinking but becoming more mobile and personalized ("Changing the Channel" 2010: 1–14; OECD 2007b: 177; Ofcom 2010: 160).

In the United States, the total television universe is worth an estimated US$136.9 billion (2010) versus US$89.4 billion in 1998. Worldwide, the total television universe grew from US$203 billion to US$351.3 billion during this time. Film revenues also grew in the United States (including Canada) from US$24.9 billion to US$38.4 billion, while total film industry revenues worldwide nearly doubled. DVD sales and video rentals *have* tumbled but have been roughly compensated for by online subscriptions and digital downloads. The bottom line is that the television and film industries have grown considerably, and their share of the vastly enlarged total network media economy is now only slightly smaller than it was 12 years ago (34 vs 37 percent) (PWC 2003: 29–43, 2010: 41–5). Table I.4 shows the trends.

The logic of the television industry is passing from one based on advertising and state subsidies to the "direct commodification" model. The pay-per model of television has grown far faster than advertising-supported television (7 vs 1.5 percent per annum), and overall the amount of television revenues accounted for by advertising has fallen from 54 to 45 percent during the past decade. The ascent of the "publishing" and "club" models is also clear, as television programs are detached from specific platforms and assembled as part of a catalog of content delivered to audiences one by one. This is the "logic" of the Apple iTunes model and it being adopted by public service (e.g. the BBC's iPlayer) and commercial media alike (e.g. Hulu and the "Television Everywhere" strategy in the United States) (Ammori 2010; see Chapter 6 in this book regarding Canada). These changes raise issues about the role of public service broadcasters in the digital media world and how their activities will be financed, if they are permitted at all, as Chapter 10 discusses. In the United Kingdom, News Corp., the British Publishing Association, and

Table I.4 Worldwide TV and film industry revenues, 1998–2010 (millions, US$)

	1998	2000	2004	2008	2009	2010 (estimate)	% Change
TV	202,893	243,322	279,971	342,509	334,461	351,300	+73
Film	46,484	52,803	82,834	82,619	85,137	87,385	+88
Total	249,377	296,125	362,805	425,128	419,598	438,685	+76

Sources: PWC (2003, 2009, 2010).

Newspaper Publishers Association, for example, have derided the BBC's efforts to carve out a place for itself in the digital media universe. As the director of the latter association, David Newell, argues, the BBC's ambitions "threaten to strangle an important new market for news and information" (quoted in "Call to Block BBC iPhone Apps" 2010). The basic assumption appears to be that new media should be reserved for commercial media, while public service media remain lashed to the mast of a sinking ship, that is, the "flow" model.

In contrast to the continued hostilities between commercial and public service media operators, the tensions between traditional media players and companies such as Google appear to be abating, despite periodic flare-ups (IDATE 2009; PWC 2010). The trend is well illustrated by the judgment in Google's favor in the long-drawn-out "blockbuster" Viacom versus Google case in 2010, where the latter's video sharing site, YouTube, was accused of facilitating unauthorized uses of commercial television programs. The case, however, revealed that some divisions within Viacom, notably MTV, were secretly uploading vast amounts of video to YouTube and, more to the point, that Google had signed agreements with Viacom, NBC-Universal, Sony BMG, Time Warner, and News Corp. *before* it acquired YouTube for US$1.65 billion in 2006. According to the arrangements made, Google would (1) implement content identification technology, (2) share access to its technology, and crucially, (3) share advertising revenue (*Viacom International, et al. v. YouTube, Inc., YouTube LLC, and Google, Inc.* 2010).[8] Google, in sum, was working hand and glove with the traditional media conglomerates to preserve their copyright interests, not against them. The online movie streaming service, Netflix, has also signed agreements with Paramount (Viacom), MGM (Disney), and Lions Gate that point in a similar direction. Crucially, these arrangements are built around *the* cornerstone of the television and film industries' "business model": time- and territory-based "distribution windows" (Wasko 2004a). Netflix is already becoming a serious new "distribution window" for the film industry (Sandoval 2010b). In these arrangements, movies first appear in theaters, then pay-TV services a year later, and 90 days afterwards Netflix can stream them over the internet for another year before they are broadcast on basic cable (Nakashima and Liedtke 2010: B10).

Although the television and film industries have grown substantially, their growth rates pale alongside those of internet access and advertising, as Table I.5 highlights. Even the growth of these latter two sectors, however, stalled in the face of the global financial crisis. Moreover, despite all of the talk about the migration of advertising to the internet cannibalizing the revenue base of the "old media," internet advertising still only represents about 5 to 6 percent of the total network media economy, as Table I.5 indicates.

Table I.5 Worldwide internet industry revenues, 1998–2010 (millions, US$)

	1998	2000	2004	2008	2009	2010 (estimate)	% change
Internet access	15,556	35,483	110,370	210,788	228,060	247,453	+1,490
Internet advertising	953	6,533	17,922	58,068	60,568	66,176	+6,844

Sources: PWC (2003, 2009, 2010).

Internet access is probably more important than internet advertising in the general scheme of things. Indeed, it is an index of the growing centrality of communication networks, as some of the following examples suggest. The number of telephone users worldwide, for example, rose from 800 million in 1998 to 4.2 billion in 2009, while the number of mobile phone users soared to 4.5 billion subscribers. A total of 2 billion people use the internet in 2010, about 10 times the number in 1998. Today, 28.7 percent of the world's population has internet access, up greatly from 5 percent 12 years ago, although it is still sobering that 70 percent of people have no access whatsoever. In 1996, two-thirds of all internet users lived in the United States; since 2009, China has had the most internet users, although citizens in the United States are more than twice as likely (77 percent) to have internet access than their counterparts in China (30 percent). The gap between the "info rich" and the "info poor" is still very significant, within countries and worldwide. People who live, for instance, in the "advanced capitalist economies" are more than *300 times* likely to have broadband internet access than people in the poorest regions (ITU/UNCTAD 2007: 22; ITU 2010: 195–202; Internet World Stats 2010). Overall, however, the *primary* trend, according to a joint study by ITU/UNCTAD (2007: 26), is of "*growing* equality over time in the global distributions of internet users, mobile and fixed [phone] lines." Figure I.5 shows the distribution of internet users in 2010.

These changes are also accompanied by a more general reorganization of the "world communication order." Table I.6 depicts some of this change by showing the growth in the 10 largest *national* media economies over time. As Table I.6 demonstrates, media markets in all 10 countries have grown substantially. It also shows that the United States is still the biggest media market and is in fact larger than the next four media markets combined: Japan, Germany, China, and the United Kingdom. In total, 6 of the 10 biggest transnational media conglomerates (Disney, Comcast, News Corp., Viacom–CBS, Time Warner, NBC-Universal) are still United States based, while the other four are located in Japan, Germany, Canada, and the United Kingdom (Sony, Bertelsmann, Thomson Reuters, Pearson) (see Table I.1). Firms from the core capitalist economies continue to dominate the telecoms, ICT, and internet industries, as Oliver Boyd-Barrett (2006) also stresses in his effort to recast the media imperialism thesis in a contemporary light. However, the world no

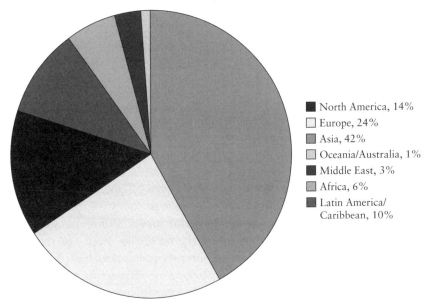

North America, 14%
Europe, 24%
Asia, 42%
Oceania/Australia, 1%
Middle East, 3%
Africa, 6%
Latin America/
Caribbean, 10%

Figure I.5 Global distribution of internet users by region, 2010
Source: Internet World Stats (2010). Available at www.worldinternetstats.com

Table I.6 Top 10 network media, entertainment, and internet markets by country, 1998–2010 (millions, US$)

	1998	2000	2004	2008	2009	2010 (estimate)	% change
United States	336,885	395,695	395,936	420,397	406,733	411,357	+22
Japan	94,255	100,799	114,330	141,340	156,120	157,985	+68
Germany	59,919	68,981	79,877	84,635	84,100	89,905	+50
China	23,057	27,599	32,631	66,310	72,024	81,005	+251
United Kingdom	56,738	65,319	75,637	72,346	70,478	72,605	+28
France	39,984	46,031	53,302	63,863	58,841	59,587	+49
Italy	29,626	34,107	34,494	41,528	39,890	39,924	+35
Canada	18,346	21,432	25,842	31,287	30,701	31,229	+70
S. Korea	17,687	18,492	22,760	26,672	27,394	28,589	+62
Spain	19,219	22,132	25,622	28,736	27,200	27,479	+43
Total	695,716	797,358	860,431	977,114	973,481	999,665	+44

Sources: PWC (2003, 2009, 2010).

longer orbits so tightly around the US axis as it once did, and "cyberspace," as we will see shortly, is by no stretch of the imagination the exclusive dominion of Western-based transnational communications corporations. The United States' "mature market" is growing slower than the others and is in relative decline. In 1998, the US media market accounted for one half of all worldwide media revenues; in 2010, the figure was less than a third. The four largest Anglo-American markets—United States (1), United Kingdom (5), Canada (8), and Australia (12)—still account for about 44 percent of media revenues worldwide, but this is a drop from 60 percent in the late 1990s. The average foreign revenues of the big 10 media (42.5 percent), internet (25 percent), and telecoms companies (31 percent) are significant, but less than ICTs (65 percent), and not a solid and unambiguous index of "strong globalization." Internet companies are actually *less* global than traditional media companies on the basis of revenues. The most global of the media conglomerates are Thomson Reuters, Pearson, Bertelsmann, and News Corp., in that order (see Table I.1).

The steady rise of China among the major media economies along with Japan (2) and South Korea (9) is tilting the center of gravity of the global media decisively toward Asia. National internet companies dominate in each of these countries, allowing them to carve out a significant spot for themselves among second-tier firms, with five Chinese internet companies standing out in this regard: Glam Media (14th), Tencent (16th), Baidu (17th), NetShelter Technology Media (19th), and Alibaba (20th) (Comscore 2010a: s.03). Moving beyond the "big ten" national rankings also shows that there is considerable diversification among smaller media economies and firms: Brazil and India rank 11th and 14th in terms of the size of their media economies, for instance, while several so-called small media economies figure quite prominently, that is, Canada (8), South Korea (9), Australia (12). These are not, thus, quite the "small national media economies" they are often made out to be, and therefore, the reigning orthodoxy that they require a few massive media groups is not as compelling as some might like to think.

Table I.7 maps some of the differences between "national network media spaces" along six key dimensions: (1) online time/user/month, (2) top internet company, (3) top search engine, (4) top two social network sites (SNS), (5) number of online videos viewed per month, and (6) Wikipedia ranking. In terms of time and the number of online videos watched per person, Canadians are the heaviest internet users in the world. Wikipedia ranks among the 10 most visited websites in all of the countries addressed, except South Korea (16th), Brazil (17th) as well as China, where it does not even rank in the top 100 (Alexa.com). Google looms largely in several categories in many countries but not all categories everywhere. Brazilians have embraced Google to an unusual degree, as illustrated by its hold across four out of the six categories. Globally, Google dominates the search engine category, accounting for 67 percent of all searches in a tight oligopolistic market where Google and three others—Yahoo! (7.1 percent), Baidu (6.4 percent), and Microsoft (3.1 percent)—account for 84 percent of all search traffic. This figure is rising over time, not falling. In the United States, Britain, Canada, Australia, Germany, France, India, and

Brazil, Google controls 80 to 90 percent of the search engine category, while ranking highly in other categories through its social networking site Orkut (Brazil and India) or its online video site, YouTube (Canada, Brazil, Australia). In Australia, 93 percent of all searches in 2010 used Google, while the top four search engines accounted for 97 percent—up from 91 percent 9 years earlier (Papandrea 2010).

In several countries, however, Google and other "Western" companies play minor roles and operate mainly in the shadows of "national champions" as is the case in South Korea, Russia, China, and Japan. In South Korea, the NHN Corporation (naver.com) as well as CyWorld, a branch of South Korea Telecom, dominate the national network media space. Google, in contrast, accounts for only 8 percent of searches; Facebook lags far behind CyWorld in social network sites. In other words, the network global media system shows characteristics of diversification between some countries but high levels of concentration in all countries.

There is nothing about digital networks that render them immune to concentration. Concentration at a relatively small number of nodes in the network media environment enables control—economic, political, and cultural—and helps to explain why Wikipedia is unavailable in China, for example, whereas it ranks highly almost everywhere else, that is, it is blocked. That this power is leveraged to control national media spaces is undeniable (Diebert, Palfrey, Rohozinski, and Zittrain 2010). Market dominance also means that Google, Facebook, Microsoft, and MySpace, for example, possess a great deal of power to set *de facto* standards for privacy, copyright, the distribution of advertising revenues, and the parameters of "audience behavior."[9] The concentration of control over network media is a function of money and power (Baker 2007; Noam 2009; McChesney 2008), but the idea of "network effects"—that is, the value of the network to each user increases exponentially as more "conversational partners" join the network—also biases network evolution toward concentration at key points. Furthermore, communication networks also tend to collect large volumes of traffic, people, messages, and so forth at a relatively small number of nodes, followed afterward by a "long tail" of sites receding into lesser and lesser visibility. This is known as "power law" and it can be a good thing in the network media environment because it helps to "gather attention" and create a "structure of importance" on the basis of "soft factors," such as trust, communities of interest, hyperlinks, credibility, and so forth, that allow intelligibility, relevance, and mutual understanding to emerge amidst a babble of voices, cultural fragmentation, and the potential for money and power to run roughshod over online communication (Benkler 2006; Shirky 2003). The upshot, nonetheless, is that it is more important than ever to keep digital networks as open and free from money and power as possible so that the processes of social and communicative interaction can unfold in as undistorted a fashion as possible.

Table I.7 New world media order? Global homogeneity and "varieties of capitalism" in the network media

	Minutes online per user per month	Top internet companies (% reach)	Top search engine (Google share)	Top two SNS (% reach)	# of online videos per viewer per month (YouTube share)	Wikipedia rank
Canada	2,750	Google, 92%	Google (81%)	Facebook, 79% Windows Live, NA	185 (49%)	7
United States	2,050	Yahoo!, 84%	Google (66%)	Facebook, 62% Google, 19%	196 (26%)	6
S. Korea	1,974	NHN naver.com, 85%	NHN (8%)	SK Tel (CyWorld), 56% Facebook, 8%	NA	16
United Kingdom	1,800	Google, 87%	Google (80%)	Facebook, 76% Windows Live, 16%	185 (45%)	9
France	1,625	Google, NA	Google (90%)	Facebook, NA Windows Live, NA	138 (NA)	10
Brazil	1,550	Google, 90%	Google (63%)	Orkut (Google), 72% Facebook, 20%	95 (80%)	17
Germany	1,475	Google, NA	Google (93%)	Facebook, NA Twitter, NA	193 (50%)	6
Japan	1,450	Yahoo!, 89%	Yahoo! (48%)	Mixi JP, 19% Facebook, 6%	154 (44%)	6
Australia	1,325	Microsoft, 93%	Google (92.5%)	Facebook, 74% Windows Live, NA	92 (55%)	8
Russia	1,250	Yandex, 79.3%	Yandex (39%)	VKontakte, 73% Facebook, 8%	NA	6
China	780	Tencent, 65%	Baidu (13%)	Baidu (QQ), 16% Kaixin, 7%	50 (5%)	NA
India	750	Google, 94%	Google (86%)	Facebook, NA Orkut (Google), NA	NA	8

Sources: Comscore (2010a,b), Alexa.com (2010), and Experien Hitwise Canada (2010) (all sources last accessed October 20, 2010).

The internet is not the same "thing" in every place; nor has it been the same "thing" over time (Braman 2010). For instance, Elizabeth van Couvering, in Chapter 8 in this book, sketches three phases in the development of the internet since its popularization after the introduction of the world wide web in 1993: first, a phase of technological and commercial innovation (1994–7), followed by attempts to consolidate ownership and control over the internet by media and telecoms firms (1997–2001), and finally the rise of a commercial internet model based on the searchable web, syndicated search engines, user-created content, and selling access to audiences (2002–). The fact that the internet changes over time and space also suggests that its potential impact on other media will vary over time and place.

As I have shown, the traditional media are largely thriving, growing more diverse, yet becoming concentrated in key areas. The strongest potential counterpoints to this portrait, however, are the newspaper and music industries. Newspapers are still the third largest segment of the network media industries, with revenues significantly higher than the film industry, about double those of the music industry and nearly 3 times as high as video games (see Table I.2). Some, however, argue that the press is in terminal decline. There is no doubt that *some* elements of the press have been battered badly in recent years. In the United Kingdom, for instance, the internet accounted for 24 percent of all advertising revenue in 2009, up greatly from 3 percent just 5 years earlier (Ofcom 2010: 10). This is far more than the worldwide average of 5 to 6 percent and substantially greater than in the United States (17 percent) and Canada (14 percent)—two other countries where the flow of advertising to the internet is relatively high. This is undoubtedly part of the reason why the United States, United Kingdom, and Canada are among just five countries that have seen *medium-term* newspaper revenues decline since 2005 (Japan and the Netherlands are the other two).[10] In the United States and United Kingdom, revenues plummeted by about 30 and 21 percent, respectively, between 2007 and 2009. Newspaper revenues fell in *every* OECD country during the "crisis years" but at a more modest pace (e.g. about 9 percent) (OECD 2010: 17–18; PWC 2010: 29).

The consequences of these trends for journalists and newspaper workers have been harsh. In the United States, the number of full-time journalists dropped from 53,000 in 2007 to 40,000 by early 2010. There were one-quarter fewer full-time journalists in 2009 than at the turn of the twenty-first century. Many US newspapers have been closed or forced into bankruptcy, while coverage of foreign affairs, Washington, state legislatures, science, and so forth has been slashed. The "crisis of journalism" is also allowing spin and official news sources to gain greater control over the news agenda and the primary definition of events, with baneful effects for the role that journalism and media are suppose to play in democratic societies (McChesney and Nichols 2010: ix; Project for Excellence in Journalism (PEJ) 2010; Starr 2009).

Despite the severity of these issues, however, the OECD's (2010) report, "The Evolution of News and the Internet," concludes that it is too early "to make the case for 'the death of the newspaper'" (OECD 2010: 6). Why? First, only five countries have suffered *mid-term* revenue losses (i.e. since 2005–6). For the rest of the OECD countries, the decline has been *short term* and not nearly as severe. In fact, and second, "most OECD countries have seen a growth of their newspaper market between 2004 and 2008" (OECD 2010: 17). This pattern is actually the "norm" on a global basis, where the number of daily newspaper titles *doubled* in the past decade and revenues expanded substantially. In Brazil, China, India, Indonesia, and South Africa, newspaper circulation grew, on average, by 35 percent from 2000 to 2008 (OECD 2010: 24). Third, there has been no downward spike in daily newspaper circulation due to the internet, and newspaper revenues grew even in the worst-hit countries until the mid-2000s. Fourth, newspapers are still often highly profitable, as Chapter 6 shows with respect to Canada. Even in the United States, three out of the four newspaper groups that filed for bankruptcy between 2008 and 2010—Media Group, Freedom Communications, and the Tribune Company—were profitable (the fourth is Philadelphia Newspapers). Bankruptcy allowed them to remove debt, journalists, and old assets from balance sheets that had been warped by the logic of financialization ("Update 1—Big US Newspaper" 2010; Picard 2009: 5). Table I.8 shows the global trend for newspaper revenues for the past 12 years.

The point is not to deny that some elements of the press have fallen on extremely hard times but to suggest that we must qualify the diagnosis and understand that the recent instability is part of the much broader dismantling and reorganization of the traditional media—even though it does appear to be most severe in this sector. Still, it cannot be ignored that, in many countries, the press is enjoying something of a renaissance. Finally, Yochai Benkler (2010), among several others, strikes a less ominous note by suggesting that a revamped press may be in the making, with the following elements at its core: (1) a large role for traditional media organizations that successfully grasp the "new logic" of digital media, (2) many small-scale commercial media (Talking Points Memo, Huffington Post, GlobalPost), (3) volunteer, partisan media (Indymedia), (4) effective nonprofit media (Wikipedia), and (5) a networked public sphere of citizen bloggers and journalists (also see PEJ 2010).

Table I.8 Worldwide newspaper industry revenues, 1998–2010 (millions, US$)

	1998	2000	2004	2008	2009	2010 (estimate)	% change
Newspapers	142,794	156,641	174,395	174,723	154,887	149,317	+4.6

Sources: PWC (2003, 2009, 2010).

The music industry is often cast as being in equally dire straits. Indeed, the notoriety of file-sharing and peer-to-peer (P2P) networks from Napster in the late 1990s to Grokster, Pirate Bay, and the closing of Limewire as I write provides the stuff of legends. The fact that new sites emerge as quickly as old ones are closed down reinforces the view that the music industry is under siege from rampant piracy, digitization, and the internet and that this will only get worse as broadband internet becomes widely used. For about a decade and a half, the Recording Industry Association of America (RIAA) and the International Federation of Phonographic Industries (IFPI)—the two most important lobby groups for the music industry—have consistently argued that the industry's revenues are in decline and that it is a portent of things to come for the rest of the media. As the IFPI (2010) states in its most recent *Digital Music Report*, digital piracy is wreaking havoc on all of the "creative industries" and will soon create "a world where copyright has no value" (IFPI 2010: 20). Given that "digitization" has progressed further in the music industries (27 percent of revenues from digital media) than film (5 percent of revenues), newspapers (4 percent), and all other media sectors, except video games, it should not be surprising that the effects of digitization have been severe in this sector (IFPI 2010: 10).

According to the IFPI, music industry revenues have fallen in lockstep with the advent of the internet. As its *Digital Music Report* for 2010 states, "overall music sales fell by around 30 percent between 2004 and 2009" (IFPI 2010: 18). Figure I.6 below shows the trend.

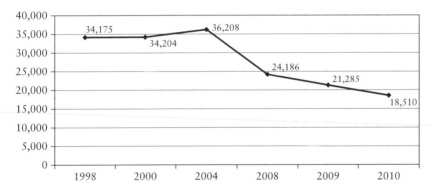

Figure I.6 Worldwide "recorded music industry" revenues, 1998–2010 (millions, US$)

This image of a beleaguered industry, however, is badly flawed because it refers to only one element of the industry and lets that stand for the whole. Indeed, the only way that the music industry can be presented to be in dire shape is to show *only* the revenues from the "recorded music" segment of the business. Figure I.7, however, shows the trend going in exactly the opposite direction once the three fastest growing segments of the industry are included: (1) *concerts and live performances*, (2) *internet and mobile phones* as well as

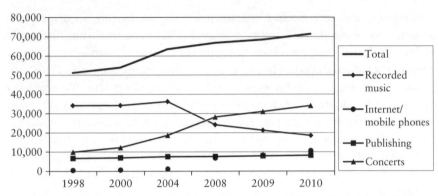

Figure I.7 Worldwide "total music industry" revenues, 1998–2010 (millions, US$)
Sources: PWC (2003, 2009, 2010) and IDATE (2009).

(3) *publishing* (lending rights + digital and network distribution platforms, broader global markets in some cases) (PWC 2009: 274–5).[11]

The "total music industry" is *not* in decline. Instead, its revenues have grown *substantially* from US$51 billion in 1998 to just over US$71 billion in 2010—consistent with other sectors of the network media, with the partial exception of newspapers. The IFPI's use of 2004 as its baseline is also dishonest because this was not a typical year but a relative high point for "recorded music" sales. By definition, anomalies skew averages and in this case the narrow measure is being skewed to advance a policy agenda. That policy agenda has been remarkably successful over the past decade and a half, with copyright laws in one country after another being made longer, broader, and more punitive (e.g. the World Intellectual Property Organization (1996), US Digital Millennium Copyright Act (1998), and Copyright Directive (2001)). This agenda has also been augmented, until recently, through the addition of digital rights management technologies that circumscribe what digital media can and cannot be used for, albeit with results, even from the industry's perspective, that can best be described as ambivalent. Currently, the core of that policy agenda aims to legally require ISPs to restrict, and even cut off, people's access to P2P networks, unlicensed MP3 pay sites, MP3 search engines as well as fan forums and blogs that link to "cyber-lockers" of unauthorized music stashes (IFPI 2010: 19). The IFPI has already chalked up many "wins" for this agenda in several countries that have passed legislation along such lines: France, United Kingdom, Sweden, South Korea, Taiwan, and with many others in line to adopt similar measures (IFPI 2010: 25–7). The thrust of these initiatives is to leverage control over networks to exert greater control over copyright for content. This turns the historical practice of separating control over the medium from the message on its head and poses substantial threats to creative expression by relocating editorial and gatekeeping power back in the center of networks instead of leaving those choices at the ends of networks and in the hands of users (Benkler 2006; Lessig 2004; Vaidhyanathan 2004).

As the screws tighten on BitTorrent and other P2P sites, new commercial digital media services are moving closer to the center of the industry. The emergence of "legitimate" online digital music services is of considerable benefit to the music industry, but they also pose further challenges to traditional players. The long-standing "big four" firms in the music industry—Warner, Universal, Sony, EMI—are in disarray. All have been spun off from their former media conglomerate parents, except Sony, and their share of the market has fallen considerably over the past decade (Noam 2009). In 2009, there were 400 "legitimate" commercial online digital music services (IFPI 2010: 28–9; OECD 2008: 268). The vast majority of these entities have no formal ownership links to incumbent interests (e.g. Spotify, Deezer 3). Many of them are well funded by venture capitalists. This is extremely important because it means that they do not just compete with the incumbent interests in the marketplace for audiences but for capital, observes Hesmondhalgh (2009b: 60). Others are divisions of major telecoms and ICT firms (e.g. MSN Music/Microsoft, iTunes/Apple, TDC Play/TeleDenmark, Sonora/Telefonica, CWM/Nokia). Nonetheless, there are still other services that are owned by the well-established media conglomerates (e.g. Myspace/News Corp., Last.fm/Viacom–CBS, Vevo/Universal, Sony, Google, Abu Dhabi Media).

This is a crowded, complicated, and sometimes competitive field, which makes it easier to explain why the incumbents' sense of being under siege is not allayed by significant revenue growth. At the same time, we must also remember that despite so many different interests and vectors of development, even digital online music services are not immune to concentration. With 100 million subscribers in 23 countries, Apple's iTunes dominates digital music downloads globally; in the United States, it accounts for about one-quarter of such sales (IFPI 2010: 4, 10). Again concentration and fragmentation emerge as two sides of the same coin and thus ought to be considered a defining characteristic of the network media similar to the "publishing model" during the "industrial media age."

Some closing thoughts

To bring this introductory essay full circle, we can conclude by saying that incumbents in the media and telecoms industries have not been able to simply graft the internet and digital media onto their existing operations. However, catastrophic claims regarding the "death," "crisis," and so on of one or another medium, with the partial exception of the press, are at odds with the evidence. In the current conjuncture, digital media, the crisis of capitalism, and a flood of new players entering into an evermore common commercial and cultural field *do* pose significant challenges to well-established players across the network media generally. The discourse of "crisis" and use of the romantic image of "struggling artists" to front for the media industries' bid to apply stronger-than-ever restrictions on the internet and digital media, however, skate over the reality that music, like most other areas of culture, is thriving as an artistic and cultural form and as popular culture commodities. The fact, however, that all media industries are based on "strange commodities" that have been force-fit into the commodity mold with extreme difficulty since the late nineteenth century is a significant cause of never-ending uncertainty (Babe 1995; Boyle 1996). This conundrum has been brought to a head because digitization seems to excavate the "social ecology of information" (lifeworld) from its natural setting and subject it to the processes of commodification to a greater extent than ever in the past. That process, in turn, has been given added momentum by the intense drive for new outlets for capital investment under the guise of the financialization of capitalist economies—a trend that has been very pronounced in the telecoms, media, ICT, and internet sectors relative to other sectors. These processes, however, and as we have seen, do not flatten out all significant social, political, and cultural differences but in some instances magnify them as, for example, the divergent situation of newspapers and "national network media spaces" in different countries helped to illustrate.

Each sector of the media industries, and these industries as a whole, has its own interests that compel them to cloak self-interest in the guise of a problem affecting us all. Pointing the finger at technological change, and one as ubiquitous as the internet, is easy, but also terribly flawed, and based on methodological sleights of hand that take partial elements of a particular media sector and allow it to stand for the whole. The tendency to wrap self-interests in societal concerns has gained more traction in the aftermath of the global financial crisis of 2007–8. However, radical and heterodox political economists have always emphasized that the consequences and costs of capitalism are born by citizens, while splitting over whether these tendencies can be ameliorated through reform or the belief that the system is so congenitally flawed that only its complete overthrow offers a decent way forward. We are once again at such a "fork-in-the-road" moment. While it is neither possible nor desirable to predict how things will transpire, the chapters in this book are animated by the conviction that the rich intellectual traditions in political economies of the media and an open mind are essential to shedding light on the crucial issues of our time.

Notes

1   The IMCRP is directed by Columbia University professor of finance and economics Eli Noam. It includes 40 researchers, including Guillermo Mastrini and Martín Becerra who have chapters in this book, investigating trends in media concentration in every sector of the media and telecoms industries in 40 countries since 1984. It is funded by a modest grant from the Soros Foundation's Open Society Institute.

2   By the number of users and as of December 2009, according to Comscore (2010a).

3   This account of disembedding, social stocks of knowledge, and mediated flows draws from Polanyi (1944/1957), Lash and Urry (1994), Benkler (2006), and Castells (2009).

4   Miège's criticisms were related directly to Theodore Adorno and Max Horkheimer's culture industry thesis, but the surrounding discussion makes clear that the criticisms apply to the then dominant versions of neoclassical economics (e.g. Baumol) and the monopoly capitalism school (e.g. H. Schiller as well as Baran and Sweezy 1966) as well.

5   I am indebted to Peter A. Thompson for a series of discussions that deeply inform this paragraph.

6   Among others, the key members of this school include Bernard Miège, Patrice Flichy, Gaetan Tremblay, Jean-Guy Lacroix, Enrique Bustamante, Philippe Bouquillion, Christina Pradie, Yolande Combes, David Hesmondhalgh, and Nicholas Garnham.

7   As also indicated in the annual reports of these firms for 2006.

8   Google is leveraging its market power in a range of media and cultural policy matters (see Chapter 6 regarding Google's role in Canadian broadcasting regulatory hearings). Google has also attempted an end run around copyright reform in the US Congress by setting its own standards with book publishers (the Google Books Settlement case)—a move that triggered opposition from the governments of Germany, France, the US Department of Justice, and hundreds of others (Darnton 2009; Samuelson 2010). There are many benefits to the proposed Google Books Settlement, but they come at a very steep price in terms of existing legal and cultural standards regarding the preservation, use, sale, and distribution of books and other cultural goods.

9   See Chapter 6 for an assessment of conditions in Canada. Newspaper revenues in the United States, Japan, United Kingdom, Canada, and the Netherlands fell by 20, 9, 7, 2, and 1 percent, respectively, over this period.

10 See Note 3.

11 Note on method for Table I.2: The music category is constructed using data from PWC and IDATE. PWC's *Outlook* does not include publishing rights, concerts, merchandizing, and advertising in its definition of the music segment, even though it observes that these are the fastest growing segments of the music industry (PWC 2010: 275). IDATE does include these elements. I have done three things to arrive at "total revenues" for the music industry: first, averaged the slightly different figures these sources identified for "recorded music"; second, I added the additional categories from IDATE to come up with a total; and third, based

on average growth rates for these "additional categories" I worked backward from the 2006 figures to come up with estimates for previous years. The "internet access" and "internet advertising" sectors are not disaggregated before 2004 in the *Outlook* report. The "book publishing" is drawn more narrowly after 2004 by eliminating professional and training books. In order to make the data consistent across time, I use the definitions from the 2009 edition and then arrive at figures for prior years by extrapolating based on average annual growth rates identified in the *Outlook* report. The 2009 *Outlook* drops "theme parks" and "sports." I have deleted them from earlier years as well to maintain consistency over time. Data for 2010 here and throughout the introduction are based on PWC estimates in the 2010 edition of the *Outlook*.

PART TWO

From the Singular to the Plural: Theorizing the Digital and Networked Media Industries in the Twenty-First Century

1

Principal Ongoing Mutations of Cultural and Informational Industries

Bernand Miège
University Stendhal of Grenoble (France)

The "mutations of cultural, informational, and communications industries" research program

For over three decades, a group of scholars has developed the Cultural Industries School.[1] Some of the key figures, main contours, and diffusion of this school, especially in Europe, Latin America, and parts of Canada, are outlined well enough in the Introduction and in Chapter 2, so they do not need to be repeated here. Instead, this chapter provides an update on a collective research program organized by practitioners of this approach in 2004 at a seminar at MSH Paris Nord. Its participants call this research program "Mutations des CICI" or, translated into English, "Mutations of Cultural, Informational, and Communications Industries." This research project is the next step in a trajectory of research that others and I have carried out for many years under the framework of the cultural industries approach. The goal is to grasp the contemporary mutations affecting the cultural, information, and communications industries. Sometime in the future, we also intend to examine whether it makes sense to distinguish between the now fashionable notion of the creative industries and our focus on the cultural industries. For the time being, however, it can safely be said that we are skeptical that much would be gained by a change in nomenclature at this time.

Our current approach reflects the reality that, intellectually, the conditions in the humanities and social science research remain unsettled. Furthermore, our "objects of study" are likewise in a heightened state of flux. Reflecting this unsettled state of affairs, it is necessary to indicate that the task in front of us is a daunting one and can only be partial and tentative in the conclusions that it draws. The temporality of the phenomena under study is too quick to do otherwise. In other words, things are far from complete, and to proceed otherwise would impose a false sense of surety on the insights that we do offer. Media professionals, industrialists, and decision makers in the public sphere, of course, would like faster answers, but this is simply not possible, at least not in an honest way. Despite these demands to supply ready-made formulaic answers, what is being observed here does not take place over a short span of time. Instead, it brings together a number of tendencies that, however congruent and related to one another, do not in any way lend themselves to being identified as a unitary phenomenon. There are no neat-and-tidy answers to appease those who want to know, *exactly*, what we should conclude or do in practical terms about the contemporary condition of the cultural, information, and communications industries. To put this another way, it is as if the compositional elements of the mutations in question are following their own rhythm and are only partially self-regulating; it would be rather bold to suggest that they form something like a system. Nonetheless, we can be sure of one thing: that they are directly implicated in the changes in cultural and informational production and consumption.

Since 2004, we have focused on the question of cultural diversity[2] (to be discussed momentarily in greater detail). This focus has been on a coherent grouping of issues that appeared not long after the beginning of the new century (on the heels of strong protest against World Trade Organization (WTO) policy regarding cultural markets) and were felt by many to have the potential to serve as a normative offset to the ever-expanding, market-based approach to cultural and informational products, both domestically and in international trade. Certainly, cultural diversity works, in some ways, beyond any temporal frame for research. It is also easily overrun by the immediate course of events, as has been obvious since the world economic and financial crisis, with its diverse effects on the regions of the world. Yet, over the past two decades, there has been a steady fixation by the different powers-that-be on not just the creation of a world market economy but an accompanying information and communications framework for just such an entity: *convergence* (among networks, hardware, and content), the *information highway*, *information societies*, and now *creative industries* (or *creative economies*)—and this list will surely grow.

All of these projects, to different degrees, concern the future of cultural and informational industries (though not only this) as well as their place in contemporary capitalism. All, as well, position the cultural and informational industries vis-à-vis (or, more aptly, against) powerful network and computer hardware industries. At the same time, however, the truly significant features of these developments have been given a reflective gloss by slogans and performative injunctions that, primarily, serve as vehicles for ideological discourse. Such slogans and ideological discourses should be named as such.

These syntagms (though differently in each case, as a result of which analysis must be performed repeatedly) are so important because they are at the heart of beliefs that are being translated into action, strategies, and policy; they are mobilizers and, importantly, act across cultures and borders. Pulling apart their exaggerations and simplifications, their tropisms and omissions, their stereotypes and superficialities is indispensable work in all cases. This, however, is not enough because these "programs" are taken up by "decision makers," although not only by them. There is no shortage of, for example, boosterism around quasi-amateur independent production and the importance of social networks for musicians and their publics.

Sorting out the effects of beliefs from real effects is an intellectual undertaking that existing research methodologies cannot ever totally guarantee. Research can, however, show that the social actions that take place in the name of these syntagms, and which are translated into programs of action, have a distinct social logic. This, in turn, underpins the trajectories of development as well as the mutations that characterize the communication, informational, and cultural industries (CICIs). We need simultaneously a comprehensive and global analyses of this sector just as much as we need analyses of the particular industries within it, always going about this work with a certain anxiety about (prudence toward?) the incompleteness of the results and a full awareness that whatever results we do have are provisional. This, then, crystallizes the essential focus of the Mutations des CICI research program: That is, beyond the successive recycling of a relatively coherent set of beliefs and ideologies (syntagm) under somewhat different labels, what social logics are giving rise to durable mutations in the media content industries? Beyond superficial and short-lived effects, how does the expression of these social logics permit a glimpse at long-term changes that are taking place, here understood as mutations?

With regard to *cultural diversity* (and to be clear, all of what is behind this notion), it is useful to insist on the expression's multiple meanings. In play here, and mostly unchecked, are scholarly meanings (as used by liberal cultural economists and anthropologists alike in the area of cultural trade and exchange), trivial meanings (reiterated by cultural movers or artists), and recently constructed politico-strategic meanings (reiterated to a large degree in UNESCO's 2005 "cultural diversity" declaration or built into the "cultural industry" clauses of numerous bilateral conventions). Undoubtedly more so than with other analogous expressions, when we speak of cultural diversity, confusion is common, and slippage between meanings is permanent. The many distortions surrounding the notion of cultural diversity in official and academic discourse are made all the worse by the relatively short history of this syntagm's uptake in "official bodies." Now, even previous scholarly usages of the term seem to have disappeared in a way almost totally unnoticed. It is incumbent on us to question whether cultural diversity will continue to draw interest in the realm of international trade.

Guessing at the answer to such a question would be dangerous. The recent financial and economic crisis represents a certain set of limits on the attempts to build a world economy and will put the brakes on this kind of trend. One can also reason the opposite too, however, as soon as we remember that the increase in trade in areas related to cultural diversity is quite large and runs parallel to the growth seen in trade in the area of digital products, where values have also greatly increased. We know, too, that similar trends have seen long ebbs (and have even been totally eclipsed) before flowing anew: This was the case with the idea of information societies. Cultural goods, in other words, can simultaneously constitute objective limits to economic expansion, while also serving as a vast new frontier of capital accumulation.

Five major trends and trajectories in the development in the CICIs

What can the discussion of cultural diversity tell us about CICIs? What is revealed by the strategies deployed by the various actors that operate under its aegis? Still further, in what way can we see cultural diversity as a darkroom in which we can develop a picture of these industries? On what elements do authorities inside the relevant international organizations and those working in particular professional milieus place the greatest emphasis?

There seem to be five main elements at the forefront of these discussions, all of which translate into an equal number of deep mutations that are currently taking place and congealing within the CICIs (e.g. through public policy, and probably more so through regulatory changes, but equally through the rationalization of distribution, intensification of promotion, etc., processes that can easily be described in relation to the specific industries targeted by the research program: film and audiovisual, book publishing, music production, general information and newspapers, video games). Each of these will be taken up successively, with a focus on their principal aspects.

Mutation 1: the current globalization of, and expansion in, market consumption (of culture and information)

Two things help us to explain the emergence of cultural diversity within international trade and its significance as a trade-related regulatory concept, especially during the early 2000s. First, there has been a very strong incentive and push to open new markets for informational and cultural industry (ICI) products. Second, there has been an emphasis on marketizing cultural and informational products.

However, there is a paradox in both of these processes, which I have proposed should be considered as social logics of communication precisely because they are, along with a few others, at the heart of what organizes information and communication over the long term. In reality, however, these processes have not actually taken such a long time to be realized between more and less developed countries. Those checks that might seem to oppose them present very little in the way of insurmountable obstacles. Some see the CICIs, and the content industries in particular, as being of an inherently political and cultural nature, whose unique status as such should not be surpassed or simply flattened by the advance of the market. Others, however, rely on the remaining relics of a dated brand of cultural protectionism. For the former, culture and information are not and should not become goods. The proponents of the former view cling to a nonnegotiable stance despite decades of evidence to the contrary. The latter conservatively cling to the idea that cultural identity and heritage are crucial and should not be trammeled by the rush to include culture as just another element of trade regimes. In other words, in the public discussions that accompanied and followed the protests over the policies that the WTO sought to impose, those opposed to such moves considered the socio-symbolic components of "cultural goods" as being of foremost concern, and decisive, either because they constituted a "public domain" that ought to stay outside the market or because they wanted to protect and preserve heritage trophies.

Does this mean there are no significant economic stakes at issue, nor particularly, any strong boost sought to world commerce of cultural and informational products? Clearly, such an end is indeed sought, but it does not hold the same significance for every region of the world. For developed countries and the firms that depend on and remain dominant in them, the opening of new markets in developing countries and those of the southern hemisphere is of paramount importance. Such efforts have become all the more trying in light of the emergence and maturation of Indian, Brazilian, Mexican, and even Egyptian competitors, all of which seek to win such opportunities for themselves. The clear hope is for new areas of expansion, but whether this can actually be achieved is far from certain. Marketizing culture and information has always been difficult, and this continues to be the case despite the development of informational and communications technologies (ICTs) better able to regulate access to content and to measure and value information and culture goods. The seriousness of these difficulties has only been compounded by the fact that growth margins for informational and cultural content industries have shrunk, especially since 2009.

Beyond this set of questions, what matters here is not just the place of cultural industries in the development of contemporary economies but actually the position of formerly industrialized countries in the face of polarization occurring in many directions in these same economies. In other words, it is not only a question of knowing whether the industrial and capitalist valuing of culture and information is as strategic as has been claimed by some experts but also whether this is a means by which long-standing groups and firms in industrialized countries can maintain dominance in a time when their status is being contested in many segments of the industries that they pioneered.

Mutation 2: the increasing dominance of communications industries over content industries

This search for expansion while confronting objective limits is not new. But it has accelerated. Recently, we can observe a particular rise in the position of hardware manufacturers, telecom firms, access providers, web players, software industries, and so on. The disproportion in terms of capitalist valuing and economic activity between some of these sectors and others no longer surprises anyone; it is flagrant and rarely analyzed as such. This has begun to give rise to structural effects, to the point that the future of some of the constitutive elements of the cultural and informational industries have come into question.

The increasing industrialization of culture and information leads to a paradoxical observation: The social value of these domains continues to depend on one another, and it is also true that the distinctive conditions of production for specific types of media and cultural goods remain intact. However, the *dissemination* of informational and cultural products is being drawn ever closer together. Previously, different media forms were easy to distinguish from one another by their socio-symbolic functions, consumption patterns, ownership, and regulation. These distinctions are becoming less and less obvious as media and cultural practices themselves become more individualized, especially on account of the proliferating number of ICT devices used in the circulation and consumption of such goods. Moreover, the cultural goods on offer increasingly come from the same multimedia industry groups, although even their operations must cut across the boundaries of the fundamental models that have defined different segments of the cultural industries (i.e. the publishing model, flow model, etc.) for a long time. Finally, the cultural and information industries are distinct from the communications industries, even if they have close relationships with them and are sometimes under their sway by way of ownership, strategic agreements, and so forth. Communications industries are extensions of the telecommunications industries, consisting of the technological networks that enable individuals or groups to remotely communicate with one another.

Communications industries are themselves diverse, and it is dangerous to generalize. However, one fact intrudes on our assumptions: The scenario many once envisioned has not held. This scenario foresaw, first, that communications industries would position themselves, as it were, behind content industries, using these as a cover to justify the distribution of their tools and network access and, second, that the financial control of these same industries via multimedia conglomerates would emerge as sure as day follows night, given the synergies presumed to exist between the two industries. Of course, a few prudent groupings having gained a footing after some sensational failures at the very beginning of the 2000s, but the "realists scenario" so easily assumed in the past is no longer certain today. And so, what is?

First, take Apple, the commercial success of which in some ways established the new reality, where makers bind content and services to technical tools that it provides. In this scenario, Apple, and others in the hardware and telecoms industries like it, is very much involved in music and other areas of information industries but without actively participating in content making. Next, certain telecom companies (e.g. Telefonica and Vivendi) have entered into audiovisual and film production, which, in the relatively short term, upsets how financing and production of film and series is done. Finally, following the example of the dominant purveyor of information on the web (namely, Google), there is distribution and redistribution of content, without concern for what links it to its creation and, despite some lesser agreements reached between producers and copyright holders, there is a stated desire for control of all information. In each of these situations, different as they are (with more or less respect paid to the ways things have been done before and to regulation), there is nonetheless a similarity in that these communications industries have instigated a power struggle headed in their favor. Since the different ICT markets have matured, there is no longer much talk of negotiating with content providers.

Mutation 3: the power of ICTs (digital) over cultural and informational practices

For consumer users, interactions with and uses of ICTs are multiple: access and consultation, archival work, amateur practices, DIY production, social uses, participation in public activities—and the forms of interaction evolve constantly. They are modeled quite closely on—we might even say conform to—the tendencies inherent in these very practices, that is, reinforcement of the logic of individual action; maintenance of social and cultural distinctions; increasingly systematic generational differentiation; enmeshing of public, private, and even professional spheres; as well as increasing marketization, even as the latter, normally highly attuned to information consumption, hurts (for now) the consumption of not-for-profit informational and cultural products. Even awaiting statistical confirmation, we can likely safely add that the present phase is in all likelihood a moment of development for usages that are difficult to evaluate because they are so dispersed and varied in character, occasional, erratic, and therefore still unstable. For most classes of consumer users, this is a time of trial and error.

As such, it would not do to declare the supremacy of ICTs over content. We are not only talking about digital consumption of culture and information, meaning only consumption supported by digital technologies. What has arisen in most branches of this sector is more coexistence than competition: Movie ticket sales are still selling briskly, and neither e-books nor video-on-demand have yet taken a firm hold; newspapers owe their difficulties more to their own past shortcomings and to free venues for information than to the emergence of new digital modes of access and searches for the information that they provide. The latter's efforts to break into new "digital domains" are unstable and of uncertain interest to younger people. Current development in usages and the trial-and-error character of this period thus encourage coexistence between emerging and well-established patterns of media consumption. Paradoxically, the (brutal) domination of the communications industries, or at least of some of these, weakens their capacity to adapt to change in any seriously anticipatory fashion. In many instances, they have become lumbering giants. Conversely, it is true that the major players in the recording industry, despite being the most severely affected by the drop in consumption of CDs since 2003, are, without saying so, in the process of a very real and successful transition to digital platforms.

Mutation 4: maintenance of content industries but emergence of common interindustry characteristics

We will do well to insist on this point, one that will yield surprising results that run contrary to many predictions. How is it that these different industries (music, film and audiovisual, book publishing, news, and even the new video game industry) have been able to maintain or even reinforce the core strength they have held for decades: namely, the existence of a tight industrial oligopoly at the center of each of these industries while being surrounded by a dispersed multitude of players of all kinds of sizes and forms at the fringes?

To this question, we can sketch several complementary answers but still without fully doing justice to the diverse elements in play. Unquestionably, there is the fact that the digital world has not (not yet?) introduced a new product or form to trump those that have emerged over the history of communication and expression. Multimedia is no more than a composite, and at that not a very compelling one, of known forms: Creativity and innovation have not been invited to that party. To be sure, such media open many new possibilities for images, sound, data, and graphics to coexist, while promoting hypertext pathways and allowing interactive access. These developments, of course, underpin much of the hope for innovation, and even revolution, in the methods of creating cultural goods and information products. Despite some meaningful and interesting advances in this direction, most notably in the field of gaming, such potentials have fallen short of our expectations. Most often, websites are not the place of a real renewal of cultural forms but merely texts now displayed on an expanded array of screens and poorly integrated with other modes of expression. But should we be surprised? Film took a considerable amount of time to differentiate itself from theater and photography from which it borrowed.

Meanwhile, as determined as the dominant communications and software firms may be to gain a footing for their own technological systems in the emerging media ecology, they generally ignore content, either directly or even indirectly (through the biases built into agreements with the providers of this content). In other words, these increasingly powerful players lack a strategic stance on content, which they tend to poorly understand and fail to distinguish meaningful differences between distinctive cultural forms. Cultural goods, from this standpoint, tend to be perceived as archaic curiosities steeped in their own history and professional culture. This strategic vision seems particularly lacking when we consider that the commercial interests at stake are considerable and of global proportions. This is why we can expect, in the end, to see agreements develop between these firms and content firms as well as with public agencies.

At the same time, common features between branches of the ICI sector[3] are increasing, characterized by concentration of investment in the production of key content products, rationalization based on methods emerging from distribution broadcast, creation of portals (an area that, in the long run, could be important for exploiting cultural and informational products), and so on.

Mutation 5: difficulties and growing pressures faced by social agents, producers, and in particular, artists and intellectuals within the various branches of the cultural and informational industries

This pressure on creation and production flows from what has just been discussed: the constraints imposed by network and software industries, the ease of multiple disseminations, the rationalization of promotion and distribution, the possibility of direct trade that bypasses retail—these are new factors that upset standard practice in all these branches of industry more or less systematically (for the moment, the music industry has been the site of the greatest number of changes, less so in film and audiovisual). But other perhaps subtler mutations are beginning.

For a start, if the possibility of producing works or editing them is unquestionably greater, and the diversity of what is on offer, as we can see in all these industries, has measurably increased, conditions for production have worsened, and this mutation is far from done: More must be produced (with the same means) faster and with less assured outlets due to the advent of new competitors who pay perhaps less respect to professional considerations. Increased productivity in artistic or intellectual work, precariousness of employment, and the relative devaluing of works thus characterize what is falsely deemed the "digital" era. Those areas where revenues were relatively stable before (e.g. among the majors of the music industry, who, during past moments of technological change, could set prices in which a favorable margin for producers was built in) are less impacted than within more fragile industries, such as book publishing and newspapers, where retail prices might also now be adjusted—downwards. Contrary to what is sometimes claimed, however, this does not necessarily benefit consumers, because the new diversity of products is poorly distributed, and new logics whose value is ambivalent are coming into play (cf. what we can call the "blockbuster/niche" logic).

As well, pressures are increasing on artists and intellectuals at the level of creativity (artistic conception). Not only have most seen their working conditions worsen and their pay become yet more abysmal (made even worse by the resurgence of wage-claw-back mechanisms such as temp work), but the dividing line (as well as social and cultural distinctions) between professionalism and amateurism have shifted to such an extent that they are hard to spot and virtually incomprehensible. The simplification of the creative process results in productions that are deemed "independent" (or "alternative"), being carried out by individuals who in the past would very likely have been required to work much longer to demonstrate their creative talent and abilities. It is true that for more than a century, cultural and informational industries have depended on pools of artists for hire. Indeed, such large pools of precariously employed cultural workers have long been essential to these industries, guaranteeing creative innovation or at least renewal in forms and genres. However, we must wonder if even these pools will continue to be sustainable if there is no longer any guarantee of entry to a professional life for even a portion of the hopefuls?

Three decisive questions and one new orientation in perspective

What lessons and conclusions can be legitimately drawn from these observations for the study of cultural industries? Which recurring themes,[4] originally having taken shape in the eighteenth century but developed throughout the twentieth, are in play in the mutations described above? Sticking to the basics, we can identify three such themes and point to a fourth, only now beginning, but which is poised to take on greater and greater importance.

Theme 1 ICTs should neither be considered technological supports nor strictly content vehicles. Our focus should be on the (somewhat systematic) relationships between production practices, technical means (supports), and content. True, these relationships[5] have been the object of attention (from researchers, specialists, and practitioners) for some time, but no one has yet elucidated all the consequences that arise from them. The result has generally been a mixed set of parallel but uncoordinated approaches separated by a series of distinctions: between practice and technology (networks or tools), between content (on offer) and technologies, between content (on offer) and practice. Our theoretical and practical ignorance in comparison to the strategies and production modes used by actors in each of these areas is no longer acceptable, but nonetheless it persists in spite of blatant asymmetries and shows of dominance.

In the end, neither comparisons between the economic importance of network and software industries relative to the cultural and informational industries nor an evaluation of the relative primacy of ICTs in shaping the practices of the latter (cf. above) can fully explain communicative developments in the present conjuncture. A number of examples of what is really happening abound: Direct trade practices in music are not independent of strategic realignments going on in the music industry and their reorientation toward a diversity of means for accessing their products; end users, be they hackers, activists, or demanding consumers, beyond the free spaces or initiatives they occupy, still interact with and exhibit a kind of dependency toward the strategic orientations of the principal firms in question; with regard to practice, which are increasingly individualized and strongly reflective of specific cultural identities, these relate not only to technological advancements (e.g. the more collaborative Web 2.0 or 3.0) but also to the contents offered and distributed by these means. Triangulation between all of these disparate trends, mutations, and trajectories of developments must thus be a centrally important concern.

Theme 2 The shift from a flow-and-catalog dialectic to a "blockbuster/niche" logic is also a defining feature of our times. The expression "flow-and-catalog dialectic" was coined in 1978 by the authors of *Capitalisme et Industries Culturelles* (Capitalism and the Culture Industries) to name a long-standing practice in book publishing, the record industry, and in film by which successes (small in number but spectacular) are used to compensate for failures (in the strict commercial sense) and losses. Editors and producers realized that they had to, first, offer a range of products in a kind of catalog that far exceeded market demand, second, to calculate their basic operating income, and finally, to determine commercial gains not title by title but by the whole catalog of titles held by any given entity. Because successes were hard to predict (despite marketing), they spread their risk and hopes for it across the entire range of titles. Obviously, the ideal did not always hold in practice, and most producers had a tendency, especially in lean times, to narrow the gap between their field of offerings and market demand, that is, to diminish the importance of the catalog's capacity to pay over time. Over the course of the twentieth century, nonetheless, the dialectic did prove itself as a practice, in part, because to abandon it was extremely costly: For example, for a book editor, to get no prize nominations in a given year was perilous, and it was smarter to maximize their chances through larger production, a choice that also let them test out new talent.

This practice, specific to the publishing and film parts of the culture industries (it does not work the same way for other media), has not been abandoned. However, it is being supplanted/augmented, at different rates depending on the specific branch of informational and cultural production, by a more or less observable kind of double movement: On the one hand, there is a concentration of means (as much financial as artistic, technical, and promotional, not to mention over distribution channels) on a small number of titles through the organization and predetermination of distribution (through advance sales, etc.); on the other hand, clearly there are more specialized niches being created (through limited editions and with carefully targeted potential audiences) with low profit margins (and concurrent recourse to other compensating revenue streams, including requests for public funding, sponsorships, minimal sales guarantees by sellers, etc.). This "double movement" has begun but is still far from complete.

This kind of production suits the conditions created by the digital world (this is already the case with, among others, independently produced music groups). In the end, cultural or informational production is not actually restricted by this double movement; quite the opposite, in book publishing, music, and even film production, the annual number of titles is growing (as well as reaching a now-global audience), but there is no longer any compensation between one movement and the other, with predictable economic consequences but also with new modes of cultural and social discrimination.

Theme 3   The online portals: A conception–production–consumption logic for cultural and informational products is increasingly becoming a model. The question of the evolution of future models is part of a larger analysis of the cultural industries and their place in contemporary capitalism. Either we see these industries as being at the heart of capitalist development, and consequently assume a stance that is typically loathe to admit to any specificities or uniqueness among cultural commodities, or we see them as dated relics of the past rapidly on the way to extinction. Or yet again, we can see such commodities, and especially when they are linked to ICTs (platforms, particularly communications tools and devices), as so many differentiated modes of exploitation and "management" procedures that constitute little more than what the professionals call "business models."

But here we must insist on the fact that the models for production—consumption defined by several writers (among them, yours truly) in the past, including editorial, flow, club, online portals, and brokerage models—are ideals and are not limited to the dimensions of financing the production of cultural merchandise. In very real ways, these models also grease the entire chain of conception–production–consumption, while also leaving their mark on user/consumer practices. Certainly, the conditions of cultural production (among them, financing) are far from indifferent to the making and consumption of merchandise. However, it would be too constricting to limit ourselves to this dimension only or to foreground it by isolating strategies used by different types of producers in their search for viability and *a fortiori* the profitability of new products. This is why, for my part, I do not label these as socioeconomic models (which would be much too reductive). I see the editorial and flow models as being generic models that have stood the test of time, while the club, online portals, brokerage, and print-bound form of the press represent for me a logic (because stable over the long term) that do not quite fit the designation of being unique "models."

The present situation is difficult to interpret because it is moving toward diverse disruptive or emerging phenomena, several of which have been mentioned above. These phenomena consist of, first, the increase or, rather, the enlargement in the range of industrialized cultural and informational products on offer by the different industrial branches of the CICI and in the development of an entirely new industry and online video games; second, the expansion of media and new media; third, bitter competition between artists, intellectual creators, producers, and distributors for those resources that consumers of these products allocate, which are necessarily limited (particularly as public funds are frozen or in decline); fourth, the difficulty of raising or even maintaining prices (which were too high before and included a quasi-rent, as in the case of CDs, etc.); and fifth, diversification in the means of accessing products, which considerably extends the breadth of possible access points, from a single user acquiring a good through a technical support (e.g. a book) to online use of online content (watching a talk show on a commercial network), and a whole slew of different means in between, the most significant of which is pay per view—an exemplary case of the new "metered economy" and based in a reworking of the urban service economy; and finally, sixth, demand, especially by the youngest consumers and those in developing settings, for free access to content, which is assisted by both the technical possibilities of the tools at their disposal and the ways intellectual production is remunerated. This is a defining feature of the computer industry, which thereby becomes a significant new player in the culture and information industries as a result.

All of this constitutes a complex situation indeed, one that will be transitory for some time. This is to be expected due to the multiple and divergent interests at stake, including those of major players (cf. see Mutations 2 and 5). Nonetheless, we can still identify and label the principal logics in play. For the generic models, the publishing and flow models maintain a strong position; coming between them is a neo-club model, highly diversified, arising as much from the televisual club as from new platforms (more or less in relation to provision of internet access). But it is useful to add that the publishing model, as well as flow and club, is now taking on the form of adapted hybrids, with the evermore insistent presence of advertising (not strictly related to media) and sponsorship deals. This change leaves (for now?) very little room for brokering. As for the online portals model, it is on the ascendant, but only recently, and in experimental forms; thus, we can hypothesize that it is on its way to becoming a generic model, equal to publishing and flow models, provided it is not limited to the distribution of products and that it leaves its mark on production, including at the conception stage.

Theme 4   Finally, there is an increasing tension in intellectual property rights that is pitting author's rights against the general form of copyright. This question merits immediate attention, since it could eventually disrupt one of the major functions of the cultural and informational industries. The intensifying tensions in intellectual property rights are arising from many sides: It is emerging from the computer industry's increasing interventions in the cultural and informational spheres. The WTO's efforts to remake cultural and informational products into goods like any other and to transnationalize them are also behind the process. The emphasis of big companies specializing in blockbusters is yielding similar results. In emerging economies that have no settled custom of integrating the particularities and demands of author's rights, firms that still largely function on an in-house basis (such as Indian film companies) are also bringing tensions within intellectual property rights into sharp relief. More recently, the emergence of the "creative industries" project and, more fundamentally, the push to foster the so-called "creative economy," first in the United Kingdom in the 1990s and now in many parts of the world, have propelled the extension of intellectual property rights into an extremely wide array of activities and territories now covered under the rubric of the new creative industries. All these forces are disrupting the conventions that have ruled industrialized cultural and informational production for two and half centuries. New settlements will surely emerge over time, but in whose favor and with what consequences for cultural and informational production remain an open question.

Conclusion

Throughout the twentieth century, cultural and information industries have been changing constantly and have undergone some significant innovations. Of the three themes and the issue of intellectual property rights just discussed, it is extremely difficult to envisage the ultimate destiny of the developments now under way. Already, and especially in the past one to two decades, they have led to significant changes in the organization of the CICI and to new alignments between the participants and players in these industries. New modes of consumption are proliferating, and the dissemination of cultural and information products is converging around a small number of networks. Still, abiding distinctions between the production of cultural forms still persist and are not easily erased by a single "master logic" such as digitization, convergence, commodification, and globalization. One common observation, however, is that all aspects of the CICIs are now at the forefront of attention in not only the developed capitalist world economy but also emerging countries and even the poorest countries alike.

Notes

1   This chapter builds on previous work published as "Nouvelles considérations et propositions méthodologiques sur les mutations en cours dans les industries culturelles et informationnelles" [New Considerations and Methodological Concerns Regarding Current Mutations in the Cultural and Informational Industries] in Miège (2007b). It will appear, in a slightly altered form, as "Les mutations en cours des industries culturelles et informationnelles (Suite)" [Current Mutations in the Cultural and Informational Industries] in Miège (2011b). We would like to especially thank the editors, who have agreed for this chapter to appear in translation.

2   At the turn of the new century, cultural diversity (and its preservation) became at once a paradigm for international trade of cultural products and a normative tool (as written into UNESCO's 2001 Universal Declaration on Cultural Diversity and attendant conventions) aimed at guaranteeing multiculturalism. In reality, this idea has been interpreted in numerous and even contradictory ways, and following Armand Mattelart, it can be seen at once as a support to criticisms of translational cultural industries and as *une caution du nouveau mode de gestion du marché global* (a prop for a new style of managing global markets).

3   For a complete and detailed picture of recent developments of different branches within the ICI sector, see the assessment made of these (in French) at http://www.observatoire-omic.org/fr.

4   If, to explore this point, we turn only to my own work, we can consider the following two publications (each with a usefully full bibliography): *Les industries du contenu face à l'ordre informationnel* [Content Industries in the Information Order] (Miège 2000; particularly, pp. 15–34) and "The Cultural Industry Theory: Reconsiderations, Persistent Specificities and Adapting Modalities to Contemporary Issues" (Miège, 2011a).

5   Miège (2007a).

2

Media Ownership, Oligarchies, and Globalization

Media concentration in South America

Guillermo Mastrini and Martín Becerra
University of Buenos Aires

Introduction

This chapter begins by reviewing different lines of thinking within the political economy approach to the media industries and communication.[1] It then sketches the main historical processes that have shaped the media in Argentina, Brazil, Chile, and Uruguay—the Southern Cone countries of Latin America—and compares media concentration trends in these countries over the past decade. Lastly, we analyze the variety of strategies used by the main actors in the media markets of the region.

Studying the media industries, and media ownership in particular, in Latin America is important for several reasons. For one, the region has one of the highest levels of media concentration in the world (as this chapter will show) but is difficult to study because Latin American countries lack reliable statistics from either the State or the media companies themselves.[2] There are many studies available about media ownership, but most have been national in scope and lack a consistent research methodology.[3]

Underlying all of our research is the belief that any theory about the consequences of concentration must first establish the real structure of the media system. We have set out to do this by systematically surveying the structure of media markets, their concentration levels, and the main media groups in each country of the region using data from three different points in time (2000, 2004, and 2008).[4] This research project has already helped to illuminate the main tendencies with respect to media ownership concentration and has set critical precedents for linking the analysis of media structure to the development of communication policies in Latin America over the past 5 years (see Mastrini and Becerra 2006; Becerra and Mastrini 2009).

This chapter extends our research project by setting out the main characteristics and tendencies of the media industries in the Southern Cone countries. We pay particular attention to the strategies used by telecommunication companies such as Telmex and Telefonica to expand their influence across Latin America in the twenty-first century, largely as a result of technological developments, especially digitalization, that have blurred the traditional barriers between telecommunications and media (especially radio and television). We also show that the close historical ties between media owners and the State is changing with the rise of the "regulatory state," a trend that has been magnified by the rise of left-wing, center-left, and populist governments in the regions (Brazil, Chile, Bolivia, Ecuador, Venezuela, Nicaragua, Uruguay, and partially Argentina) that have been keen to flex some regulatory authority.

We are particularly interested in showing how the large communication groups of the region are adapting themselves to the new environment. They are doing so by finishing the transition from family-owned businesses to media conglomerate structures. Some have also taken advantage of globalization to diversify their interests in other countries (especially Televisa, Cisneros, and Globo). At the same time, however, we argue that large media groups in Latin America are at a crossroads, with ample opportunities to expand but with their strategies hemmed in by more assertive regulators, on the one hand, and as powerful telecommunications-based rivals enter their domains, on the other.

Approaches to media concentration

Media markets in Latin America are both international and dynamic, and most media companies are now at a crossroads where future growth depends on acquiring smaller companies or being taken over by an international group. The increase in mergers and acquisitions of info-communication companies as a result has turned the traditional structure of firms into a new structure of groups. Spanish scholars such as Enrique Bustamante (1999), Ramón Zallo (1992), and J.C. Miguel de Bustos (1993) have developed a solid body of research that provides a wealth of detailed analysis on the structure and strategies of the main communication groups in the region. Our research builds on that tradition and other internationally well-known approaches to the political economy of the media and cultural industries.

In general, there are three approaches to media concentration. The first one, marketing oriented, is not concerned about the concentration processes except for monopoly cases and the impact of consolidation on advertising rates. The second is the pluralist school, which recognizes the risks of concentration and supports State intervention to restrict ownership concentration but usually does not share the broader criticism of the critical approach. Finally, the critical school characterizes media ownership concentration as a dynamic process shaped by and through markets, political decisions, technology and cultural influences, as well as one of the main mechanisms through which capitalism achieves legitimization.

Adam Thierer (2005) proposes a drastic version of the market-oriented thesis when he suggests that criticism of media concentration rests *entirely* on myths. In his view, information is abundant, not scarce, in the information society, and ownership concentration, even if does exist, does not necessarily imply a reduction in informative options given the pace of ongoing technological change. His position supports the least possible State intervention and the market as the best way to guarantee diversity: "[F]ar from living in a world of media monopoly we now live in a world of media multiplicity" (Thierer 2005: 18). For Thierer, we live in a golden age of media diversity. Benjamin Compaine (2005) similarly states that there is no empirical evidence to relate the effects of concentration of ownership to the decline of diversity of media content.

Eli Noam (2006: 1) explains that "[p]luralism is important. But, there is no conceptual, practical or legal way to officially define and measure the vigour of a marketplace in ideas. The best one can do is to count voices, and assume that in a competitive system, diversity of information increases with the number of its sources." In order to better analyze the impact of media ownership concentration, Noam proposes to divide the Herfindahl–Hirschman Index (HHI) that shows the power of the market, by "the square root of the number of voices." The resulting index, according to Noam, would measure the diversity of the markets more accurately and also make it easier to develop policies according to the prevailing political and cultural standards of the time and place.

The critical school has strongly condemned the processes of ownership concentration. In a pioneering study, Ben Bagdikian (1986) tried to demonstrate that the media in the United States are concentrated and that media owners promote their values and interests through the outlets they control. Interference in journalistic work can be indirect when influencing editors through self-censorship or direct in cases in which media texts are changed or spiked. The key point is that ownership concentration jeopardizes the expression of critical voices. More recently, Robert McChesney (1999) has raised the alarm about the risks of communication concentration at a global level. According to McChesney, market logic and convergence are turning a global media oligopoly into an even larger communication oligopoly. Graham Murdock eloquently states why we should be concerned about these trends when he observes,

> [P]ress freedom was [originally] seen as a logical extension of the general defense of free speech. This was plausible so long as most proprietors owned only one title and the costs of entering the market were relatively low … By the beginning of this century the age of chain ownership and the press barons had arrived, prompting liberal democratic commentators to acknowledge a contradiction between the idealized role of the press as a key resource for citizenship and its economic base in private ownership. (Murdock 1990: 1)

Arsenault and Castells adjust the focus of the critical school by recognizing the effects of media concentration within a global framework but give greater weight to the idea that the groups standing at the core of the global media system are not stand-alone entities but complex multinational companies that operate through a global network of relationships. According to Arsenault and Castells, those networks are capable of producing diverse content, especially when taking advantage of the benefits of digitalization. In order to understand power, therefore, we need to comprehend a dual process that combines networks of control by big corporations with the creative capacity of new producers. Moreover, we need to see media conglomerates as being compelled by the threat of extinction, or exclusion from the network, to be agile and determined to discover new business models that will sustain them into the future (Arsenault and Castells 2008b: 744).

Our research has gathered contributions mainly from the critical theory approach. From this perspective, the assessment of ownership concentration and consolidation constitutes one of the entry points for understanding the processes of social signification on a massive scale. The structure of the communication system is a vitally important dimension in the process of meaning making and circulation, and needs to be analyzed along with other mediations. Moreover, this task is especially urgent in Latin America, where it must not be forgotten or ignored that it was impossible to discuss this topic in either academia or government during the 1980s and 1990s.

The issue of diversity

A general consensus exists among communication scholars, reinforced in recent years, about the importance of preserving and strengthening cultural diversity.[5] However, beyond the most general level of agreement on this point, opinions and approaches to the issue diverge sharply.

There are no fixed rules regarding the number of products or proprietors necessary to guarantee pluralism in a society. At the most basic level, the key issue is whether or not concentration of the media has a negative influence on the range and flow of information and ideas (Vivanco Martínez 2007: 14). The relationship between concentration and pluralism, however, is neither simple nor linear since there are many factors to account for, that is, the size of a particular market and the availability of resources, media market structure, diversity of content, sources, and innovation tendencies (Doyle 2002a: 15). Gillian Doyle underscores the difficulty of linking the number of owners to the range of voices available. As she states, it is reasonable to think that big companies are in a better position to innovate in products and content than small firms. That being the case, concentration could conceivably increase levels of pluralism. A concentrated market with few proprietors could have a more efficient cost-benefit margin and, therefore, more resources to innovate and to increase the quality of its products. However, she also counters that "[p]luralism is not simply about the presence of several different products in a given market, or even separate suppliers, for their own sake. The need for pluralism is, ultimately, about providing society a whole representation of the different political viewpoints and forms of cultural expression" (Doyle 2002a: 14).

Napoli agrees that diversity and public policies are part of a larger goal of the State to ensure the development of a well-nourished "marketplace of ideas" as a necessary condition for the exercise of the rights and duties of citizenship (Napoli 1999: 9).[6] However, after studying communication policies in the United States for the past two decades, he asserts that many State decisions have assumed a cause–effect connection between source diversity and content diversity (limited concentration brings more diversity) but have failed to empirically demonstrate such a relationship. Napoli (1999: 12) states that focusing on the number of proprietors can provide a useful tool for approximating the diversity of information sources available, but he also argues that any examination of the concept of diversity must also consider whether the market allows broadcasters reasonable access to audiences. Such an approach, he argues, should focus on the distribution of the market share ("diversity exposure") in order to assess the exposure of audiences to different content.

Van der Wurff and Van Cuilenburg (2001) analyze the effects of concentration by combining industrial organization theory—particularly, the concept of "competitive strategies"—together with the Schumpeterian emphasis on innovation as the key element to ensure diversity and pluralism in media systems. Diversity, in this case, encompasses two key dimensions:

1 *Reflective diversity:* the ratio of media content that represents ideas and issues requested by the audience.

2 *Open diversity:* evaluates the ratio of the media that expresses the ideas and points of view that circulate in society, beyond the audience's demand.

For Van der Wurff and Van Cuilenburg (2001: 214), an "optimum" media system exists when it achieves a "balance" between "reflective" and "open" diversity. The most likely route to that balance, they argue, is through an oligopoly media market structure that allows for *moderate competition* while avoiding *ruinous competition.* From this point of view, moderate concentration can encourage media companies to adopt strategies that promote product differentiation and the use of resources in ways that offer acceptable levels of reflective and open diversity, while increasing audience size and maximizing benefits overall. It would also, however, restrict the entry of new competitors to the system.

Measurement techniques

According to Doyle and Frith (2004), most studies of media economics and concentration focus narrowly on specific issues in specific media industry sectors. Consequently, we end up with a variety of inconsistent results derived from the techniques and theoretical approaches of a wide range of disciplines running the gamut from sociology and political science to economics and industrial organization theory. On their own, none of these approaches by themselves offer a common approach or adequately address the specificity of cultural and communicational products. The success of inquiries, as a result, turns on our ability to assess the strengths and weaknesses of these perspectives and the methodological tools they use.

The HHI is one of the most widely used techniques to measure media concentration. This index can be used to measure the market share of each proprietor among the total number of media companies under consideration and can give an approximation of existing levels of diversity on the basis of the relative weight of each source within whatever media sectors a researcher chooses to select. Napoli (1999: 20) recognizes the value of the HHI on the grounds that studies of diversity and pluralism need quantifiable evidence, but he also argues that there is still not enough empirical evidence to conclusively demonstrate a causal relationship between the number of sources and diversity.

Albarran and Mierzejewska (2004) also highlight the crucial role played by the availability of information and survey techniques in North American and European markets. This point has broader application and applies especially to Latin America, where the lack of reliable State statistics and the scarcity of data provided by media companies pose severe challenges to researchers. For our studies, we have chosen the CR4 concentration ratio, which measures the market share of the top four operators. Although this technique may not be as accurate as the HHI, it adjusts better to the limited information available in Latin American markets. This choice is also supported by Albarran and Dimmick (1996: 44), who state that "the best measure of concentration is the HHI. The index is more accurate than concentration ratios, but to calculate the HHI one must have data on every firm contributing to total revenues in an industry ... [Absent such data] concentration ratios are the most useful when analyzing trends over time." Our analysis covers the years 2000, 2004, and 2008, and our fieldwork is complemented by an analysis of the revenue sources by media sector for each of the main companies in the region over time.[7] This approach allows us to assess concentration trends during the first decade of the twenty-first century.

The media in the Southern Cone

Generally speaking, the communication model in Latin America follows the main characteristics of the North American model. Broadcasting was taken over by the private sector from the outset and has stayed that way with some competition and near complete reliance on advertising for financial support ever since.

Both radio and television have shown a strong tendency to centralize their content production in major urban centers. Free-to-view television depended heavily on North American content for many years, but since the early 1990s the ability to produce national content has steadily grown, and now even prime-time fiction genres have been captured by national productions (although Uruguay is an exception due to the small size of its market). Foreign content, however, is still predominant on cable television, with several movie and series channels relying entirely on a flow of content from Hollywood.

There is one key difference between Latin America and the United States, however, and this is the existence of State-owned television channels. Chile is perhaps the most outstanding case in this regard, where television channels were run by the State and universities until the 1990s. A similar case took place in Colombia, although despite these differences in ownership the overall business model hewed closely to the business models adopted across the rest of the continent.

In a comprehensive study of Latin American television, John Sinclair (1999: 77) highlighted the extent to which ownership and control in the industry is based exclusively on family structures with strong patriarchal figures. Although this model is still relevant, the internationalization of the audiovisual markets has also led to the arrival of a new generation of large media groups. As we stated in a previous study, "the descendants of the patriarchs still exercise family control over the media groups but they apply new management styles. The old 'national champions' are turning into important actors in a globalized world" (Mastrini and Becerra 2001: 180). Fox and Waisbord (2002: 9), who have systematically chronicled the main changes in the media system since the 1990s, paint a portrait whereby "the main trends in Latin American media have been the formation of multimedia corporations; the decline of family-owned companies; the articulation between local, regional, and international capitals; the intensification of cross-regional trade of investment and content; and the increase in the production and export of television programming." Media have also changed their supply. As Bustamante and Miguel (2005: 13) state, media groups "originally based on distribution and diffusion ... have learned to take charge of important national productions with strong local demand (like TV fiction), but they have also abandoned or weakly cultivated the most dominant markets, like cinematography or record companies, where they have developed alliance policies with global groups."

As regards the relationship between the media and the political system, governments historically have generally adopted lax standards with respect to media ownership and other standard policies in exchange for a certain level of political control over media content. Elizabeth Fox (1990) describes this model as a politically docile commercial media system. The predominance of neoliberal policies since the 1990s promoted an even more lax environment, with ownership concentration increasing as a result and greater cross-ownership setting the stage for the rise of large media conglomerates. This situation is especially apparent in large markets such as Brazil and Argentina.[8]

During the first decade of the new century, however, the neoliberal postulates of the Washington Consensus have waned and a new agenda is arising, where media have a prominent status. Some changes in media policies have increased regulatory intervention and to the adoption of at least some modest limits to ownership concentration. Likewise, there has been more encouragement for civil society to participate in the arena of policies and media ownership.[9] Media proprietors have responded immediately and vociferously, denouncing government regulation as a constraint on their independence and freedom of speech. This is in line with their stance for decades, where any proposed effort to increase access to new actors has been steadfastly opposed. The previous cozy relationship between media owners and political power described by Fox has increasingly been turned into an antagonistic one in most Latin American countries over the past decade, with television channels, radio, and the press leading the political opposition against democratic governments. In the following sections, we offer a brief overview of the media structure of each country in the Southern Cone region.

Argentina

The definition of communication policies in Argentina involves a paradox: a strong State but with few policies promoting the public interest. The State has had a decisive influence in the broadcasting sector (defining licenses, granting subsidies, sanctioning the legal frame, etc.) but, at the same time, has lacked sustained public policies.

The media system structure is based on private-owned broadcasters that control the media in the main cities in the country. The State/government media complement this structure, although coverage only includes Buenos Aires and areas of low-density population; meanwhile, the main urban centers are not served by public media.

The media structure until the 1980s showed no cases of press and broadcasting cross-ownership. After the 1990s and the neoliberal policies of Carlos Menem's administration, however, the legal framework of broadcasting was modified to allow the creation of media conglomerates. Since then, media ownership concentration has grown steadily. Clarin is the main media group in the country with direct control over the leading newspaper in terms of sales (*La Nación*), and through local partnership agreements, it also controls several newspapers in the rest of the country (e.g. *La voz del Interior* and *Los Andes*). The Clarin Group owns one of the main TV channels in Buenos Aires (Canal 13) and many others across the country, a radio network, the main cable service provider, and several cable channels. The group also participates in other areas of the cultural industries, including newsprint paper production (as a State partner), cinematography production, news agencies, and as a broadband internet service provider. The most significant threat to the Clarin Group's position in the media market is the telephone companies, especially Telefonica from Spain, which dominates the fixed telephone market as a duopoly. Besides Telefonica and Telecom (linked to Telecom from Italy), Telmex from Mexico is increasing its presence. Both Telefonica and Telmex want to enter the cable television business but are currently banned from doing so. The annual revenue of these companies vastly exceeds those of the Clarin Group.

Since 2008, the government and large media groups, especially the Clarin Group, have clashed repeatedly, and especially, over the passing of a new audiovisual media law that sets limits to media ownership concentration. The main argument of media proprietors has been, once again, that regulation restricts freedom of expression.

Brazil

Brazil is the largest media market in Latin America. Cultural industries have an enormous potential development in this country due to its population of over 180 million inhabitants. In absolute terms, cultural consumption in Brazil remarkably exceeds any other country of the region, even though estimates consider that one-third of the population lives in extreme poverty.

Over 500 newspapers circulate in Brazil, most of them regional in scope since there is almost no printing press with a national reach. Media concentration in the main city centers (Sao Paulo, Rio de Janeiro, and Salvador) exists for radio and television, and the shared distribution of content among "media chains" across the country aggravates this situation, even though each member paper in such chains is usually not commonly owned. In other words, while the structure of ownership is distributed among different interests in the major cities, content is shared throughout the whole country.

The Globo Group, whose origins date back to the 1960s, stands out in the Brazilian media market structure. In the mid-1960s, the Marinho family's holdings (headed by the O Globo newspaper) emerged as the dominant player in the television market. According to Fox (1990: 72), TV Globo originated during the dictatorship established in 1964 and served the regime's conservative modernization project very well. After receiving investment from the US-based Time Life Group, Globo displaced its competitors and has become the main national player. Its subsequent growth resulted from substantial investments made by the State in an effort to develop telecommunications through the Brazilian Telecommunications Company. The Group's horizontal and vertical integration was an advantage for the production of a new product with a distinct national pedigree, "telenovelas" (soap operas), which subsequently become Globo's "raw material" for expansion into the international market.

Globo Group also owns the second largest newspaper in Brazil in terms of circulation, the main television channel (with booster stations in most of the territory), and the main cable company in association with Televisa from Mexico. Globo Group has also been keen to expand through partnerships with foreign media companies to counter the mounting threats posed by the possibility that telephone companies such as Telefonica and Telmex will soon enter the main media markets in Brazil and throughout Latin America (Possebon 2007: 302).

In terms of media policies, President Lula's administration (2002–present) has been restrained; in fact, for a long period of time, the communications minister was a journalist Helio Costas, a man with long-standing ties to the Globo chain. The main policy of the government addressed the promotion of public broadcasting through the creation of the Brazilian Communication Company, but that venture has not gathered much momentum. The National Conference on Communications convened by a heterogeneous group of civil society organizations in December 2009 tried to give further impetus to media reforms and the democratic regulation of communication by proposing over 600 projects, but it is uncertain whether or not the administration will update media regulations that date back to the last dictatorship.

Chile

The Chilean Republic has been the most stable economy from the last decade of the twentieth century until the beginning of the twenty-first century. Chile is the only "successful" case of neoliberal policies in the region, in terms of not only economic growth but also some degree of wealth distribution. Though this fact can be attributed to the nonorthodox characteristics of those policies, at least since the recovery of the constitutional regime in 1989 (part of the structural reforms that took place in the 1980s during the dictatorship of Augusto Pinochet). Since then, however, and until March 2010, the country has been run by presidents from the Chilean Social Party.

The cultural industries market in Chile is one of the least regulated in the region. There are almost no legal restrictions for media ownership concentration or for foreign investment in the info-communication sector. The structure of media organizations, especially in the press, was strongly linked to political allegiances until the 1970s. Moreover, television channels were owned by the State and universities. The dictatorship of Augusto Pinochet (1973–89) imposed ideological control over media, censorship, and in many cases closure, all the while buttressing a duopoly between the Mercurio Group (Edwards family) and COPESA Group (La Tercera).

Since the beginning of the 1990s, together with the recovery of democracy, there has been a liberalization and privatization of the info-communication sector. In contrast to the period before the 1990s when the entire media system was controlled by the State and the universities, democratic neoliberalism has allowed private media firms to expand and media concentration to increase. Greater levels of foreign investment have also been permitted, and there is a fairly strong presence of foreign capital in the broadcasting industry. Over the past two decades, the historically high level of concentration found in the Chilean press has spread to other sectors of the media, although media concentration in Chile is still lower than either Argentina or Brazil. At the same time, however, the Concertacion government has adopted policies that constrain the potential for government intervention in the media while also striving to increase the role of public television in the overall media landscape. As a result of the latter efforts, public television in Chile now has higher audience ratings than any of the privately owned media.

Uruguay

For many years, Uruguay has been considered the Switzerland of South America. In fact, besides an oversized banking system renowned for its accounting information secrecy, the socio-demographic characteristics of Uruguay are similar to many European countries. The media system has a strong presence in Uruguayan society, but the small size of the market (less than 4 million inhabitants) prevents the development of scale economies. Moreover, there is a high dependency on content produced in neighboring countries such as Argentina and Brazil.

The media is highly concentrated in Uruguay, although there are no significant, large media groups. In terms of both the press and audiovisual sectors, three groups control the market. Even cable television services have been developed by these three companies. It is important to mention that Uruguay is the only country in the region that has maintained a monopoly for all fixed telephone operations and a central role for the State mobile communications company.

The center-left-oriented Frente Amplio government won the election in 2005 for the first time, but has not adopted any communication policies that have significantly affected the interests of the commercial sector. Nevertheless, a new broadcast regulation for community media was passed in 2008 that is considered to be one of the most innovative of its kind worldwide.

Concentration in the Southern Cone today

As outlined earlier in this chapter, our research has collected data on media concentration levels for the years 2000, 2004, and 2008 in order to identify prevailing trends during the first decade of the twenty-first century. We have already published two books to account for the situation in 2000 and 2004

(Mastrini and Becerra 2006; Becerra and Mastrini 2009), but this chapter updates that work by including evidence from 2008.

Because there are no systematic collections of public or private statistics about the economic behavior of the media, data presented in this chapter have been collected from diverse sources that did not always follow the same criteria but which we have accounted for by cross-checking our data against multiple sources. Beyond some possible inaccuracies of figures, this study systematizes information that has been extremely difficult to find and collate in a meaningful way. Although our broader project analyzes all communication markets (press, radio, television, cable, fixed telephony, mobile, internet broadband), this chapter focuses on the daily press, free-to-view television, and mobile telephony, with data and examples from each. The internet market did not really begin to grow significantly until the first years of the new century and, consequently, data for internet remain limited and incomplete.

Press concentration levels differ in each country. While in Brazil[10] the revenue of the top four newspapers is less than 40 percent of the market share, in Argentina it is over 60 percent, and Chile and Uruguay have a concentration index that is even higher (Figure 2.1). This data confirms previous studies that link editorial market diversity with market size. Simply put, a high volume of readership provides the scale economies that a newspaper needs to operate efficiently. The implications of this point are clearly demonstrated in Brazil where a population that is triple that of Argentina, Chile, and Uruguay combined is able to sustain a larger number of newspaper groups. In terms of the direction of trends, concentration levels have held steady over time.

The television market in Latin America also shows high levels of concentration. According to the data obtained (Figure 2.2), it constitutes an oligopoly market. In all countries of the Southern Cone, the top four television channels control at least 50 percent of the total revenue of the sector. Thus, it can be asserted that the reported levels of concentration are high. Brazil's concentration index, however, is lower than its neighboring countries. It is important to mention

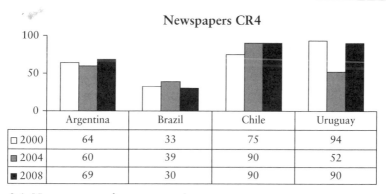

Figure 2.1 **Newspaper market concentration**
Note: Figures represent the percentage of market share accounted for by the top four ownership groups.

that even though the number of licenses in each country varies remarkably—with over 300 in Brazil and less than 50 in Argentina—concentration levels are high in both cases. This would suggest that those who gain dominant positions with audiences early on are able to maintain the most significant part of the market over time. Unlike the press sector, the data show a gradual increase in concentration in the television market of the Southern Cone.

The mobile telephone market is the most concentrated of the markets we assessed. All countries of the Southern Cone reach the CR4 maximum, that is, 100 percent (Figure 2.3). In fact, it is curious that neoliberal policies that

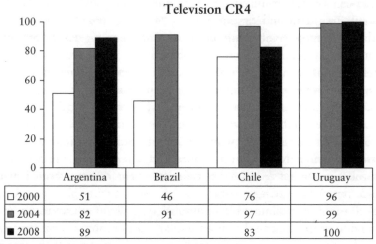

Television CR4

	Argentina	Brazil	Chile	Uruguay
□ 2000	51	46	76	96
■ 2004	82	91	97	99
■ 2008	89		83	100

Figure 2.2 Television market concentration
Note: Figures represent the percentage of market share accounted for by the top four ownership groups.

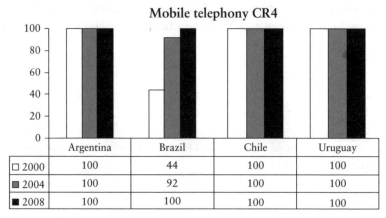

Mobile telephony CR4

	Argentina	Brazil	Chile	Uruguay
□ 2000	100	44	100	100
■ 2004	100	92	100	100
■ 2008	100	100	100	100

Figure 2.3 Mobile phone market concentration
Note: Figures represent the percentage of market share accounted for by the top four ownership groups.

eliminated telecommunications public monopolies at the outset of the 1990s have since spawned a strong private oligopoly (in some cases, duopoly). Even the mobile telephone market, which developed in a "competitive" environment, does not seem to be able to support more than four operators. This situation is also present in Brazil, which showed a lower concentration index at the beginning of the century but which has since seen the demise of most competitors.

The extremely high levels of concentration in the telephone market deserve deeper analysis. As Elizabeth Fox and Silvio Waisbord (2002: 11) point out, "Privatization and liberalization in the telecommunications industry also contributed to the formation of conglomerates. It is impossible to analyze the evolution and structure of contemporary media industries without addressing developments in telecommunications."

Two companies have launched strategies to capture the Latin American market since the beginning of the twenty-first century: Telefonica from Spain and Telmex from Mexico. The Telefonica Group has had a significant presence in most Latin American countries since the beginning of privatization in the 1990s (see Figure 2.4). The Telmex Group (Figure 2.5), which took over the Mexican telecommunications system in 1990–1, began this race later than its rival (Figure 2.6), but it has gained ground and surpassed Telefonica in terms of regional revenue in 2008.

It is also important to compare the relative size of the telecommunication groups and those in the traditional media to underscore the economic importance of the former. As Figure 2.6 shows, in 2008, the revenue of Telefonica in Latin America was nearly 10 times higher than those of all the newspapers in Argentina, Brazil, Chile, and Uruguay combined, 6 times higher than cable television, and triple those of free-to-view television. In fact, the revenue of Telefonica and Telmex combined was US$73 billion for the region, an amount that vastly exceeds the US$21 billion in revenue for the press, free-to-view television,

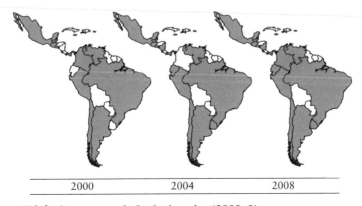

| 2000 | 2004 | 2008 |

Figure 2.4 Telefonica presence in Latin America (2000–8)
Note: Shaded areas equal the growing footprint of Telefonica's presence over time.

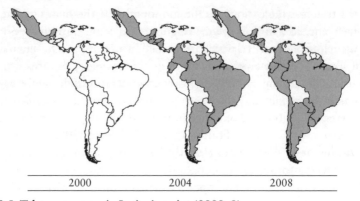

	2000	2004	2008

Figure 2.5 Telmex presence in Latin America (2000–8)
Note: Shaded areas equal the growing footprint of Telmex's presence over time.
Source: Own elaboration from company balances.

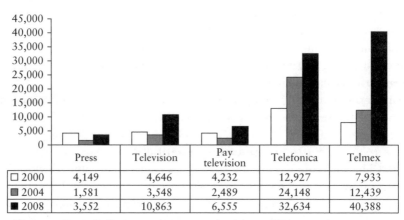

	Press	Television	Pay television	Telefonica	Telmex
☐ 2000	4,149	4,646	4,232	12,927	7,933
◼ 2004	1,581	3,548	2,489	24,148	12,439
◼ 2008	3,552	10,863	6,555	32,634	40,388

Figure 2.6 Media and telephone sector comparative revenue
Note: Data are expressed in millions (US$).

and cable television services combined in the four countries under study. In other words, the capital available for the telecommunications groups vastly exceeds those of the media groups, and this gives them inordinate power when they decide to use it to implement their strategies, policies, and developments across the region. Indeed, that scenario is now coming to fruition with Telmex and Telefonica's recent decisions to expand into cable television to reap the potential benefits of digital convergence. This issue is beyond the scope of this study, but data from Figure 2.6 reveal the potential threat that these initiatives pose to the current proprietors of cable systems in the Southern Cone.

It is also necessary to consider that telephone companies follow the logic of global markets and participate in it on a different scale than traditional media operators (McChesney 1998). Crucially, their global ambitions and reach exceed the traditional frameworks for commercial media operations that have largely been confined to the territorial boundaries of the nation-state. In other words, companies such as Telefonica and Telmex are the most influential actors and will likely be the main beneficiaries of the changes that are now taking place within the framework of the so-called Global Information Society.

According to McChesney, there are three levels in the commercial global system of information and communication. The first level belongs to 10 transnational groups that operate worldwide. The second includes the 50 largest groups based in Europe, United States, or Japan that have businesses spanning several regions and countries worldwide. Telefonica and Telmex are part of this second group. The third level covers groups that lead national domestic markets or subregions and encompasses around 90 corporations, from which Globo Group from Brazil and Clarin from Argentina are the most important in the Southern Cone. The entrance of the telephone companies to the paid television market presumes a dispute between actors from the second and third group, where the telephone companies have stronger financial resources, although the national groups have closer ties with the political world and deeper knowledge of the cultural idiosyncrasies of local media system. There are also thousands of smaller cultural companies, but they do not directly affect the global market, even though their cultural productions are important at a local level.

Concluding comments

As we started out by saying, concentration is a complex, multifaceted, and diverse process. And media are complex, double-sided institutions that mediate both political and economic interests. The sort of commodities they work with have a material as well as a symbolic value. This turns them into special actors whose activities have specific consequences. They intervene, affect, and constitute (although not determine) the public sphere, which is also a political sphere. As economic actors and, due to the very high fixed costs and very low variable costs associated with their activities, the media industries are strongly predisposed toward concentration. The major players organize their activities within this framework, and this has the potential to create entry barriers for other market actors. In order to counteract this tendency, many States have decided over the course of the past century or more to use antitrust policies to stimulate different sources and editorial perspectives.

With regard to the Latin American situation, Bustamante and Miguel (2005: 13) consider that "in terms of the general structure of the cultural industries sector, several conclusions seem to be clear: concentration in Latin American countries, favored and catalyzed through political interference and in an absence of public action to counter them, raises significant concerns in terms of political pluralism in each country, with numerous moments when politicians have assumed unbearable arrogance."

The study has sought to further understanding of the media structure in the Southern Cone, especially through the analysis of the concentration index in the most relevant sectors. Based on the widely accepted standard that concentration exists and is considered high when the top four operators control over 50 percent of the total market share (Albarran and Dimmick 1996: 44), our analysis shows that in all cases (except for the Brazilian press) concentration ratios are high. Although we have shown some of the different points of view on this issue, our methodological tools do not yet permit us to say what the implications of these high levels of ownership concentration are for diversity. That debate is still open.

Finally, a third aspect to consider is the increasing integration between the logics and dominant actors of the communication sector in the Southern Cone and those that lead the market worldwide. As an inherent quality of this process, it is worth emphasizing that overcoming both geographical and industrial borders creates an objective articulation between the global and convergent characteristics of the media and telecommunications sectors. In this respect, Arsenault and Castells (2008b) propose that

> [m]edia content is both diversified and globalized: media ownership is concentrated and organized around networked forms of production and distribution, the backbone of which is provided by a core of multi-national media corporations that operate through a global network of media networks. The majority of media businesses follow a networking logic so that all nodes of the network are necessary to fulfil the ultimate goals of their program: the commoditization of mediated culture and the subordination of all forms of communication to profit making in the market place. (Arsenault and Castells 2008b: 743)

Seen in that light, the greatest challenge for media in the Southern Cone, and especially for its societies, is to somehow mesh with the requirements of a globalized world while trying to avoid the loss of significant cultural diversity at the hands of a highly concentrated media system that such dynamics seem to inexorably entail.

Notes

1   Part of the research for this chapter has been supported by the Press and Society Institute (Instituto Prensa y Sociedad in Spanish, www.ipys.org), a nongovernmental organization based in Lima, Peru, concerned with the defense of freedom of expression and which sees media ownership concentration as a threat to free journalism.

2   One of the consequences of conglomeration processes is that as media companies entered the stock market, they were compelled to provide more information about their financial status—although this only applies to the big media groups that are publicly traded.

3   To the traditional studies of the 1970s (Muraro), we can add recent studies in English: Sinclair (1999), Fox and Waisbord (2002), and in Spanish: Mastrini and Becerra (2006), Becerra and Mastrini (2009), and Trejo Delarbre (2010), among others.

4   The survey collected data of all countries in Latin America from 2003 to the present, including the following markets: editorial, record companies, cinematography, press, radio, television (free-to-view and cable), and telephony (landline and mobile).

5   All member countries of UNESCO, with the exception of United States and Israel, adopted the Convention on Protection and Promotion of Diversity of Cultural Expression in 2005. In Argentina, the House of Representatives passed law 26.305 on November 14, 2007, ratifying the Convention. This is the only international treaty that strives to safeguard cultural expressions in opposition to the movement toward the free trade of cultural goods that takes place in other international organizations, especially the World Trade Organization (WTO).

6   This concept reflects the First Amendment of the United States Constitution, adopted in 1791, which states that "Congress shall make no law respecting an establishment of religion, or prohibiting the free exercise thereof; or abridging the freedom of speech, or of the press; or the right of the people peaceably to assemble, and to petition the Government for a redress of grievances."

7   In previous studies (Mastrini and Becerra 2006; Becerra and Mastrini 2009), we have measured the concentration levels with CR4 ratio, both for companies' revenue and consumption. Nevertheless, we will only work with revenue data for this chapter because the updated information about consumption is not available yet.

8   The same applies to Mexico, Colombia, and Venezuela, but these countries are not part of this study.

9   Analyzing the change of scope of the policies exceeds the remit of this chapter. We will briefly mention a few cases: A new law was passed to regulate the audiovisual sector in Argentina and Venezuela. Bolivia and Ecuador have modified their Constitutions to incorporate the notion of communication rights. Uruguay has passed a new broadcasting law for community media. Brazil organized the National Conference of Communication, attended by thousands of people. The role of public television has been reinforced in Chile.

10 Unfortunately, it was not possible to obtain the revenue data of Brazilian newspapers for 2008.

3

Media as Creative Industries

Conglomeration and globalization as accumulation strategies in an age of digital media

Terry Flew
Queensland University of Technology

Introduction: which media economics?

As the contributors to this collection have made clear, an understanding of the economic dynamics of media forms and industries matters. Questions arising from media ownership and organizational structure, private investment and the debt levels of media businesses, the changing nature of media markets, the globalization of media and cultural production as well as its products, and the impact of digital media technologies on the future of media jobs and professions, as well as media content, all draw out the profound and ongoing significance of economic analysis to understanding the media. But while the importance of understanding media from an economic point of view can be readily acknowledged, there are nonetheless limits to applying such insights in practice. One set of issues arises from the normative expectations we have of media. Whether understood in terms of the "Fourth Estate" watchdog on political power, as the putative site for a Habermasian public sphere (Dahlgren 1995), or as being "central to our capacity to define ourselves as citizens" (Schultz 1994), a prevailing view exists that there are many aspects of media structure, conduct, and performance that are too important to simply be determined by commercial markets. Consequently, extensive government regulation of media remains a priority as a safeguard for liberal-democratic politics and discourse.

Another issue is that media economics as a sub-branch of economic theory has often not been particularly helpful in understanding how actual media forms and markets operate. Influential texts in the field define media economics as "the study of how media industries use scarce resources to produce content that is distributed among consumers in a society to satisfy various wants and needs" (Albarran 1996: 5) and "how media operators meet the informational and entertainment wants and needs of audiences, advertisers, and society with available resources" (Picard 1989: 5). In these texts, media economics is essentially about the application of conventional neoclassical microeconomic theory, and to a lesser extent macroeconomic theory, to the media industries. Such accounts tend to take economics to be synonymous with the *neoclassical paradigm* as it has developed from the 1870s onward, particularly around its methodological individualism, its bracketing off of "markets" and "culture," and its understanding of the central economic problem as being primarily about how producers meet the needs and wants of consumers through the buying and selling of goods in the overarching context of scarce resources. As the cultural economist David Throsby has observed, "Despite its intellectual imperialism, neoclassical economics is in fact quite restrictive in its assumptions, highly constrained in its mechanics and ultimately limited in its explanatory power. It has been subject to a vigorous critique from both within and without the discipline" (Throsby 2001: 2). Such limitations have been pointed out by critical political economists such as Graham Murdock and Peter Golding, who argue that "while mainstream economics focuses on sovereign individuals, critical political economy starts with sets of social relations and the play of power" (Murdock and Golding 2005: 62), and Mosco (2009a), who argues that mainstream media economics has been "limited to taking up incremental change within one given set of institutional relations," and that "it tends to ignore the relationship of power to wealth and thereby neglects the power of institutions to control markets" (Mosco 2009a: 62).

A key moment in illustrating both the power of economic ideas in relation to media and the need to think beyond inherited orthodoxies was seen in British debates in the 1980s over the future of public service broadcasting. The Thatcher government's review into the current and future financing of the British Broadcasting Corporation (BBC)—the Peacock Committee chaired by the economist Professor (later Sir) Alan Peacock—was highly skeptical of arguments for a compulsory license fee as the primary basis of BBC financing, and considered privatization of the BBC, or at the very least a radical deregulation of British broadcasting to promote new competitors. Rather than defend the BBC in terms of its cultural value, Collins, Garnham, and Locksley (1988) instead responded to the Peacock Committee in economic terms, arguing that Peacock's framework of liberal welfare economics failed to adequately comprehend the specific features of the broadcasting commodity and how this shaped broadcasting markets and industries. Among the distinctive features of the broadcasting commodity they identified were the immaterial nature of the commodity and the intangible use-value that consumers derive from it, the public good attributes of broadcast programs and the near-zero marginal costs of distribution, and the high sunk costs in new programs as well as the need to generate continuous program innovation and product novelty (Collins *et al.* 1988: 6–10). Their argument for continuation of the compulsory license fee as the primary source of income for the BBC was made not on the basis of the institution's cultural superiority to "the Philistine influence of economic analysis" (Collins *et al.* 1988: 2) but rather upon applied economic analysis, albeit of a nature that did not simply replicate the assumptions of mainstream economics.

A second major area in which economic analysis has had an impact on media studies in the 2000s has been in the debates surrounding *creative industries*. From this perspective, media and design are moving to the center stage of knowledge economies in an era of globalization (Venturelli 2005), and the arts are increasingly serving as incubators of creativity and repositories of cultural value (Throsby 2008). This has given rise to a great deal of attention on the specificities of the creative industries and the policy implications of identifying such economic features (see Flew 2011 for an extended discussion of creative industries policy discourses). Richard Caves (2000) utilized new institutional economics to consider the pervasiveness of contracts as a defining feature of the creative industries, characterized by endemic risk, profound demand uncertainty, and the high sunk costs associated with complex team-based production processes and the need for continuous product novelty. Potts and Cunningham (2008) have also drawn upon Schumpeterian innovation economics to propose that, rather than being sectors that are subsidized from the "real economy" to achieve cultural or social goals, the value of creative industries increasingly lies in their role as generators of new ideas and processes that have impacts across the economy as a whole. In this account, the more that economies become higher income, postindustrial, and technology driven, the greater the size and significance of the creative industries within them become. As the German economist Ernst Engel observed as early as the 1850s, the proportion of income spent on basics such as food tends to fall as incomes rise, suggesting that the balance of spending flows more toward specialist goods and services as incomes rise. This insight has been applied more recently by Andy Pratt (2009), who observes the resilience of Britain's creative industries since the onset of the global financial crisis in 2008. In other words, the development of the creative industries is not simply an outgrowth of the boom times that prevailed in the UK financial sector in the 2000s, but are now a core part of the base of the British economy.

An important feature of creative industries, first identified by Garnham (1990) in relation to media, is the *hourglass structure* of these sectors. They are characterized by a high number of cultural producers and an infinite number of consumers, but they have historically been constrained by the high costs associated with content distribution, meaning that economic power resides with those firms that control distribution and the delivery of cultural content to markets. Furthermore, high barriers to entry have enabled those firms that control distribution channels to exert monopoly or oligopoly power over other aspects of the media industries. With the rapid adoption of fast-evolving digital media technologies that substantially reduce these distributional bottlenecks, a major question arising out of creative industries theories is whether the economic power conferred by control over distribution channels and networks is diminishing over time or is being reconfigured around alternative sources of economic rents, such as highly restrictive copyright and intellectual property regimes (Benkler 2006). The debate about whether economic power in the creative industries is shifting over time toward producers and consumers and away from corporations, or whether new monopolies are emerging in the sphere of distribution, is one with substantial implications for the future development of political economy in media studies.

The curse of bigness: monopoly, competition, and the media

As noted above, the limitations of mainstream media economics have been readily observed by the *critical political economy* school of media theorists. Vincent Mosco contrasts political economy to mainstream economics, proposing that political economy involves analyzing "the social relations, particularly the power relations, that mutually constitute the production, distribution, and consumption of resources," as part of a broader "study of control and survival in social life" (Mosco 2009a: 24–5). Janet Wasko also observed that "a primary concern of political economists is with the allocation of resources (material concerns) within capitalist societies. Through studies of ownership and control, political economists document and analyze relations of power, a class system, and structural inequalities" (Wasko 2004b: 311). These definitions indicate how a concern with corporate power and how the concentration of ownership and control in media industries and markets impacts—largely in a negative sense—upon the role played by media in public communication, particularly in liberal-democratic capitalist societies. Murdock and Golding (2005) summarize the argument in these terms:

> Media production has been increasingly commandeered by large corporations and moulded to their interests and strategies. This has … been considerably extended in recent years by the sale of public assets to private investors (privatization), the introduction of competition into markets that were previously commanded by public monopolies (liberalization), and the continuing squeeze on publicly funded cultural institutions. Corporations dominate the cultural landscape in two ways. Firstly, an increasing proportion of cultural production is directly accounted for by major conglomerates with interests in a range of sectors, from newspapers and magazines to television, film, music and leisure goods and services. Secondly, corporations that are not directly involved in the cultural industries as producers can exercise considerable control over the direction of cultural activity through their role as advertisers and sponsors. (Murdock and Golding 2005: 64)

It is the first of these two propositions that I wish to critically interrogate here. The media conglomerate with its vast, sprawling tentacles insidiously spread across the political, economic, and cultural landscapes is an enduring feature of our times, as the all-powerful and sinister media mogul has reigned supreme in popular consciousness, from the central figure of *Citizen Kane* to the Bond villain of *Die Another Day* who bore a strange resemblance to Rupert Murdoch. The media conglomerate is one of a number of "big" institutions that can inspire populist outrage, along with bankers who give themselves excessive bonuses or the "out of touch" political elites of Washington, Westminster, Brussels, and elsewhere. But on the case of media, the concerns about concentrated and unaccountable power exist alongside a set of assumptions about how the existence of large, diversified corporations in the industry landscape impacts upon how media markets operate, which require both explication and some empirical evaluation.

Both the neoclassical and critical political economy paradigms draw upon *industrial organization theory* in order to understand how the level of competition in different media and creative industries markets shapes the behavior of firms in that industry. Industrial organization theory has made use of what is known as the *structure–conduct–performance* (SCP) model to determine how the number of firms in a market, the types of products they produce, and the extent of barriers to entry for new competitors, shape a range of conduct and performance variables in that industry. A model of the SCP framework is provided in Figure 3.1.

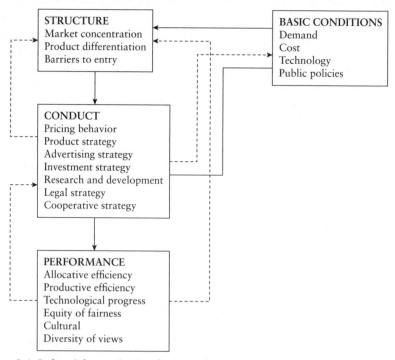

Figure 3.1 Industrial organization framework
Source: Hoskins *et al.* (2004: 145).

This SCP framework generates different types of market structures based on number of firms and type of product, ranging from pure monopoly (one supplier only) to oligopoly (few suppliers, homogeneous product), monopolistic competition (few to many suppliers but differentiated products), and perfect competition (many suppliers, homogeneous product).

The important point that arises from industrial organization theory is that most media and media-related industries are oligopolies, where a very small number of firms account for the majority of market share. Industry economists use what are known as *concentration ratios* to measure market concentration, such as the percentage of total market share accounted for by the four largest firms (CR4) and that accounted for by the eight largest firms (CR8). Based on an examination of trends in the United States in the mid-1990s and again during the first decade of the twenty-first century, Albarran and Dimmick (1996) and Noam (2009) found that the US media and media-related industries are characterized by oligopoly or monopolistic competition, with the broadcast television, cable/pay TV, film, and recorded music industries all having CR4 ratios of over 60 percent (i.e. the four largest firms accounted for over 60 percent of total market share). Indeed, all of the industries they surveyed, except for the newspaper and magazine industries, had CR8 ratios of over 70 percent. Noam also argues that trends over the past decade have been toward somewhat greater concentration and that new media (internet service providers, search engines, internet advertising, web browsers, etc.) are not immune to the forces of consolidation either. Similar evidence of market concentration can be found in most other advanced industrial economies. According to the SCP model, we can expect this market structure to influence aspects of *market conduct* (including pricing behavior, product development strategy, advertising strategy, and new product strategy as well as the propensity to cooperate or compete), and this has further market performance implications that may warrant government regulation to deal with consequences of imperfectly competitive markets, notably over-investment in similar products alongside underinvestment in others (e.g. specialist programs and those of interest to minorities) or the potential for political power to arise from excessive market power (Picard 1989: 94–9).

While industrial organization theory provides a starting point to understanding media markets, and particularly the much-discussed question of whether there is greater concentration of media over time, it has some significant limitations. One concerns the direction of causality. As Hoskins, McFayden, and Finn observe, activity that is associated with market conduct, such as heavy advertising or predatory pricing, could constitute a barrier to entry, although it is not directly related to market structure (Hoskins *et al.* 2004: 152). Moreover, concentration ratios have traditionally only measured media concentration within industries, whereas the dominant strategies of the largest media corporations have been to operate across multiple industries, generating market advantages arising from vertical integration (e.g. ownership of both film studios and television networks) or expanding their range of operations through diversification or conglomeration. Winseck addresses the question of whether concentration ratios continue to be useful in an era of media conglomeration in Chapter 6.

The SCP paradigm is a product of neoclassical economics and its approach to competition. At the core of the neoclassical model are individual producers and consumers, whose interactions in markets determine the formation of prices and the allocation of resources. In this model, the optimal state is held to be that of *perfect competition*, where no individual consumer or firm can have market power, and where prices are set purely by these interactions. The paradox of neoclassical theories as they developed from the mid-nineteenth century onward was that, as the theory of perfect competition was progressively refined at a theoretical level, the evolution of capitalist economies worldwide was increasingly toward the rise of large corporations and the concentration of industries, along with the rise of industries and practices that were clearly associated with strategies to shape market outcomes—the rise of advertising being an obvious and highly visible case (McNulty 1967). As a result, theories of perfect competition have always been open to the charge of being unrealistic in relation to how competition is actually occurring in markets and industries today.

One line of response has been theories of *imperfect competition*, where firms have some control over prices and outputs but not as much as a monopolist would have. The SCP paradigm is based on the "how much control" question and posits an inverse relationship between market structure (as measured by concentration ratios) and firm behavior: The more concentrated the market, the more capacity firms have to exert control over it (Auerbach 1988: 13–22). Many radical critics of corporate media rely on a similar approach but derive their views of imperfect competition from Marxian theories of *monopoly capitalism*. This theory, originally associated with Rudolf Hilferding and V.I. Lenin, has subsequently been applied in its contemporary form by economists such as Paul Sweezy and journals such as *Monthly Review* (Sweezy 1968; Baran and Sweezy 1966; Foster 2000). This latter work has transformed theories of imperfect competition into the more far-reaching Marxist critique of capitalism. The key argument from this perspective is that large corporations have become increasingly able to "tame" the capitalist market and insulate themselves from competitive forces through corporate planning and the use of advertising and marketing, among other things, to manage consumer demand. John Bellamy Foster describes this process as follows:

> With the rise of the giant firm, price competition ceased to take place in any significant sense within mature monopolistic industries. ... In this strange, semi-regulated world of monopoly capital, there is no longer a life-or-death competition threatening the survival of the mature capitalist enterprise. ... Rather, the giant

corporations that dominate the contemporary economy engage primarily in struggles over market share. ... It remains a competitive world for corporations in many respects, but the goal is always the creation or perpetuation of monopoly power—that is, the power to generate persistent, high, economic profits through a mark-up on prime production costs. (Foster 2000: 6–7)

A complicating factor in these debates arises from two quite divergent approaches to competition in economic theory. While Adam Smith and the Classical economists identified competition as being central to an understanding of capitalism, this was subsequently interpreted in two quite distinct ways. The dominant neoclassical approach understood competition as generating a system of relative prices and resource allocation. It is from this tradition that media economics has developed (Albarran 2010) and from which the concept of monopoly emerges as the negation of competition. The concentration ratio, for instance, aims to track the degree of divergence from a perfectly competitive market, where CR = 0 when there is perfect competition and CR = 1 in cases of pure monopoly. This is quite different to the second, minority, tradition that focuses upon *competition as a process*. This latter conception sees competition as "the attempt to out-do one's rivals in securing goods or customers or revenue or profit" (High 2001: xiv) and is less interested in questions such as relative prices than in the relationship between competition and innovation or competition and regulation. The view is also closer to how business people themselves have understood competition. It was also central to Joseph Schumpeter's conception of capitalism as a dynamic economic system driven by intermittent episodes of *creative destruction* (Schumpeter 1950) and figures largely in the economics of Friedrich von Hayek and the Austrian economists. For Schumpeter, the problem with neoclassical models of competition and their emphasis on equilibrium price settings was that they failed to focus on the dynamic and often cutthroat nature of the competitive process, being "like *Hamlet* without the Danish prince" (Schumpeter 1950: 86). Interestingly, there is also a tradition in Marxist political economy that differs from the monopoly capitalism thesis, arguing that competition and monopoly are not diametrically opposed concepts but rather that competition for capital itself acts as a force on firms requiring them to engage in competitive behavior in ways not primarily determined by concentration ratios or market structures (Eatwell 1982).

These views have also been given new life in the work on *competitive strategy* associated with business economists such as Michael Porter (1980). Understood this way, we have the possibility that competition may increase over time, driven by disruptive forces such as technological change, developments in capital and financial markets, and economic globalization (Auerbach 1988). This is not to say that the results will better achieve social or cultural outcomes—they may be less likely to do so—but it is to say that there is no simple movement from competitive to monopolistic markets in the media sector.

Conglomeration as a media corporate strategy

Any listing of the world's largest media corporations reveals that they are complex entities that often operate across multiple industries and markets. Winseck (2008) has demonstrated the extent to which these corporations operate as media conglomerates, and it is increasingly the case, as Dimmick observes, that "the media firm that produces a single product in a single market is largely a relic of the 19th century" (Dimmick 2006: 357). For all of the empirical observation of such trends, however, the amount of actual research into media conglomerates is surprisingly thin and typically based around single companies, such as Wasko's (2001) pioneering analysis of Disney. One thing behind the rise of large media corporations has been the process of *horizontal expansion*, where the potential to obtain economies of scale and scope can be considerable. Furthermore, "first-mover" advantages and the "high sunk" costs of investment in both media infrastructure and content can also present significant barriers to new would-be competitors. The case for *conglomeration*, or what Albarran and Dimmick (2006) refer to as "multiformity" and Doyle (2002b) calls "diagonal expansion," is even more complex and harder to define. At the heart of this latter strategy, however, is the much used (and abused) term "synergy." A concept that refers to five hypothetical possibilities for a corporation to derive economic benefits from conglomeration across media and media-related industries.

First, there are advantages associated with *diversification* and the spreading of risks and opportunities across multiple industries and markets. While this is a clear feature of some companies that have their origins in media but have evolved into something quite different, such as Richard Branson's Virgin Group (which started as a record company), the most significant expansions of this sort have been between media and telecommunications companies, as the convergence of digital content and platforms have brought these hitherto distinctive industries—e.g. cable television, internet portals, and content for mobile phones—ever closer together over the 1990s and 2000s. Second, there is the scope to repurpose media content for multiple platforms, particularly as the digitization of content significantly reduces the costs associated with reusing content in another format. As Nicholas Negroponte observed in *Being Digital*, "Companies are determined to repurpose their (digital) bits at a seemingly small marginal cost and at a likely large profit" (Negroponte 1995: 63). Third, there is scope to cross-promote media content across platforms, such as a television station promoting new films being produced by another division of the company and music on a company's record label being promoted by radio and TV stations owned by the company. Fourth, *branding* media content means that successful media, and the characters associated with it, can be exploited across multiple media and nonmedia platforms. As *The Economist* observed,

The brand is a lump of content ... which can be exploited through film, broadcast and cable television, publishing, theme parks, music, the internet and merchandising. Such a strategy ... is [like] a wheel, with the brand at the hub and each of the spokes a means of exploiting it. Exploitation produces both a stream of revenue and further strengthens the brand. (Wasko 2001: 71)

Disney has historically been the master of cross-promotional synergy for its media brands and properties. Content digitization and the identification of ever more tightly defined consumer niches have both seen media conglomerates such as Disney evolve from, as Simone Murray puts it, "a household brand to a house *of* brands" (Murray 2005: 422). This relates to the fifth potential advantage of conglomeration, which is the ability to exploit *subsidiary rights* that, as anyone with young children would be particularly aware, can operate across a plethora of nonmedia products, from clothes to lunch boxes to bed sheets. It must be noted that this is often driven as much by the artists as it is by the companies involved: Established musical acts such as The Rolling Stones, AC/DC, and KISS are among those who have demonstrated a capacity over many years to generate revenue streams from subsidiary merchandising that sit very enticingly alongside the income they generate from sales of their music and concert tickets (Doyle 2008). What Winseck refers to in this volume as the "law of relatively constant media expenditures" indicates that generating products and services that sit over the top of media content serves to minimize the inherent risks associated with the development of new forms of media content.

Does conglomeration work?

So does media conglomeration work? Caves (2000) makes the point that critics of media conglomerates see them as agglomerations of barely constrained market power, while those heading the conglomerates themselves have images of these businesses as "inexhaustible cash machines," extracting economic rents across multiple platforms. These claims are premised upon a proposition that conglomeration works, which is not necessarily borne out by the evidence of media conglomerates in practice. It is frequently the case, in fact, that all parties would do better from arm's-length contractual arrangements than from exclusive dealings within one organization, and this is more true the more successful the media product.

The strategies of three of the largest media corporations in the world—Time Warner, Disney, and News Corporation—provide insights into the pros and cons of conglomeration strategies in the media sector. It is often the case that media conglomerates that grow through takeovers and mergers bring together management teams that lack compatibility or have expertize in related fields. The merger of America Online (AOL) and Time Warner was the most conspicuous case of this; it created an entity whose combined value was estimated at US$350 billion, but it ultimately proved almost impossible in practice to achieve the much-vaunted content synergies across the two very distinct corporate entities. By the time that AOL was quietly spun off from Time Warner at the end of 2009 as a separate public company, its value was a fraction of what it had been at the time of its famous 2001 merger with Time Warner (Arango 2010).

Another example of how the benefits of conglomeration can be illusory is seen with the hit TV comedy *Seinfeld*. *Seinfeld* was produced by Castle Rock Entertainment, which was acquired by Time Warner, but first runs of the program were screened on the NBC network rather than Time Warner's own WB network or one of Time Warner's cable channels. The reason is not surprising: NBC was at that time the highest rating US television network, and *Seinfeld* was an integral part of this ratings success. All parties did much better out of the program screening on NBC than would have been the case had it run on WB, which has smaller audiences and less audience reach, or on one of Time Warner's many other cable channels. To take another example, in 2001 Time Warner's largest advertising client was in fact Time Warner, with US$468 million worth of advertising being spent to cross-promote the company's products on one or another of Time Warner's many media platforms (Fine and Elkin 2002). While this may be presented as evidence of synergy in action, it is in fact revenue foregone, as this churn of money within the organization is an alternative to bringing in real money from other advertisers for the sale of these slots (Flew and Gilmour 2003). Time Warner continued to face the question of whether it should be both a distribution company and a content company, and in 2009 it divested itself of AOL and Time Warner Cable, focusing more upon its perceived core strengths in media content.

Disney is generally seen to be the exemplar of a media company that successfully achieves cross-platform synergies for its media products, and Janet Wasko has traced how it became "the quintessential example of synergy in the media/entertainment industry" (Wasko 2001: 71). There are, however, important differences between its internally generated synergies—best seen in its tightly managed branded products that range from *High School Musical* to *Cars* to *Disney Fairies*—and its mergers and acquisitions strategy. The acquisition of Capital Cities/ABC in 1996 has only generated mixed results, and the successes or failures of the US ABC Network have only a tangential connection to its relationships to Disney. By contrast, the acquisition of the animation company Pixar is widely credited with putting new creative life into Disney's animated products, which had become formulaic and reflective of a factory-like concept development process, unlike the director-driven approach that had brought so much success to Pixar ("Magic Restored" 2008). The success of the Disney–Pixar partnership can be seen as reflective of the fact that animation is clearly in the core capabilities of Disney; in fact, they pioneered the development of business models to bring animated material to mass markets.

This sense of mergers and acquisitions working best when they build upon established core capabilities is also seen with News Corporation. The 2007 takeover of the *The Wall Street Journal* has provided News Corp. with a significant masthead from which to pursue its strategy of shifting access to online news from advertiser financing and free access to "paywall" models and subscription-based access, which News intends to base all of its online publications around. At the same time, while its takeover of social media site MySpace was hailed in 2005 as a case of News Corp.'s owner Rupert Murdoch finally "getting" new media, in practice it has presented greater corporate losses for News than its much more debated "old media" assets such as newspapers. In the fast-moving world of social networking sites, the number of unique hits on MySpace fell from 61.2 million to 42 million between March 2008 and March 2010, while those for Facebook went from 25 million to 117 million over the same period, and Twitter hits were 24 million in March 2010, having barely existed in the public realm in 2008 (Friedman 2010).

The literature on the role of managers in corporations indicates that they frequently identify their own interests as being in the expansion of companies for its own sake, as their salaries are frequently tied to share market performance, which can be connected to the perceived benefits of expansion, even if this is contrary to the longer term interests of shareholders or the firm itself (Fama 1980). Foster and McChesney believe that this has become an economy-wide phenomenon in the current phase of US capitalism in particular (Foster and McChesney 2009). With such a focus on managers as engineers of corporate growth, a great deal of attention is given to the original decision to expand a media corporation or take over another, and far less attention is given to how the merged entity actually performs, meaning that we may well be prone to overstate the success of conglomeration strategies in the media and entertainment industries. Indeed, as Richard Caves concludes,

> The basic traits of creative industries cast a pall of skepticism over the growth of entertainment conglomerates. The synergies they pursue are probably illusory when they seek to improve on the rent-extracting power of auctions. They at best offer defensive value when they unite media content with distribution channels. To create greater value from their integration of functions requires complex collaboration in the development of creative inputs, which requires a water-and-oil mixture of creative talents with bureaucratic planners. (Caves 2000: 328)

Globalization of media corporations: myths and legends

It is frequently taken as a given that the largest media corporations have either become or are becoming truly global entities and that global expansion has been a highly profitable option for them, driven primarily by access to new markets and cheaper labor. Robert McChesney has observed that "global media giants are the quintessential multinational firms, with shareholders, headquarters, and operations scattered across the globe" (McChesney 2001: 16). Manfred Steger also argues that "[t]o a very large extent, the global cultural flows of our time are generated and directed by global media empires that rely on powerful communication technologies to spread their message ... [and] a small group of very large TNCs [transnational corporations] have come to dominate the global market for entertainment, news, television and film" (Steger 2003: 76).

The available evidence on these points, however, is far less clear-cut than is commonly assumed. Part of the problem is a tendency to overstate the extent to which the operations of these companies are truly global. Using the UNCTAD (United Nations Conference on Trade and Development) Transnationality Index, my own research found that, in 2005, companies such as Time Warner, Viacom, and Disney were deriving about 20 to 25 percent of their revenue from outside of North America (Flew 2007: 86–7). While this is a moderate level of globalization—certainly higher for all of these firms than was the case 10–15 years earlier—it is not high enough to justify classifying these firms as "functionally integrated global corporations"; rather they are what economic geographer Peter Dicken refers to as "national corporations with international operations" (Dicken 2003: 225). The outrider here, and the company with the strongest claims to being a truly global media corporation, is News Corp., which generates 44 percent of its revenues outside of North America. But the picture here is complicated, as News was until 2004 an Australian company, generating over 90 percent of its revenues outside of its home country (Flew 2007: 85–8), indicating that the size of the home market is a relevant variable in determining how "global" media companies actually are. Even in the case of News, however, it still needs to be made clear that much of its corporate success continues to be in English-speaking countries; by contrast, the long struggle to establish a base in China has cost the company billions (Curtin 2005; Dover 2008).

There are three issues to be considered in assessing the implications of the globalization of media corporations:

1   The relative significance of reducing costs to internationalization strategies.

2   The relationship they have to nation-states in the host countries.

3   The extent of competition faced from nationally based media corporations.

Theories based on the new international division of cultural labor model, most famously developed by Miller, Govil, McMurria, and Maxwell (2001) and inspired by Frobel, Heinrichs, and Kreye (1980), propose that the ownership advantages possessed by multinational corporations (MNCs), such as their globally integrated supply chains and high-profile brands, would see them triumph over nationally based competitors. They also view their foreign investment activities as being primarily a mix of factors such as access to primary resources, access to new markets, the availability of low-cost labor, and incentives, such as tax incentives or lower levels of worker or environmental regulation, being offered by governments. In this scenario, economic globalization is seen as a "race to the bottom," disadvantaging governments and workers in both their home countries and the host countries, as corporations "increasingly ... play workers, communities, and nations off against one another as they demand tax, regulation, and wage concessions while threatening to move" (Crotty, Epstein, and Kelly 1998: 118).

An issue raised in recent work on the economic geography of MNCs (Dunning 2001; Dicken 2003) was *why* such large firms would undertake such foreign direct investment in the first place, given that they understand these markets less well than their home base, skilled local labor is harder to recruit, and there are a range of potential political risks. There are other, less risky, options open for large corporations to access new markets and/or unique resources that do not involve the direct investment of physical capital, including equity investment in local partners, import/export arrangements with local distributors, and various forms of strategic partnerships. Dunning (2001) proposed that what had not been given much consideration in earlier models of MNC investment behavior was the role of what he referred to as *internalization advantages* or the ability to capture local sources of knowledge as part of developing a more global knowledge base for the corporation. Such advantages can include organizational learning, cultural awareness, new innovation opportunities, and opportunities to augment existing intellectual assets and minimize the problems of "cultural distance" that act as barriers to the promotion of global products and brands. Dunning's key point was that the primary goal of MNCs in international expansion has been shifting over time from one driven primarily by the opportunities to extract more profits from existing assets (e.g. by lowering labor costs) to strategies that focus upon "the creation, as well as the use, of resources and capabilities ... [to] organize their activities in order to create future assets" (Dunning 2001: 100).

Once we incorporate this perspective into questions of why media corporations expand their international operations—noting the earlier caveat of simply assuming that they are global media corporations—three research questions present themselves. The first relates to the type of product and the forms of production process involved. Michael Storper (1997, 2000) has argued that what he refers to as *deterritorialization*, or the offshoring of production of generic commodities in order to develop a lower cost global value chain, is only one of the possible features of global production systems, one characterized by *flow-based production systems* where resources are easily substitutable between one place and another, and assets can, therefore, be distributed across multiple locations. This is contrasted to *territorialized economic development*, defined as "economic activity that is dependent on territorially specific resources" (Storper 1997: 170), including specific practices, routines, and relationships that have evolved over time in particular locations. The argument is that these are not disappearing with economic globalization: On the contrary, as the locational dimensions of innovation are recognized (as in the literature on economic clusters), and as demand is generated for "de-standardized" commodities, or those products that can attract a price premium based upon real or implied distinctiveness, space can become more, not less, significant as an economic variable in the context of globalization. Little work has taken place that considers the implications of this for the economic geography of global media, but we can note the questions that Goldsmith and O'Regan (2003) have asked about the assumption that cost factors are the primary drivers of international film production decisions as well as the consideration given in the work of Michael Curtin (2007, 2009) to the rise of Asian media capitals as competitors to "Global Hollywood."

The second set of research questions concerns the relationships between media corporations and nation-states. The assumption that these companies simply "roll over" governments by virtue of their global reach is not supported by either the recent literature on MNCs (e.g. Dicken 2003; Rugman and Brewer 2003) or that on global production networks (Ernst and Kim 2002; Henderson, Dicken, Hess, Coe, and Yeung 2002). Rather, this work suggests a series of ongoing game-like relationships, where the relative strength of each party varies over time and across countries. The "race to the bottom" scenario is only one of a range of possibilities, with ongoing knowledge and technology transfer being another. It is also important to note that MNCs are at their strongest at the point prior to an investment decision being made, but that power and influence accrues to the host country the more the fixed capital is invested and production relationships become embedded. It also makes little sense to be seeing nation-states as diverse as, say, China and Honduras as being in equivalent bargaining positions vis-à-vis foreign media corporations. The study of such media policy issues requires consideration of different levels of state capacity in bargaining with MNCs, as it does in other business fields. Keane (2006) has begun to map the relationship between global media and the emergence of new production centers in East Asia, drawing attention to a spectrum of possible outcomes between being simply a "fly-in/fly-out" component of cost-driven "world factory" audiovisual production on the one hand, and developing sustainable agglomeration advantages associated with being a "creative cluster" or "media capital" on the other.

Finally, the question remains of whether we have been too quick to use globalization theories to write off nationally based media. Just as the extension of access to "global" media content does not lead to a homogeneous global media culture (Tomlinson 2007), and the vast bulk of the world's media content remains local or national in its circulation (Tunstall 2008), nationally based incumbent media continue to have significant advantages in their own markets, regardless of the superior resources and brand leadership of the big global media companies (Straubhaar 2008). These include accrued knowledge of local audiences, the absorption of sunk costs associated with establishing the service, the most recognized local media personalities, and long-standing links to political parties and government decision-makers. It can be too easy to assume that globalization entails a unilinear shift from the local to the national to the international, rather than a complex, multiscalar set of processes in which the space of the nation retains a vital economic, political, and sociocultural significance (Amin 2002).

Conclusion

In this chapter, I have aimed to draw upon diverse strands of media economics to tell a slightly counterintuitive tale. As we have watched the largest media corporations become larger, more internationalized, and more diversified, there is a tendency to presume that this points to an inexorable expansion of their market power and a resultant diminution of competition in media markets. I have pointed to three reasons why this may not necessarily be the case. The first is that understanding competition primarily in terms of the number of competitors in a particular market is only one way of thinking about the competitive process, and there are influential traditions that focus more upon competitive strategy and the dynamics of technological innovation and what Jospeh Schumpeter termed "creative destruction." It is no surprise that these nonmainstream traditions in competition research are becoming more significant at the present time, as we are in an era of fundamental change in the techno-economic paradigms that underpin media industries, associated with convergence, digitization, and network economics: Some of these dynamics are captured in the emergent creative industries' analytical framework (see Flew, 2011, for further discussion).

Second, I have pointed to a series of potential downsides of media conglomeration that needs to be considered in any account of the phenomenon and the risks of assuming that we can take corporate media managers at their word on proclaiming the success of media synergies. As *The Economist*, the international bible of the corporate world has put it, when these media giants start talking about synergies, "run to the hills" ("Media Companies' High Spirits" 2010). There is very often a gap between what is presented as the favorable outcomes of such strategies at the time of their gestation (e.g. when mergers are proposed or initial stock offerings occur), and what actually materializes in practice. While we talk of the successful application of synergies in a company such as Disney, we forget the many instances where such ventures simply fail because corporate history tends to focus upon instances of success rather than those of failure or even mixed results.

Finally, I have argued that the proposition that the internationalization strategies of large media corporations need to be subjected to more empirical analysis, to better understand the motivations that underpin international expansion, the relative success of these strategies, the relationships that emerge with the nation-states of the host countries, and the effectiveness of the competition they face from local incumbents. Much recent work in economic geography suggests that older paradigms that saw the MNC as all-powerful against its local competitors have underestimated the advantages that accrue to local incumbents. This is particularly important in media industries, where significant cultural discount applies to the consumption decisions made around nonlocal media content. In all of these cases, the arguments I have put forward point to the need for more empirical work, and a greater degree of circumspection, in relation to claims about the economic power of the global media giants than has hitherto been the case in global media and communication studies.

4

The Structure and Dynamics of Communications Business Networks in an Era of Convergence

Mapping the global networks of the information business

Amelia Arsenault
Annenberg School, University of Pennsylvania

Disney Corporation boasted a market capitalization of US$63.7 billion, employed 144,000 employees around the world, and earned US$37.8 billion in revenue in 2009.[1] It owns the major movie studios Walt Disney Pictures, Miramax, Pixar Animation, and Touchstone Pictures and television channels available in 190 countries, including the Disney Channel, ABC networks, ESPN, SOAPNet, Lifetime (37.5 percent), Jetix (Latin America and Europe), SuperRTL (Europe), and Hungama (India). In addition to these media outlets, Disney maintains theme parks, resorts, and cruise lines and produces merchandise ranging from books to home décor. What can we infer from this long list of properties? Are large communications conglomerates like Disney, News Corp., and Time Warner worthy of consideration because they own countless numbers of studios and television stations in countries and markets around the world? Or should we evaluate their power in terms of how much money they make, their political influence, or their market share?

A number of scholars have documented the increased size, market concentration, and vertical and horizontal integration of global communications business conglomerates.[2] This chapter takes a slightly different approach by examining the implications of media ownership concentration through the theoretical lens of networks. Scholars such as Eli Noam (2001) and Yochai Benkler (2006) have wrestled with the transformational power of computer-mediated networks. However, there has been little substantive engagement by political economists with the body of theoretical and empirical work that considers networks as a set of socially embedded processes and the defining feature of contemporary social organization rather than an exogenous variable (e.g. Castells 2000, 2009; Latour 2005). As this chapter will argue, technological and accompanying social, organizational, and economic changes have made networks *the* defining feature of contemporary media and communications businesses, and as such a consideration of networks should be incorporated into political economic inquiry.

While theoretical consideration of networks predates the radical transformations wrought by the digitization of information, the majority of network theorists agree that technological innovations have propelled the reconfiguration of contemporary society into networks. Castells (1996) goes so far as to posit that we are living in a "network society " and that

> Dominant functions and processes in the Information Age are increasingly organized around networks. While the networking form of social organization has existed in other times, the new information technology paradigm provides the material basis for its pervasive expansion throughout the entire social structure. (Castells 2000: 500)

Similarly, Actor–Network–Theory (ANT), most closely associated with the work of Bruno Latour, maintains that while technology has intensified the importance of looking at network associations, the social has always been organized around networks. Therefore, sociology should be redefined as the tracing of network associations (Latour 2005: 5).

Building upon these theories, in this chapter, I identify networks as the dominant social structure guiding the operations of contemporary communications businesses. This investigation approach complements rather than replaces more traditional political economic approaches. Key thinkers from Marx to Schumpeter called attention to the central role of technology in driving innovation, organizational change, and relationships between individuals and mechanisms of production. Schumpeter (1943/1996), for example, argued that technological innovation, not capital, was the key driver of innovation, a "perennial gale of creative destruction" that "incessantly revolutionizes the economic structure from within, incessantly destroying the old one, incessantly creating a new one" (Schumpeter 1943/1996: 84). Following Schumpeter, we can identify the technology and social transformations of the second half of the twentieth century as part of this continual process of "creative destruction" leading to the emergence of networks as the principal structural form around which media and communications businesses are organized. Therefore, in this chapter, I adopt what might be called a network political economy approach.

The network political economy approach differs from traditional political economy approaches in a number of respects. First, the primary focus of analysis is on the processes, programs, and structures that constitute a given network rather than capital or markets. While we may talk about television networks or computer networks, "networks" in this chapter refer to social architecture rather than purely tangible structures. A network is a series of nodes (these nodes can be businesses, offices, individuals, or even machines) that are linked to one another. These links may take many forms, including interpersonal interactions, strategic corporate alliances, and flows of information between and within groups. Nodes and associations are constituent elements of the network, but their specific characteristics are made relevant or redundant according to the program (i.e. goals) of the network at hand. Thus, networks as a framework for academic analysis are bounded by the overarching consideration of who is (or is not) associated with whom, why, and to what social effect.

Second, traditional political economy tends to focus on how organizations expand their hierarchical control over properties or markets through mergers and acquisitions, that is, the takeover of other firms. The network approach, however, sees power as embedded in networks rather than something that is a function of corporate hierarchies. A corporation may amass hierarchical control over a stable of media properties, but its ability to do so successfully is predicated upon its ability to leverage the larger network within which it is embedded. Power is thus not necessarily concentrated within any single company but embedded in the processes of association between key nodes in the network, which may include regulators, relevant political agencies, and equipment manufacturers. These key nodes may change, while the network itself continues to thrive.

Third, traditional political economy focuses on competition and, perhaps even more so, consolidation within media markets. Competitive practices are a subject of concern, but the network approach assigns equal, if not greater, significance to the processes of collaboration between actors. Fourth, in examining media and communications networks, we are concerned with many of the same measures used by other political economists, such as strategic alliances, joint ventures, and the movement of capital. However, these measures are used and individual institutions (i.e. nodes) or subnetworks are examined with the ultimate goal of better understanding systems-level network *processes*. Even a cursory glance at the evolution of communications corporations over the past decade illustrates that there are few constant players, and those that remain undergo constant metamorphosis, suggesting that it is particularly instructive to understand the programs guiding the network within which they operate. Individual media companies, particularly large ones like Disney, wield significant influence. However, the processes of power at play within the global network of communications networks are greater than the sum of the bottom line of individual media or telecommunications companies or the movement of capital. Mapping the network, neither individual companies nor resources, is thus the focus of this approach.

As this chapter will demonstrate, contemporary media and communications companies are organized around a core global network of diversified multinational communications organizations that are interlinked with large national and regional companies and to their local counterparts in different areas of the world. Disney, to return to our opening example for a moment, is a large multinational corporation that has offices and businesses around the world connected by formal contracts, the exchange of money, and person-to-person interactions. While Disney may operate as a network *internally*, it simultaneously serves as a central node in a larger *external* network of communications business networks with multiple associations with other multinational corporations and local communications businesses as well as to political, financial, and creative networks.

Over the course of this chapter, I will examine the contemporary global media environment through the network approach to political economy over the course of three sections. In the first section, I will explore the nature of communications networks in an era of technological convergence. The second section examines the collaborative structures of competition and collusion between multimedia companies, internet, hardware, and telecommunications companies. Finally, I will investigate some of the ways in which global communications companies influence the operations of regionally and locally based communications businesses and vice versa.

Communications networks in an era of convergence

Multinational diversified communications companies are the products and the agents of three broader concurrent and interrelated trends: digitization, deregulation, and corporatization. In order to understand the structure and dynamics of these companies, we must first understand the importance of these trends.

First, the larger movement toward deregulation of industry at both the national and global level has had a pivotal influence on the media and communications sector. The United States was a policy trendsetter in this respect (Cowhey and Aronson 2009). Among other things, the Federal Communications Commission repealed the Financial Interest and Syndication Rules (Fin/Syn) in 1993, which allowed television networks to merge with television and film studios (e.g. NBC TV Studios and Universal Pictures). Regulatory changes at the end of the decade also created favorable conditions for cable companies to become major internet service providers (e.g. Time Warner and America Online [AOL]). The United States was also a key proponent of the General Agreement on Trade in Services (GATS), which required signatories to commit to opening up their telecommunications sector to competition, issue additional licenses to private communications operators, and to expand opportunities for foreign investment. The ensuing changes helped to denationalize the means of production and distribution of communications content and infrastructure. Such trends were also reinforced as governments across the political and economic spectrum began to call for greater investment in communications as part and parcel of their bids to create and compete in the "information economy." This could be seen, for example, as Singapore strove to become an "intelligent island" and as the European Union laid the groundwork for the creation of a common market for telecommunications services and equipment between 1987 and 1992 (Singh 2002: 8). Similarly, in the United States, the Clinton Administration, seeking to solidify US dominance in information and communication technologies (ICTs), pushed to advance the development of the National Information Infrastructure (NII) in the early to mid-1990s. All of these initiatives granted investors and market strategies a much bigger role in reconfiguring communications and also left communications corporations largely free to pursue profits across markets and countries.

Second, this movement toward deregulation facilitated a global trend toward privatization, corporatization, and monetization of communications content and infrastructure (Bagdikian 2004; Cowhey and Aronson 2009; EUMap 2008). Countries around the world (e.g. Ethiopia and South Africa) moved to privatize or partially privatize their telecommunications systems, partly in response to pressure by the United States and other proponents of privatization at the bilateral and multilateral level. In the ensuing years, both private and publicly owned communications businesses have been under increased pressure to deliver profits due to shrinking state subsidies and expanding market competition. Even public service broadcasters such as the BBC have adopted hybridized revenue models. While the BBC remains the largest public service broadcaster in the world, and receives subsidies in the form of licensing fees, in 1995, under government pressure to decrease dependence on public funds, it initiated BBC Worldwide, a corporate arm that includes television, internet, and publishing investments and initiatives around the world.[3] These trends are not limited to the West. In 1991, India had one state-owned television station, Doordarshan (Thussu 2007: 594). In order to compete with over 200 new private satellite television stations, Doordarshan has since expanded its operations to include 11 regional and 8 national satellite and terrestrial broadcast stations—funded in large part by advertising revenue. Media and communications corporations like the BBC do not exist in a vacuum; their organizational decision making is embedded within and influenced by their ability to leverage trends and behaviors of the larger network of communications networks.

Finally, the technological convergence of different communications technologies has amplified the importance of connections between and across businesses formerly restricted to distinct sectors of the communication and media industries. Rather than leading to more egalitarian ownership and control of both the content and infrastructure of communications, convergence, instead, has empowered an ever-shrinking pool of consolidated companies that have the ability to influence and control the deployment of *multiple* communication platforms. In the past, gaming, computing, internet, media, and telecommunications corporate networks operated relatively autonomously. Companies concerned with broadcast technologies (e.g. one-to-many platforms like TV, movies, and radio) were also subject to separate legal and regulatory regimes from those involved with networking technologies (e.g. one-to-one platforms like telephones and personal computers).[4] With digitization, these boundaries have largely disappeared (Warner 2008). You can listen to radio through your computer or access the internet through your mobile phone or Nintendo Wii game console. Consequently, the key players in what have hitherto been relatively autonomous industries are now moving into the territories of others, so we can no longer talk about media business and telecommunications business networks in isolation.

Deregulation, corporatization, and digitization have facilitated (and been facilitated by) communications companies' ability to adapt their products and services according to the demands of the market. Even in cases where states attempt to regulate or restrict linkages to global business communications networks, increasingly sophisticated hardware, web innovations, and the proliferation of satellites have posed strong challenges to information sovereignty. In the face of these changes and the increasingly networked communications environment, the activities of one company (e.g. Disney) or industry (e.g. newspaper publishing) take on more meaning when contextualized within the network of actors that determine the overall media ecology.

The core of the global network of communications networks

While concentration of ownership in the communications sector is nothing new, the concentration of influence by large mega-corporations over networks of communication has intensified (Bagdikian 2004; Noam 2009). Convergence, deregulation, and privatization have enhanced the ability of global communications corporations to network both with each other and with regional and local actors, which compounds their influence. There is a tendency to talk about global communications corporations to distinguish them from smaller companies with regional or local holdings. However, the rise of networked forms of organization means that no corporations are truly global and few if any are truly local, nor can they be examined in isolation. This section concentrates upon the largest diversified multinational communications corporations that provide the backbone of the global network of communications networks (measured by their 2009 revenue). Figure 4.1 provides an overview of this global core of communications networks.

Figure 4.1 identifies the global core as being comprised of a diverse group of the largest multinational, multimedia companies (i.e. Bertelsmann, CBS, Comcast, Disney, News Corp., Time Warner, and Viacom), telecommunications firms (i.e. AT&T, Verizon, Nippon Telegraph & Telephone [NTT], Deutsche Telekom, Telefonica, France Telecom, Vodafone, China Mobile, Telecom Italia,

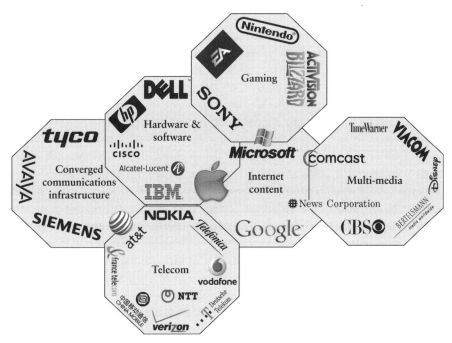

Figure 4.1 The global core of communications networks
Source: Author's elaboration.

and Sprint Nextel), hardware and software production companies (i.e. Dell, Hewlett-Packard, IBM, Alcatel-Lucent, and Apple), internet content companies (i.e. Google, Apple, News Corp., Comcast, and Microsoft), Gaming (Nintendo, Activision-Blizzard, EA, Sony, and Microsoft), and converged communications infrastructure firms (i.e. Tyco, Avaya, Siemens, Cisco, IBM, Alcatel-Lucent, Nokia, and AT&T).[5] Interestingly, there are several repetitions in this list, illustrating the extent to which firms are no longer locked into distinct, and separate, sectors of the communication and media industries. For example, Microsoft, which began as a computer software company, now ranks among the world's largest gaming and internet companies. This is just one indication of the interconnections and commonalities between the companies explored in this section. This global core of the global network of communications networks shares similar networked forms of organization, including four interrelated characteristics: (1) concentration of ownership; (2) diversification of products, platforms, and services; (3) the flexible reconfiguration of holdings, products, and services; and (4) strong linkages to parallel networks.

Concentration of ownership

Political economists often use the Herfindahl–Hirschman Index (HHI) to measure levels of market concentration. On the basis of this method, markets with an HHI of less than 1,000 are considered to be competitive, while those between 1,000 and 1,800 points are considered to be moderately concentrated, and those in excess of 1,800 points are considered to be concentrated. In a recent study of the American communications industries, Eli Noam found that in 1984, the top five firms amassed 13 percent of the revenue, but by 2004 that number had more than doubled to 29 percent. Moreover, HHI levels were even more pronounced in the telecom, computer, and internet subindustries, all of which ranked well above 1,800 (Noam 2008: 149–52). Beyond the United States, IBISWorld (2009) estimates that the top four mobile telecommunications carriers achieved a collective global industry share of approximately 24.6 percent in 2008 (Noams 2009: 8). A majority of the top 15 global video games publishers are also based either in Japan or in the United States, but even among these giants Nintendo and EA alone control 29 percent of the global market for gaming hardware devices (Business Insights 2009b: 13). In terms of music production, despite the proliferation of independent music distribution via the internet, Vivendi (which owns Universal Music), Sony Entertainment, the EMI Group, and the Warner Music Group (which spun off from Time Warner in 2004) still account for 48 percent of global music revenue (IBISWorld 2010b).

The companies depicted in Figure 4.1 own a disproportionate percentage of both content creators and communications infrastructure. While these companies often compete for new properties and seek ever-expanding profit margins, cooperation with their competitors is typically critical to their expansion. Even companies that are often depicted as rivals, such as Microsoft and Apple, are connected through a dense web of partnerships, cross-investments, and personnel. For example, in 1998, Microsoft entered into a 5-year patent licensing agreement with Apple that included US$150 million in special shares of Apple stock. In the telecoms industry, NTT owns 15 percent of AT&T Japan, and Alcatel-Lucent and Ericsson supply the infrastructure for AT&T's radio access network. These connections extend across different communications industries. Steve Jobs, Apple CEO, for instance, sits on the board of Disney. Charles H. Noski, a former AT&T executive, sits on the board of Microsoft. In another example, Sony produced "in-world" (i.e. in-game) advertisements for major companies like 20th Century Fox and Intel.

These multimedia conglomerates simultaneously compete and collude on a case-by-case basis according to their business needs. Levels of competition increase or decrease according to the exigencies of particular markets. As their property portfolios ebb and flow, so do the form and content of these interconnections. When certain corporations amass disproportionate control over certain content delivery or production mechanisms, other businesses seek to break this bottleneck through investment or the development of rival properties. For example, when Google's YouTube cornered a disproportionate percentage of the online streaming video market, News Corp. and NBC-Universal (now 51 percent owned by Comcast) launched Hulu—an online portal for professional media content. Shortly thereafter, News Corp. signed a US$900 million deal with Google to provide search and contextual ads for its MySpace social networking site. In the network society, large size matters more because it amplifies the ability of these actors to pursue favorable policies and programs according to the exigencies of the market. However, ownership and influence are not necessarily commensurate. Ownership concentration creates a domino effect. Size leads to the ability to leverage partnerships and broker favorable deals and, as will be discussed in the latter half of this chapter, the ability to influence the business practices of other corporations within the global network of communications networks.

Diversification

The global core companies own more properties than ever before, and the content that these companies create is delivered via an increasing variety of platforms, many of which they also own. Figure 4.2 provides an overview of the main properties currently owned or partially owned by the seven largest global multimedia organizations.

All of the companies depicted in Figure 4.2 are vertically and horizontally integrated. News Corp. is perhaps the most horizontally integrated company of all, owning 47 TV stations in the United States, the MySpace social networking platform, satellite delivery platforms in five continents, 20th Century Fox Studios and Home Entertainment, and numerous regional TV channels (Arsenault and Castells 2008a). As previously mentioned, digitization has amplified diversification. Media companies seek to secure access to multiple platforms from traditional media to newer mobile- and internet-based platforms so that they are well placed to adapt to fluctuations in consumer demand. Similarly, telephone and cable companies now offer phone, internet, and television in bundled packages. Even in the gaming industry, which one might think of as relatively specialized, companies such as Nintendo, Sony, and EA are following similar policies of diversification. Gaming corporations have invested heavily in online and mobile gaming and diversified their revenue streams through the adoption of in-game advertising and micro-transactions (Business Insights 2009a). Conversely, other communications corporations have diversified into gaming. In 2002, Microsoft, in its first step toward becoming one of the world's largest gaming companies, released the Xbox and in 2006 purchased the in-game advertising company Massive Incorporated. As brick and mortar stores are bypassed, the pipes—the internet pathways through which customers purchase games and add-ons— become evermore important access points. Reflecting this, all of the major gaming companies have invested in ISPs, internet portals, aggregators, and mobile phone companies to ensure successful delivery of gaming products to their target markets (Business Insights 2009a: 16).

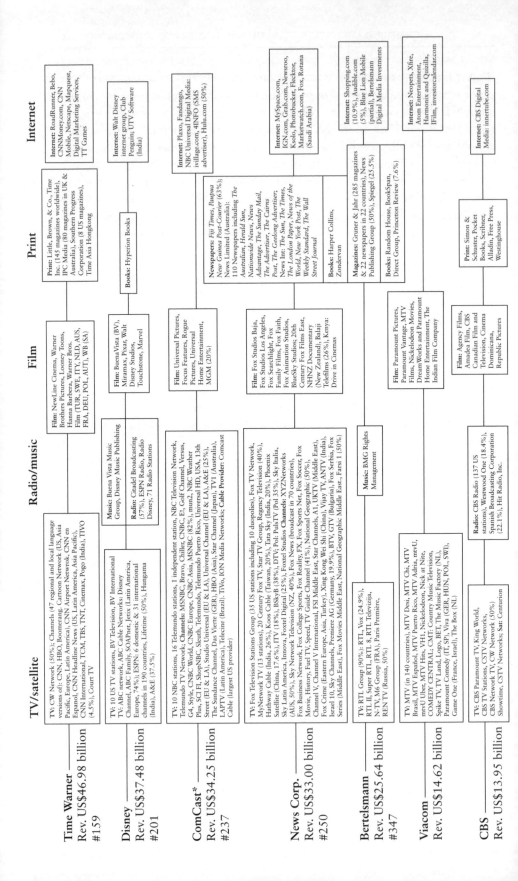

Media ownership chart

Column headings: **TV/satellite** | **Radio/music** | **Film** | **Print** | **Internet**

Time Warner — Rev. US$46.98 billion — #159

- **TV:** CW Network (50%); Channels (47 regional and local language versions of): CNN, HBO, Boomerang, Cartoon Network (US, Asia Pacific, Europe, Latin America), CNN Airport Network, CNN en Espanol, CNN Headline News (US, Latin America, Asia Pacific), CNN International, TCM, TBS, TNT, Cinemax, Pogo (India), TIVO (4.5%), Court TV
- **Film:** NewLine Cinema, Warner Brothers Pictures, Looney Toons, Hanna Barbera, Warner Bros. Film (TUR, SWE, ITY, NLD, AUS, FRA, DEU, POL, AUT), WB (SA)
- **Print:** Little, Brown, & Co., Time Inc. (145 magazines worldwide); IPC Media (80 magazines in UK & Australia), Southern Progress Corporation (8 US magazines), Time Asia Hongkong
- **Internet:** RoadRunner, Bebo, CNNMoney.com, CNN Mobile, Netscape, Mapquest, Digital Marketing Services, TT Games

---

Disney — Rev. US$37.48 billion — #201

- **TV:** 10 US TV stations, BV Television, BV International. TV: ABC network, ABC Cable Networks: Disney Channel, ABC Family, SOAPnet, Jetix (Latin America, Europe, 74%); ESPN: 6 domestic & 31 international channels in 190 countries, Lifetime (50%), Hungama (India), A&E (37.5%)
- **Music:** Buena Vista Music Group, Disney Music Publishing
- **Radio:** Citadel Broadcasting (57%), ESPN Radio, Radio Disney, 71 Radio Stations
- **Film:** BuenaVista (BV), Miramax, Pixar, Walt Disney Studios, Touchstone, Marvel
- **Books:** Hyperion Books
- **Internet:** Walt Disney internet group, Club Penguin, UTV Software (India)

ComCast* — Rev. US$34.25 billion — #237

- **TV:** 10 NBC stations, 16 Telemundo stations, 1 independent station, NBC Television Network, Telemundo TV Network; Channels: MSNBC, Bravo, Chiller, CNBC, E!, Golf Channel, Versus, G4, Style, SCI FI, ShopNBC, Sleuth, CNBC Europe, CNBC Asia, MSNBC (82%), mun2, NBC Weather Plus, SCI FI World, CNBC World, CNBC Europe, Universal HD, USA, 13th Street (EU & LA), Studio Universal (EU & LA), Universal Channel (EU & LA, A&E (25%), The Sundance Channel, Das Vierte (GER), HBO (Asia), Star Channel (Japan), TV1 (Australia), LAPTV (Latin America), Telecine (Brazil): TiVo, ION Media Networks; Cable Provider: Comcast Cable (largest US provider)
- **Film:** Universal Pictures, Focus Features, Rogue Pictures, Universal Home Entertainment, MGM (20%)
- **Internet:** Plaxo, Fandango, NBC Universal Digital Media: ivillage.com, 4INFO (SMS advertiser), Hulu.com (50%)

News Corp. — Rev. US$33.00 billion — #250

- **TV:** Fox Television Stations Group (35 US stations including 10 duopolies), Fox TV Networks, MyNetwork TV (13 stations), 20 Century Fox TV, Star TV Group, Regency Television (40%), Phoenix Hathway Cable (India, 26%), Koos Cable (Taiwan, 20%), Tata Sky (India, 20%), Phoenix Satellite (China, 17.6%), ITV (18%), BSkyB (38%), DTV: Pol: PulsTV (Pol 35%), Sky Italia, Sky Latin America, Innova, Foxtel Digital (25%), Foxtel Studios Channels: XYZNetworks (AUS, 50%), Sky Network Television (NZ, 40%), Fox News (broadcast in 70 countries), Fox Business Network, Fox College Sports, TV Guide Channel (41%), National Geographic (50%), Movie, History, Fuel TV, Speed, TV Guide Channel, FX, Fox Sports Net, Fox Soccer, Fox Channel V, Channel V International, FSI Middle East, Star Channels, A1, UKTV (Middle East), Fox Crime (Eastern Europe, Asia, Turkey), Xing Kong Wei Shi (China), Vijay TV, ANTV (India), Israel 10, Sky Channels, Premiere AG (Germany, 19.9%), BTV, GTV (Bulgaria), Fox Serbia, Fox Series (Middle East], Fox Movies Middle East, National Geographic Middle East, Farsi 1 (50%)
- **Music:** BMG Rights Management
- **Film:** Fox Studios Baja, Fox Studios Los Angeles, Fox Searchlight, Fox Family Films, Fox Faith, Fox Animation Studios, BlueSky Studios; 20th Century Fox Films East, NHNZ Documentary (New Zealand), Balaji Telefilms (26%), Kenya: Drive in Cinemas
- **Newspapers:** Fiji Times, Papua New Guinea Post-Courier (63%); News Limited (Australia): 110 Newspapers including The Australian, Herald Sun, Nationwide News, News Advantage, The Sunday Mail, The Advertiser, The Cairns Post, The Geelong Advertiser; News Int: The Sun, The Times, The London Paper, News of the World, New York Post, The Weekly Standard, The Wall Street Journal
- **Books:** Harper Collins, Zondervan
- **Internet:** MySpace.com, IGN.com, Grab.com, Newsroo, Ksolo, Photobucket, Flecktor, Marketwatch.com, Fox, Rotana (Saudi Arabia)

Bertelsmann — Rev. US$25.64 billion — #347

- **TV:** RTL Group (90%): RTL, Vox (24.9%), RTL II, Super RTL, RTL 8, RTL Televizija, N-TV, M6 Group (FRA), Paris Première, REN TV (Russia, 50%)
- **Music:** BMG Rights Management
- **Magazines:** Gruner & Jahr (285 magazines & 22 newspapers in 22 countries); News Publishing Group (50%), Spiegel (25.5%)
- **Books:** Random House, BookSpan, Direct Group, Princeton Review (7.6%)
- **Internet:** Shopping.com (10.9%), Audible.com (5%), Blue Lion Mobile (partial), Bertelsmann Digital Media Investments

---

Viacom — Rev. US$14.62 billion

- **TV:** MTV (in 140 countries), MTV Desi, MTV Chi, MTV Brasil, MTV Español, MTV Puerto Rico, MTV Adria, mtvU, mtvU Uber, MTV Hits, VH1, Nickelodeon, Nick at Nite, COMEDY CENTRAL; CMT: Country Music Television, Spike TV, TV Land, Logo, BET, The Music Factory (NL), Paramount Comedy (IT, SP), Viva (GER, HUN, POL, SWI), Game One (France, Israel), The Box (NL).
- **Film:** Paramount Pictures, Paramount Vantage, MTV Films, Nickelodeon Movies, DreamWorks and Paramount Home Entertainment, The Indian Film Company
- **Internet:** Neopets, Xfire, Atom Entertainment, Harmonixx and Quizilla, IFilm, investorcalendar.com

---

CBS — Rev. US$13.95 billion

- **TV:** CBS Paramount TV, King World, CBS TV Stations, CSTV Networks, CBS Network TV, CW Network (50%) Showtime, CSTV Networks; Sat: Centurion
- **Radio:** CBS Radio (137 US stations), Westwood One (18.4%), Spanish Broadcasting Corporation (22.1%), Hit Radio, Inc.
- **Film:** Agency Films, Amadea Film, CBS Canadian Film and Television, Cinema Dominicana, Republic Pictures
- **Print:** Simon & Schuster, Pocket Books, Scribner, Alladin, Free Press, Westinghouse
- **Internet:** CBS Digital Media: innertube.com

Flexibility and synergy

Diversification also engenders network flexibility. Networks are defined equally by who is included and who is excluded from the network. Redundant technologies and nodes based on those technologies are thus quickly discarded. The News Corp. of today is not the News Corp. of yesteryear, and it will look completely different in 5 years time.[6] If, for instance, a particular medium or a particular market declines, communications corporations quickly reconfigure their operations, adding newer, more profitable associations and nodes, and shutting down or selling off those that are less desirable. For instance, despite the American newspaper industry crisis, the Washington Post Company profits rose 68 percent in the third quarter of 2009—mostly because of its movement into cable and educational entertainment investments (Ahrens 2010). In another example, 10 years ago, interests in the Middle East were minute and China loomed as the next big market. However, as developed markets reached penetration and the Chinese government became increasingly inhospitable to foreign investment in its communications sector, companies have turned their attention toward the Middle Eastern region. News Corp., for example, purchased a 10 percent stake in Rotana (one of the largest communications companies in the Middle East) in December 2009. Concurrently, Time Warner developed contracts to deliver a stable of channels across several Middle East satellite service providers. AT&T also aggressively expanded its presence in the Middle East and India through the establishment of global network nodes in Qatar, Kuwait, Dubai, and Saudi Arabia, and with a minority stake in the Asia America Gateway (AAG) telecommunications cable.

The ability to successfully leverage economies of scale, diversity of platforms, and customization of content reflects the strong impact of "economies of synergy" within the media and communications industries (Arsenault and Castells 2008b). In economics, synergy traditionally refers to the ability of corporations to sell variations on a particular product (e.g. a song) through all the various subsidiaries and platforms owned by a corporation. When examining communications companies in the context of networks, an economy of synergy refers to the ability of diversified corporations to successfully integrate formal and informal network programs across their various holdings. This may include the marketing of goods (e.g. a particular television program) via different platforms; but more importantly, it includes the ability of a corporation to successfully merge cultural customs, machine code, methods of operation, and external network associations across multiple holdings. The configuration of the internal network organization of major media organizations is critical in this regard. Sometimes certain network configurations do not work, as both Jin (this volume) and Winseck (this volume) show with respect to the record-breaking merger between AOL and Time Warner in 2000. The partnership between AOL, an internet company, and Time Warner, mainly a media company, never worked, and thus in 2008–10, after a decade of paring back its operations, Time Warner finally spun off its cable operations and the AOL franchise. In a society structured around networks, incorporating networked forms of organization rather than integrating the day-to-day operations is key, allowing companies to easily adapt, achieving optimal economies of synergy vis-à-vis various exigencies. As the global credit crisis began to unfold in 2008, communications companies shed unprofitable business across a range of industries in order to maintain profit margins. Even internet companies like Google and Yahoo! followed this path. The most successful global communications corporations are those like News Corp. and AT&T that maintain loose-networked forms of organization. Because these global communications corporations are organized according to networks rather than hierarchies, nodes that do not adapt are easily shed while the larger corporate network moves forward unimpeded (Arsenault and Castells 2008a).

Leveraging complementary networks

The fact that global communications corporations are flexible and adaptable supports and is supported by the ability of communications companies to leverage connections with other parallel networks of interest. Communications networks are central to contemporary society because they serve as the primary transmission belt between political, business, social, and cultural actor networks. At the same time, they depend upon connections to those networks to expand market share and maximize profits. In this section, I focus on the linkages between the largest global communications companies and advertising, financial, and political networks.

First, the largest global communications companies are bolstered by their connections to financial networks. The majority of the boards of trustees of multinational communications corporations are populated by individuals in leadership positions at large nonmedia, multinational corporations, investment banks, and private equity firms, and/or hold positions of importance in such organizations as NASDAQ and the New York Stock Exchange. Indeed, communications companies constitute a significant component of the networks of financial capital. Of the Global Fortune 500 companies, as ranked by *Fortune Magazine* in 2009, 21 are telecommunications companies, 35 are electronic hardware and software producers, and 5 are entertainment multimedia companies. Moreover, communications companies depend upon their ability to attract investors and private equity (see Crain 2009).

Second, the successful operation and expansion of communications corporations depend upon connections to the global network of advertising providers and vice versa. As of 2009, the global advertising industry employed over 1.6 million people and accounted for US$427.47 billion in revenue (ZenithOptimedia 2010). In terms of ownership, the industry is highly globalized and networked, with each of the major players (i.e. ICG, WPP, Omnicom, and Publicis) controlling a network of agency subsidiaries across the globe (IBISWorld 2010a). Developments within the global advertising network are intertwined with communications business networks. Changes in the advertising industry also propel movements away from declining markets toward more favorable ones. In 2009, global advertising revenues shrank by 10.2 percent, the greatest decline since the Great Depression (Standard and Poor 2010). Advertising spending in every medium declined by between 9 and 20 percent—except internet and video game advertising, which increased by 4.2 and 16.2 percent, respectively (PriceWaterhouseCoopers (PWC) 2010: 31). Figure 4.3 provides an overview of advertising spending by medium between 2000 and 2009.

As Figure 4.3 demonstrates, while newspaper and television are still the dominant advertising markets, digital advertising has been gaining year-on-year and now accounts for 15 percent of all global advertising spending, up from 3.4 percent in 2003 (PWC 2010; IBISWorld 2010a: 8). Propelled by this shift in market demand, traditional media companies have purchased new digital properties and introduced numerous efforts to market traditional media content through online, advertising-supported portals. Similarly, in recent years, developing countries have accounted for increasingly significant percentages of global advertising spending (PWC 2010). As a sign of this shift, global advertising firms significantly expanded their operations in non-Western markets. For example, Publicis Groupe SA, a French advertising agency, was in line to generate

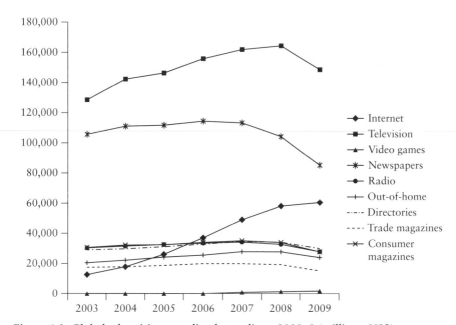

Figure 4.3 Global advertising spending by medium, 2003–9 (millions, US$)
Sources: Data from PWC (2008, 2010).

50 percent of total revenue in emerging markets and digital advertisements by the end of 2010, up from 42 percent (23 percent in emerging markets and 19 percent digital) at the end of 2008 (Standard and Poor 2010: 1). Not coincidentally, communications corporations have followed similar trajectories seeking new investments in regions with greater advertising growth potential. As a result of this reconfiguration, a major resurgence in advertising revenue is predicted for 2011 (Standard and Poor 2010; IBISWorld 2010b).

This is not unique to media companies. As communications companies diversify their holdings, advertising has become an increasingly important source of revenue for gaming, telecommunications, and internet companies alike. Gaming companies are experimenting with embedding advertising within the virtual game worlds. Telecommunications companies have traditionally relied on selling hardware (e.g. handsets) and connectivity (e.g. monthly phone or cable subscriptions). However, they have also expanded their range of services, offering ad-supported streaming video and other services. Communications corporations depend on advertising, but the advertising industry also depends on the communications industry. Communications corporations are responsible for over 30 percent of the global advertising industry's revenue (Media, 16 percent; Computer and electronics, 16 percent; Telecommunications, 4 percent) (IBISWorld 2010b: 8).

Third, as mentioned above, contemporary global communications companies are supported by their multifaceted connections to political networks. They leverage political connections to gain favorable regulations and access to new markets, while political actors benefit from the direct and indirect support of communications companies. One of the most direct connections between political networks and media and communications networks is through the exchange of money (Dunbar 2008). The communications industry ranks among the top four most active industries in terms of political lobbying in the United States. In 2009 alone, the industry donated US$360.5 million to American politicians, up from US$185 million in 1998 (Center for Responsive Politics (CRP) 2010).

The importance of connections with political networks is also evidenced in national attempts to court multimedia businesses and invite infrastructure development and through state lobbying on behalf of domestic multimedia businesses abroad, as briefly outlined earlier in this chapter.[7] While political networks have been active collaborators with communications business networks, the exponential growth of communication channels and products has simultaneously broadened the range of legal and regulatory issues that are negotiated by states at the national, bilateral, and multilateral level. Governments link communications infrastructure to economic interests. They enforce intellectual property rights and invite or export the means of production or disposal of communications equipment.

Political and communications networks also frequently directly intersect. Throughout history, state actors have initiated or purchased communications facilities in order to further their instrumental power (see Hallin and Mancini 2004). While deregulation and privatization have facilitated new business models for communications corporations, political actors maintain a direct interest in the communications infrastructure. For instance, Italy's longest serving Prime Minister Silvio Berlusconi, founded and maintains a 38 percent stake in MediaSet, the largest commercial broadcaster in Italy with investments in numerous other media properties around Europe. State interests in the telecommunications sector are even more pronounced. For instance, China Mobile, the world's largest mobile phone provider, is nearly three-quarters owned by the Chinese government.

Already, we can see that the diversification of platforms, concentration of ownership, and flexibility and synergy make the major communications companies particularly well situated to leverage connections with parallel networks to facilitate favorable financial terms and conditions, rules and regulations, and to obtain lucrative contracts. As the following section demonstrates, the internal configuration of these global communications corporations is also heavily contingent upon their ability to leverage and connect to regional, national, local, and individual media and communications actors.

The global network of communications networks

The largest global communications companies wield a great deal of influence when it comes to programming the national and global networks of information that constitute the global information environment (Arsenault and Castells 2008a,b; Castells 2009). The expansion of communications companies depends upon their ability to form successful structures of collaboration with other nodes in the global network of mediated communication. Processes of networked production and distribution, the portability of content and function from one device to another, and the collaboration of global and local companies further solidify these networks by encouraging the adoption of similar formats and models of production.

Collaboration

Global multinationals are not necessarily truly global. The majority of them are headquartered in the West and concentrate on one or two regions. However, their reach is global due to their ability to either deliver services directly in particular areas of the world or to connect to regional and local companies. AT&T, for example, operates in 160 countries but is only able to do so because of partnerships with local companies. For example, it became the first foreign telecommunications company operating in China through a joint venture with Shanghai Telecom launched in 1999. In 2004, it improved its network interconnection in Latin America through an agreement with Alestra in Mexico. It also established a node in Jeddah, Saudi Arabia, in 2008 in cooperation with the Saudi Telecommunications Company (STC). Similarly, News Corp. reaches 75 percent of the world's audiences, but its global reach is conditioned by its ability to form synergistic partnerships with different companies around the world (Arsenault and Castells 2008a).

These partnerships between global and smaller companies facilitate and are facilitated by the customization and localization of content and services. Communications companies follow profits and do so by looking for new market opportunities and new beneficial partnerships. However, global corporations need to tailor their products to local conditions, while local or regionally based companies need access to the global core to market their products internationally. The operations of global corporations depend upon their ability to provide services tailored to local markets. In 2009, Google controlled 38.6 percent of the global search market, largely because it provided search engine services in 130 languages and 136 country-specific domain names (e.g. google.fr in France) (ComScore 2010c). Microsoft provides Windows 7 software and operating systems in 59 languages and counting (Microsoft 2009). In another example, reality television, one of the most popular television formats around the world, is almost always tailored to local audiences. In other genres, media giants deliver localized products to some markets and global content to others. For example, MTV International is hugely popular in the Czech Republic, but MTV only realized success in India with a channel customized to local cultural and music tastes.

This collaboration does not benefit only the global core. Instead, regional and national companies look for ways to market their products and expand their relationships with the global core of communications companies. Prince Alwaleed, the major owner of Rotana media, one of the largest communications companies in the Middle East, for example, owns roughly 7 percent of News Corp. through Kingdom Holdings, his personal investment company. News Corp., in turn, purchased 10 percent of Rotana media in 2009 and expanded the range of partnerships between the two companies. This *quid quo pro* access to others' network of operations improves Rotana's standing in the Middle East, while also expanding News Corp.'s footprint in the region. The linkages between global corporations and local and regional companies are thus a mutually beneficial process for all of the parties involved.

Replication

Global giants break into new markets and effectively reprogram the regional market toward a commercial format. However, the so-called global corporations are not simply subsuming local and regional communications companies.

Rather, global companies are leveraging partnerships and cross-border investments with national, regional, and local companies to facilitate market expansion *and* vice versa. Regional players are actively importing global business models and localizing them, while global media organizations are pursing local partners in order to deliver customized services to audiences. No individual media corporation is truly global; just as few, if any, are truly local. What is truly global is the network, the social structure through which these firms are organized.

The most obvious example of the global influence on local media markets is through the direct import of programming and channels such as HBO, E!, Fox, and other transnational media channels (Bielby and Harrington 2008). More pervasive is the fact that multinational media companies have helped to diffuse a corporate-driven media model. The introduction of corporate media products creates a further demand for these products and propels players farther down the food chain to participate in similar behavior. These companies all tend to follow a similar networking logic to their larger multinational counterpart. Space restrictions prohibit a detailed analysis of the organizational behaviors of all media and communications companies outside the global core. However, we might take for an example, Naspers, a multimedia company headquartered in South Africa, as suggestive of this trend.

Over the past 20 years, Naspers has evolved from being a rather specialized owner of mainly South African newspapers and some Afrikaans language magazines to become primarily a pay-TV and internet company. Naspers owns MultiChoice, the operator of DStv, and M-Net, the only pay-TV option in South Africa. It has also invested heavily in emerging markets, with a print media operation, Abril, in Brazil and minority stakes in a host of internet businesses, such as Tencent in China. Figure 4.3 provides an overview of Naspers' major holdings.

As Figure 4.4 demonstrates, while not as lengthy, Naspers key holdings mirror the same sort of diversification noted among the global core in Figure 4.2. Naspers' linkages to the global core of communications companies grant it greater leverage over regional and local companies. It has obtained the rights to programs for its pay-television broadcasting across many areas of Africa from the world's major television and film studios, including Disney, Warner Brothers, Columbia Pictures, Sony, Miramax, Fox, Universal, MCA, Paramount, MGM, and DreamWorks. As Teer-Tomaselli, Wasserman, and de Beer (2007) point out in their analysis of the South African position within the African media market overall,

> [T]he South African media occupy a marginal position in the global media arena, [but] as a market for media products owned and produced outside its borders, they extend their influence (albeit on a much smaller scale) as a powerful role-player into the region and further on the continent. (Teer-Tomaselli *et al.* 2007: 154)

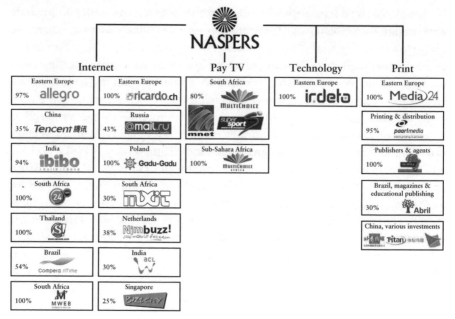

Figure 4.4   Naspers major international holdings (2009)
Source: Naspers (2009).

These same patterns of diversification are seen in other regional media companies such as Abril (a Brazilian company in which Naspers owns 30 percent), Kingdom Holdings (Saudi Arabia), MediaSet (Italy), Phoenix (China), and Televisa (Mexico) (Arsenault and Castells 2008b: 725). Smaller national and local companies also follow similar patterns and are increasingly interconnected both via contracts with the global core of communications companies and between themselves. Local telecommunications companies, for instance, are more attractive to customers when they sign interconnection deals with larger companies that extend their service range and lower consumer costs. The same logic applies to media companies. For example, one of Columbia's two private television stations, Radio Cadena Nacional (RCN) made a fortune by licensing franchises of its popular telenovela "Betty La Fea" to more than 70 production houses around the world, including ABC (owned by Disney) and Televisa. At the same time, it sought profitability by exporting content abroad, and it maximized its ability to compete locally through importing content from the global core via activities like signing a strategic partnership with Microsoft to form www.rcnmsn.com. In another example, in 2008, members of the Nigerian film industry established the Nollywood Foundation in Los Angeles, in an effort to market Nigerian films to global audiences, and hold an annual convention to attract foreign investors and collaborators into the country. All in all, we can see that global, regional, and local players are linked through a dense web of collaborative structures, each depending on the other. In this networked environment, individual corporations are more than the sum of their individual properties and bottom lines. Their influence is more clearly articulated when contextualized within the networks upon which they operate.

Conclusion

Throughout history, media and communications industries have been to varying degrees characterized by concentrated ownership and global relationships of production and distribution. However, the digitization of information, the proliferation of global networking technologies, and broader trends toward deregulation have induced new forms of organization, production, and distribution centered around networks. Examining this global network of communications networks through the lens of networked political economy highlights several features that might otherwise be overlooked. First, in this environment, collaboration with so-called rivals is as central, if not more so, as competition. Media, telecommunications, computer, internet, and gaming companies are connected to one another and bolstered by political, economic, and social networks through a complex set of partnership agreements, cross-investments, interpersonal connections, and much more. Second, as the regulatory, technological, and market-based walls separating media companies from computer and internet, telecommunications, and gaming companies come tumbling down, flexibility and synergy often trump market share as the most important predictor of the influence of an individual company. They are all driven by attempts to find optimal economies of synergy in light of the shifting balance between broadcasting and networking. And finally, in a world built upon networks, in assessing the dominance or influence of a particular company, we must look beyond traditional measures of the political economic power of media, such as allocational, economic, and attention scarcity. In this environment, power is equally evidenced in an actor's ability to institute network program changes in the media and communications sector and its ability to influence and leverage connections to parallel networks.

Notes

1   This chapter builds upon the theoretical work begun with my colleague Manuel Castells in our article Arsenault and Castells (2008b).

2   See, for example, Bagdikian (1983, 2004), Flew (2007), McChesney (2008), and Rice (2008).

3   Prior to 1995, BBC operated BBC Enterprises, a much more modest commercial arm established in 1986.

4   There have been several notable exceptions throughout history. For example, in the 1880s, Western Union consolidated control over the world's telegraph cables as well as the Associated Press—one of the world's largest news agencies (Noam 2008: 146).

5   Converged communication refers to the integration of all communication traffic types (i.e. voice, data, and video) into a single IP network (Business Insights 2009a).

6   In 1952, at the age of 21, Rupert Murdoch inherited the *Adelaide News* from his father, Sir Keith Murdoch. Using this paper as a launch pad, Murdoch gradually expanded his holdings into News Corp., which was formally incorporated in 1980. As of 1980, News Corp. mainly specialized in print media but gradually expanded into television, film, and internet holdings that now reach approximately 75 percent of the world's population (Arsenault and Castells 2008b).

7   This is not a new trend. Michael Hogan (1977) looking at the role of business interests in foreign policy during the early twentieth century illustrated how these "private networks of cooperation" supplemented rather than undermined the nation-state from which they originated. The British government welcomed Reuter's efforts to wire the world, considering the global expansion of telegraph networks key to empire, intruding only to encourage lower rates to facilitate further usage. Both the British and the Americans provided subsidies for under-ocean telegraph cables (Winseck and Pike 2007).

PART THREE

The Conquest of Capital or Creative Gales of Destruction?

5

Hard Jobs in Hollywood

How concentration in distribution affects the production side of the media entertainment industry

Susan Christopherson
Cornell University

Introduction

While studies of the creative economy and creative work have exploded since the mid-1990s, it is only recently that creative production and creative work have been analyzed as embedded in *industries*, with particular dynamics of capital accumulation (Deuze 2007). In the economics literature on creative industries (Caves 2000), as well as in more expansive, "catch-all" definitions of creative work (Florida 2002), the focus has been on the characteristics of individual creative workers and their values. With some important exceptions (Bielby and Bielby 1992, 1996; McKercher and Mosco 2008; Mosco 2009b), the analysis of creative work—who does it, how they are remunerated, and how and where it takes place—has been disengaged from the decisions of industry firms about how to make profits. This has been true even in those industries such as television, in which work has taken place in corporate environments where firm decisions have been, historically at least, more visible. In general, the industries in which creative talents are employed have been treated as unchanging, except for the ups and downs of business cycles. As a consequence, the contemporary literature on creative work has focused on labor *supply* and the characteristics of individual creative workers without adequate consideration of the *demand* side—the long-term structural changes affecting the environments within which creative workers enter the workforce, access jobs, and build careers.

In this chapter, I examine what an approach focused on the industry context can offer as a way to understand creative work, especially in the entertainment media. To illustrate how industry structure shapes the conditions for creative work, I describe how demand has changed in the US film and television industries since the 1980s, in conjunction with concentration among film and television distributors, "financialization" of the media industries, and access to new high-profit opportunities in emerging markets. I argue that to understand what directors, actors, writers, and other skilled film and television workers do, we need to understand the links between the increasingly concentrated distribution side of the industry and the production side of the industry, which remains highly fragmented and dominated by small firms and self-employed workers.

I then look at how media consolidation and the "financialization" of the industry have altered the profit strategies of the key media distribution conglomerates. Over time, these new strategies have translated into a different structure of demand and altered what happens on the production side. I present evidence to show that the conditions under which film and television workers carry out their crafts have deteriorated as entertainment conglomerates have changed their investment strategies. Finally, I look at how the workforce has responded to these new conditions and their implications for the Los Angeles industry production center. Overall, my findings raise questions about the sustainability of this agglomeration under conditions in which conglomerates search for ways to reduce production costs by favoring low-cost products for key markets and encourage production outside leading industry production centers such as Los Angeles and New York.

The industrial context of creative work

The most common depiction of a career in an industry that produces creative products emphasizes self-organization, intense competition mediated by "gatekeepers," and the central role of project-based work. Almost all depictions of creative work emphasize that it is risky, offering little in the way of conventional security as defined by a regular paycheck or a pension. The individual is at the heart of the creative career, a self-expressive entrepreneur, and this model distinguishes work that engages self-expression and creative skills from humdrum work driven by economic motives. While adaptability and flexibility in response to change are considered key attributes of creative workers, the sources of change and their effects on opportunity are rarely examined. They are assumed to lie in unpredictable, consumer tastes rather than in the regulations and financial markets that shape the environments within which creative work takes place.

From an industry perspective, however, both economic and creative motivations shape individual and organizational strategies. The fine artist has different motivations than the gallery owner or publicist, though all are engaged in careers that require a sensibility open to creativity and innovation. The artist develops a range of economic activities to sustain a career that also enables creative self-expression (Markusen, Gilmore, Johnson, Levi, and Martinez

2006; Menger 1999). In all creative industries, there are also occupations that do not fall into the creative category, while they may be skilled. These include administrative aides, accountants, lawyers, or electricians.

In some creative industries—including entertainment media, advertising, fashion, and music—the drive for self-expression and economic success (or at least sustainability) is often present in equal measure. And because workers in these industries direct their self-enterprise to the needs of firms buying their services, rather than directly to their audience or market, firm strategies drive access to jobs and opportunities to build sustainable careers. In this subset of the creative economy, the competitive strategies of the firm are more likely to drive the strategies of the workforce (Ursell 2000, 2003).

Thus, freelance entrepreneurial creative workers are in an interdependent relationship with firms in the industries in which they work, whether fashion houses, advertising agencies, galleries, or motion picture distributors (Christopherson 2002; McRobbie 2002; Neff, Wissinger, and Zukin 2005; Rantisi 2004). It is difficult to understand either the nature of a creative worker's "flexibility" or the degree to which self-expression and economic motives are balanced in their work lives without understanding the business strategies of the firms to whom they sell their products or services.

In this respect, research on media entertainment and new media is exceptional because it frequently incorporates perspectives that reach beyond the individual creative worker. The social dimensions of creative work are likely to be brought into the picture (Bielby and Bielby 2003; duGay 1996; McRobbie 2002; Perrons 2003; Ursell 2000, 2003) as well as the technological and political/economic context (Hesmondhalgh 2002; Deuze 2007; Miller, Govil, McMurria, and Maxwell 2001; McDonald and Wasko 2008). This industry-sensitive research, along with data on employment patterns and conditions, can be used to illuminate the changes in creative work in light of the changes in the industries in which workers build their careers.

To examine how industry structure creates a context for creative work, I will look at how the entertainment media industry has been altered by concentration in distribution of profit-making products and by financial pressures produced by mergers and acquisitions. While typically examined in isolation, the combination of conglomerate market power with intensified efforts to reduce risks and maintain stockholder returns has had serious consequences for the production side of the industry and for the workforce.

Entertainment media in the United States, especially in film production, has always been carried out with an international audience in mind and so was appropriately characterized as a "global" industry. But what that means is now changing. The current strategies of the dominant distribution firms that have evolved since the late 1990s go beyond marketing into international market products that were first released in the US national market. First, the emphasis now is on financing media products for a global audience while *moving away from* investment in riskier and potentially less profitable productions for the US national market. Second, the now "decentered" global media conglomerate is using its market power within the United States and in relation to other nations instrumentally, to foster the "socialization" and absorption of production costs by governments who *perceive* themselves as global competitors and to reduce the use of higher cost production centers such as Los Angeles.

In the next section, I look at the processes that have led to this market power and the emergence of the decentered, "financialized" media conglomerate— processes that arguably create a new phase in the globalization of media entertainment production, with significant implications for US production centers and their media workforce.

How the bargaining position of content producers changed with increasing distributor bargaining power

There is now a fulsome analysis of the origins and consequences of concentration in the US media entertainment industries (cf. Cooper 2009; Noam 2009; Schatz 2008), including the chapters in this volume. For the purposes of this chapter, however, the subject of concentration has to be viewed from a particular perspective—that is, how does concentration on the distribution side of entertainment media affect content production, which is vertically disintegrated and carried out by networks of small companies and self-employed individuals. As Noam (2009: 22) notes (quoting Edwin Baker), content creation and production and the delivery of content are different products. This distinction is particularly important in understanding the impact of concentration in the film industry, which has had a vertically disintegrated *production* organization since the early 1960s (Christopherson and Storper 1986).

The declining bargaining power of independent producers and of the workforce in film and television began in the mid-1980s with the deregulation of the entertainment media industries, and it demonstrates how policies leading to concentration in distribution can gradually change production and working conditions even in a highly fragmented, project-oriented production process.

The history of entertainment media production, particularly in film, is typically divided into two periods: first, the "studio system," in which production and distribution were integrated via ownership of production and distribution by the major studios; and second, the period of vertical disintegration of production following the Paramount decision and introduction of television (Storper and Christopherson 1984).

Between the 1960s and the mid-1980s, however, there was an important period in which the entertainment media industry was characterized by significant competition on the *distribution* side. New product distribution markets were opening in cable and DVD, and syndicators, such as Lorimar, were searching for new content. The financial syndication rules were still in place, forcing television networks to find and buy content on the market rather than producing it themselves. During this relatively brief period, the content production side of the industry had considerable autonomy in its relationship to distributors (Storper and Christopherson 1984). Because of what in hindsight looks like considerable competition on the distribution side of the industry, content producers—independent producers and the skilled workforce—had unusual bargaining power in relation to product distributors. Not surprisingly, this period was also a "golden age" as measured by the variety and creativity of production.

This competitive situation changed dramatically in the mid-1980s with the abrogation of the Paramount decision (which had legally separated content production and distribution and content exhibition). This decision was followed in the 1990s by a series of regulatory decisions, most notably the end of the so-called "financial syndication rules," enabling the distributors to regain their powerful position vis-à-vis content producers (Christopherson 1996).

Thus, the history of the relationship between content production and distribution has been more complex than the two-phase model suggests. The contingent and critical factor shaping the relative bargaining power of content producers as against content distributors has been the regulatory policy.

Cooper (2009), for example, lays out two critical processes that have emerged from media distribution concentration: increasing monopsony (few buyers for supplier inputs) and the thinning of alternative sources of production inputs as vertically integrated firms tighten their supply networks:

> The leverage that the vertically integrated core of the industry acquired … dramatically changed the terms of trade between the independents and vertically integrated conglomerates. With a small number of vertically integrated buyers and a large number of much smaller product sellers, the core oligopoly gains monopsony power. They can impose onerous terms on the supplier, appropriating maximum surplus. With all of the major distribution channels under their control, the vertically integrated oligopoly can slash the amount they are willing to pay for independent product. (Cooper 2009: 373)

The impact of distribution concentration on the bargaining power of independent content producers—the myriad small firms that contribute to film and television production—and on the workforce has been magnified by the processes of "financialization" that arose in response to expanded global financial opportunities beginning in the 1990s (Epstein 2010; Milberg and Winkler 2010). As authors in this volume illuminate, financialization was more significant in entertainment media than in other industries. In particular, media distribution companies leveraged their considerable assets to acquire or merge with their competitors or suppliers, thus tightening their grip on the overall media entertainment market (Greenwald, Knee, and Seave 2009). This merger and acquisition mania increased their debt load, and as both Winseck and Flew (this volume) indicate, it is not at all clear that they are stronger corporations because of their increased size and reach. The vulnerability of the media distribution conglomerates may, in fact, be an important factor in the strategies they have undertaken to (1) cut costs in feeding their US distribution platforms, (2) reduce risks by emphasizing products aimed at a narrow segment of a global audience, and (3) take risks to explore and invest in potentially high-profit media distribution markets such as those in India.

While the six US-based media distribution conglomerates—Time Warner, Disney, News Corporation, Viacom, GE (NBC-Universal), and Sony—are on shaky ground financially, there are bright spots. Possibly the most important and consistently growing source of revenue has come from international film markets. In 2009, for example, global movie ticket sales by the six conglomerates increased 7.6 percent to almost US$30 billion, with the most growth in the Asia Pacific region. The Asia Pacific box office increased 12.3 percent, mostly in Japan and China, generating US$7.7 billion in ticket sales (Dobuzinskis 2010). Again, this shift has been occurring for some time: In 2001, international box-office sales accounted for 51 percent of the worldwide total that year (US$16.7 billion); in 2008, they had grown to 65 percent of the worldwide total (US$28.1 billion) (MacDonald 2010). Although the net profits derived from the growth in global box office may not be as large as these figures would indicate, the trend is clear. Profit *growth* opportunities lie in the emerging country markets, not in the mature markets such as the United States, Canada, Australia, or Europe.

The exponential shift in the potential profit opportunities from producing event films such as *Dark Knight*, *Avatar*, and *How to Train Your Dragon* for a global market, and the potential advertising revenues from television production and distribution in emerging markets, has accelerated the reshaping of media conglomerate investment strategies. This shift supports the financial objectives of corporations, including General Electric and Sony, who own key media entertainment distribution companies. While still nationally based, the US conglomerates that distribute entertainment media products are also becoming, as Desai (2009) describes it, "decentered"—shifting their attention and investment to markets where superprofits are possible. At the same time, however, they are maintaining their grip on the now "mature" US national market.

As potential geographic markets have expanded, the entertainment media distributors have focused on a narrower audience demographic. The target market is the young moviegoer, either children or young males (Motion Picture Association of America (MPAA) 2010). There are complex reasons for focusing on very high-budget films for a global family or young male audience. Possibly the most important is that they open opportunities to market ancillary products, including toys and games. Because of their capital assets, the studios owned by the conglomerates have a competitive advantage in producing global entertainment/product marketing vehicles. These megaproject films are, in many ways, less risky than a medium-budget film made for an adult audience in the United States. The conglomerates cooperate in coproduction deals to share the costs and the profits, and set release dates so as not to step on each other's profits. Foreign release dates are chosen to maximize global results and now may occur before a US release date. For the conglomerates, bigger is indeed better.

In large measure, the shift to the global family and young male markets has come about as a result of increasing personal incomes in emerging markets such as China and India, privatization of formerly state-regulated media, and the opening of private investment opportunities in production centers such as "Bollywood." All the major entertainment media distribution conglomerates are now significantly invested in India. In 2009, the MPAA—the multinational enterprise's (MNE) trade and lobbying association—opened an office in Mumbai under the name of the Motion Picture Distribution Association. With growing pay-TV viewership and advertising revenues, the attraction of the Indian market is obvious. Critics of this strategy note, however, that the barriers to entry in markets such as India are much lower than in the United States, and the US conglomerates are therefore entering a potentially highly competitive situation (Greenwald et al. 2009).

So, how are the "vulnerable," highly leveraged media distribution conglomerates financing their acquisitions and forays into potentially lucrative international markets? To answer this question, we need to look at the other half of their business strategy—to reduce costs in the distribution markets and platforms they already dominate and to transfer risks to content producers for those markets. In the next section, I look at what these strategies mean for what is produced and how it is produced.

How distribution concentration is shaping what gets made by content producers

To understand how concentration on the distribution side of the industry and the strategies of the distribution conglomerates affect the content production side, we need to look at what the conglomerates are demanding from their content suppliers. As was noted earlier in this chapter, creative media workers and content producers cannot produce what they want (at least if they want to earn a living). They must respond to what the conglomerates want to distribute on their platforms, whether cable or broadcast television or film.

For example, as US-based distribution conglomerates reduce costs in order to pay for mergers and acquisitions and invest in potentially highly profitable emerging markets; they are reducing investment in less profitable and more fickle, medium-budget, adult-oriented products in their own national market.

Theoretically, this conglomerate focus on narrow segments of a global market should be good news for independent content producers—*if* they can find financing for middle-budget (about US$50 million) films for those segments of the market not served by the global "blockbuster" strategy. For example, when in the 1950s and early 1960s, the then "major studios" turned to a blockbuster strategy of producing fewer but much more costly films (e.g. *Ben Hur, Cleopatra*), Italian and French films developed significant audiences in the United States by playing in exhibition houses that were looking for more films to exhibit. This time around, however, the picture appears to be mixed and inconclusive. Non-US production centers in Europe and Asia have been growing slowly (Scott 2004) even as nontheatrical distribution channels such as Netflix have opened markets for films lacking a US theatrical release.

Without theatrical release, however, a film is unlikely to get enough attention to produce a substantial "request-based" audience, such as that available through Netflix. And, despite the market gap, the percentage of foreign films released in the United States has declined. In the 1960s, imported films accounted for 10 percent of the US box office; in the 1980s, it was 7 percent; in the 2000s, it has declined to less than 1 percent. Why? Because films made outside the United States do not fit into the conglomerate strategy—synergies across their multiple distribution gateways of theatrical exhibition, broadcast, cable, DVD, and ancillary markets—and so do not get distributed on key platforms, even if they are excellent films that win international awards.

What about other geographic markets? Here, too, the conglomerate power to pay for marketing a film globally has enormous significance. The dynamic is similar to that in the book distribution and retailing industry, where the marketing money behind a "best seller" crowds out attention and shelf space for a wider diversity of titles and publishers. And like a small bookstore, a small theater that shows foreign films finds it difficult to survive without getting revenue from the occasional "blockbuster." As long as film producers have difficulty getting distribution deals in major markets, such as those in North America, their opportunities to garner audiences in global markets are decreased.

A significant by-product of (1) the mergers and acquisitions that enabled media distribution concentration and (2) the financialization that placed media distributors in a highly leveraged and vulnerable financial position is the "squeeze" in which the content producers of media entertainment find themselves. As a consequence of their control of distribution gateways, the conglomerates and their corporate parents are able to press producers (the suppliers of content) to reduce the costs of production (Cooper 2009).

The place where this pressure is most visible in the United States is in the production center, Los Angeles. In the early 2000s, long before the beginning of the current "great recession" in 2007, the Los Angeles-based film and television industry began to suffer from production declines, cost-cutting, and the redistribution of risk to program and film producers (Christopherson 2008; MacDonald 2010). The MPAA, which represents conglomerate-owned media entertainment companies, indicates that its member studios released 28 percent of all films in 2009. In 1999, that figure stood at 44 percent. While the total number of films released increased over the decade of the 2000s (from 479 to 558), there was a significant drop in films released by MPAA studio subsidiaries (MPAA 2010). So a larger proportion of films are being financed and released by independent production companies. Because they lack access to the MPAA-controlled distribution platforms, however, only a few of these independently made films are profitable (Epstein 2010). The MPAA attributes this decline to recent union actions, contending that changes in production and distribution can be attributed to industry strikes in 2007 as well as to the recent economic downturn. Their own statistics, however, indicate a longer term decline in productions released by their members that parallel the restructuring of the industry and the distribution firms' shifting investment strategies since the early 1990s.

The acceleration of the distribution conglomerate's foreign investment and global product agenda is (in combination with falling profit rates in the United States in key segments such as broadcast television) behind significant shifts in what is produced in the United States and how it is produced. This has important implications for the workforce, including the large concentration of entertainment industry workers in the Los Angeles entertainment industry "agglomeration." In the following sections, I look at some indicators of how the Los Angeles entertainment production industry is being affected by the business strategies of the distribution conglomerates. I then examine the US political response to changes in what is produced and where.

The restructuring of US entertainment media work

Based on record-setting box-office revenues and an expanding labor supply, media entertainment looks like a healthy global industry that, true to its reputation, is "recession proof." And, for the small number of people working in that portion of the industry producing digital special effects, games, and global blockbusters aimed at family and young male consumers all over the world, the future may be bright. For the majority of the US workforce, however—those engaged in producing content aimed primarily at a US national market—pressures have increased to produce more with less and to find financing from unconventional sources. These pressures are reflected in four processes: (1) the downsizing and reorienting of corporate broadcast television operations and expansion of low-cost production for cable operations; (2) the expansion of a contract workforce that works project by project for all production types; (3) measures to reduce labor and overall production costs across production types, including shortened production schedules, extended production days, and reorganization to eliminate the influence of unions; and (4) reduced production of products that can support a middle-income workforce because of reduced distribution opportunities for high-value film and television aimed primarily at US audiences. All of these processes are manifested in the industry center in Los Angeles and are gradually undermining its creative and productive strengths.

The data that can illuminate how distribution firm strategies are changing and the consequences for the workforce are difficult to piece together because of the project nature of the industry—companies are established for particular production projects and then dissolved when the television or film project is completed. Publicly available data (which typically are collected on firms) are a highly imperfect source of information on the entertainment media production industry and its workforce trends. Data on firms suggest stable employment and misrepresent employment in an industry dominated by project-based production with a high proportion of self-employed independent contractors. To get a more complete (though still partial) picture of trends, I use multiple sources to derive shifts in industry structure, risk allocation, and workforce adaptation. Some evidence is derived from a study of industry patterns that included 40 interviews with directors, producers, leaders in both unions and guilds, and studio owners as well as analysis of proprietary data and publicly available data on industry production trends and employment (Christopherson, Figueroa, Gray, Parrott, Richardson, and Rightor 2006). Additional interviews were conducted in 2007 along with an analysis of change in key occupations and self-employment from publicly available secondary data.

Corporate downsizing and increased use of independent contractors

Work in television remained distinctively different from that in the film industry until the mid-1980s because of the corporate organization of broadcast television. Bielby and Bielby (1992, 1996) have described the greater stability of corporate television work and how that provided advantages to some groups, such as women writers, who faced greater barriers in the project-based work environment of film. Apart from the "talent" portion of the workforce, the broadcast network workforce was employed in long-term jobs in large corporations (CBS, NBC, ABC) and highly unionized. With the deregulation of the industry, beginning in the 1980s, the broadcast networks were acquired by multinational firms, in which they were only minor units in a diversified portfolio of profit centers. These firms (including Viacom, General Electric, and Disney) also moved rapidly to acquire cable networks, to cut costs in the broadcast network segment in response to cable's competition for viewers and segmenting of the mass audience and in order to finance their acquisitions. As broadcast television faced more competition from other media distribution platforms, corporate owners began a series of cutbacks in personnel. According to Raphael (1997),

> Feeling the squeeze on profits, production companies and the networks initiated a series of cost-cutting strategies that translated into an attack on labor, mainly on below-the-line workers such as technicians, engineers, and extras. The first move was a wave of staff cutbacks at studios and network news departments. In the mid-1980s, Fox cut 20% of its studio staff, Capital Cities/ABC 10% of its staff, CBS 30% of its administrative staff and 10% of its News Division. NBC resisted a 17-week strike by the National Association of Broadcast Employees and Technicians (NABET) in 1987, shedding 200 union jobs. By 1992, NBC had eliminated 30% of its News Division through layoffs and bureau closings. (Raphael 1997: 3)

These restructuring and labor reduction initiatives continued for two decades, and have accelerated again since 2008, with estimated overall cuts of 4 percent in broadcast television. Disney, for example, recently eliminated 200 jobs at ABC, amounting to 5 percent of total staff.

Job cuts have not been the only strategy to reduce labor costs, however. In the midst of stalled negotiations with the Communications Workers of America that began in 2009, NBC announced plans to close operations in the industry centers (Burbank, CA, and New York City) and transfer them to nonunion facilities in New Jersey. While "runaway production" has received the lion's share of the media attention, such corporate decisions regarding their skilled craft employees demonstrate how production location has become a key tool in the restructuring of work.

Overall, with the conglomeration of film and television distribution companies since the 1980s, the stable corporate television sector has declined in size and significance, and TV production processes and employment conditions have gradually come to resemble those in the project-oriented film industry (Raphael 1997; Christopherson 2006).

The expansion of the "for-hire" workforce in an industry losing middle-income work

Since the end of the "studio system" in the 1950s, film industry production has been carried out by crews made up of self-employed independent contractors (Christopherson 2002). As a consequence of corporate downsizing, however, more of the television and film workforce than ever before is made up of freelance independent contractors. Individuals reporting themselves as *self-employed* in the Motion Picture and Video Industries (as reported by US federal income tax filings) grew by 28.4 percent between 2002 and 2006 (United States, Department of Commerce, Bureau of the Census 2002, 2006). As in many other industries in the United States, large media firms are paring down their production workforces to an essential core and using temporary workers and self-employed workers on an as-needed basis.

At the same time, data from the Occupational Employment Statistics (United States, Bureau of Labor Statistics 2002, 2006) show dramatic increases in the number of people who place themselves in key entertainment industry occupations. Between 2002 and 2006, there was a 14 percent increase in the number of individuals identified as producers or directors, a 7 percent increase in individuals identified as actors, and a 9 percent increase in those who identified themselves as camera operators for television and motion pictures.[1]

This shift to independent contractors has occurred in the context of an expansion of the labor supply, stimulated in part by the success of higher education media training programs. In these programs, which have proliferated in Los Angeles and New York as well as in other cities, students learn a wide variety of production skills and are introduced to new technologies that traverse conventional union professional and craft jurisdictions. They learn how to produce on "shoestring" budgets and to work very rapidly under severe time constraints. They learn to work in efficient multifunctional production teams. When they graduate, they are "hybrids"—writer–directors or director–camera-operator–editors—who make up a flexible workforce of independent contractors perfectly suited to the high growth segment of the media industry—production for cable television (Wyatt 2009).

In some respects, this workforce has more in common with their young colleagues in website or digital design media than they do with their elders who worked in broadcast television and medium- to high-budget film (Batt, Christopherson, Rightor, and Van Jaarsveld 2001). Working style, expectations, and a cultivated amateurism separate this "free agent," entrepreneurial workforce from the establishment professionals who populate the traditional entertainment media guilds and unions. Although there is still considerable intersection (and even some merging) between the professional worker with a defined role and the multifunctional media production team member, the contemporary workforce appears more segmented and differentiated (by age, gender, and race) than it did in the 1980s when the major divide in the US entertainment media workforce was defined by union versus nonunion status (Christopherson and Storper 1989).

The expansion of an independent contractor workforce has taken place as the film and television media distributors have moved "down-market." As the higher prestige and more highly paid jobs, such as those in broadcast television and mid-budget feature films, have been reduced, jobs have been growing in the low-cost environment of cable television. For example, while 4 percent of broadcast jobs have been eliminated since 2008, cable has added 3 percent.

The availability of large numbers of entrepreneurial self-employed workers with at least some level of skill provides media entertainment firms with a strong incentive to subcontract low-end production, particularly if they are providing product for the cable market where production values are of less importance and budget constraints are significant. And the concentration of this unorganized and low-cost workforce in a major production center like Los Angeles gives those firms good reason to funnel low-end production there. In fact, virtually all the recent job growth in the major media centers of Los Angeles has been in production for cable television (Los Angeles County Economic Development Corporation (LAEDC) 2010).

The new working environment for media workers is not only risky but also increasingly difficult. While long working hours are legendary in media production, the boundaries that circumscribed abuse appear to have broken down as unions have lost power over industry practices, and the proportion of productions made on "shoestring" budgets has increased. Hourly wages in the media industries remain high for the smaller number of union members, but reports from the International Alliance of Theatrical and Stage Employees (IATSE) unions indicate that the work has become more arduous and less predictable than it was in the early 1990s. IATSE members commonly complain that producers attempt to cut costs by reducing shooting days while requiring overtime work from the production crew. On the talent side, the Casting Data Report from the Screen Actors Guild (SAG) reports on roles (jobs) and days worked by production type. Between 2004 and 2006, the total number of roles (jobs) was up 10 percent, but the average number of days worked per role was down 7 percent. In nonepisodic television, average days worked declined by 19 percent (Screen Actors Guild 2007). In addition, the largest increase (20.2 percent) in roles (jobs) nationwide was in the low-budget "theatrical" category (Screen Actors Guild 2007). While such figures are only available for actors, they describe a common pattern in the media entertainment industries: a tendency to reduce production time and squeeze the workforce to produce more with fewer resources.

The weakening of the Los Angeles agglomeration

The available evidence indicates that, in Los Angeles, where 45 percent of the total US film and television industry is employed, changes in what and how much is produced have been dramatic (United States, Bureau of Labour Statistics 2008).

First, there is a long-term trend toward less production in Los Angeles, particularly higher budget productions. One of the few available indicators is permitted production days—the number of days of shooting on-location, away from studio facilities, in the Los Angeles area. This surrogate provides some measure of overall production volume year to year and of trends in particular production categories. It shows, for example, total permitted production days in greater Los Angeles rose from 7,831 in 1995 to a steady 12,000–15,000 per year in the mid-2000s, peaked in 2008, and then dropped to near 1995 levels within 2 years. Feature film on-location shooting reached a high of 13,980 days in 1996; by 2009 it was only 4,976 days (LAEDC 2010). By contrast, location activity for TV reached a high of 25,277 days in 2008, reflecting the expansion of low-cost reality and dramatic productions for cable television. However, on-location television production days dropped almost 17 percent in 2009.

These figures indicate a decrease in the volume of higher value production— in mid-range feature films and scripted television, particularly for broadcast— and suggest that the industry workforce is facing a long-term structural change rather than a cyclical downturn.

While blame for such changes is frequently attributed to union actions (particularly as the 14-week Writers Guild strike in 2007–8) or to "runaway production," those explanations strain to cover a seismic shift in the volume of production, the product mix, and the conduct of production activity simultaneously. The scope of change has been so extensive that even the normally sanguine Los Angeles economic development officials are recognizing its structural origins.

A study by the LAEDC (2010), for example, indicates that the number of workers employed in film, television, and commercials in Los Angeles County decreased 6 percent in 2009 to 132,442, the lowest number since 2001. According to the director of the economic development corporation, California state employment numbers actually undercount employment losses in the entertainment industry agglomeration in Los Angeles: They do not include unemployment of part-time workers (nearly a quarter of the industry workforce), nor unemployment in ancillary business services such as prop houses and equipment rental shops, which depend on Los Angeles productions for their employment and profits.

The result has been heightened anxiety over income expectations, dismay over a loss of creativity, and anger over the pressure to produce too much too fast (Christopherson 2008). Even in this historically high-risk industry, the recent period has been one in which the rewards of working in media entertainment are more elusive than ever.

How can this be happening in an industry agglomeration that, because of its flexibility, creativity, and high skills, is an exemplar of the global knowledge economy. One answer is that the strengths of agglomeration are *production* strengths. They lie in cooperation between production companies, networks of skilled and creative workers, and the regional institutions that support them. If these skilled content producers, including the entire skilled talent and craft workforce, cannot distribute products in markets that support them financially, the health of the entire creative production complex and its capacity to replenish and sustain its workforce is at risk.

What is important to recognize is that the *distribution* side of the industry could not have had this effect in the 1970s and early 1980s, when there was more competition among distributors. Creative producers then had multiple markets for their products. Concentration and conglomeration since the mid-1980s have increased the relative power of distributors over the creative content producers. This power and the distributor conglomerates' strategy of restructuring and disinvestment are slowly undermining the viability of the production complex and its creative workforce.

The fragmentation of the labor supply and the inability of unions to organize and represent a larger and more diverse workforce have had profound and negative implications for their ability to craft a coherent response to the real changes facing entertainment industry production. Furthermore, responses have been shaped by divided union representation and fear of conglomerate reactions to any direct challenge to their control of distribution markets. Consequently, one of the most visible labor responses to disinvestment has taken the form of an alliance with the conglomerates to support "socialization" of production costs through State and municipal subsidies to production companies.

How workforce responses to MNE disinvestment are further undermining the Los Angeles agglomeration

Changes in entertainment media production and work have been interpreted differently by the so-called "talent" or "above-the-line" workforce, and the skilled craft workers who compose the "below-the-line" workforce. At the top end of the creative entertainment media workforce, producers, writers, and directors are more aware and knowledgeable about changes in industry structure and investment patterns. They complain about the loss of creative control, about tighter production deadlines and budgets, and about the loss of residual payments that sustain them financially during the dry periods when they are not employed on a project. The Independent Film and Television Alliance, which represents independent producers and directors, for example, devotes a section of its website to analyzing the impact of media distribution conglomeration and to proposals for regulatory action that would reestablish competition (http://www.ifta-online.org/media-concentration-and-internet-access). According to one veteran filmmaker,

> In cable, residuals (payments for each showing of the product) for writers, actors, and directors are a percent of the producer's gross. But if that producer is a network who self-deals the rights to their cable company ... there is no compensation for that. Suddenly you discover that the eleven or twelve per cent gross residual among the three guilds that has been fought over for so many decades is virtually meaningless, as rights are simply self-dealt among related entities. (Hill 2004: 20)

The 2009–10 discussions between the SAG and the American Federation of Television and Radio Artists (AFTRA) over whether to merge and what issues to bring to the negotiation table with the Alliance of Motion Picture and Television Producers (AMPTP) (which is dominated by the conglomerates) also indicate how divided the unions are within their own membership about how to react to concentration on the distribution side (Handel 2010). Anne-Marie Johnson, first vice president of the SAG, described the impact of distribution concentration in her testimony at the Federal Communications Commission Hearings:

> As actors, we find the continued consolidation of media companies has drastically limited our ability to individually bargain our personal services agreements ... the networks decide what the top-of-the show rates are, in a parallel practice. Some networks will even tell you they only pay 50 per cent of the going rate. Take it or leave it. This salary compression cripples the middle class actor's ability to make a living. (Screen Actors Guild 2006)

"Below-the-line labor," by contrast, has generally ignored structural change in the film and television industries and focused on "runaway production" (or outsourcing, in particular to Canada) as the cause of increasing unemployment and the loss of good industry jobs and project work in the United States, particularly in major centers such as Los Angeles. One analysis of media labor responses to the search for financing and lower production costs by film and television producers also found that the less-skilled and less-geographically mobile craft workers developed a coalition to initiate restrictions on outsourcing, while the "talent" portion of the workforce rejected strategies to limit outsourcing, presumably because they could follow productions wherever they were being made (Chase 2008).

Chase's analysis of the political-economic responses to "globalization," however, is limited to the demonstration of a split between segments of labor regarding support for the Film and Television Action Committee's (FTAC) agenda favoring trade regulation restrictions. While the FTAC story is significant, it narrowly depicts the dynamics that the labor force is facing and what they perceive as their alternatives. In fact, the FTAC agenda was rapidly eclipsed by a political project, namely, "the film incentives agenda," that captured support from all segments of the industry—capital, craft workers, and talent. This agenda began with the idea of matching subsidies and cost differentials in production locations outside the United States with federal and State subsidies to finance productions inside the United States. It has morphed into something quite different—the promotion of public subsidization of entertainment media production on the grounds that such subsidies can create new film and television production industries in states with little or no industry base or experience, like Michigan, Connecticut, or Georgia. In 2010, incentives of various forms were offered in 43 US states (Entertainment Partners, http://www.entertainmentpartners.com/).

The film incentive-based financing strategy has attracted broad support within the industry because it provides something for everyone. For the major media conglomerates, film and television production subsidies lower the cost of US productions, enabling them to fill out a roster of film and television products with less investment and to free up capital for investment in lower risk products or where future profits may be higher. For talent, it provides opportunities to work and develop careers in an era when these opportunities have significantly diminished. For craft workers, it multiplies opportunities to work, even if they involve moving from state to state to do so. Ultimately, state film incentives programs shore up the national industry by providing a financing alternative for productions that take place in the United States.

The film incentives agenda is led by the conglomerate-owned distribution companies (through MPAA), in collaboration with craft workers (through IATSE). Although talent workers describe the problem somewhat differently, focusing on the underlying sources of structural unemployment rather than outsourcing, they support the film incentives agenda. This is particularly true of those segments of the workforce, such as members of the SAG, whose incomes and opportunities for work have been particularly affected by decisions to limit financing and distribution of feature films and high-value scripted television series (Christopherson 2008). The MPAA, in fact, uses labor to make the argument for subsidies at state houses and in public hearings across the United States. Ironically, this agenda appears to have blunted pressure from labor to stop the outsourcing of production, which has not declined (MacDonald 2010). In addition, although incentive programs are rationalized as producing economic development, the preponderance of the evidence indicates that they constitute a net cost to the citizens of the states in which they exist (Christopherson and Rightor 2010; MacDonald 2010). In fact, film incentives constitute a production subsidy to entertainment media, which is captured by the conglomerate distributors who have more and better quality products to distribute without having to invest in their production.

Perhaps ironically, one of the side effects of this incentive-driven production-financing strategy is that the industrial commons that support the industry and the labor force in its primary production center, Los Angeles, are being further undermined. Thus, the rational actions of individual firms (and unions) in response to the challenges presented by deregulation, trade liberalization, and financialization are undermining the complex and place-specific strengths of a major US industry—television and film production.

Conclusion

Our ideas about creative work and creative workers have been shaped by a literature that focuses on the supply side of the picture—that is, on the characteristics of individual workers and their motivations. In this literature, personal motivation and capacity for creative production determine why a person enters a creative industry and whether they persist in a creative career. While these personal characteristics and motivations are critical to what happens in high-risk, entrepreneurial creative production markets, they do not tell the whole story.

Many creative workers, such as those in advertising, music, and media, do their creative work in industries dominated by firms whose shares trade on international capital markets and whose success is measured in shareholder rather than creative value. In the US entertainment media, it is the firms that *distribute* entertainment products that confront the pressures and reap the opportunities measured by short-term stockholder value. For reasons that can be traced back to the breakup of the studio system in the 1950s, the production side of the industry is overwhelmingly composed of small firms and independent contractors who are assembled and then reassembled for particular projects. In this chapter, I have described the changing relationship between the *distribution* side of the industry, as it has become more concentrated across distribution platforms, and the *production* side—the marketplace where creative media workers produce their products. One of my central contentions is that relationship between distributors and creative producers is not fixed, as has been implied in some analyses of the relationship of production and distribution (Aksoy and Robbins 1992; Storper 1993). In fact, there is not one Hollywood but two—producers of content and distributors of content, continuously in conflict and sometimes in uneasy alliance. The power of the distributors has increased dramatically since the mid-1980s as a consequence of deregulation. Their increased power is a result of political decisions, not the result of inherent structural properties of the industry.

In the contemporary US media entertainment industry, concentration and conglomeration among entertainment product distributors, enhanced by the pressures of financialization, have resulted in the consolidation of those platforms that distribute the types of products that provide good, career-sustaining jobs to the film and television workforce. This process of consolidation has had profound consequences for product demand—what is produced, where, and by whom. In addition, responsibility for financing production has been redistributed downward to the still largely vertically disintegrated production system, composed of networks of firms and workers, highly concentrated in Los Angeles and to a much lesser extent, New York.

In response to conglomerate disinvestment in US-produced entertainment media products, the US entertainment media industry workforce has joined *with* the conglomerates in efforts, state-by-state, to advocate for film and television production subsidies. While these joint initiatives have retained some production in the United States, they do not address the critical underlying issues: industry restructuring and conglomerate power in distribution markets. They instead socialize production costs for firms that are highly leveraged financially, though achieving peak revenues in the global film market. Over the long term, the incentives battle may undermine the "industrial commons" that has sustained this project-based industry since its last great transformation to a vertically disintegrated production organization in the 1950s.

Note

1   These figures are based on averages over the 2002–6 period.

6

Financialization and the "Crisis of the Media"

The rise and fall of (some) media conglomerates in Canada

Dwayne Winseck
Carleton University

This chapter examines the crosscutting dynamics that have reshaped the network media industries in Canada over the course of the past 15 years, with occasional glances back to the 1980s. Three questions are at its core: First, do new digital technologies, especially the internet, pose fundamental threats to well-established media players or create a larger media economy within which they can expand? Second, have media markets become more concentrated or less? Third, are the media "in crisis"?

I argue, first, that the media economy has grown substantially and that the rise of new players such as YouTube (Google), Apple, Facebook, MySpace (News Corp.), and Wikipedia has been especially strong in Canada and added to the media economy, without cannibalizing the economic base of traditional media. Second, I show that the media have become more concentrated and that a half-dozen media conglomerates now form the centerpiece of the network media economy in Canada. Adding four other second-tier firms to the list yields what I call the "big 10" media firms: Rogers, Shaw, Quebecor, CTVglobemedia, Bell, Canwest, Torstar, Astral Media, Canadian Broadcasting Corporation (CBC), and Cogeco.

Finally, I argue that massive increase in the capitalization of media firms since the mid-1990s has fundamentally altered the organizational structure of media firms and the "operating logic" of the media industries overall (Bouquillion 2008; Miège 1989). The media are in a heightened state of flux, but I argue that the current woes besetting *some* media enterprises are not primarily due to the steady onslaught of the internet or declining revenues as advertising shifts from "old" to "new" media. Instead, I argue that contemporary conditions reflect a short-term, cyclical decline in advertising caused by the economic downturn, the accumulated results of two waves of consolidation (1995–2000 and 2003–7), and the "financialization of the media."

The concept of financialization directs our attention to the capitalization of the media industries alongside the traditional focus of critical media political economy on media ownership, markets, regulation, commodification, digitization, and so on. The concept highlights the extraordinary growth in the size of the financial sector and financial assets relative to the industrial and other sectors of the economy over the past 25 years, especially since the mid-1990s. These developments have been enabled by the steady liberalization of financial markets, the search for new modalities of capital accumulation in the face of persistently low levels of overall economic growth in the Western capitalist economies since the 1970s, the rapid growth of network information and communication technologies, and accelerated global flows of capital. It also refers to a condition where financial capital and, crucially, financial models drive the strategies and evolution of the rest of the economy, as has been especially evident with respect to the telecom, internet, and media sectors globally and, as this chapter demonstrates, in Canada (Duménil and Lévy 2005; Foster and Magdoff 2009; Phillips 2009). Paying close attention to the dynamics and discourses of financialization also offers a potential bridge between critical political economy and critical *cultural* political economy insofar as it highlights how the discourses and models of financial actors constitute an *image* of reality around which financial actors organize their behavior, including allocating enormous sums of capital investment to financial market trading, mergers and acquisitions, corporate restructuring, and so forth—even if the desired aims fail to materialize or, worse, lead to calamitous consequences, as attested by the ongoing global credit crisis that began in 2008 (Jessop 2008; Sayer 2001; Thompson 2010a).

The logic of financialization is particularly important to recent developments across the media industries because it has, paradoxically, not only created greater media concentration but also bloated media giants that have sometimes stumbled badly and occasionally been brought to their knees by the two global financial crises of the twenty-first century (2000–2; 2008–). Indeed, several bastions of the "old order" assembled just before or after the turn of the millennium subsequently have been restructured (Bertelsmann, ITV) or dismantled (AT&T, Vivendi), have collapsed in financial ruin (Canwest, Craig, Kirch), or have abandoned early visions of convergence altogether (Bell Globemedia, Time Warner). The woes of these entities offer a cautionary tale regarding the impact of financialization on the media, rather than a tale in which the internet, changing media behaviors, and declining advertising have precipitated a "crisis of the media." These trends are global in scope, but as this chapter shows, the conditions in Canada are unique (Scherer 2010).

A bigger pie? The vast expansion of the network media economy, 1984–2009

That the media are in crisis often appears to be a given, with no shortage of examples that seem to prove the case. To take just a few of these for examples, Canwest and CTVglobemedia closed several television stations in 2009, while workers of the former acquired one of its stations in Victoria, BC, and another in Hamilton, Ontario, was sold. TQS, the second largest private French-language television network, was sold to Remstar in 2008 by the consortium of Cogeco, the Canadian Imperial Bank of Commerce (CIBC), and BCE that had previously backed the beleaguered network. Even the CBC's advertising revenue dropped significantly in 2007–8. Profits for private conventional television fell to zero in 2008, and revenues declined from $2.2 billion to $2.1 billion (Canadian Radio-television and Telecommunications Commission (CRTC), 2009b). Daily newspapers also seem to have been hit hard, and several—*National Post, Brockville Recorder and Times, The Chatham Daily News,* and *The Daily Observer* (Pembroke)—pared back their weekly publishing schedule in 2009 from 6 days to 5. Newspaper revenues declined slightly, and daily circulation fell yet again from 4.3 to 4.1 million between 2008 and 2009 (Canadian Newspaper Association (CNA) 2010). A slew of layoffs by Rogers at its Citytv stations in 2009 and 2010 (140 jobs), CTVglobemedia in 2009 (248 jobs), and Canwest in 2008 (500 jobs) and 2009 (an additional 15 percent cut in the workforce or 1,400 jobs) only seems to reinforce the view that a secular wave of destruction has pummeled the traditional media (Canwest 2009; Toughill 2009).

Broadcasters' incessant pleas to the CRTC to shore up their supposed faltering economic base have been met with several modest initiatives, including the implementation of a "local programming improvement fund," more flexibility for broadcasters to negotiate fee-for-carriage arrangements with cable and satellite distributors, permission to include advertising in video-on-demand services, and a willingness by the regulator to entertain the potential for all television distributors—including currently exempt internet service providers, wireless service providers, and content aggregators such as Apple, Google's YouTube, and Zip.ca—to be required to financially support Canadian content (CRTC 2009c, 2010).[1] At the same time, the regulator's decisions regarding "network neutrality" and media concentration have favored established telecom and media providers, on the dubious grounds that they possess the deep pockets and inclination to invest in network infrastructure and high-quality journalism and programming (CRTC 2008, 2009d). Clearly, the "media in crisis" argument is being mobilized, but policy responses thus far have been subdued relative to the anguish hanging over the press in the United States and television news in Britain or relative to the $850 million newspaper bailout in

France in 2009 (Benkler, Faris, Gasser, Miyakawa, and Schultze 2010; Nichols and McChesney 2009; Scherer 2010).

It is one thing, however, to recognize that the media industries face tumultuous times but another altogether to see current conditions as cataclysmic (Picard 2009). In fact, notions that the media are in crisis must contend with the reality that they have grown immensely over the past 25 years, as Figure 6.1 demonstrates.[2]

Figure 6.1 indicates that the total telecoms and network media economy expanded enormously over this period. In real dollar terms adjusted for inflation, the size of the media economy in Canada expanded from $38 billion in 1984 to $56.6 billion in 2000 to $73.6 billion in 2008.[3] Even after removing the wired and wireless telecoms sectors, the remaining seven sectors of what I call the network media industries—television, cable and satellite distribution, newspapers, internet access, internet advertising, radio, and magazines— expanded substantially from $21.4 billion to $32 billion between 2000 and 2008. Newspaper revenues have stayed flat; almost all sectors of the media have survived well (radio, television, magazines), while some have flourished (cable and satellite television); and internet access and internet advertising have exploded. The decline in wired telecoms from 2000 to 2008 is substantial, but not without precedent (e.g. 1984–92), and it has been offset by the immense growth in wireless and internet services. In fact, almost all new revenue from the latter services goes to incumbents: BCE, Telus, Manitoba Telecom Services

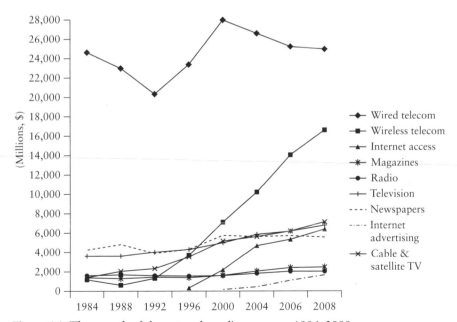

Figure 6.1 The growth of the network media economy, 1984–2008

Sources: CRTC, *Communication Monitoring Report*, 2009a and various years; Canadian Newspaper Association, *Ownership of Canadian Newspapers*, 2009 and various years; Internet Advertising Bureau, *Canada Online Advertising Revenue Survey*, 2009; Corporate Annual Reports.

(MTS), SaskTel, Rogers, Shaw, Quebecor, and Cogeco. These firms are not in crisis.

Claims that television is in desperate straits typically highlight the relative decline of conventional advertising-supported television, where profits fell from 11 percent in 2005 to 5 percent in 2007 to zero in 2008. This argument is disingenuous. For one, it confuses short-term events with long-term patterns. Profits for conventional television hovered between 10 and 15 percent from 1996 to 2006 and have declined for only the 2 most recent years. In addition, revenues have been steady for the past half a decade and have not fallen except for a slight decline in 2008. Moreover, the television universe as a whole has grown enormously. New distribution channels, as well as cable and satellite television, pay-per-view, video-on-demand, the internet, and so forth, have proliferated and are exceptionally lucrative. There were 48 cable and satellite television services in 2000; today there are 189. Indeed, revenues for these services ($3.1 billion) in 2008 were nearly four times those of a decade ago and slightly less than those for conventional television (if the CBC's annual subsidy is included) (CRTC 2004, 2009a).

Overall, profits for specialty- and pay-television services have hovered between 21 and 25 percent annually since 2002—roughly two-and-a-half times the rate of profit for all industries as a whole and equaled by just three other economic sectors: banking (25.2 percent), alcohol and tobacco (23.6 percent), and real estate (20.9 percent) (Statistics Canada 2010a). Even at the height of the financial crisis in 2008 and 2009, specialty- and pay-television profits were 22 and 23 percent, respectively. Cable and satellite distributors are equally lucrative (CRTC 2004, 2009a). As a whole, the television universe has expanded from a $5 billion market in 1984 to $10.1 billion in 2000 and $13.9 billion in 2008 (see Figure 6.1). Thus, television is not in crisis but one of the fastest growing and most lucrative sectors of the economy!

The newspaper business offers the most challenging test to the arguments that I am making, but its current state is better described as a continuation of long-term trends, rather than a crisis. Picard (2009) and Goldstein (2009) argue that daily newspaper circulation has been in long-term decline relative to the total population in the United States, Britain, and Canada since the 1950s, partly due to the steady rise of new sources of news over this period (e.g. television beginning in the 1950s, cable news channels in the 1980s, and the internet in the 1990s). Measured in absolute terms, however, daily circulation in Canada rose until 2000, when 5 million copies were sold, before falling to 4.7 million in 2005 and 4.1 million in 2009 (CNA 2010; Goldstein 2009). There has been no downward spike in circulation attributable to the advent of the internet. In fact, there are indications that the tide is turning as internet newspaper readership begins to yield some new subscribers. The catch, of course, is that internet audiences are worth a tiny fraction of the value of "hard-copy" readers. Still, the Project for Excellence in Journalism (PEJ) lays a good part of the blame for the state of the press on a complacent industry that has been slow to adjust to the internet over the past decade (Picard 2009; PEJ 2009, 2010; Zamaria and Fletcher 2008).

Newspaper revenues in Canada have not plunged. They fluctuated between 1984 and 1992, grew steadily afterward from $3.9 billion (1992) to $5.7 billion in 2000, then fell to $5.5 billion in 2008. In addition, with operating profits of 12 to 15 percent between 2000 and 2008, newspapers are comparatively profitable outlets for investment (Statistics Canada 2010b). The profits for Torstar—owner of the *Toronto Star* and closest to a "pure" newspaper publisher in Canada—ranged from 16 to 18 percent annually between 2000 and 2005, then declined from 13 to 14.5 percent between 2006 and 2009. Looked at from a slightly different angle, however, the image of the press and media industries being in peril did have some basis in reality in recent years as net profits and return on equity plunged briefly for Astral (2009), Canwest (2008–9), Cogeco (2009), Quebecor (2007–8), and Torstar (2008). These are 5 of the top 10 media firms in the country, and therefore this is significant. Except for Canwest, however, the shock was short, sharp, and confined to 1 or 2 years between 2007 and 2009, depending on the firm.

Figure 6.2 illustrates the operating profit trends for the top eight firms in the network media industries from 1995 to 2009. As this figure shows, mid- and long-term profits for Canada's leading media companies have been high, not

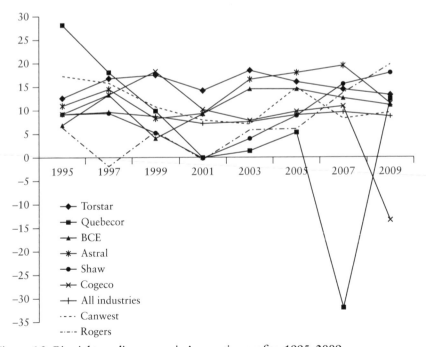

Figure 6.2 Big eight media companies' operating profits, 1995–2009
Sources: Company *Annual Reports*; Bloomberg Professional; Statistics Canada (2010a and various years), *Financial and Taxation Statistics for Enterprises*.

low. Moreover, it also indicates that the occasional woes of some media firms have been transitory and have coincided with the two economic crises of the past decade, suggesting that broad economic forces, not the internet, are the source of their problems. Indeed, recent troubles have been compounded by their close proximity to the crash of the telecom–media–technology (TMT) bubble between 2001 and 2003 (Picard 2009).

Clearly, the network media economy has not shrunk, but it has grown and consistently allowed companies to achieve well-above-average profits. The pleadings of the industry, however, begin to make a bit more sense once we realize that some of the overall growth that has occurred has been ambiguous in the sense that it has occurred not in terms of money but *time*. Indeed, "total media time" for internet users (over three-quarters of the population) surged from 46 to 62 hours per week between 2004 and 2007 (Zamaria and Fletcher 2008). Canadians have long been intensive media users, and this is still the case, as their use of the internet, online video, social networking, and blogs exceeds that of their counterparts in Britain, France, Germany, and the United States, although the growth of the media economy "in time" is also visible in these and other countries (Benkler *et al.* 2010; "Changing the Channel" 2010; Comscore 2009). A steady rise in spending on connectivity further highlights this trend, while spending on media content and cultural goods, conversely, has stayed remarkably flat for the past quarter of a century, as Figure 6.3 shows.[4]

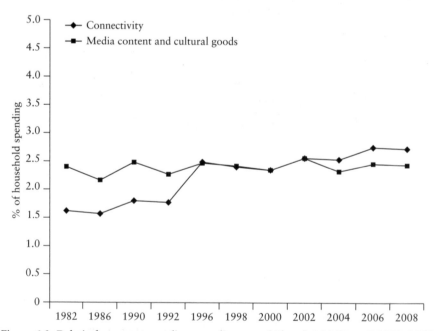

Figure 6.3 **Relatively constant media expenditures and "bandwidth kings," 1982–2008**
Sources: Statistics Canada (2008 and various years), *Survey of Household Spending* (Catalog No. 62M0004XCB). Ottawa: Statistics Canada.

The fact that spending on content and cultural goods in 2008 was the same as it was in 1982 (2.4 percent) suggests that people are using "bandwidth" and "connectivity" for their own purposes rather than consuming more commercial media content. If so, bandwidth, not content, may be king in the network media ecology. Such trends also coincide with the growing visibility of "mass self-expression" (Castells 2009) and the "social economy of information" that has been enabled by distributed networked media (Benkler 2006). This is an important point because it helps to illuminate the "multiple economies" of the network media ecology. As Aristotle observed over 2,000 years ago, the production of *things*, in this case communication and media goods, does not have a singular purpose. Instead, we create things for ourselves (self-production), for exchange (markets), and for others (the community). It may be this reality that is essential to grasping the relationship between the commercial network media economy, mass self-expression, and the social economy of information. In other words, the growth of self-production and the social economy of information are likely behind traditional media players' concerns that they are being deprived of their "fair share" of the "new media economy." But if Aristotle was right, then the greater mediation of everyday life has only brought to the fore the multiple economies of cultural production that were already there. While this may be a difficult concept to wrap our minds around, Wikipedia can usefully be seen as the poster child for some of its core values. The collaborative online encyclopedia was launched in 2001 with 800 "stubs" to be developed by volunteer contributors. By 2010, it held more than 15,000,000 articles written in 270 languages by 91,000 regular contributors—all based on values of "self-production," shared editing, and an alternative model of property, that is, the GNU Free Documentation License, which lets everybody use one another's work and even download the entire database for free. Canadians, on a per capita basis, are generous contributors to the venture (Wikipedia 2010).

All in all, these trends express the multiple economies of digital capitalism, and while nestled firmly within the "belly of the beast," so to speak, they should not be conflated with the logic of market exchange. The key point is that these trends *add* to the media economy, rather than taking away from it. People are using traditional media somewhat less, but this applies to all media users. As Zamaria and Fletcher (2008) observe,

> Online activities appear to supplement rather than displace traditional media use. In general, new media … activities are being added to an existing media diet that includes substantial time spent with conventional media, even for youth and younger internet users. (Zamaria and Fletcher 2008: 9)

The Canadian television industry has been slow off the mark in coming to terms with these new realities, but this may be beginning to change. Perhaps this complacency is not all that surprising, given that only 3 percent of television viewing occurs on the internet, while mobile devices account for much, much less (CBC/Media Technology Monitor (MTM) 2009; "Changing the Channel" 2010). Yet "digital download stores" (e.g. Apple), content aggregators (e.g. Google's YouTube), and peer-to-peer networks (e.g. BitTorrent) are expanding rapidly, albeit from a low base, and a flurry of activity is occurring that will shape the future of the media. Indeed, there have been many attempts to transform nascent trends into viable services. The BBC's iPlayer, created in 2008, now obtains 70,000 views a day, and Hulu, the jointly owned internet television service of News Corp., Disney, and NBC-Universal, is now one of the leading online video services in the United States. None of these ventures, however, is profitable, others have folded (Joost), and still others are expected to be short-lived (Netflix) (CBC/MTM 2009; Canadian Film and Television Production Association (CFTPA) 2010). Broadcasters in Canada finally joined the fray in 2007/8 when they began their own substantial video portals in a sustained way (e.g. CBC.ca, CTV.ca, and GlobalTV.com) and started to offer programs through Apple's iTunes store and YouTube. Behind-the-scenes clips also increasingly accompany scheduled fare, although imported programs such as "The O.C." (aired by CTV) are more likely to use Facebook, YouTube, and MySpace pages than Canadian programs. "Degrassi: The Next Generation" (CTV), "Star Académie" (Quebecor's TVA), and the independently produced "Sanctuary" are notable, but extremely rare, exceptions (Grant 2008; Miller 2007; Nordicity 2007).

The main thrust, however, has been to prevent the rise of the internet as an alternative medium for television. To this end, telecom and cable providers restrict peer-to-peer traffic and regulate their networks with a heavy hand, as the CBC discovered when Bell hobbled its attempt to use BitTorrent to distribute an episode of "Canada's Next Great Prime Minister" in 2008. Geo-gating and content rights management technologies are also being used to shore up "national borders." The US cable companies' "TV Everywhere" strategy is an excellent example of this. Created in 2009, it was quickly imported by Bell and Rogers as the basis for their own broadband video portals. Broadcasters have offered more programs to these services in response but, as in the United States, exclusively to existing cable and satellite subscribers. Geo-blocking and content rights management technologies are also being used to preserve the window-based model that has forever been central to the television and film industries, where the release of films and television programming is staggered over time and across territorial borders in order to maintain separate markets for the theater, specialty and pay TV, DVD, conventional television, and so on. Deals have been struck with Google, Apple, ISPs, wireless service providers, and so on, but they have been hedged by broadcasters' demand that the CRTC require all of these "new media" providers to contribute to Canadian television production funds (CRTC 2009c; Grant 2008; Miller 2007). Of course, Google Inc. (2009) and Apple Inc. (2008), with ISPs at their side, staunchly oppose such a move, arguing that they offer additional channels of distribution that benefit not just traditional commercial media providers but independents and the hordes of people involved in mass cultural production.

Financialization and consolidation of the network media industries

Instead of investing in cutting-edge network infrastructure and adapting to new media forms, incumbent media and telecom firms have mostly spent the past decade and a half amalgamating and subsequently retrenching under the weight of fairy-tale levels of capitalization, enormous debt, and dubious business strategies (Benkler *et al.* 2010; Organisation for Economic Co-operation and Development (OECD) 2008). The process of consolidation is usually explained as a response to new digital technologies, permissive regulation, and globalization, but the financialization of media is another phenomenon that has arguably been even more important and understudied. Kevin Phillips (2009) defines financialization as a function of the swelling role of the financial sector in the United States from 11 to 12 percent of GNP in the 1980s "to a stunning 20–21 percent ... by 2004–2005 ... while manufacturing slipped from about 25 percent to just 12 percent" (Phillips 2009: xiii). Duménil and Lévy (2005) highlight "the tight and hierarchical relationship between industrial capital and banking capital" as its signature feature. Foster and Magdoff (2009) define it as the growing reliance of the economy on the financial sector in response to general economic stagnation and overproduction—the "normal state of the monopoly capitalist economy" (Foster and Magdoff 2009: 14) but also a source of chronic instability. Crotty (2005) and Shiller (2001) argue that such processes have been pronounced in the telecom, media, and internet sectors, with detrimental effects ("The Great Telecoms Crash" 2002).

The financialization of the media and telecom industries also occurred in Canada in the latter half of the 1990s, as investment poured into mergers and acquisitions, yielding huge media conglomerates with unheard-of capitalization levels and enormous debts. Figure 6.4 reveals the spike of acquisitions in the telecoms and media industries between 1996 and 2000 and again, albeit more modestly, from 2003 to 2007 as well as the sharp rise in the market capitalization of the leading media firms in Canada.[5]

Media transactions alone in 2000 ($7.1 billion) were more than eight times greater than 5 years earlier, while telecoms and internet acquisitions were more than 10 times that amount. Indeed, primed by the easy cash of the TMT boom, media convergence, and the permissive policies of the Liberal government, media and telecom companies went on a buying spree. BCE acquired CTV and *The Globe and Mail* ($3.4 billion) in 2000, and Quebecor bought Vidéotron, TVA, and the Sun "Media" newspaper chain ($7.4 billion) between 1998 and

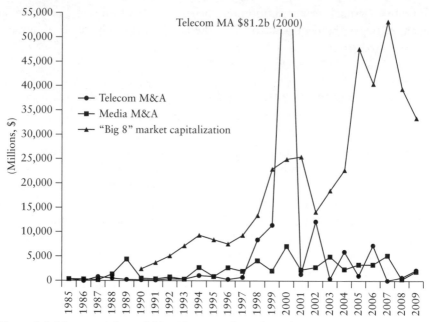

Figure 6.4 Mergers and acquisitions in network media industries, 1984–2009
Sources: Thomson Financial, 2009; FPInformart, 2010; Bloomberg Professional.

2001, making it Quebec's biggest media conglomerate. Canwest purchased Western International Communications ($800 million) in 1998, followed 2 years afterward by the Hollinger newspaper chain and the *National Post* ($3.2 billion). The capitalization levels of the largest eight publicly traded media firms soared alongside these trends, from $8.5 billion in 1995 to $25 billion in 2000. As the TMT bubble collapsed, however, their capital structure tumbled by nearly 45 percent, while rival telecoms and internet firms created in the late 1990s went bankrupt or "ceased to exist" altogether (CRTC 2002: 21).

This caused a lull of activity, but by 2003–4 the process regained steam. Already struggling to bring its debt under control, Canwest sold several smaller newspapers to Transcontinental and Osprey Media (2002–3). With financing from the US-based private equity fund Providence Equity Partners, Craig Media expanded its modest A-Channel and created a new station, Toronto One (2003). The effort, however, failed; Craig was forced into bankruptcy, Toronto One sold to Quebecor, and the A-Channel system bought by CHUM (2004)—the fifth largest broadcaster in Canada and owner of Citytv. That too was short-lived, however, and the debt-laden CHUM was sold after its founder's death to Bell Globemedia in 2006 ($1.6 billion). But even Bell Globemedia was in disarray, and the company abandoned its convergence strategy by scaling back its stake in CTV and *The Globe and Mail* (from 71 to 15 percent) in late

2006 and selling its stake in TQS the next year. A re-branded CTVglobemedia emerged from this restructuring with the Thomson family at the helm (40 percent) and the Ontario Teachers' Pension Fund (25 percent), Torstar (20 percent), and Bell (15 percent) all holding minority interests.[6] The last step in this tangled web of affairs occurred as the CRTC allowed CTVglobemedia to keep the A-Channel stations as well as the specialty- and pay-television services that it had acquired from CHUM but forced it to sell the Citytv stations (CRTC 2006). Rogers snapped them up within the year ($375 million).

Three other transactions occurred in 2007 that set the course for the rest of the decade. Astral Media bought Standard Broadcasting. Osprey was sold to Quebecor. Lastly, Canwest and the New York–based investment bank Goldman Sachs bought Alliance Atlantis for $2.3 billion. The CRTC blessed this transaction based on the fiction that Canwest maintained ownership control of the entity as required by the *Broadcasting Act*'s foreign-ownership rules, despite the fact that Goldman Sachs held two-thirds of the equity in the acquired specialty- and pay-television services, and with few qualms for the rise in concentration the deal entailed. Some argued that the huge debt levels involved would not be sustainable and that the increased media concentration that would result was unacceptable. This was all for naught, however, and Canwest's takeover of Alliance Atlantis gave it ownership of 13 specialty- and pay-television channels (such as BBC Canada, HGTV, National Geographic, and Showcase). Goldman Sachs assumed half the stakes in Alliance Atlantis' highly touted "CSI" series (with Viacom/CBS holding the other half) as well as a 51 percent stake in its film and television production venture (Communication Energy Paperworkers 2007; CRTC 2007; Goldstein 2007). All in all, media acquisitions neared their dot-com highs and the market capitalization of the leading eight media firms outstripped even the levels set in 2000 to reach $53.3 billion, but this figure, too, began to plummet with the onset of the global financial crisis of 2008.

The scale and speed of these events suggest that the media were swept up not only in the financialization of the economy but also on the cutting edge of this process. The intensity of investment driving media consolidation has been wholly out of proportion to the media industries' weight in the "real economy." The dynamics are also important because, as Picard (2002) notes, institutional investors prefer firms that possess a reach across many media sectors and a deep treasure trove of content. The outcomes yielded a half-dozen media conglomerates and four other significant entities that now form the "big 10" media firms in Canada, as ranked by market capitalization and revenues, outlined in Table 6.1.[7]

Table 6.1 highlights the sheer size of the leading media conglomerates, but as Terry Flew (2007) states, this tells us little about whether media markets have become more or less concentrated over time. Others also argue that media

Table 6.1 The big 10 media firms in Canada, 2008 (millions, US$)

	Owner	Market capitalization (2009)	Total revenue (US$)	Conventional TV	Specialty & pay TV	Cable & satellite distribution	Press	Radio	Internet access
Shaw (Corus)	Shaw	8,084.2	3,487.6		449	2,040.5		272	726.1
Rogers	Rogers	19,440.1	3,238	216.4	402.4	1,500.2	184	240	695
QMI	Péladeau	1,750.7	3,284.1	309.9	57.6	1,079.9	1,398.6		438.1
Bell	Diversified	1,560.7	2,944.6	51.8	51.8	1,450			1,391
CTVgm	Thomson (40%), TPF (25%), Torstar (20%), BCE (15%)	NA	2,288.1	932.9	806.4		388.8	160	
Canwest	Asper	24.9	2,739	608	459.2		1,495.8	176	
CBC	Public	NA	1,590	1,023.2	169.3			397.5	
Astral	Greenberg	1,780	779.2		456.2			323	
Torstar	Atkinson, Thall, Hindmarsh, Campbell, Honderich	500.1	750.6				750.6		
Cogeco	Audet Family (80%), Rogers (20%)	336.1	888	111.3	2	561.5			213.2
Total industries, US$			31,148.00	3,565.8	3,045	6,953.5	5,400	2,000	6,200
C4			41.6	80.6	71.3	87.6	77.3	61.7	54.6
HHI			615.4	1929	1,588.3	2,094.7	1,819.3	1,151.9	926

Sources: Corporate Annual Reports; CRTC *Communication Monitoring Report* (2009 and various years); Canadian Newspaper Association (2009 and various years).

ownership no longer really matters because most media companies are now owned by shareholders and controlled by managers. As Demers and Merskin (2000) argue, the managerial revolution signals the death knell of the media mogul, and this is a good thing because corporate media managers do not have ideological axes to grind, but they do have deep pockets and the expertise needed to support better media performance and higher quality journalism than owner-controlled companies. Others go even further and argue that the vast expansion of the television universe, explosive growth of the internet, and the rise of YouTube, MySpace, Google, and so on render worries about media concentration anachronistic. Indeed, Benjamin Compaine (2001) assures us that "the democracy of the marketplace may be flawed, but it is getting better, not worse." Finally, Kenneth Goldstein (2007) argues that the issue is not concentration but the fragmentation of audiences. Audience fragmentation is a problem because it threatens to yield a tower of babble as strident voices swamp civil discourse and the mutual understanding that democracies depend on to survive (Sunstein 2007).

The upshot from all of this is that the media are more competitive and fragmented than ever. Or are they? The fact that all of the "big 10" media firms are owner controlled, except Bell and the CBC, suggests that Demers and Merskin's (2000) case does not fit the Canadian context. Furthermore, their data from the early 1990s highlight a process of steady, incremental change, whereas the financialization thesis reveals a sharp, dramatic bout of transformation beginning in the latter half of the decade that led to a sharp rise in concentration, albeit without substantially altering the structure of media ownership.

To help determine whether the media have become more or less concentrated, I collected data from company reports, the CRTC's Monitoring Reports, industry associations, and other sources for each sector of the network media between 1984 and 2008 (see Note 2). Data on the number of media owners and market share were gathered at 4-year intervals and then analyzed using concentration ratios (CR) and the Herfindahl–Hirschman Index (HHI). The data were then pooled to create a portrait of the network media. The CR method adds the shares of each firm in a market and makes judgments on the basis of widely accepted thresholds, with 25 percent market share by three firms (C3), 50 percent or more by four firms (C4), and 75 percent or more by eight firms (C8), indicating high levels of concentration. The HHI squares the market share of each firm and then adds them to arrive at a total that will range from 100 (i.e. 100 firms each with a 1 percent market share—perfect competition) to 10,000 (one firm with 100 percent of a market share—monopoly) (Noam 2009). The US Department of Justice as well as Canadian competition authorities use the following thresholds to help determine whether markets are more or less concentrated:

HHI <1,000	Unconcentrated
HHI >1,000 but <1,800	Moderately concentrated
HHI >1,800	Highly concentrated

Overall, the "big 10" media firms' share of all revenues in 2000 and 2008 hovered around 71 to 72 percent in both years—a substantial rise from 61 percent in 1996 and a still further increase from 54 percent in 1992. Taken individually, each sector was highly concentrated in 2008 on the basis of the CR method (Figure 6.6). The picture according to the HHI is slightly more mixed. Cable and satellite distribution (2,094.7), conventional television (1,929), and newspapers (1,819) were highly concentrated in 2008, while specialty- and pay-television services (1,588) and radio (1,151) were moderately so. Only internet access (926) and the network media as a whole (616) were unconcentrated. The pooled network media score rose steadily to 667 in 2000, where it stayed until declining to its current level after BCE and Cogeco scaled back their convergence strategies in 2006–7 and new players (the Thomson family and Remstar, respectively) filled the breach. As an aside, Thomson's takeover of Reuters—the world's largest news and financial information agency—2 years later transformed CTVglobemedia into a subdivision of the eighth largest global media empire. In short, media concentration has grown in specific sectors and plateaued at historically high levels after 2000 for the network media as a whole, with the sharpest increase occurring after 1996. Figures 6.5 and 6.6 illustrate the trends.

In some ways, this portrait understates media concentration. The national measure used does not fully capture the extent to which, for instance, Quebecor dominates the French-language media. The shares of media conglomerates in the English-language market would be higher as well if this factor was taken into account but not to the same degree. A web of alliances between key players also blunts the sharp edge of competition. *The Globe and Mail* and Torstar, for instance, are rivals in some markets, but the latter has a stake (20 percent) in CTVglobemedia and a director on its board. Rogers owns 20 percent of Cogeco and has a director on its board, while CTVglobemedia, Rogers, Quebecor, Shaw (Corus), Astral, and Cogeco jointly own a dozen cable and satellite television channels (CRTC 2009a).

Many argue that the internet obviates such concerns, but the internet is not immune to consolidation. Roughly 94 percent of Canadian high-speed internet subscribers gain access from incumbent cable and telecoms providers (CRTC 2009a). Google's *growing* dominance of the search engine market further illustrates the trend, where it accounts for 81.4 percent of searches. Trailing far behind are Microsoft (6.8 percent), Yahoo! (5 percent), and Ask.com (4 percent), yielding a CR4 of 97 percent and an HHI of 6,713—far outstripping

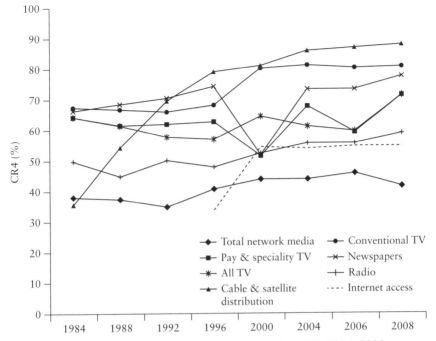

Figure 6.5 Network media industries concentration ratios (CR), 1984–2008

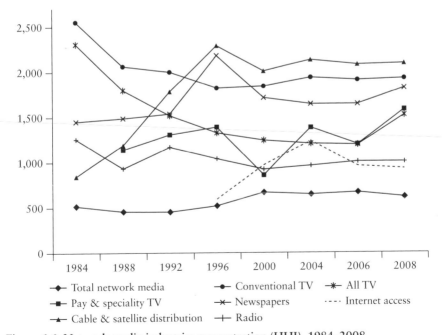

Figure 6.6 Network media industries concentration (HHI), 1984–2008

the standards of concentration outlined earlier. Social networking sites display a similar trend, with Facebook accounting for 63.2 percent of time spent on such sites, trailed by Google's YouTube (20.4 percent), Microsoft (1.2 percent), Twitter (0.7 percent), and News Corp.'s MySpace (0.6 percent) (Experien Hitwise Canada 2010). Again, the CR4 score of 86 percent and HHI score of 4,426 reveal that social networking sites are highly concentrated in Canada. Google's dominance in the search engine market and pivotal place in social networking help to explain why it is such a powerful force in defining the relationship between "old" and "new" media.

The number of websites, blogs, and so forth continues to proliferate, but the amount of time that internet users spend on the top 10 sites has nearly doubled from 20 percent in 2003 to 38 percent in 2008 (Comscore 2009). In Canada, 8 of the top 15 internet news sites belong to traditional media firms: cbc.ca, Quebecor, CTV, *The Globe and Mail*, Radio-Canada, the *Toronto Star*, Canwest, and Power Corporation; CNN, BBC, Reuters, MSN, Google, and Yahoo! cover almost all of the rest (Zamaria and Fletcher 2008). A similar pattern prevails in the United States (PEJ 2010), and Chris Paterson (2005) argues that concentration is even higher, given that 40 to 60 percent of foreign stories published by internet news sites originate from Reuters or Associated Press.

The problem, therefore, is not the "fragmentation" of audiences, as Sunstein (2007) and Goldstein (2007) fear, but the concentration of attention. While Noam (2009) argues that this reflects the continued power of money and brands in structuring the internet, Benkler (2006) argues that the concentration of attention on the internet reflects the workings of "power law distribution." According to this idea, most networks—communication, social, and transportation—have just a few nodes, blogs, websites, and so on that attract most of the traffic, attention, people, and so on, after which a steep drop-off occurs, followed by a "long tail" that accounts for ever tinier slices of attention. Benkler believes that this could be a good thing if communication networks remain open and processes of communication and social interaction, versus power and money, function to foster understanding out of the "tower of babble." While strongly opposed to the trend toward closed and controlled communication networks, he sees popular sites arising out of the internet's hyperlinking structure, where relevance, credibility, trust, and communities of interest help to organize attention on the internet. The outcome is not ideologically sealed "echo chambers" and a "tower of babble" but a substantial improvement in understanding and knowledge relative to the standards set by the "industrial media" of the past. The upshot, however, is not that this diminishes worries about concentration but that the suppleness of these structuring practices makes maintaining open networks and curbing the influence of money, power, and "business models" over network media more important than ever.

Debt, delusions, and the crisis facing the network media ecology

There is a giant, tangled paradox in all of this in that while media conglomerates have become larger and continue to be very profitable, and markets have become more concentrated, there are obvious signs of disarray all about us. Why? In addition to the impact of two economic crises and excessively capitalized corporate structures, part of the answer lies in the irony that convergence was embraced in Canada precisely as it was losing its luster elsewhere. Indeed, by the turn of the twenty-first century, all the major regional telecom firms in the United States —SBC, Bell Atlantic, US West, and BellSouth— had drawn back from the close alliances they had forged with television and film studios over the course of the past decade. Microsoft has also wound down the stakes in cable and telecom systems WebTV and MSNBC that it acquired in the late 1990s, while its CEO, Steve Ballmer, lamented entering the media and telecoms businesses directly as early as 2001 (Olsen 2001). AT&T sold off all of its cable interests in 2003, just 5 years after embracing the "convergence strategy," and was sold to SBC in 2005. Time Warner is, ironically, the poster child of the failures of convergence, having dropped AOL from its moniker in 2003, sold the Warner Music Group in 2004, labored under fraud charges for years until settling with the Securities Exchange Commission in 2005, and spun off its cable systems in 2008. Indeed, in 2009, its market value stood at $78 billion—about a fourth of its value in 2000, when the merger between AOL and Time Warner was the biggest in corporate history and supposedly a sign of things to come (Time Warner 2009). The collapse of KirchMedia in Germany, the travails of ITV in Britain, and the continued dismantling of Vivendi in France are further examples of crestfallen media conglomerates formed amid the *fin de siécle* convergence hype.

So too have the "field of dreams" visions of convergence floundered in Canada. BCE's capitalization soared from $15 billion in 1995 to $89 billion in 1999 but plunged to $26 billion 3 years later (Bloomberg 2010). By the time the renamed CTVglobemedia was sold in 2006, it was worth roughly half of the $4 billion assigned to the venture 6 years earlier (BCE 2003, 2007; CRTC 2006; see Note 6). "Broadband multimedia trials" continue to come and go at other regional telecom providers in Canada, but they play tiny roles in the media. Canwest's collapse in 2009–10, the sale of its 13 dailies and the *National Post* to "old hands" in the Canadian newspaper business (Paul Godfrey) backed by a private equity fund in the United States, and the tentative sale of its television operations to Shaw provide yet another example of consolidation gone bad. Quebecor has also struggled with enormous debt, but it has enjoyed considerable success presiding over the star system in Québec, with newscasts that rival those of the CBC's Réseau de l'information (RDI) and popular programs such as *Star Académie*. Quebecor's case also reveals a striking feature that applies to all the "big 10" media firms: namely, that if profitability is a good proxy for success, then they have been very successful except for the sharp but short shocks felt by some media companies after the crash of the TMT bubble and the financial crisis of 2008 (see Figure 6.2). Even Canwest has been profitable, sometimes extremely so, every year since 1991 in terms of operating profits and all but 2 years (2004 and 2008) in terms of return on equity. The industry's favorite "bragging rights" measure of profit—earnings before interest, taxes, depreciation, and amortization (EBITDA)—also reveals that its profits were in the low- to mid-20 percent range for the past decade before falling to 16 percent on the eve of its demise in 2009. How is it possible for highly profitable firms to be in such disarray? The answer is debt. Figures 6.7 and 6.8 put the issue of debt in historical perspective.

As Figure 6.8 illustrates, the mountain of debt acquired by the eight major media companies soared from $8.8 billion in 1995 to $24.8 billion in 2001 and continues to hang about the industry to this day. There are no hard-and-fast rules as to when there is too much debt. However, Figure 6.8 demonstrates a clear break with historical norms after the mid-1990s, although Rogers and Quebecor were already pacesetters for the trend to come. Likewise, there are no fixed rules regarding appropriate debt-to-equity ratios; however, historical norms and informed views provide a useful guide. Before 1996, most firms maintained a debt-to-equity ratio of less than 1, and this is still the case for Astral and Torstar, which are considered to be fiscally conservative entities. The Bank of Canada (2009) gives a sense of appropriate debt levels when it applauds

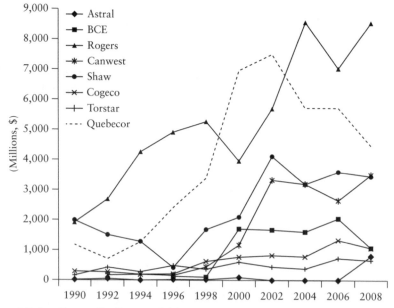

Figure 6.7 Leading media firms and debt, 1990–2008
Sources: Company Reports; Bloomberg Professional.

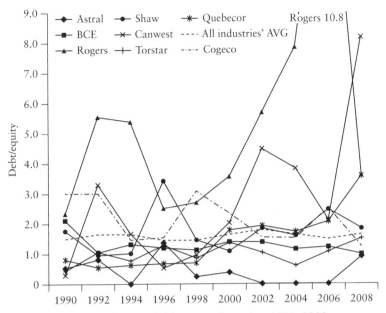

Figure 6.8 Leading media firms and debt-to-equity ratios, 1990–2008
Sources: Company Reports; Bloomberg Professional.

the decline of corporate leverage from over 1 in the early 2000s to roughly 0.85 in 2009, while urging an even greater return to corporate fiscal probity. William Melody (2007b) argues that a debt-to-equity ratio above 80 percent "is unsustainable in the long term [and that] running a firm's debt up to an unsustainable level … is simply acquiring short-term cash at the expense of long-term development and increased financial risk and costs" (Melody 2007b: 2).

According to this standard, most major media firms in Canada throughout the 2000s, except Astral, Torstar, and to some extent BCE, have been bloated corporate entities, run as "cash cows" rather than companies capable of sustained investment and innovation. Indeed, while the cost to specific firms has been high, the cost to the economy, society, journalism, and the network media ecology has been higher, as the following discussion illustrates. At the end of the 1990s, a slew of new rivals in telecoms and the internet did lead to an unprecedented surge of investment in network infrastructure that put Canada near the top of "global league" rankings for basic communication and broadband internet services. Most of those rivals vanished long ago, however, and their facilities were absorbed by the incumbents (CRTC 2002). The result has been stagnating investment in network infrastructure and weak competition, buttressed by weak regulation and policies. As a result, in the past decade, Canada fell to the middle or bottom of the rankings relative to other OECD countries in terms of the state of high-speed broadband networks; wireless connectivity; bundled telephone, cell phone, television, and internet services; and public Wi-Fi services (Benkler *et al.* 2010). Figure 6.9 charts long-term investment trends in network infrastructure.

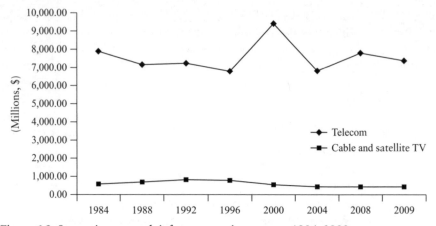

Figure 6.9 Stagnating network infrastructure investment, 1984–2009
Sources: Statistics Canada (2010b), *Capital and Repair Expenditures—Broadcasting and Telecommunications* (2001–2009) Cansim Table 029-0013 and Statistics Canada (2010c) *Capital and Repair Expenditures on Construction and Machinery—Broadcasting and Telephone* (1984–1993), Table 029-0033; CRTC (2002). *Status of Competition in Canadian Telecommunications Markets.*

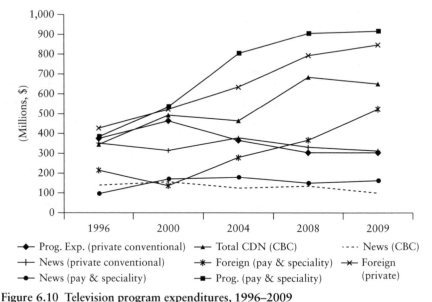

Figure 6.10 Television program expenditures, 1996–2009
Sources: CRTC, *Communications Monitoring Report*, various years; Statistics Canada (2007), *Television broadcasting industry, by North American Industry Classification System (NAICS), annual—Survey of Program Details, 1995–2007.*

Spending on conventional television news and programming shows similar trends, while expenditures on foreign (mostly United States) programs have risen sharply to feed the expanded fleet of cable and satellite television services. Indeed, the trends shown in Figure 6.10 comport with many studies that show that commitments to domestic television production continue to fall short of the pledges made by companies during regulatory reviews and when their acquisitions were approved (Auer 2007; McQueen 2003). Total television production grew slightly from $1.8 billion in 1998 to $2 billion a decade later in response to the growth of cable and satellite television channels, although full-time production jobs fell slightly (CFTPA 2010). This parsimonious approach, however, has come back to haunt the industry by making it more vulnerable to rights holders who have no qualms about playing off "old" and "new" media providers against each other for television and internet distribution rights, while leaving broadcasters badly equipped to benefit from the huge growth of television worldwide (Miller 2007; Grant 2008). In other words, this is one more small reason for the current woes facing *some* media firms.

Quebecor and Canwest are especially notorious for their "slash and burn" approach to the restructuring that inevitably follows the consolidation of ownership. Throughout the past decade, they have failed to meet pledges for television program production, eliminated journalists, centralized operations, and lost editors in chief and publishers under clouds of acrimony (Jim Jennings at the *Toronto Sun*; Russell Mills at the *Ottawa Citizen*) (Soderlund and Hildebrandt 2005). To be sure, CTVglobemedia and Torstar have also sought to revamp the conditions of media work, albeit with a little more finesse. Indeed, 281 positions were cut at CHUM on the day it was acquired by CTVglobemedia, while another 248 jobs were cut across the operations of the latter in 2009 (Toughill 2009). In contrast, Canwest riled journalists and the public alike by withdrawing from the Canadian Press news service and initiating its national editorial policy, a move that ultimately collapsed under the weight of its own stupidity (Soderlund and Hildebrandt 2005). Canwest also cut the number of its foreign news bureaus from 11 in 2000 to just 2 a few years later—exactly the opposite of what Canadians need as the country becomes deeply embroiled in complex and contested world affairs and military conflicts. The CBC, in contrast, has 14 foreign bureaus. In addition, just as Canwest was lining up its bid with Goldman Sachs for Atlantis Alliance, it eliminated 300 media jobs in the fall of 2007 and centralized its news operations in its Winnipeg, Vancouver, Montréal, and Toronto facilities. Despite all of this flailing about, uncontrolled debt finally triggered the fall of Canwest in 2009–10.

Similar forces have continuously pushed Quebecor to the brink but without ultimately pushing it over. Nonetheless, massive debt caused Quebecor to delay investment in its cable networks in the early 2000s (Marotte 2000) and to push through aggressive changes to working conditions in the face of staunch opposition from journalists and other media workers. The *Ryerson Review of Journalism* refers to Quebecor's "hatchet job" at *The Sun* in 2006, with another 120 jobs slashed and its production and printing operations centralized—a move that led Jim Jennings, the internationally experienced editor in chief of the *Toronto Sun*, to resign (Magarrey 2006). Such conditions have created conflict between media workers and executives of the likes not previously seen in Québec or Canada. There have been at least nine lockouts in the past decade at Quebecor operations, including a protracted 15-month standoff at *Le Journal de Québec* that ended only after the Québec Commission des Relations du Travail (2008) ruled that its activities were illegal. Unbowed, Quebecor Inc. (2009) locked out reporters at the *Journal de Montréal* a few weeks later, arguing that newspapers everywhere were "in a state of crisis, given that the entire world is experiencing an economic crisis and is eager to embrace change." Yet such opportunistic claims ignore the fact that, far from being innocents caught up in events not of their making, Quebecor, Canwest, Cogeco, Bell Globemedia, and so on took the lead in fostering the financialization of the media to begin with. It is this reality that has come back to haunt them, while others are left to grapple with the underdevelopment of the network media system that has followed.

Concluding comments

Ultimately, this chapter has shown that the network media ecology has become larger and, by and large, remains highly profitable. The declining costs of information creation and distribution have yielded important new players and rendered the multiple economies of the network media ecology more visible. These same considerations, however, have also amplified economies of scale and scope, leading to greater concentration and the rise of media conglomerates. Google's dominance of search activities and its sizeable stake in social networking sites alongside Facebook also shows that the internet is not immune to consolidation.

Yet the "fly in the ointment" from the perspective of the media industries is that while the cost of reproducing the immaterial stuff of information may be zero in a hypothetical world, this potential is difficult to achieve in practice. The OECD's observations about the music industry are relevant to most media on this point:

> Contrary to earlier expectations, distribution of digital music is complex and far from costless … [and] requires … the digitalization of content, the clearing of rights, … online music storefronts, secure billing systems and new digital intermediaries (e.g. digital rights clearance, software such as Windows DRM, online billing). (OECD 2008: 269)

To put this in more familiar terms to media scholars, different media work by different rules, and these distinctions are not easily reconciled within a single firm (Garnham 1990; Miège 1989). Mediation is a constitutive element of modern societies and economies that is magnified, not diminished, by communications media (Calhoun 1992). This also helps to explain why Google stands midstream between the "new" and "old" media. It furthermore reminds us, as Bernard Miège (1989) observed long ago, that the distinctive qualities of media and cultural activities can and often do throw up obstacles to the "capitalization of the cultural industries." The financialization of the media and the formation of media conglomerates according to the "slick rationality" of synergies ignored such realities, but the folly of doing so has been laid bare. To grasp contemporary conditions, it is essential to pay attention to this dialectical interplay between efforts to expand and accelerate the circuits of capital accumulation, on the one hand, and the distinctive aspects of media and cultural goods, on the other, as well as to the recursive effects of "discursive models" on the worlds that they represent and strive to create. These are also key elements for a critical cultural political economy of the media formulated along the lines that I have begun to sketch out in this chapter (Jessop 2008; Sayer 2001; Thompson 2010a).

In the end, we can conclude that there are no clear cases in which specific media sectors are "in crisis," although the two major global economic crises of the twenty-first century have dealt punishing blows to *some* media conglomerates. In fact, at the core of the network media industries are a number of stumbling media behemoths that are ill-equipped to create the kind of open, digital network media system needed for the twenty-first century. Canwest is the poster child of the bankrupt media conglomerate in Canada, but others such as TQS, Craig Media, and CHUM demonstrate the stern lessons of hubris, empire-building, and debt. Add Bell Globemedia's retreat from convergence and the perennially indentured state of Quebecor, Rogers, and Shaw to this portrait, and it is abundantly clear that media conglomerates can, and sometimes do, fail. Ultimately, if free and open media really are essential to democracy, then surely we cannot let the fortunes of the latter hinge any more than they already have on those who have done so much to drive the current media system into the ground.

Notes

1 The latter, however, has been deferred to the federal courts to ensure that the CRTC has the authority to regulate "new media" in this way.

2 All of the tables, figures, and data in this chapter are based on the annual reports of the "big 10," the Bloomberg Professional electronic financial news service, FP Infomart and Mergent profiles, industry association reports, CRTC monitoring reports, and so on, unless otherwise stated. Citing these sources for each use would clutter the text, but readers can check my analysis against them. Only revenues from Canada and sectors that fit the definition of the network media industries established at the outset of this chapter are included. Bell figures include its DTH service, internet access, and CTV and *The Globe and Mail* between 2000 and 2006. Data for CTVglobemedia are limited after 2006

because it changed ownership and became a privately held company at this time. Revenues for the television industry include the CBC's annual parliamentary appropriation.

3   Unless otherwise noted, all dollar values are in real dollar terms, with 2010 as the base year. Using current dollars would make my arguments easier by showing even more pronounced growth. All dollar figures in this chapter are in Can$.

4   Connectivity includes spending on telephone, cell phone and internet access services, and computers. The "media content and culture" category covers cable and satellite subscriptions, newspapers, magazines, movie theaters, audiovisual equipment, and attendance at sports, arts, and culture events.

5   In Figure 6.4, I use data obtained from a custom analysis of "Announced Mergers and Acquisitions (1/1/1984–3/19/2009)," assembled at my request by an analyst at Thomson Reuters. Data are on file with the author and available upon request. The remainder of 2009 was filled in using Factiva to search for all completed mergers and acquisitions in these sectors for 2009. Market capitalization as of December 31st for each year covered and for each of the major Canadian media companies included in my "big 10" category was obtained from the Bloomberg Professional financial information service.

6   Bell sold 55 percent of its stake in the re-branded CTVglobemedia for approximately $1 billion, with roughly $685 million allotted to the CTV portion and an estimated $300 million to *The Globe and Mail*. Altogether, this was about quarter of the value of $4 billion originally assigned to the entity in 2000 (BCE 2001; CRTC 2006).

7   Data for magazines are incomplete, so specific firm revenues are not reflected, except for Rogers ($184 million), which is placed under newspapers. Magazine-sector revenues ($2,394 million) are included in the total revenues for the "network media." Including magazine revenues for specific firms, notably Quebecor, would raise the big 10's share of total revenue.

7

Deconvergence and Deconsolidation in the Global Media Industries

The rise and fall of (some) media conglomerates

Dal Yong Jin
Simon Fraser University

Introduction

Over the past two decades, the promise of economies of scale, synergy, and the lure of potential benefits from the coordinated production and distribution of diverse cultural products led many communication and media corporations to embrace the strategy of media convergence. This became especially apparent in the late 1990s. From small software developers to global media giants, convergence became a core paradigm and was touted as the next big leap in the digital era (Ip 2008). "Big is beautiful" has indeed been the business motto, and through vertical and horizontal integration, communication companies expanded in a bid to become leaders in the digital communication era.

Since the early twenty-first century, however, a countertrend has emerged as several mega-media and telecommunications companies, including Disney, Time Warner, and Viacom have turned to deconvergence as a new business model. Many communication giants have adopted a strategy of focusing on a few core business areas and have split-off and/or spun-off other aspects of their operations. Thus, whereas mergers and acquisitions (M&As) among media and communication companies were the norm during the high tide of neoliberal reforms in the 1990s, during the past decade spin-offs, split-offs, and deconsolidation have become significant trends in the communication market. This change is occurring mainly because media convergence has met with several serious problems, including plummeting stock prices, feeble content, and the fact that new forms of mediation mean that synergies are not as easily achieved as the "visionaries of convergence" once thought. Such trends raise the question as to whether this process will fundamentally change the ownership structure of the media and communication industries and, in essence, supersede convergence as the governing paradigm for these industries.

The approach that I adopt in this chapter is mainly informed by the critical political economy of communication perspective. As Robert McChesney (2000) states, "the political economy of communication looks at how ownership, support mechanisms such as advertising, and government policies influence media behavior and content" (p. 110). The approach is also uniquely positioned to take an integrated approach to "traditional" and "new media," and to relate these to society and larger processes of social change as a whole. Dan Schiller (1996) makes just such a point when he observes in his seminal book, *Theorizing Communication: A History*, that studying communication is concerned with more than just a restricted set of media. Crucially, as he states, "The potential of communication study, in short, has converged directly and at many points with analysis and critique of existing society across its span" (Schiller 1996: vii). Giving these starting points, this chapter starts with an overview of media convergence in the 1990s up until the turn of the millennium. It then investigates the countertrend of deconvergence that has increasingly taken hold since then, mapping out how and explaining why deconsolidation and spin-offs have become central strategies and key elements of new business models in the communication industries. It also asks whether these changes to the communication and media industries will enhance the goals of competition, diversity, and democratic discourse that are at the heart of antitrust laws and media regulation in many countries.

How to understand convergence and deconvergence

Media convergence is not a simple phenomenon and has multiple meanings.[1] According to Henry Jenkins (2006a: 2–3), media convergence can be conceptualized in three ways: first, as the flow of content across multiple media platforms; second, as the coming together of multiple media industries; and third, as a consequence of the migratory behavior of media audiences who will go almost anywhere in search of the kinds of entertainment experience they want. Other scholars (Baldwin, McVoy, and Steinfield 1996; Wirtz 2001) view media convergence from three different perspectives: consolidation through industry alliances and mergers, the combination of technology and network platforms, and integration between services and markets. Regardless of their differences, these views share the idea that convergence brings about a closer relationship between media structure and content, a closer integration of production for old and new media forms, and the consolidation of firms across different sectors of the communication and media industries.

Communication corporations have pursued convergence due in large part to the belief that vertical and horizontal integration would create synergy effects and, thus, help to maximize profits (Chambers and Howard 2005;

Chan-Olmsted 1998). Many traditional media firms also saw convergence as a way to venture into the internet market and to take advantage of evermore pervasive digital technologies and neoliberal communication policies (Bar and Sandvig 2008; Huang and Heider 2008: 105). For traditional media industries, such as network broadcasters and newspaper companies, convergence is a great opportunity to integrate with the new media sector and to deploy multimedia and multifunctional networks that will allow (digital) hardware and software (content) to be integrated across the full span of their operations (Noll 2003; Schiller 2007). While some see convergence as primarily being about the technological integration of media technologies (Jenkins 2006a), large integrated companies actually play a fundamental role in shaping the dynamics of the convergence process (Mosco 2009a). Some corporations have horizontally integrated within similar media sectors, for example, between traditional network broadcasters and/or among internet companies, while others have vertically integrated, for example, between the broadcasting and film industries and/or between telecommunications and broadcasting industries.

The promotion and adoption of neoliberal communication policies since the 1980s have strongly encouraged vertical and horizontal integration (McChesney 2001). Since that time, most governments, not only in the United States but also in non-Western countries, have introduced economic liberalization measures, including the reduction of government intervention in communication markets, opening the domestic market to competition and foreign investment, and privatizing telecommunications and broadcasting providers. The aggressive promotion of neoliberal reform by the United States and the United Kingdom early on in this process led to telecommunications and broadcasting companies being privatized in many countries and changed the map of the media industry as a result (Murdock 2006).

Before the ascent of neoliberal globalization, most media companies focused on their core business areas, partially because government policies, including antitrust laws and cross-ownership restraints, sought to define them distinctly and to keep them separate (Baldwin et al. 1996). Indeed, the dangers of ownership concentration in the communication industry were addressed by a combination of antitrust and regulatory policies that attempted to attenuate the amalgamation of corporate power. In particular, corporate mergers and the consolidation of ownership have long been sources of concern because of their potential to limit the diversity of voices. US regulatory and antitrust policy traditionally attempted to address the potential negative implications of concentrated media power by adopting structural limits on media ownership consolidation (Horwitz 2005: 181–2). For example, prior to the 1990s, Time Inc. was known as a publication company, Viacom was famous for its TV syndication and cable businesses, whereas News Corporation was mostly a newspaper company based in Australia.

Pro-business neoliberal communication policies changed all that by lifting the barriers between media sectors. This has resulted in the consolidation of media ownership into the hands of a few media giants (McChesney 2008). Vertical and horizontal integration work to help secure corporations' access to new markets and new sectors of the communication industries, although the consequence is the oligopolistic control of the world communication market by a few giant corporations (Jin 2007). The loosening of cross-ownership rules, in particular, has been one of the most significant factors that have allowed communication and media firms to expand beyond their traditional core business realms into additional sectors of the media (Thussu 2006). Thus, media corporations have become larger and presumably more powerful as ownership regulations have weakened over the past two decades (Horwitz 2005).

Nevertheless, despite the supportive role played by digital technologies, neoliberal regulatory reforms, and ownership consolidation, media convergence has often failed to achieve many of the promised benefits. As Albarran and Gormly (2004) argue, historically, fewer than half of all mergers survive. A few scholars also documented the process of disintegration in the communication industry in the mid-1990s (Gilder 1994; cited in Mueller 1999). These authors also point to the failures of AOL–Time Warner and Vivendi-Universal after the turn of the twenty-first century as further evidence that convergence has given way to divergence or demergers (Albarran and Gormly 2004: 43). Their discussion, however, has not been developed widely, most likely because the deconvergence process has only come fully into its own in just the past few years.

Given the recency of these trends, there is no clear definition of deconvergence. This chapter defines deconvergence as referring mainly to companies' strategic decision to decrease the scale and complexity of their operations in order to regain profits and restore their public image, while deploying new strategies to survive in the continuously changing communication and media industries. In other words, deconvergence occurs when media and communication corporations spin off or sell parts of the company to others.[2] Spin-offs and/or spilt-offs separate particular divisions from a parent corporation and allow them to act independently in the market, although the parent company may often still hold some of the shares in the new entity. This is most evident in the case of Viacom–CBS, where these entities were formally separated from one another at the end of 2005 but without actually diluting the fact that Sumner Redstone continues to be the dominant shareholder in both entities—a point I will examine further below.

Convergence: an old trend in the communication industries

The global communication industries have entered a period of unprecedented change on account of digital technologies that enable moving pictures, sound, and text to be transmitted over the same transmission media, the liberalization of national communication markets as well as the integration of individual national markets into a vastly enlarged global communications market. M&As are another form of convergence and have been propelled by two major historical events: the 1996 Telecommunications Act in the United States that allowed cross-investment between the telecommunications and cable industries and the 1997 World Trade Organization (WTO) agreement that reinforced the trend toward market liberalization worldwide. With the momentum of these efforts behind them, telecommunications and broadcasting industries invested in one another on a large scale, and Western communication companies invested massively in developing countries, such as South Korea and China. The Telecommunications Act withdrew prohibitions on cross-media ownership and rendered antitrust criteria evermore fuzzy as to just what they covered and what rationales and values guided their use (Schiller 2007: 108–9). As the Federal Communications Commission (FCC) put it, by implementing "the 1996 Act, Congress sought to establish a precompetitive and de-regulatory national policy framework for the U.S. communications industry" (McFadden 1997).

Previously, multiple ownership rules limited the total number of television and radio stations an entity could own nationally, irrespective of location; however, those changed under the new act. As originally promulgated in the 1940s, the multiple ownership rules prohibited common ownership of more than three television stations, and then from the 1950s onward the number of television and AM and FM radio stations that a single entity could own was capped at seven in each of these media (Horwitz 2005: 188). However, in 1984 the FCC increased the ceiling to 12 AM radio, 12 FM radio, and 12 television stations, and these measures have been loosened even further over the past two decades. The Telecommunications Act of 1996 repealed all national ownership limits for radio; the Act also repealed the 12 stations per owner national cap for television, although a single company may not own stations that reach more than 35 percent of the nationwide television audience (Section 202 in the Act). In short, the Telecommunications Act played a significant role in the neoliberalization process.[3]

Against this backdrop, mega-media companies that control content and hardware together in order to maximize their value, image, and profit emerged. These mega-media giants can secure the outlets for their content, including television programs and films, through vertical and horizontal integration, and through international alliances (Jin 2008: 370). They understand that synergies accruing from common ownership, especially when they are internet-related outlets means that outlets under a single corporate umbrella function mostly to promote, not compete with, other outlets (Horwitz 2005: 186). Convergence also occurs within the same communications sectors, for instance, as broadcasting companies merge with one another and as telecommunications companies combine. Meanwhile, consolidation in the global broadcasting industry has also reflected neoliberal reforms and the growing importance of broadcasting, cable television distribution networks, and specialty and pay television services in the digital era.

The global expansion of media convergence through M&As in the 1990s and the early twenty-first century occurred as Western-based transnational media corporations invested an enormous amount of money in the global communication industry. Indeed, this sector became one of the most profitable sectors of the world economy. For example, the United States exported US$13,598 million worth of film and television programs to other countries, whereas imported only US$1,878 million in 2008. The net profits for the United States were more than US$11,720 (Department of Commerce 2009). The WTO agreement reduced barriers to trade and encouraged countries to adopt an export-driven, corporate-based economic system and targeted local media content rules for elimination. Unlike telecommunications, the WTO agreement did not explicitly include the broadcasting industry as its target area for free trade; however, it has certainly influenced the liberalization process of the media industry in many countries (Pauwels and Loisen 2003). WTO member states have continually pushed to expand the reach of the General Agreement of Trade in Services (GATS) in this respect (White 2008). Even where countries have not made specific commitments to the WTO, there has still been pressure to harmonize domestic laws and rules with the standards set by the WTO. Canada, for example, relaxed and harmonized its rules governing foreign ownership in the broadcasting sector with those of the telecommunications sector in 1997, that is, by limiting direct and indirect ownership of broadcasting and telecommunications firms to 46.7 percent (Transport Canada 2003). Given that the division between telecommunications and broadcasting is gradually dissolving due to the forces of convergence, many countries, including Canada, continue to consider additional steps that would relax foreign ownership restrictions in the telecommunications and broadcasting industries even further.

The continued steady growth of the internet and digital technology as well as the pursuit of neoliberal reform means that convergence continues to loom large even today. However, in the twenty-first century, that strategy has waned and the consolidation of global broadcasting has actually begun to diminish in recent years. The total number of deals fell from 858 in 2000, the highest in history, to just 444 cases in 2002 and 471 in 2003. M&As once again increased thereafter until 2007 but fell off in 2008 and 2009 (569 cases) as the global financial crisis kicked into high gear. This is a far cry from the 800 cases per year that was typical of the late 1990s.[4] The fall of M&As also coincides with the emergence of deconvergence, as I will show below (Watkins 2008).

Several political-economic factors help to account for the decrease in national and global M&As in the communication industries: the terrorist attacks on the United States in 2001, the economic recession starting in the early twenty-first century as well as the market saturation right after the Telecommunications Act of 1996 and the 1997 WTO agreements. The unparalleled global downturn in advertising in the wake of the dot-com crash and the events of September 11, 2001, have also been offered as explanations for why some media conglomerates have failed, including Time Warner (Murray 2005). The 2007–8 global financial crisis has also become one of the major factors behind recent turmoil in the media market. The collapse and/or rescue of major investment banks, the lack of interbank liquidity, and the resulting impact upon stock markets, production systems, national economies, and workforces reveal essential elements of market instability (Chakravartty and Schiller 2010; Hope 2010).

In sum, communication companies rapidly jumped into the deal market, tempted by the potential rewards of synergy and economies of scale held forth by the idea of media convergence; however, with only a few exceptions, this has not come to pass. Instead, major media giants that seemed to stand astride the world at the turn of the twenty-first century, such as Time Warner, Viacom–CBS, and Disney, have seen their convergence strategies flounder badly. Instead of being runaway successes, these entities have experienced plummeting stock price, falling revenues and profits, and deteriorating corporate images, leading them to reconsider, postpone, or even abandon convergence. It is in this context that deconvergence emerged as the media and communication industries' new "golden" strategy.

Deconvergence: the emergence of a new trend in the communication industries

Convergence has not achieved what it was meant to in many cases, and now mega-media giants appear to be turning to the pursuit of a deconvergence strategy. As Manuel Castells (2001) pointed out,[5]

> [T]he business experiments on media convergence carried on since the early 1990s have ended in failure. Most of the forms of convergence did not make money. Indeed, traditional media companies are not generating any profits from their internet ventures. (Castells 2001: 188–90)

Deconvergence has appeared in several ways: the sale of profit-losing companies, spin-offs, and split-offs and massive layoffs, none of which are mutually exclusive. Deconvergence has expanded greatly, especially in the content and entertainment sectors more than new media areas. This is likely because traditional media corporations' hopes that merging with other entities in the new media industries would be hugely profitable have, for the most part, not come to pass.

In the twenty-first century, restructuring through deconvergence began with Viacom—formerly the second largest media company after Time Warner. As is well chronicled, in September 1999, Viacom bought CBS, which was one of the largest network broadcasting companies, for $40 billion. The merger brought together the extensive motion picture and television production, cable network, video retailing, television station, and publishing assets of Viacom, Inc. with the television network, radio stations, and cable programming holdings of CBS, Inc. (Waterman 2000). The merger of Viacom and CBS primarily reflected a strategy of vertical integration, in the hope that the combined entity would realize significant synergy effects.

However, just 5 years later, Viacom began to separate from CBS. Viacom–CBS was thus broken up into two independent media companies: Viacom would focus on new media, while CBS was to emphasize traditional media. In other words, Viacom would be the "engine" of growth, retaining mainly cable and film entities, including MTV, BET, and Paramount Pictures, while CBS would oversee the slower growth but cash-flow-rich television and radio broadcasting, publishing, and outdoor advertising divisions (Sherman 2006). Prior to this, the Paramount Pictures division of Viacom already spun off its video rental chain Blockbuster in 2004, leaving Viacom to mainly focus more on production rather than distribution and exhibition. Viacom, nonetheless, continues to be a formidable entity, owning the largest international music broadcast company MTV, Nickelodeon, Showtime and Comedy Central, Spike TV, and VH1. Viacom also controls more than 150 cable channels worldwide, reflecting the new company's focus on new media, compared to traditional network broadcasting companies (Viacom 2008).

At a glance, the deconsolidation of Viacom–CBS changes the media environment by increasing diversity and lessening concentration of ownership. As in many large-scale mergers between media corporations, the merger between Viacom and CBS in 1999 raised several critical issues about the potential undesirable economic and social effects that it could have. Among the main issues raised were whether the merger would lead to excessive market power or to a reduction in the diversity of voices within particular media market segments, such as in broadcast networking or in local radio and television station markets. Another broader concern about the merger involved the growing size of media corporations in the United States because the Viacom–CBS merger would take a significant step toward the concentration of control of all the media into too few hands (Waterman 2000: 532).

The breakup of Viacom, however, has little to do with diversity and media democracy, or with addressing the concerns of consumer and public interest groups. The deconvergence process is a matter of pure economics for Viacom: Share prices were languishing and the media conglomerate seemed to be a concept that might have had its day. When the merger between Viacom–CBS occurred, Viacom shares were trading at $46.3. They peaked 2 years later at almost $75 but plummeted to $38.8 in March 2005 (Teather 2005). Sumner Redstone, the CEO of Viacom, broke up the media conglomerate on the grounds that two separate companies could be worth more than the combined entity (Sherman 2006). Redstone also told the cable news channel CNBC that "synergy," if not dead as an idea, was certainly in its "death throes" (Teather 2005: 22). Moreover, as he stated at a dinner meeting for media industry VIPs in San Francisco, the move was really about introducing a new business model into the heart of the media industries:

> [C]onvergence, the bigger-is-better concept that dominated the industry for most of the past 10 years, is falling apart. As some of you know, divorce [deconvergence] is sometimes better than marriage [convergence]. (Maich 2005: 33)

Although he did not explicitly say so, Redstone's comments marked the rapid growth of the deconvergence age—a new direction that repudiates much of what his audience were already grudgingly accepting (Maich 2005).

Many observers, including government officials, media practitioners, business strategists, and even critical media scholars, believed that there would be no turning back from the heyday of convergence, but the breakup of Viacom–CBS confounded the common wisdom. Indeed, the whole concept of deconvergence was considered highly unlikely for at least two reasons. On the one hand, it would involve the restructuring of many billions of dollars in equity. On the other hand, it defies the logic of digital production. Media and telecommunications companies have merged for the expressed purpose of selling digital content and having control over both the network and content. Moreover, telephone, internet, radio, and television services are now carried on the same cable or telephone line and are functionally inseparable. Just from a technological viewpoint, therefore, divestiture seemed to be an unfathomable idea (White 2008: 43). Instead of accepting falling values of corporations as inevitable, however, media firms adopted deconvergence as a new business strategy and began turning back to their core businesses in the midst of the crisis of convergence. Others will surely follow.

Viacom is indeed only one of several media empires now being broken up into smaller media companies. The most notable such example in the United States is the giant media conglomerate, Time Warner. Time Warner became the largest media company when its takeover by AOL in 2001 created a massive media conglomerate that was expected to be worth $350 billion—the largest corporate amalgamation in US history. Through the deal, AOL secured access to the premier content of Time Warner as well as a broadband distribution platform for its interactive services, while Time Warner would be able to accelerate the marketing of its products over the internet—an exemplary case of synergy effects, if there ever was one (Wirtz 2001). Time Warner's stock more than doubled between 1998 and the announcement of the company's merger with AOL in January 2000. Since AOL completed its $165 billion takeover of Time Warner in 2001, however, the shares of the combined entity have plunged, and the company is now considered a textbook example of a disastrous media merger. Time Warner's 22 percent drop in stock price in 2007 put it among the 10 biggest losers in the S&P 100 Index of large US companies for the year (Wee 2007a). Under pressure from investors to boost its stock price, Time Warner has had little choice but to separate itself into several small companies.[6] The media giant has changed CEOs several times, and hoped-for synergy effects have fallen far short of expectations. Time Warner is now a leading example of the deconvergence strategy along the lines pursued by Viacom (Arango 2007). As David Henry (2002) suggests, there are common reasons why these mergers fail:

> [C]ompanies sabotage their deals by making the same mistake again and again: [they] overpay by offering a sizable premium, which hands the bulk of future economic gains from the merger to shareholders in the target company, [they] overestimate the likely cost of savings and synergies. (Henry 2002: 64)

Current Time Warner chief executive Jeffrey Bewkes is clearly responding to pressure from investors in his efforts to emphasize the company's entertainment businesses and to turn around the flagging AOL internet unit (Klemming and Sondag 2008). Movement along this path was already evident when Time Warner removed AOL from its moniker in 2003 and sold off the Warner Bros. music division in 2004. In 2008, the Time Warner Cable unit was also spun-off, and it is now planning to separate AOL and Time (publication sector). Once completed, Time Warner will be a reborn company focusing on content-based media, including film and a few cable companies. As Jeffrey Bewkes stated when Time Warner Cable—the second largest cable operator in the United States—was being spun-off in May 2008, "we've decided that a complete structural separation of Time Warner Cable is in the best interests of both companies' shareholders" (Time Warner 2008).[7] In other words, Time Warner dismantled itself not because of pressure from civic groups or citizens who want media diversity and democracy but because of intense pressure from shareholders, in particular, large institutional shareholders. A recent statement by Time Warner makes the point:

> [T]his is the right step for Time-Warner and Timer Warner Cable stockholders. After the transaction, each company will have greater strategic, financial and operational flexibility and will be better positioned to compete. Separating the two companies also will help their management teams focus on realizing the full potential of the respective businesses and will provide investors with greater choice in how they own this portfolio of assets. (Time Warner 2008)

> [O]nce the transaction is completed, Time Warner will have a streamlined portfolio of leading businesses focused on creating and distributing our branded content across traditional and digital platforms worldwide. (Time Warner 2008)

The fate of AOL within the Time Warner corporate-fold remains unsettled, but Bewkes has never been a fan of the original AOL's takeover of Time Warner.

Indeed, unlike his "media convergence visionary" predecessors, Stephen Chase and Gerald Levin, Bewkes has seen that venture as the ultimate failure in media convergence (Wee 2007b). The decision to drop AOL from the company name in 2003 was already a significant symbolic gesture that the mega-merger of the dot-com boom was en route to becoming one of history's biggest corporate calamities (*The Times* 2003). Back then, Jonathan Miller, chairman of AOL, asked AOL–Time Warner chief executive Richard D. Parsons to propose a name change to the board of directors. Miller states,

> [T]he AOL brand name has been hurt since the merger when it became shorthand for the media conglomerate, which has experienced a precipitous stock drop, the launching of two federal investigations into AOL's accounting, the accrual of more than $24 billion in debt, the departure of top executives, the selling of corporate assets and a nearly $100 billion loss in 2002, the largest in U.S. corporate history. (Ahrens and Klein 2003)

Beyond Viacom and Time Warner, several other substantial media firms have pursued a similar course of deconvergence. For example, Liberty Media, separated from AT&T in 2001, spun off its international cable businesses into a separately traded company in 2003 and then spun off its ownership in the Ascent Media Group and Discovery Communications, Inc., in 2004 (Liberty Media 2008). Clear Channel, the country's largest radio broadcaster with about 1,200 radio stations and several television stations until recently and the epitome of the mega-media company made possible by the 1996 Telecommunications Act, announced that it would spin off its live entertainment division and sell 10 percent of its outdoor advertising business in an initial public offering in May 2005 amidst a steep decline in revenues and profits (McClintock 2005). The takeover of the firm by the private equity group Thomas H. Lee and Bain Capital Partners in 2006 ultimately led to all of its television stations and 161 of its radio stations outside the top-100 US markets being sold to another private equity group, Providence Equity ("Clear Channel sells … " 2007).

According to a Lexis-Nexis search, the total number of deconvergence cases has substantially increased over the past several years. Using spin-offs and split-offs as the key terms in the search, there were only 218 deconvergence cases in the US media industry in 1995; by 2008, this number had jumped to 407 cases— and 87 percent increase (Table 7.1).[8] The trend toward media deconsolidation is no longer just a passing fad; it is a full-fledged trend reshaping the US communication industries. Deconvergence has also been visible in the United Kingdom, France, and Canada during this time. Vivendi, one of the largest media conglomerates in France, for example, sold Universal Entertainment in 2005. In Canada, CanWest Global Communications contemplated packaging its newspaper assets into an income trust that would be sold in an initial public offering. Thus, even before being forced by bankruptcy to dismantle the company in 2009/10, CanWest had considered splitting off its newspapers

Table 7.1 Increase in deconvergence in the US media industry, 1995–2009

Year	Spin-off	Split-off	Total
1995	82	136	218
2001	181	192	373
2002	152	181	333
2003	151	176	327
2004	170	246	416
2005	193	249	442
2006	165	252	417
2007	162	218	380
2008	177	230	407
2009	102	179	281

Source: Lexis-Nexis.

from its core TV operations (before changes in tax law rendered that option undesirable). Although deconvergence in mid-sized economies such as South America and Canada, as Chapters 2 and 6 in this volume suggest, is not as strong as in the United States, it has nonetheless constituted a clear and significant business trend in recent years. Table 7.1 charts the de-covergence trend over the past decade and a half in the US market.

It is worth repeating that the deconvergence trend is a response to the limited success of the mega-mergers that characterized the late-1990s before these firms quickly became lumbering dinosaurs that could not survive as their economic models and stock market valuations crumbled. Forced by this turn of events, they have tried to morph into small or mid-sized companies. This rather abrupt change in course reflects the stern discipline of disgruntled investors and the drying up of capital markets. First and foremost, it is the logic and demand of capital, rather than *any* concern with restoring competition and a diversity of voices at the center of the public sphere.

Implications of deconvergence in the communication industries

Deconvergence has changed the structure and dynamics of the communication and media industries in several ways, most notably, perhaps, by changing the traditional business model. Viacom and Time Warner certainly believed that the merger would increase access to know-how and content, and even astute critical media political economists such as Robert McChesney (1999: 22) believed that this pursuit would be business success, albeit disastrous for the future of the media, good journalism, and democracy itself. However, with recent experience in hand, and perhaps the exception of the takeover of *The Wall Street Journal* by News Corporation in 2007, the majority of M&As have been disastrous on any measure, business or otherwise.

Comcast's bids for Disney in 2004, for example, did not work out. While Comcast had a successful track record of acquisitions on the cable side, this has not been so on the content side. If the deal had succeeded, Comcast, the nation's biggest cable operator, would have owned the ABC broadcast network as well as the Disney film studio, ESPN, Pixar, and other Disney assets. However, already alert to other unsuccessful mergers, Disney rebuffed Comcast's (CNN/Money 2004).[9] Instead, instances of media convergence that have taken place since have focused mostly on horizontal integration between production corporations, particularly new media corporations, as the cases of Google and YouTube (2006) and between Disney and Pixar Animation (2005) demonstrate. Comcast, however, has not put the convergence dream to rest, and in 2009 it made a move to acquire NBC-Universal from GE. While this complicates the general trend that I am identifying here, it is also one of those "exceptions that proves the rule" cases. Besides, it is also an example of a spin-off and de-diversification, given that the prototypical general conglomerate, GE, is selling off its controlling share in NBC-Universal.

Deconvergence has also led to a newfound emphasis among major media corporations on their core businesses, particularly content. It may be that "content is king" because media audiences care more about having convenient access to quality content regardless of medium (Jenkins 2006a). In this scenario, audiences' changing media behavior drives media convergence. With clear evidence that convergence often fails but also that audiences will switch allegiances at the drop of a hat, media corporations are now fixing their strategy on horizontal consolidation, where core competencies can be strengthened and, critically, the internet-related new media sector. Of course, this does not mean that media corporations that focus on content must hold all their interests under the same roof. Indeed, it is already clear that when a specific division fails to perform, they are cut loose, as Disney is currently doing with Miramax—the art-house studio—which it acquired in 1993. Miramax was valued at approximately $2 billion in 2005, but even after its two Oscar-winning, box-office hits in 2007 (*No Country for Old Men* and *There Will Be Blood*), it has been difficult to find new buyers for the studio. As of April 2010, Bob and Harvey Weinstein, the brothers who founded Miramax in 1979, are reported to be the front-runners with their bid of about $600 million to take the studio off Walt Disney's hands (Frean 2010). The point, in short, is that even mega-sized, content-rich Disney has realized that it must reduce corporate sprawl in order to achieve greater business success.

Finally, deconvergence is changing the lineup of major players in media markets. Over the past 15 years, the communication market has witnessed the rise of sprawling media giants of the likes of Time Warner, Disney,

Table 7.2 Top six US media and entertainment companies (2007)

Media companies	Revenues in 2004 (billions)	Revenues in 2007 (billions)
Time Warner	42.8	46.6
Walt Disney	30.7	35.9
News Corporation	20.8	28.7
NBC-Universal	NA	15.4
CBS	NA	14.1
Viacom	27.0	13.5

Sources: Fortune (2005, 2008). Data of NBC-Universal comes from GE 2008 Annual Report (2009).

News Corporation, NBC-Universal (independent of GE), CBS, and Viacom (the "Big Six") that have dominated domestic and global media markets. Now, however, we must ask whether this will continue as deconvergence proceeds apace? According to *Fortune 500* (2008), Time Warner has been the largest media corporation in recent years; however, with the separation of Time Warner Cable and potentially part of AOL in the near future, Disney could become the largest media conglomerate within a few years. Viacom, the second largest media corporation until the early twenty-first century, already ranked sixth, while CBS became the fifth largest right after NBC-Universal, in 2007. However, whilst the rank ordering of the "big six" (Table 7.2) may change in the years ahead, there is scant evidence that major media giants will be giving up their dominance in the communication market any time soon as they move toward more diverse ownership structures. Instead, current trends suggest that these media empires are pursuing a strategy of deconvergence, not because of protests by civic groups, or on account of government regulations that place a premium on the maximum dispersal of "media power" as a key factor in creating a healthy democracy, but on account of economic imperatives and changing business fashions. Seen in this light, the basic philosophy of deconvergence differs little from that of convergence. Deconvergence changes the ownership and organizational structure of the media industry, from concentration to deconcentration, at least for a while, but fundamental changes to the media still remain far off in the distance.

Discussion and conclusions

Convergence fundamentally changed the structure of the communication and media industries in the 1990s, but deconvergence and deconsolidation have stepped into that role in the twenty-first century. It is too early to refer to this as the "Age of Deconvergence," however, but not risky to say that deconvergence has become one of the major business paradigms in the communication industry, largely in response to the failures of convergence. The 1990s saw the triumph of systemic belief in the virtues of synergy and economies of scale and scope without end, and regulators and politicians fanned the flames with weak regulations and neoliberal policies. In the twenty-first century, however, the media market has witnessed buyout teams busy unwinding those very deals. The pieces are worth more than the whole (Jubak 2002). The draconian media paradigm driven by both neoliberal communication policies and digital technologies, thus, has substantially lost its power, or at least its hegemonic allure, and the communication sector has witnessed the birth of a new business model as a result. The deconvergence strategy now being pursued by Viacom and Time Warner, most notably, but many others as well, has become the new standard *d'jour*, perhaps because these media behemoths still set the pace and determine the rules and models that prevail in the business at any given point in time. Furthermore, convergence will not disappear altogether because demands for information and entertainment as well as the internet remain high (Dennis 2003). The fall of convergence does not mean that the dominant paradigm is dead or that it will be entirely without signs of life. Media companies will still seek consolidation if for no other reason than to dampen the risk and uncertainties endemic to the media business. This was true of the industrial media in the twentieth century, and it is likely to be true of the emerging digitally networked media of the twenty-first century.

Deconvergence will change the communication market and the ownership structure of these industries. According to traditional antitrust measures, deconvergence has been welcomed and desirable because corporate media ownership concentrated among a handful of media giants means treating media as economic properties, pure and simple, without the traditional tension between profit and public service (Horwitz 2005). However, it must be restated in no uncertain terms that deconvergence has nothing to do with the concerns of society, the diversity of voices, democracy, competitive markets, and so forth. It is, through and through, a new business model with little other than the thoroughgoing commodification of content and culture in mind. Seen in this light, it is "old wine" in a "new bottle." The current wave of deconvergence is real, but we still face a lack of diversity of voices from visible minorities, mainly because new shareholders of deconsolidated media firms are mostly other large agglomerations of capital, that is, institutional investors, corporations, private equity groups, and so forth. As long as the current trend of deconvergence is driven by economic imperatives and these actors, the goal of improving the public sphere and revitalizing democracy will prove elusive. Split-offs and spin-offs, and other markers of deconvergence, will be further expanded in the midst of the global financial downturn that presently defines much of the world economy, to be sure, but we should not pin our hopes on the idea that economic calamities will somehow create the kind of media that democracies need and people want.

Notes

1 Although the term "convergence" has become popular in recent years, it has a long history. For example, Winseck and Pike (2007) demonstrate that convergence is as old as the telegraph and that the promises and challenges we associate with the internet were anticipated by that mid-nineteenth-century technology.

2 Spin-off is a type of divestiture where an independent company is created through the sale or distribution of new shares of an existing business of a parent company. Meanwhile, split-off is a type of corporate reorganization whereby the stock of a subsidiary is exchanged for shares in a parent company.

3 One of the major legal forces to control the concentration of media ownership has been the limitation of the cross-ownership between newspaper and broadcasting firms. However, in December 2007, the FCC voted to eliminate the cross-ownership rules despite severe public opposition. In response to the FCC's efforts to dismantle ownership limits, the Senate introduced a resolution disapproving of the FCC rule changes and seeking to nullify them. The resolution is under consideration in the 3rd US Circuit Court of Appeals in Philadelphia as of May 2010 (Blethen 2010).

4 This chapter used the Securities Data Company (SDC) Platinum Database for basic data on M&As in the communication and media sectors, which includes all corporate transactions, private as well as public, involving at least 5 percent of ownership of a company between 1990 and 2009.

5 Detailed reasons for the failure of convergence in terms of technological convergence between television and the internet are discussed in Castells (2000: 189–90).

6 Several factors have been offered to explain why consolidation between AOL and Time Warner failed, including the conflict of corporate cultures between the two media companies, the economic recession in the early part of the twenty-first century, and the decline in the number of AOL service subscribers (Albarran and Gormly 2004).

7 Time Warner obtained a $9.25 billion, one-time cash dividend from its Time Warner Cable, Inc. unit before spinning off the business to shareholders (Klemming & Sondag 2008).

8 This part of the chapter employs Lexis-Nexis power search to examine the overall trend of deconvergence between 1995 and 2008. Two search terms were used: One is spin-off in US media companies and the other is split-off in US media companies. Sources were restricted to *The New York Times* in order to avoid double counts.

9 The board of Walt Disney rejected the $54 billion unsolicited stock offer from Comcast because they believed it was too low. However, they also acknowledged the poor track record of other big media deals such as Vivendi-Universal and AOL–Time Warner. They knew that "on paper, marrying content with distribution makes a lot of sense but in reality it's been a tough nut to crack" (Holson and Sorkin 2004).

8

Navigational Media

The political economy of online traffic

Elizabeth Van Couvering

Leicester University

Introduction

By using documentary and archival evidence to analyze the historical emergence of search engines from 1994 to 2010, this chapter shows how search engines have used the development of automatically priced, widely syndicated, paid-performance advertising to become online media powerhouses, although they neither originate nor control content *per se*. Despite predictions from some political economists of media and communications that the internet would be controlled by large media conglomerates such as Vivendi, Disney, Time Warner, or Bertelsmann, these companies have been relatively unsuccessful in their attempts either to absorb or to compete with the search engines for a share of internet traffic or advertising revenues. The search engine conceptualization of traffic distribution as the major revenue stream has implications as other services with large audiences and search-like elements, such as Facebook and Twitter, and even retailers such as Amazon and eBay, begin to have greater influence over the distribution of cultural products and other goods. Without a doubt, navigational services will continue to gain influence as more and more content and goods are distributed by digital services and advertising money flows to the internet and other digital platforms at the expense of traditional distribution formats. However, at present, it is still an open question as to whether and how navigational media companies and traditional media companies will compete.

This chapter examines the economic and historical basis of the largest online media companies—the internet search engines operated by Google, Yahoo!, and Microsoft. In treating search engines as media companies, there is an immediate objection to overcome: Search engines *per se* produce very little in the way of media content. Employees of these companies write no stories, film no videos, record no audio programs, and take no pictures.[1] However, search engine companies are, by far, the largest venues for advertising online, and to consider online media without understanding and analyzing their role is to neglect the most central actors in the online media landscape. Given this, the task is to build a new analysis that includes search engines and other media entities that use search functionality and that still retains the sharp focus on the *implications* of the media industry on media content, while acknowledging that these entities produce little in the way of traditional media content.

This chapter is conducted within the tradition of the political economy of media and communications. This is a tradition that combines the analysis of politics and economics of the media, as practiced by political scientists and certain types of economists (notably institutional economists) with a critical focus, questioning in particular the development of capitalism as it relates to other societal concerns (e.g. of freedom or justice). For some media political economists, this means a concern with how well cultural products distributed through capitalist media outlets can serve to create a more informed citizenry, necessary for the functioning of a democracy. I would extend that to suggest that the political economy critique is essential in understanding how the capitalist media system interacts with noncapitalist and nondemocratic systems and further to suggest that it is not only our ability to be informed but also our human rights of self-expression and recognition by others that are implicated in the study of the political economy of the media.

In 1999, the political economist Dan Schiller, citing examples from search engines Yahoo! and Infoseek among others, argued that "[W]e must locate the internet within the evolving media economy. We must learn to see how it fits within, and how it modifies, an existing forcefield of institutional structures and functions" (Schiller 1999b). This article considers the ways in which traditional media and communications institutions have been involved in the search engine business and vice versa. It also considers how other large actors on the internet, such as social media networks and some e-commerce websites, such as Amazon and eBay, are involved in the trade in traffic. Thus, the chapter reveals how search engines have evolved over time to be a key part of the developing new media ecology.

Although much has been made by some scholars of the "newness" of online businesses in other areas (e.g. open source development), many attempts to characterize the economics of the online media industries have used traditional media industries as their base. For example, Carveth (2004) suggests that, in future, all traditional media content, including television, music, and print, will be distributed through the internet. Further, this "threatens the future existence of older media because the audience will not be open (or even able) to 'consume' in the traditional fashion" (Carveth 2004: 280). However, he suggests that media conglomerations will adapt, migrating content online into a converged distribution platform. This analysis of online media economics suggests very little new about online media apart from a new form of consumption. Hoskins, McFayden, and Finn (2004), whose volume concentrates on applying positive economic techniques to media firms, also see little new in online media: Content production, advertising, and other characteristic activities of media production are analyzed in a similar fashion in both online and off-line media companies. These studies seem to suggest that the online and off-line media industries are essentially the same but for differences in distribution. While clearly there are similarities, this cannot be the whole story, or why would traditional media companies, with many advantages in terms of assets and experience in the media business, have been relatively unsuccessful online?

Other scholars, while acknowledging the newness of new media, suggest that new media will simply become an extension of the corporate philosophies of traditional media: "To the extent the internet becomes part of the commercially viable media system, it seems to be under the thumb of the usual corporate suspects" (McChesney and Schiller 2003: 15). James Curran (Curran and Seaton 2003: 250) argues that the internet from the mid-1990s onward entered a commercialized phase in which mainstream companies—in particular, large media conglomerates such as Bertelsmann, Vivendi, Time Warner, News International, and Disney—began to dominate the web, owning three-quarters of the most visited news and entertainment sites. The present study, by contrast, finds that large traditional media firms are conspicuously absent from the major online media.

This chapter is based on an analysis of financial statements prepared for stock exchange authorities, press releases, reports in the trade press, archived information on early search engine websites, and interviews with senior search engine personnel that, together, were used to build up a picture of the financial and geographical organization and history of the search engine industry. This picture was supplemented with information from other sources such as ratings data and scholarly publications on search engine technology. The total corpus was well over 1,000 documents, including a large volume of corporate press releases (over 600). I also read, watched, and listened to interviews conducted with key personalities, for example, Mike "Fuzzy" Mauldin (Devlin 1996), who created the Lycos spider; Sergey Brin and Larry Page, the founders of Google (Correa 2000); and Matt Cutts (Abondance 2002; Grehan 2006), a Google engineer who often speaks publicly.

The study first gives a short history of the search engine business (for a more detailed history, see Van Couvering 2008). It then examines the centrality of traffic, or audience movement (as measured in clicks), in the search business. Next, it considers the workings of other high-traffic internet websites, including social media networking sites and retailing services. Finally, drawing on these analyses, it outlines the key elements of what this chapter terms *navigational media*.

The development of the search engine industry

The search engine industry has changed dramatically since its inception shortly after the creation of the world wide web in 1993. Figure 8.1 presents the development of the major internet search engines of the dozen years following the invention of the web. The chart consists of three periods: first, a period of *technical entrepreneurship* from 1994 to late 1997; second, a period that was characterized by *the development of portals and vertical integration* from late 1997 to the end of 2001, in which major media companies and network providers attempted to buy their way into the search arena; and finally a period of *consolidation and "virtual" integration* from 2002 to the present day. While presented as analytically distinct, these three periods, of course, overlap to a certain degree; for example, it is certainly possible to find technical entrepreneurs in the middle period (Google and Overture are excellent examples), and attempts at consolidation in the early period (e.g. Excite's early acquisition of Magellan and WebCrawler).

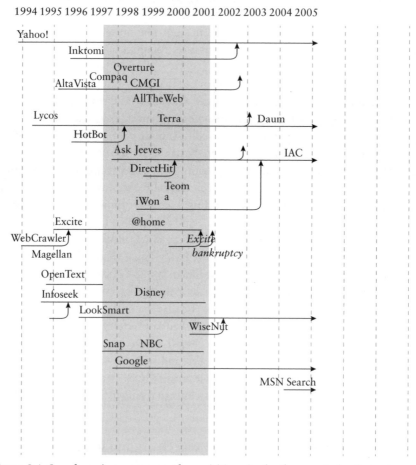

Figure 8.1 Search engine mergers and acquisitions in the three periods of search history
Source: Data from company websites and press reports, compiled by author.

The periods into which I have classified the short history of search engines are essentially based on shifts in revenue models and ownership, and give primacy to the economic history of search over its technological history. Clearly technological innovation is also important, and indeed, the shifts in revenue and economics closely coincide with technological developments and are related to preexisting structures for capitalizing on technology. But a history of technological "successes" is not sufficient to explain the dynamics of the search market, nor can it adequately characterize an industry that generated some US$10.7 billion in the United States and €6.7 billion (about US$8.8 billion) in Europe (according to the Internet Advertising Bureau)—that is to say, just under half of all internet advertising.

Of the 21 search ventures listed in Figure 8.1, only 5 remained independent entities in 2010. Of these, only four produce algorithmic search results of the whole web: Yahoo!, Google, MSN, and Ask. Lycos no longer operated a search engine but purchased search from Yahoo!

Technological entrepreneurship (1994–7)

The first period of this history shows a competitive industry with multiple companies and different technologies and strategies for navigating the web, including both directories (e.g. Yahoo! and Magellan) and search engines (e.g. Excite and Infoseek). The pattern is one of technological innovation within research centers, primarily universities, followed by commercialization, using advertising and licensing as business models and capitalization through venture capital and the stock market. The center of the industry was Silicon Valley, where a historical linkage between research, technology, and venture capital was already in place (see Zook 2005).

Portals and vertical integration (1997–2001)

The middle period of the short history of search engines online comprises the heart of the dot-com boom and bust period, that is to say late 1997 to late 2001. It is characterized by the change in focus from search engines to "portals" and the involvement of traditional media and telecommunications giants in the sector. If the first period of search can be characterized by technological innovation and the establishment of a vibrant, competitive marketplace for search technology, in this second period the search engines become focal points for a struggle to control the internet as a whole on the part of traditional media companies and telecommunications providers. Essentially, the strategy was one of growth through vertical integration in the content supply chain—that is to say, the conglomerates hoped to dominate existing portals by running their acquisitions more efficiently, exploiting economies of both scale and scope.[2]

Business texts of the time sought to promote this new kind of vertical integration, touting a concept called the "fully integrated portal" (e.g. Meisel

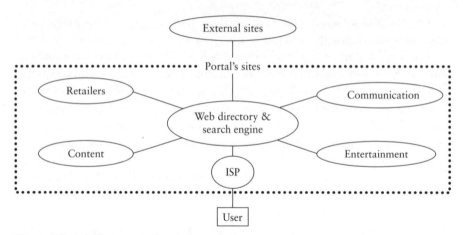

Figure 8.2 A fully integrated portal
Source: Adapted from Meisel and Sullivan (2000: 480).

and Sullivan 2000: 484). The vision of the fully integrated portal was to control the whole user experience online—it was envisaged that users would leave the portal only rarely to visit external sites (Figure 8.2).

Thus an important element that characterizes this phase of search engine development, in addition to the acquisition of many of the search engines by larger conglomerates, is the downgrading of search within the portal; the search engine itself was no longer seen as a key competitive advantage for a portal but rather as a simple requirement for doing business.

Recall that the vision of the fully integrated portal was that this mega-website would be so engrossing (or "sticky," as the industry called it) that users would never want to leave. They would arrive through the website of the service provider, browse licensed content, use branded online e-mail, and shop for purchases all within the confines of the portal. But search, of course, is the opposite of "sticky"—the whole point of a search engine is that users search for something and then leave the website. Search seemed like a giant fire hose spraying precious audience everywhere on the web but into the portal. In this period, many important early search engine companies (e.g. AltaVista, Excite, Lycos, and InfoSeek) were purchased by traditional media or telecommunications companies (e.g. AT&T, Terra Networks (Telefonica), Disney, and NBC) and developed into portals with significant corporate advertising. All of these were subsequently closed, as the dot-com money dried up with the crash of 2,000 and parent company content overwhelmed search results.

Ask Jeeves and Google also made their debuts during this period, funded out of Silicon Valley and very much along the model used by early entrants in the first period. This period also saw the very important development of pay-per-click advertising, debuted by GoTo (subsequently renamed Overture).

One of the only pioneers to survive this period was Yahoo!, which was never acquired and continued to be publically traded.

Syndication and consolidation (2002–?)

The final period of the short history of search is one of consolidation and concentration. This is due to two interconnected dynamics. First, media and infrastructure corporations ceded search to technology companies and were content to buy their search from search providers. Second, the revenues generated from pay-per-click search advertising meant that the large players were able to buy their rivals. In this period, acquisition activity of search technology businesses has been by other search providers—in fact, almost exclusively by Yahoo! Funding during this period has been characterized not by large corporate sponsorships on portals (although some do exist, particularly on Yahoo! and MSN) but via pay-per-click payments from companies both large and small on text ads on search results pages and syndicated to small sites throughout the web.

The online ad market has grown strongly in this period, increasingly funded by growth in "paid search" advertisements, that is to say the type of cost-per-click (CPC) advertisements pioneered by GoTo, linked to user traffic, whether on search engine sites or syndicated to other websites. This advertising has three key characteristics: (1) it is priced on a CPC basis; (2) it is *contextual*, linked either to page content or to the users' search term; and (3) it is *syndicated* to other websites on a revenue-sharing basis (i.e. the fee is split between the owner of the website and the provider of the paid search service). Google and Yahoo! have received by far the majority of the revenue from these ads. In addition, search services have been syndicated to a large range of ISP home pages. What these very successful syndication efforts have meant is that, effectively, Google and Yahoo! have achieved a situation where, without needing to purchase companies, their advertising is carried across the web through syndicated advertising, and audience is directed to them through syndicated search engine functionality.

By the end of this period, entrepreneurial activity within search engines became focused on specialist search engines (such as blog search engine Technorati). The only significant new entrant during this period since 2002, in terms of whole-web search, has been Microsoft, which has started afresh several times with different search engine technologies (MSN Search, MSN Live, and Bing) hoping to reproduce Google and Yahoo!'s winning formula. An oligarchic structure has been firmly established, with search engine companies engaging in a range of agreements that syndicate both their results and their advertisements to a range of websites, ensuring a constant flow of traffic both in and out of the engine. The next section introduces the concept of *traffic commodity* as a key element of understanding the short history of search as given above.

The traffic commodity

In order to understand the dynamics outlined in the previous section, we can use the vertical supply chain as a means of analysis. The vertical supply chain (sometimes referred to as the value chain) is a tool for analyzing an industry whereby activities are ordered in a sequence, which starts at the early stages of production and works its way through the various intermediaries until arriving eventually at the customer (Doyle 2002b: 18). Doyle has recently defined a vertical supply chain for media as consisting of three general phases: production, packaging, and distribution. Thus, the generic media supply chain is based upon taking *content*, that is to say, television broadcasts, news stories, pictures, and so on, as the basic unit of analysis. Most traditional media companies have some element of vertical integration along this chain. So, for example, Time Warner owns production companies, broadcast networks, and cable television stations.

However, media companies operate in what is called a dual product market. On the one hand, they sell content to audiences, and it is this content supply chain that Doyle references. On the other hand, however, media companies sell *audiences* to advertisers. On the internet, where audiences are extremely fragmented, this turns out to be a much more useful value chain to construct, since the problem is not so much getting content to your audience (a basic web page being relatively easy to construct) but audiences to your content.

To construct a value chain for media audiences, we must begin by considering how audiences get on the internet. First, they must have a computer and the software to make it run.[3] Hardware manufacturing and software providers are therefore the first two steps in the chain. Second, they must connect to the internet via some kind of an internet service provider whose signal will run over telephone lines (or, possibly, cable lines). The telephone or cable company and the ISP are therefore the third and fourth steps in the audience supply chain. Fourth, they need a browser to access the world wide web. In the early days of the internet, the browser was seen as the crucial point for audience aggregation. When Netscape went public, it was this insight that drove its market price sky high. Finally, in order for the audience to get to their destination website, they may very likely need a search engine, especially if this site is small and has little brand recognition of its own. Figure 8.3 presents the audience supply chain.[4]

This second period of search engine history, discussed above, is characterized by attempts at integration—both forward and backward—along this audience

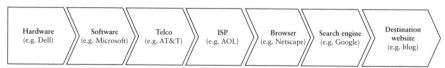

Figure 8.3 **Supply chain for search engine audiences**

supply chain. The introduction of pay-per-click advertising by GoTo (later Overture) transformed the search engine from a loss leader in the portal business to a revenue generation machine. Of Google's 2009 revenue of US$23.6 billion, advertising, nearly all of it pay-per-click, generated 97 percent. However, this type of advertisement was more than simply a brilliant business idea: It was part of a crucial shift in the search engine business. No longer would the *audience* (the traditional media commodity sold to advertisers) be at the core of the search business. Now, the online commodity of choice would be *traffic* or the flow of visitors from one website to another. When audience was the main commodity sold, the key task of online websites was to gather and keep as many audience members as possible, with the ultimate aim being—however unrealizable—to own the whole internet. But as traffic emerged as a key commodity in its own right, sites that had as much traffic as possible—that is to say, as many people coming and going as possible—became the nexus of economic wealth. Search engines were the obvious choices, and the new economic possibilities led to a resurgence of technical competence and the technically complex search product as essential elements of the large online media players we see today.

Reviewing the state of research on political economy of communication, Mosco argues for an analysis of market concentration in media markets that focuses on something more than ownership. He suggests that "networks of corporate power" might need to be investigated through "forms of corporate interaction that build powerful relationships without actually merging businesses. These forms encompass a range of 'teaming arrangements,' including *corporate partnerships* and *strategic alliances*" (Mosco 1996: 189, italics in original). In the analysis of the search engine industry, it is syndication of both results and advertising that enable the "networks of corporate power." Earlier efforts at vertical integration have been replaced by what we might term a "virtual" integration along the audience supply chain. In contrast to the fully integrated portal, the new model might be conceived as a *syndicated portal*, as in Figure 8.4.

The differences between the syndicated portal shown above and the fully integrated portal imagined by dot-com boom enthusiasts consist of not only the qualitative difference between ownership and partnership but also the quantitative differences of having multiple ISPs, multiple content providers, multiple entertainment venues, and multiple retailers attached to the portal. The lines between the search engine and its partners are of both traffic and money.

By using syndication into both advertisers and partners who are further up the supply chain such as ISPs, the new giants of search have developed a network that extends across the internet. No longer is it necessary to "own" the internet, as those who dreamed of controlling a fully integrated portal did. Rather, by means of "virtual" integration using technology to achieve

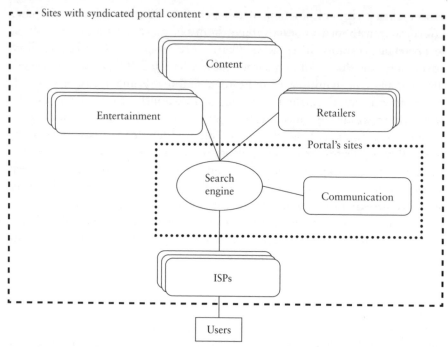

Figure 8.4 The syndicated portal

syndication, Google and Yahoo!, and to a lesser extent Ask and MSN, are able to stretch their ability to monetize (or commoditize) traffic across the web, without the need for ownership.[5]

One implication of the traffic commodity, as characterized above, is that a range of media, particularly new media but also traditional media, may begin to function differently as they seek to capitalize on the new commodity.

Search engines and social media

Beginning from about the middle of the first decade of the twenty-first century,[6] social media sites such as Facebook, MySpace, Twitter, Blogger, LiveJournal, Flickr, and YouTube began to draw considerable numbers of page views and audience engagement (measured as time spent) to their websites. By the end of 2009, Facebook page views were reported to have exceeded that of Google's search engine in the United Kingdom (although just for a few days) (Schwartz 2009). Given the large market share of search engines and their central place in the web infrastructure as discussed above, this is a fairly astonishing statistic, and the relationship of these websites to search engines deserves some consideration. The rise of social media networks has implications for search engines, but it is not clear whether search engines will end up competing with, cooperating with, or co-opting social networks.

Social media sites are diverse but have in common an infrastructure whereby users create their own content within a defined technical framework, and they also use the supplied framework to link directionally to other users, for example, by "following" them (Twitter) or "friending" them (Facebook).[7] The content allowed can be widely varied, ranging from personal web pages (MySpace, Facebook) to dated updates (Blogger, LiveJournal), to small snippets including links (Twitter), and to pictures and video (Flickr and YouTube). In many cases there is some overlap (updates via Facebook, for example), and third-party services allow people to aggregate connections via various platforms; indeed, some websites publish application programming interfaces (APIs) to facilitate this connection. In some cases, for example, Facebook, technically savvy users can also create their own small applications using these APIs and distribute them to their contacts through the interface.

These sites are not strictly search engines, but many of them incorporate search facilities as an essential element to facilitate initial connections and to enable users to follow topics as well as connect with other people. They also have other connections to the search industry. Some social media sites are owned by search engine companies: YouTube and Blogger, for example, are owned by Google, and Flickr is owned by Yahoo! Others are still independent (Facebook,[8] Twitter), while still others have affiliations with traditional media (MySpace is owned by News Inc.). While they may not be search engines, there are some areas where these sites seem to share features with the search engine industry, as I discuss below.

First, these sites share with search engines a reliance on outsourced and distributed content providers. Each of the sites listed above provided a technical interface but did not, *per se*, provide media content—texts, pictures, videos, and even small applications—although these are what its users relied on it for. Instead, rather than rely on indexing technologies, as search engines do, users are positioned as active content creators, and it is their content that forms the base upon which the social media site operates. Some of this content, unlike the content upon which the ordinary search services are based, is *exclusive* to the service in question, and this provides the service owners with an enormous asset. For example, a post on LiveJournal may only be available to other members indicated as "friends," depending upon the user settings, and a full profile will only be available to "connections" on LinkedIn. Social media sites are quite heterogeneous, so there is at least one important caveat to this: Blog content (such as that hosted by Blogger or WordPress), unlike the content produced on other social networks, tends not to be as restricted to other members of the service and is more freely available.

Second, the reliance on a network of distributed content creators gives social network providers a huge amount of frequently changing content, which is of great value to users, and thus a huge amount of traffic, which is of great value to advertisers. It cannot be stressed enough that most social networks have an *internal* traffic source (their members' content and links) and source of new members (members soliciting friends for new members) and are not as dependent on search engines for traffic as other websites. Like search engines, these services are free to users, and they typically make most of their income from advertising, although some, like LiveJournal, also charge for "premium" accounts with additional features. Advertising could be charged on a CPC basis, but unlike search engines they could also target ads to a range of demographic or personal details, which had the potential to make each click more valuable. They also had a possible additional funding model, which was the sale of access to their user-created content, including profiles and demographics, to other companies for further commercialization. In summary, the assets they have and might potentially sell to advertisers or other business partners include traffic from their network to other networks, profile information about their users, information about their users' connections and online habits, the content that their users create on their platform, and technical access to the platform (i.e. for developers to create platform content, itself potentially funded by subscription or advertising). They might also, conversely, sell services to their users such as protection from advertising on the users' personal pages, additional platform modules (e.g. games), or extended platform services (e.g. being able to message friends-of-friends directly). Having said this, at the end of 2009, there was no uniform business model.

Three examples help to clarify this: the cases of Facebook and Twitter, two independent providers of highly successful social networking websites, and Technorati, a search engine based on blogs. Facebook's funding model was to provide demographic- and interest-based targeted advertising on either a CPC or a cost-per-milli (CPM) basis. Although you could search for people or groups on a Facebook, there was no generic search—ads were purchased by demographic and interest targeting, just as is the case with traditional media, but unlike the case of search ads, which are based on user behavior in the form of clicks. Facebook's revenue stream was additionally heavily supported by Microsoft, which took a stake in the company in 2007. Microsoft's Bing search was integrated into the Facebook search pages, and only Bing was able to access information stored in Facebook's public profile pages. Twitter, by contrast, appeared to have no revenue stream at all other than investment. Speculation abounded as to how it would turn its popular service into a sustainable business, with advertising being widely tipped (Tartakoff 2010). In the latter part of 2009, Twitter took a step toward sustainable revenue by licensing the content its users create to Google, Microsoft, and Yahoo! for indexing, for rumored tens of millions of dollars per year. Technorati belonged to the class of businesses that are not social media but are made possible by social media. Technorati indexed only blog sites and implemented special search features appropriate to the format, such as ranking by date order (see Thelwall and Hasler 2006). Technorati's funding model was also based on advertising, and it announced in 2008 that it would begin selling syndicated advertising to its network of blogs (Arrington 2008).

These three examples represent quite different ways of creating and monetizing social media. With Facebook, the user's profile and interests are spelled out, and this forms a large part of the content that users and advertisers value. Twitter takes the form of a newsfeed nearly devoid of other personal information apart from linkages between followers and followees. And yet each of these two websites, in their different ways, has taken advantage of its proprietary network to include search on their own terms by charging for access to the content their users create, including content about themselves, which in turn generates traffic. Meanwhile, Technorati has followed in the footsteps of the major search engines, capitalizing on the much more loosely defined and freeform social network of bloggers. In each case, the currency of traffic remains central to understanding the business strategies of social media providers.

Finally, along with the value of traffic, comes the incentive for some users to try to manipulate the system for profit, as search engine marketers and advertisers do. Thus, there exist Facebook, Twitter, and blog optimization services; Facebook and Twitter spam, as well as straightforward Facebook and blog advertisers; and hundreds if not thousands of profiles, Twitter feeds, and blogs and blog commenters that might be called spam, all dedicated to driving traffic to private interests.

The relationship between the large search engines and these social media sites is complex. Since they have their own internal source of traffic, social networking sites can form a large proprietary traffic network with personal data that is not easily available to the search engine. They can also have search-like functionality in terms of driving traffic—many Twitter updates contain URLs, for example, so Twitter functions as a source of traffic to a range of sites, as do blogs, which often contain links and references to other sites. Social networks are clearly valuable properties: The connection of large traffic volumes with personal data is irresistible to advertisers. But they cannot remain wholly separate from the internet, and increasing the size of the network and the volume of content and traffic must be of paramount importance to network owners. Here the search engines take on their role of connecting traffic through a range of disparate technical infrastructures. Zimmer (2008) calls this mixture of personal data and search technology "Search 2.0" and raises concerns about the clear privacy implications, implications that may well prompt governments to act to restrict it. Thus, while search engines already owned many important social networking properties, an uneasy and slightly competitive relationship between the independent networks and the dominant search engines was in place at the end of 2009.

Search engines and online retail websites

Social media sites are not the only large websites that have features in common with search engines. Online retail sites also employ search professionals and extensively use search technologies to enable users to find just the product they are looking for in a sea of merchandise. The largest retail sites on the web, Amazon and eBay, are examples of this. The difference between *The New York Times* newspaper and Macy's department store is clear. Online, the lines between media company and retailer seem more fuzzy. There is some ambiguity as to whether a listing on eBay or Amazon marketplace should be considered as a sales distribution point or as an advertisement, especially when the retailers do not hold the physical goods themselves. Since eBay and Amazon both offer purchasing functionality, they are typically considered retailers. However, to understand their relationships with search engines and other large internet players, it is also helpful to consider them as potential media entities. As with the content of the search engine listings or social networking profile pages, a large part of Amazon and eBay's marketplace content is not generated by the companies in question. Instead, individuals and small businesses list their goods and services. In this way, these companies act as platforms for buyers and sellers to interact and, therefore, receive some of their value from the traffic that circulates in their network.

In 2009, Amazon.com was the largest retailer online, with US$24.5 billion in revenue. Approximately, 30 percent of unit sales in 2009 were derived from third-party sellers who use Amazon's websites to find a wider audience for their products. According to Amazon's annual report, these sales are recorded as net and are usually lower revenue, higher margin products. Even a conservative estimation, therefore, gives several billion dollars worth of revenue obtained from third parties listing their products on Amazon. Amazon also operates a syndication program to boost traffic and sales. In 2009, Amazon spent US$680 million on marketing, mostly on sponsored search results, portal advertising, and its "Associates" (syndication) program. Amazon does not pay Associates per click but rather per sale on a commission basis of between 4 and 15 percent based on volume. Portal deals may be either commission or click based (but probably click based), while search engine sponsored results are click based. Working backward, if Amazon spent, for example, half of that marketing budget on Associates' websites earning a 4 percent commission, it generated US$8.5 billion (some 35 percent) of its revenues from sales due to Associates. This is merely an estimate, as Amazon does not divulge these figures and commission rates vary, but it does show that the syndication program is likely to be highly important to Amazon's business. eBay is a more extreme example of a retailer with search-like characteristics. The primary interface to eBay is either by a search box or by a directory-like category listing. The results of the eBay search return content that a range of sellers (individuals, businesses, and agents) have contributed. eBay holds no inventory of its own, acting primarily as a retail platform supplier for buyers and sellers.[9] The traffic it hosts within its network is extremely valuable. Its marketplace segment, which includes its main auctions business plus a range of fixed-price arrangements and classified ads, generated US$5.3 billion in revenue in 2009. In contrast to a search engine, these revenues are not due to advertising. The content contributed by eBay sellers leads directly to sales, rather than indirectly via advertisements; in this it resembles early advertising-only search engines such as GoTo and Overture, with the important difference that the eBay platform includes a payment infrastructure. Thus, eBay's revenues are primarily generated by listings fees and final value fees (a commission on the known value of the sold goods). Using the audience value chain presented in Figure 8.2, eBay might be considered a search engine that has virtually forward-integrated with a range of retail destinations.

The retail networks represented by Amazon and eBay (and other similar websites) generate their own traffic, similarly to social media websites. Historically, these websites have relied on search engines extensively to generate an initial customer base (including a long-running Amazon deal with Excite and a similarly large and long-running Google spend by eBay). In the case of the online retail sites, it is tempting to conclude that their core commodity is real, physical goods, not the intangible movement of traffic. But, as the cases above have shown, these sites derive much of their income from acting as intermediaries between audience members/buyers and sellers. As Google, for example, introduces similar marketplace-based services such as Google Check-Out, the difference between search engines and online retailers may perhaps be one of emphasis. In any case, search engines both cooperate with and compete with retailers, although the traffic flow at this stage, in any case, tends to be one way.

Conclusion: the logic of navigational media

The chapter builds upon the insight that, because of the lack of traditional content production, in order to analyze the search engine industry as a media industry, we must examine the *value chain for audiences* rather than for content (e.g. news stories or television productions), as is common in the analysis of traditional media (Doyle 2002b). Online, it is technically relatively simple to produce content and make it available, and many institutions and individuals do so. What seems considerably more challenging is to attract an audience. With the inversion of the supply chain, we can begin to understand aspects of the history of search that are otherwise puzzling—for example, the failure of the large media conglomerates to dominate the search engine industry as they attempted to do. The value chain analysis shows us that the search industry is based on the creation and exploitation of a new commodity for media: *traffic* or the movement (in clicks) of visitors from one website to another.

Further examination of the trade in traffic between and within search engines, social media networks, and large online retailers suggests that a new media logic is in operation online. *Navigational media*, as I call this new logic, can be characterized by the following features. First, navigational media entities primarily produce *media platforms* or automated arenas of exchange between producers and audiences. These are the algorithmic, technical aspects of the business, and are often considered to be its core competence (although less so in the case of Amazon, which also specializes in logistics). Second, these platforms operate across *complex content pools* that are large in size, extremely varied in terms of producers, and frequently refreshed. The content producers are sometimes referred to as a "community," especially in the case of social networks. The complexity of the content pool renders the automated platform a necessity, since manual discovery of information is too time-consuming and complex. Thus, the media platform becomes the central way to mediate connections between audiences and producers. If the content pool is the network, audience traffic, enabled through the platform, are the connections within the network. These connections are used by navigational media businesses as a core, saleable asset, in the form of per-click advertising fees, referral fees, commission payments, and so on. In order to broaden the content pool and increase traffic, the *syndication* of platform-based content, whether advertising or listings, is common. Finally, the value of traffic leads also often to the introduction of services to spoof, optimize, or otherwise *manipulate traffic* as part of marketing efforts by actors other than the platform provider.

Within this logic, a powerful platform provider relates to a range of relatively powerless content providers. One concern of political economists of media and communication has been the potential lack of diversity of media content when one powerful voice is heard. In the logic of navigational media, diversity of content is, to some extent, guaranteed by the very size and complexity of the content pool, but it is only guaranteed within the parameters of the platform. On a closed platform, such as a social media website, content may be quite rigidly controlled (e.g. to 140 characters only in case of Twitter). On an open platform, such as a search engine, it is more varied. It is also the case that the platform controls (more or less tightly) access to the content pool, so that being banned from (for example) inclusion into the search index can be very serious for content providers, who may often include retailers as well as traditional media businesses or simply small producers of cultural goods such as bloggers.

A second implication of the model of the navigational media is the way in which traditional media companies and navigational media platforms relate. Throughout the short history of search, search engines have been embroiled with traditional media companies in disputes that primarily relate to the use of proprietary content as part of the platform's content pool, especially as search platforms have begun to aggregate certain types of content (e.g. news, books, scholarly articles, images, and videos) for display in specialized search interfaces like Google News or YouTube. The content providers' consistent claim has been that it is unethical for the platform provider to harvest the content and sell advertising based on that content (e.g. Agence France Press, Associated Press, and the *Chicago Tribune*—see, for example, Goldman 2007). The search engine's reply has been that they are taking only snippets of the content and subsequently providing the content originators with valuable audience for them to sell in any way they see fit, and courts in the United States have agreed with them, holding that search engine snippets fall within the "fair usage" exception to copyright protection (Grimmelman 2007: 27). Many of these suits have been settled out of court, sometimes with the search engine agreeing to pay some amount of money to the traditional media provider. But, increasingly, traditional media companies are adapting their practices to suit the search engines, with young journalists being advised to tailor their writing style to be search engine friendly (Niles 2010), and some large media companies employing the services of search engine optimizers to review their entire website strategies (Kiss 2008). Rather than the new media market being a mere extension of traditional media strategies or being co-opted by traditional media, navigational media platforms are having a profound impact on the business models and business practices of traditional media, particularly the press and the news business. The eventual configuration remains to be seen.

Notes

1   Of course, these are diverse companies, and they produce newspaper-like products, such as Yahoo! and Google news. This chapter, however, focuses primarily on the search service, which is the economic driver for these companies.

2   Economies of scale refer to the benefits that accrue for certain types of products when large numbers of them are produced. In media products, the cost of producing the first copy—for example, paying an author to write a manuscript, to edit the manuscript, to typeset the book, and to proofread the first copy—often far outweighs the costs of subsequent copies. This is even more true for digital content such as software, where copying and distribution costs are nearly zero. The technical definition is that economies of scale occur when marginal costs (the cost of producing a single copy of the work) are less than average costs—that is to say the average cost declines the more units are produced. Economies of scope refer to the benefits that accrue to companies who can reuse resources to produce a range of products. In media, you might see economies of scope when *Harry Potter* (the book) is used to provide the basis for "Harry Potter" (the film) or "Harry Potter" (the DVD). Thus, economies of scope technically occur when two (or more) products can be jointly produced and sold more cheaply rather than separately. Media industries tend to exploit both economies of scale and economies of scope, and this in turn leads to conglomerates such as Time Warner, Disney, Viacom, News International, and Vivendi (Doyle 2002a: 13–15) that have holdings in radio, television, newspapers, cable television, and so on.

3   Of course, today some audiences access the internet without having a computer— for example, from mobile phones or personal digital assistants (PDAs). However, during this period, the computer was by far the most important means of access.

4   Although this supply chain is presented horizontally, it is more correctly called a vertical supply chain. Integration along this chain would be vertical; backward integration along the chain is also called downstream integration and integration forward along the chain can be deemed upstream integration.

5   It is also worth noting that although emphasis in the industry has shifted to paid search, Yahoo! and MSN also retain more traditional "portals" with channels filled by advertiser content.

6   Social network sites had been launched earlier, as Boyd and Ellison's (2008) chronology indicates, but only began to be "mainstream" around 2003–4, with much activity happening in 2006, including the launch of Twitter.

7   This definition differs only slightly from that offered by Boyd and Ellison: "We define social network sites as web-based services that allow individuals to (1) construct a public or semipublic profile within a bounded system, (2) articulate a list of other users with whom they share a connection, and (3) view and traverse their list of connections and those made by others within the system. The nature and nomenclature of these connections may vary from site to site" (Boyd and Ellison 2008: 211). The definition in the text is slightly broader in that it includes sites where the "profile" mostly consists of visual information, such as Flickr and YouTube.

8   Facebook is not entirely independent, as Microsoft purchased a small stake in 2007.

9   eBay also has other business segments, including primarily PayPal and (until recently) Skype. These are excluded from the present analysis.

9

The Contemporary World Wide Web

Social medium or new space of accumulation?

Christian Fuchs
Uppsala University

Introduction

Many observers claim that the internet in general and the world wide web in particular have been transformed in the past years from a system that is primarily oriented toward information provision into a system that is more oriented to communication and community building.[1] The notions of "Web 2.0," "social software," and "social network(ing) sites" have emerged in this context. Web platforms such as Wikipedia, MySpace, Facebook, YouTube, Google, Blogger, Rapidshare, Wordpress, Hi5, Flickr, Photobucket, Orkut, Skyrock, and Twitter are said to exemplify this transformation of the internet.

One of the best-known definitions of "Web 2.0" has been given by Tim O'Reilly (2005):

> Web 2.0 is the network as platform, spanning all connected devices; Web 2.0 applications are those that make the most of the intrinsic advantages of that platform: delivering software as a continually-updated service that gets better the more people use it, consuming and remixing data from multiple sources, including individual users, while providing their own data and services in a form that allows remixing by others, creating network effects through an "architecture of participation," and going beyond the page metaphor of Web 1.0 to deliver rich user experiences.

The claim by O'Reilly and others is that the web has become more social, community-oriented, cooperative, and based on user-generated content. These claims have thus far hardly been empirically tested, and although there is much talk about the "social web," there are hardly any approaches based on social theory that think systematically about what sociality on the web and the internet actually means. This chapter aims to remedy that shortcoming by introducing and discussing some social theory and critical theory foundations of the world wide web. I do so in three steps. First, the notions of Web 1.0, 2.0, 3.0 will be introduced based on social theory. Then the notion of the participatory web and the role of the category of class for the web will be discussed. Finally, some conclusions are drawn.

The world wide web and social theory

For Emile Durkheim, a "social fact is every way of acting, fixed or not, capable of exercising on the individual an external constraint" (Durkheim 1982: 59). For Durkheim, social facts are ubiquitous and permanently shape our thinking and action. Max Weber had a different notion of sociality as social action: "Not every kind of action, even of overt action, is 'social' in the sense of the present discussion. Overt action is not social if it is oriented solely to the behavior of inanimate objects" (Weber 1968: 22). For Ferdinand Tönnies, the most important form of sociality is the community, which he understands as "consciousness of belonging together and the affirmation of the condition of mutual dependence" (Tönnies 1988: 69). For Karl Marx, cooperation is a fundamental mode of human social activity: "By social we understand the cooperation of several individuals, no matter under what conditions, in what manner and to what end" (Marx and Engels 1846/1970: 50).

Based on these four theoreticians, we can distinguish three modes of human sociality: cognition, communication, and cooperation. Cognition is the activity of the human mind. Cognition is social for Durkheim because it is permanently confronted with social facts and is the foundation for creating and recreating social facts. Communication is a process in which signs and symbols are given a certain meaning by a person or group of persons who share those meanings among themselves and with others who also give certain meanings to these signs and symbols. The notion of communication relates to Weber's concept of social action and stresses the role of meaning, signs, and symbols. Communication, in other words, is social action that makes use of symbols. Cooperation is a process in which several humans act together in order to achieve a goal or a process of joint actions that produces a shared consciousness of belonging together. If cooperation is understood in this way, then it expresses Marx's notion of cooperation and Tönnies' concept of community. Information can be understood as process that involves one or more of the social activities of cognition, communication, and cooperation (Hofkirchner 2008).

This notion of information allows us to distinguish three dimensions of the web (Figure 9.1). Web 1.0 is a computer-based networked system of human cognition, Web 2.0 is a computer-based networked system of human communication, and Web 3.0, a computer-based networked system of human cooperation. Web 1.0 describes cognitive aspects of the web, Web 2.0, communicative aspects, and Web 3.0, cooperative aspects. These three notions are layered one atop the other, whereby cooperation is based on but more than communication and communication is based on but more than cognition. In order to cooperate, we need to communicate, and in order to communicate we need to cognize. In Web 1.0, individuals cognize with the help of data that they obtain from a technologically networked information space. Web 2.0 as a system of communication is based on web-mediated cognition: Humans interact with the help of symbols that are stored, transmitted, and received with the help of computers and computer networks. Web-mediated cognition enables web-mediated communication and vice versa. There is no communication process without cognition. In Web 3.0, a new quality is said to emerge out of the productive capacities of communicative actions. A certain amount of cohesion between the people involved is necessary, and web-mediated communication helps to enable such mediated cooperation. To put it another way, there is no cooperation without communication and cognition. These three relatively distinct forms of sociality (cognition, communication, and cooperation) are encapsulated within one another. Each layer forms the foundation for the next one, reflecting the emergent property of each element and the "total system" as a whole. As I use the term, the "web" is meant not only to refer to the world wide web but also to any techno-social information network that enables human action and interaction. There are also feedback loops between the levels, which are indicated by the causal arrows in Figure 9.1: Cognition enables communication, communication enables further cognition, communication enables cooperation, cooperation enables further communication.

In order to assess whether there have been significant transformations and distinct stages in the evolution of the web over time, I compared the top 20 websites used in the United States between 1998 and 2010, and asked whether there are manifest differences in the technological affordances they provide for cognition, communication, and cooperation over this span of time. The statistical data in Table 9.1 show the number of unique users who accessed

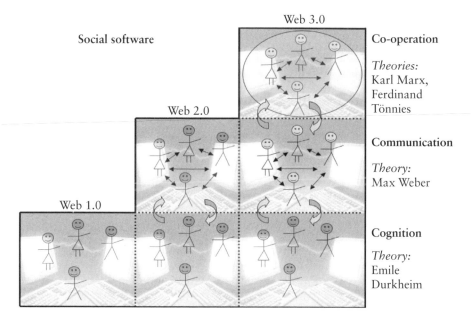

Figure 9.1 A model of social software and its three subtypes

Table 9.1 Information functions of the top 20 websites in the United States, 1998/2010

1998				2010			
Rank	Website	Unique users in '000s (December)	Primary functions	Rank	Website	Unique users in '000s (December)	Primary functions
1	aol.com	28,255	Cognition, communication	1	google.com	153,774	Cognition, communication
2	yahoo.com	26,843	Cognition, communication	2	facebook.com	133,843	Cognition, communication, cooperation
3	geocities.com	18,977	Cognition	3	youtube.com	123,585	Cognition, communication
4	msn.com	18,707	Cognition, communication	4	yahoo.com	120,081	Cognition, communication
5	netscape.com	17,548	Cognition, communication	5	amazon.com	85,311	Cognition
6	excite.com	14,386	Cognition, communication	6	twitter.com	81,631	Cognition, communication
7	lycos.com	13,152	Cognition, communication	7	msn.com	78,184	Cognition, communication
8	microsoft.com	13,010	Cognition	8	ebay.com	74,207	Cognition
9	bluemountainarts.com	12,315	Cognition, communication	9	wikipedia.org	71,952	Cognition, communication, cooperation
10	infoseek.com	11,959	Cognition, communication	10	live.com	71,348	Cognition

	1999			2011		
11	altavista.com	11,217	Cognition	microsoft.com	69,891	Cognition
12	tripod.com	10,924	Cognition	answers.com	62,192	Cognition, communication, cooperation
13	xoom.com	10,419	Cognition	blogspot.com	58,418	Cognition, communication
14	angelfire.com	9,732	Cognition	ask.com	56,249	Cognition
15	hotmail.com	9,661	Cognition, communication	blogger.com	52,673	Cognition, communication
16	Amazon.com	9,134	Cognition	aol.com	52,273	Cognition, communication
17	real.com	7,572	Cognition	bing.com	51,612	Cognition
18	zdnet.com	5,902	Cognition	ehow.com	50,590	Cognition, communication, cooperation
19	hotbot.com	5,612	Cognition	craigslist.org	45,943	Cognition, communication
20	infospace.com	5,566	Cognition	about.com	43,776	Cognition
		260,891			1,537,533	

Sources: Comcast (1999), Quantcast (2011).

a platform in a time span of 1 month. For each platform, it was assessed if it primarily supports information publishing or search (cognitive function), symbolic interaction (communicative function), or community building and knowledge cocreation (cooperative function). To help understand this relationship between different platforms and different functions, we can see, for example, that Google mainly supports information search (cognition) and communication (with its e-mail platform Gmail), while Wikipedia supports information search (cognition), interaction of users who collaborate on articles (communication), and knowledge cocreation (cooperation). The results of the analysis are shown in Table 9.1.

One initial observation is that from 1998 to 2010, the number of unique visitors in the United States to the top 20 websites multiplied by a factor of almost 6. In terms of the functional orientation of the top 20 websites, one can observe that in 1998, there were 20 instances in which information functions and 9 where communication functions were predominant. By 2010, there were still 20 information functions, but the number of communication and cooperation functions of the top 20 US websites had grown to 13 and 4, respectively. The number of websites that are oriented purely toward cognitive tasks decreased from 11 in 1998 to 7 in 2010. Thus, in 1998, and in terms of its technological structure, the world wide web was predominantly a cognitive medium (Sociality 1), although communicative features (Sociality 2) were also present. In 2010, the number of websites that also have communicative or cooperative functions is much larger than the number of "pure" information sites. This shows that the technological foundations for Sociality (2) and (3) have increased quantitatively. In other words, a feature of the web in 2010 that was not present on the top 20 websites in 1998 is the support of cooperative tasks: collaborative information production with the help of wikis (Wikipedia, answers.com) and social networking sites oriented to community building (Facebook, eHow). The development of the world wide web is thus marked by both continuity and discontinuity. Information sites are still predominant, but the importance of communicative and cooperative features has increased.

Participatory web as ideology

Changes of media and technologies have historically been connected to the emergence of certain one-sided techno-optimistic and techno-pessimistic myths. In the case of "Web 2.0" and "social software," this continues to be true. The reigning myth of the past couple of years is that the world wide web and the internet have morphed into a participatory medium, with a reinvigorated participatory culture close in tow.

THE CONTEMPORARY WORLD WIDE WEB   207

Henry Jenkins encapsulates this stance well when he argues that increasingly "the web has become a site of consumer participation" (Jenkins 2006a: 137). He claims that blogging, in particular, is "increasing cultural diversity and lowering barriers in cultural participation," "expanding the range of perspectives," and making it possible that "grassroots intermediaries" and "everyone has a chance to be heard" (Jenkins 2006b: 180–1). Axel Bruns sees the rise of produsage— the "hybrid user/producer role which inextricably interweaves both forms of participation" (Bruns 2008: 21)—as the central characteristic of Web 2.0. He argues that produsage "harnesses the collected, collective intelligence of all participants" (Bruns 2008: 1), that it allows "participation in networked culture" (Bruns 2008: 17), and that the "open participation" (Bruns 2008: 24, 240) of Web 2.0 has the potential to reconfigure democracy as we know it (Bruns 2008: 34). Clay Shirky (2008: 227–8) believes that the "linking of symmetrical participation and amateur production" in Web 2.0 spaces such as Flickr, YouTube, MySpace, and Facebook creates environments of "public participation." Shiffman (2008) sees the emergence of the "age of engage" as result of Web 2.0. Tapscott and Williams (2006: 15) similarly argue that "the new web" has resulted in "a new economic democracy ... in which we all have a lead role." Yochai Benkler (2006) points to the rise of commons-based peer production on the internet and concludes that "we can say that culture is becoming more democratic: self-reflective and participatory" (Benkler 2006: 15).

In the face of this seeming consensus, however, we must step back and ask whether the web is as participatory as many seem to think it is? To answer this question, however, we must first understand what is meant by the notion of participation. A good place to start in terms of that question is participatory democracy theory.

Held (1996: 271) argues that a primary feature of participatory democracy is the "direct participation of citizens in the regulation of the key institutions of society, including the workplace and local community." It also means "democratic rights need to be extended from the state to the economic enterprise and the other central organizations of society" (Held 1996: 268). The central idea of participatory democracy theory is that individuals should be enabled to fully take part in collective decision processes and in the control and management of structures in the economic, political, and cultural systems that concern and affect them. In other words, participatory democracy can be understood as an extension and intensification of democracy in line with the following basic principles (Macpherson 1973; Pateman 1970).

The intensification and extension of democracy

Participatory democracy involves the "democratization of authority structures" (Pateman 1970: 35) in *all* decision-making systems, such as government, the workplace, the family, education, housing, and so on. In particular, the economic system is seen as the fundamental sphere of participation, given that "most individuals spend a great deal of their lifetime at work and the business of the workplace provides an education in the management of collective affairs that it is difficult to parallel elsewhere" (Pateman 1970: 43).

The maximization of human developmental powers

Participatory democracy is not only a system of government but also a kind of society that "attains the presently attainable maximum ... level of abilities to use and develop human capacities given the presently possible human command over external Nature" (Macpherson 1973: 58). Factors that impede these powers—inadequate means of life (physical and psychological energy), lack of access to the means of labor, and a lack of protection against invasion by others—must be abolished in order to realize participatory democracy (Macpherson 1973: 59–70).

Extractive power as impediment for participatory democracy

For Macpherson (1973), capitalism is based on the individual right to unlimited accumulation of property and unlimited appropriation, a system of rights that allows some human beings to exploit others and that ultimately ends up limiting the development of human capacities in general (Macpherson 1973: 17–18). This results in an unequal distribution of property as well as inequality in terms of the "effective equal right of individuals to exert, enjoy, and develop their powers" (Macpherson 1973: 34–5). He calls this extractive power: the exercise of "power over others, the ability to extract benefit from others" (Macpherson 1973: 42).

Participatory decision making

Participatory democracy requires "(equal) participation in the making of decisions" (Pateman 1970: 43) and "a process where each individual member of a decision-making body has equal power to determine the outcome of decisions" (Pateman 1970: 71).

Participatory economy

Participatory democracy does not exclude individuals from common property but guarantees "the right to a share in the control of the massed productive resources" (Macpherson 1973: 137).

Technological productivity as material foundation of participatory democracy

A high level of technological productivity can be used to create a post-scarcity economy where all people have "economic security" (Pateman 1970: 40). As Macpherson (1973: 20f) states, "I am arguing that we are reaching a level of productivity at which the maximization of human powers, in the ethical sense, [...] can take over as the criterion of the good society, and that in the present world climate it will have to be an egalitarian maximization of powers." According to Macpherson (1973), the revolution in energy generation and communication technologies could

> releas[e] more and more time and energy from compulsive labour, allow men to think and act as enjoyers and developers of their human capacities rather than devoting themselves to labour as a necessary means of acquiring commodities. At the same time the technological revolution could enable men to discard the concept of themselves as essentially acquirers and appropriators. (Macpherson 1973: 37)

Macpherson's views that people's capabilities can be maximized through the application of technological forces rather than the latter leading to greater exploitation closely parallels Herbert Marcuse's remarks on the role of technology in liberation. Marcuse (1964) imagined that a stage

> would be reached when material production (including the necessary services) becomes automated to the extent that all vital needs can be satisfied while necessary labor time is reduced to marginal time. From this point on, technical progress would transcend the realm of necessity, where it served as the instrument of domination and exploitation which thereby limited its rationality; technology would become subject to the free play of faculties in the struggle for the pacification of nature and of society. (Marcuse 1964: 16)

This discussion shows that democracy is not limited to voting in general elections but is a condition where grassroot political participation and decision making in the economy, culture, and all spheres of society is the norm. This also includes the question of ownership, which is conceived to be undemocratic within contemporary capitalist societies because the means of production are privately owned by the capitalist class even though they are, in many respects, collectively produced. A participatory economy also requires that extractive power be reduced to zero and the establishment of "the right to a share in the control of the massed productive resources" (Macpherson 1973: 137). Furthermore, it involves "the democratizing of industrial authority structures, abolishing the permanent distinction between 'managers' and 'men'" (Pateman 1970: 43).

Given these baseline conditions, we can analyze the ownership of "Web 2.0/3.0" to determine if it is truly participatory, as I do in relation to the top 50 websites in the United States in July 2009 identified in Table 9.2. The

Table 9.2 Web 2.0/3.0 platforms that are among the top 50 websites in the United States, 2009

Rank	Website	Ownership	Country	Year of domain creation	Economic orientation	Unique US users per month (July 2009) (in millions)	Unique US users per month (December 2010) (in millions)
4	Facebook	Facebook Inc.	USA	2004	Profit, advertising	91	134
6	YouTube	Google Inc.	USA	2005	Profit, advertising	72	124
8	Wikipedia	Wikimedia Foundation	USA	2001	Nonprofit, non-advertising	67	72
9	MySpace	MySpace Inc. (News Corporation)	USA	2003	Profit, advertising	63	29
14	Blogspot	Google Inc.	USA	2000	Profit, advertising	49	57
19	Answers	Answers Corporation	USA	1996	Profit, advertising	39	62
22	Wordpress	Automattic Inc.	USA	2000	Profit, advertising	28	43
23	Photobucket	Photobucket.com LLC	USA	2003	Profit, advertising	28	25
26	Twitter	Twitter Inc.	USA	2006	Profit, no advertising	27	82
31	Flickr	Yahoo Inc.	USA	2003	Profit, advertising	21	16
32	Blogger	Google Inc.	USA	1999	Profit, advertising	20	53
44	eHow	Demand Media Inc.	USA	1998	Profit, advertising	14	51
49	eZine Articles	SparkNet Corp.	USA	1999	Profit, advertising	13	7.5

Source: Quantcast (2010).

websites are ranked according to the number of unique US visitors in 1 month of observation.

Table 9.2 uses the number of monthly unique visitors per website to show which Web 2.0/3.0 platforms were among the top 50 websites accessed in the United States in July 2009. If we define Web 2.0/3.0 platforms as those that mainly support social networking, community building, file sharing, cooperative information production, and interactive blogging—platforms that are more systems of communication and cooperation than systems of cognition—then we can analyze the role that Web 2.0/3.0 platforms play on the world wide web overall. When we do so, one thing becomes immediately clear: namely, that 13 out of the top 50 websites in 2009 can be classified as Web 2.0/3.0 platforms (i.e. 26.0 percent). In terms of total usage of these top 50 websites in the United States, these 13 platforms account for 532 million visits out of a total of 1,916 million (i.e. 27.7 percent). If just 26.0 percent of the top 50 US websites are Web 2.0 platforms, and these platforms account for only 27.7 percent of usage, then this means that claims that the web has been transformed into social medium based predominantly on sharing, cooperation, and community building are vastly overdrawn. The predominant usage type of the internet in the United States is to access information search sites and others that provide information, shopping, and e-mail services. Web 2.0/3.0 platforms have become more important, but they do not dominate the web. Furthermore, 12 out of 13 Web 2.0/3.0 platforms among the top 50 websites in the United States are profit oriented, and 11 of them are advertising supported. An exception is Wikipedia, which is nonprofit and advertising-free. Advertising and targeted-advertising are the most important business models among these Web 2.0/3.0 sites.

There are also some sites that combine this accumulation model with that of selling special services to users. So, for example, Flickr, an advertising-based photo-sharing community, allows uploading and viewing images for free but sells additional services such as photo prints, business cards, and photo books. WordPress uses advertising but also generates revenue by selling VIP blog hosting accounts that have monthly subscription rates and services such as extra storage space, customized styles, a video blogging service, ad-free blogs, and blogs with an unlimited number of community members. Until 2010, Twitter was the only profit-oriented corporation that did not have a business model based on advertising. In April 2010, however, Twitter announced that advertising will be introduced in the near future (see http://news.bbc.co.uk/2/hi/8617031.stm, accessed on July 1, 2010). In July 2010, Twitter had not-yet implemented advertising, but its privacy policy had already been changed in the preceding year in anticipation of an advertising-financed business model. As a result, Twitter's terms of use significantly grew in length and complexity, and set out the company's ownership rights with respect to user-generated content. A note that Twitter "may include advertisements, which may be targeted to the Content or information on the Services, queries made through the Services, or

Table 9.3 Ownership rights and advertising rights of the 13 most used Web 2.0/3.0 platforms in the United States

Rank	Website	Ownership of data	Advertising
4	Facebook	License to use uploaded content	Targeted advertisements
6	YouTube	License to use uploaded content	Targeted advertisements
8	Wikipedia	Creative commons	No advertising
9	MySpace	License to use uploaded content	Targeted advertisements
14	Blogspot	License to use uploaded content	Targeted advertisements
19	Answers	License to use uploaded content	Targeted advertisements
22	Wordpress	License to use uploaded content	Targeted advertisements
23	Photobucket	License to use uploaded content	Targeted advertisements
26	Twitter	No license to use uploaded content	No advertising
31	Flickr	License to use uploaded content	Targeted advertisements
32	Blogger	License to use uploaded content	Targeted advertisements
44	eHow	License to use uploaded content	Targeted advertisements
49	eZineArticles	No license to use uploaded content	Targeted advertisements

Source: Quantcast (2010).

other information" was added to Twitter's terms of service (http://www.twitter.com/tos, version effective on November 16, 2010).

The key point then is that, according to my empirical sample, 92.3 percent of the most frequently used Web 2.0/3.0 platforms in the United States and 87.4 percent of unique monthly Web 2.0/3.0 usages are corporate based. The vast majority of popular Web 2.0/3.0 platforms are mainly interested in generating monetary profits, and the corporate Web 2.0/3.0 is much more popular than the noncorporate Web 2.0/3.0.

We can also raise questions about the extent to which Web 2.0/3.0 are participatory by asking who owns the personal information gleaned from, and created by, the users of such sites? The difference between the "myth" of participatory democracy versus corporate capitalism can be seen by focusing on Google, which owns 3 of the 11 web platforms listed in Table 9.3. In terms of ownership, 18 human and corporate legal persons own 98.8 percent of Google's common stock. Google's 20,000 employees, 520 million global Google users, 303 million users of YouTube, and 142 million users of Blogspot/Blogger have no ownership stakes in Google.[2] Beyond Google, all of the analyzed Web 2.0/3.0 platforms guarantee for themselves a right to display user-generated content in any manner they see fit. This is not a tangential consideration but pivotal to how they operate their services and their business model as a whole. As Table 9.3 shows, 10 of the 13 Web 2.0/3.0 sites have user licenses and "terms of use" policies that provide them with a *de facto* ownership right over all of the data the users create, including the right to sell the content.[3] Furthermore, 11 of the 13 Web 2.0/3.0 platforms guarantee themselves the right to store, analyze, and sell the content and usage data of their users to advertising clients, who are enabled to provide targeted, personalized advertisements as a result. In sum, this means that the vast majority of the Web 2.0/3.0 companies in our sample exert ownership rights on user-generated content and behavioral data. While Web 2.0/3.0 companies own the data of the users, users do not own a share of the corporations.

To this point, we can see that corporate Web 2.0/3.0 platforms attract a large majority of users and that the corporations that operate the vast majority of these platforms are profit oriented and accumulate capital by online advertising and in some cases by selling special services. A few legal persons own the companies that operate Web 2.0/3.0 platforms, whereas millions of users have no share in ownership. This is how they accumulate capital and the cornerstone of their "business model." Web 2.0/3.0 does not extend democracy beyond the political sphere into culture and economy. Nor does it maximize the developmental powers of human beings. Instead, it mainly maximizes the developmental powers of an economic class that owns web platforms and holds the extractive power to dispossess users and to exploit workers and users in order to accumulate capital. We can conclude that from the perspective of participatory democracy theory, Web 2.0/3.0 is not a participatory techno-social system because it is based on capitalist ownership and accumulation structures that benefit the few at the expense of the many and access is stratified.

For Georg Lukács, ideology "by-passes the essence of the evolution of society and fails to pinpoint it and express it adequately" (Lukács 1971: 50). Slavoj Žižek (1994) argues that "'Ideological' is a social reality whose very existence implies the non-knowledge of its participants as to its essence" (Žižek 1994: 305). An ideology is a claim about a certain status of reality that does not correspond to actual reality. It deceives human subjects in order to forestall societal change. It is false consciousness (Lukács 1971: 83). Based on participatory democracy theory, we can argue that scholars who argue that the contemporary web or the internet is participatory advance an ideology that celebrates capitalism and does not see how capitalist interests predominantly shape the internet. Given these empirical results, it seems both necessary and feasible to theorize "Web 2.0" not as a participatory system but by employing more negative, critical terms such as class, exploitation, and surplus value.

Class and the web

Karl Marx highlights exploitation as the fundamental aspect of class by saying that "the driving motive and determining purpose" of capitalist production is "the greatest possible exploitation of labour-power by the capitalist" (Marx 1867: 449). He says that the proletariat is "a machine for the production of surplus-value," and capitalists are "a machine for the transformation of this surplus-value into surplus capital" (Marx 1867: 742). Whereas Marx had in his time to limit the notion of the proletariat to wage labor, it is today possible to conceive of the proletariat in a much broader sense as all those who directly or indirectly produce surplus value and are thereby exploited by capital. Besides wage labor, this also includes houseworkers, the unemployed, the poor, migrants, retirees, students, precarious workers, and also the users of corporate Web 2.0 platforms and other internet sites and applications. Hardt and Negri (2004) use the term "multitude" for the multidimensional proletariat of the twenty-first century.

For Marx, the profit rate is the relation of profit to investment costs: $p = s/(c + v)$ = surplus value/(constant capital (= fixed costs) + variable capital (= wages)). If internet users become productive Web 2.0 producers, then in terms of Marxian class theory this means that they become productive laborers who produce surplus value and are exploited by capital because for Marx productive labor generates surplus. Therefore, the exploitation of surplus value in cases like Google, YouTube, MySpace, or Facebook is not merely accomplished by those who are employed by these corporations for programming, updating, and maintaining the software and hardware, performing marketing activities, and so on, but by the users and the producers who engage in the production of user-generated content. New media corporations do not (or hardly) pay the users for the production of content. One accumulation strategy is to give users free access to services and platforms, let them produce content, and to accumulate a large number of producers who are then sold as a commodity to third-party advertisers. No product is sold to the users, but users are sold as a commodity to advertisers. The more users a platform has, the higher the advertising rates can be set. The productive labor time that is exploited by capital, on the one hand, involves the labor time of the paid employees and, on the other hand, all of the time that is spent online by the users. For the first type of knowledge labor, new media corporations pay salaries. The second type of knowledge is produced completely for free. There are neither variable nor constant investment costs. The formula for the profit rate can be transformed for this accumulation strategy as follows:

$$p = s/(c + v1 + v2),$$

where s is surplus value, c is constant capital, $v1$ is wages paid to fixed employees, and $v2$ is wages paid to users.

The typical situation is that $v2 \geq 0$ and that $v2$ substitutes $v1$. If the production of content and the time spent online were carried out by paid employees, the variable costs would rise and profits would therefore decrease. This shows that produsage in a capitalist society can be interpreted as the outsourcing of productive labor to users who work completely for free and who help to maximize the rate of exploitation ($e = s/v$ = surplus value/variable capital) so that profits can be raised and new media capital accumulated. Again, this situation is one of infinite overexploitation. Capitalist produsage is, thus, an extreme form of exploitation rather than the harbinger of a new "democratic" or "participatory" economy based on fundamentally different values and principles.

That surplus value generating labor is an emergent property of capitalist production means that production and accumulation will break down if this labor is withdrawn. It is an essential part of the capitalist production process. That producers conduct surplus-generating labor can also be seen by imagining what would happen if they stopped using platforms such as YouTube, MySpace, and Facebook: The number of users would drop, advertisers would stop investing because no objects for their advertising messages and, therefore, no potential customers for their products could be found, the profits of the new media corporations would drop, and they would go bankrupt. If such activities were carried out on a large scale, a new economic crisis would arise. This thought experiment shows that users are essential for generating profit in the new media economy. Furthermore, they produce and coproduce parts of the products and, therefore, parts of the use, exchange, and surplus values that are objectified in these products.

Dallas Smythe (1981/2006) suggests that in the case of advertising-based media models, the audience is sold as a commodity to advertisers: "Because audience power is produced, sold, purchased and consumed, it commands a price and is a commodity. ... You audience members contribute your unpaid work time and in exchange you receive the program material and the explicit advertisements" (Smythe 1981/2006: 233, 238). Smythe's argument is that audience labor is productive, creates surplus value, but is not materially remunerated by money. With the rise of user-generated content, free-access social networking platforms, and other free-access platforms that yield profit through online advertising—a development subsumed under categories such as

Web 2.0, social software, and social networking sites—the web seems to come close to accumulation strategies employed by capital from traditional mass media like TV or radio. When we speak of Web 2.0, however, the audience has turned into prosumers, understood as, first suggested by Toffler (1980), consumers of information, who are at the same time producers of information. The prosumers who google data, upload or watch videos on YouTube, upload or browse personal images on Flickr, or accumulate friends with whom they exchange content or communicate online via social networking platforms such as MySpace or Facebook constitute an audience commodity that is sold to advertisers. The difference between the audience commodity on traditional mass media and on the internet is that in the latter case the users are also content producers; prosumers' creative activity generates communication, community building, and content production. That the users are more active on the internet than in the reception of TV or radio content is due to the decentralized structure of the internet, which allows many-to-many communication.

The first sentence of Chapter 1 of Marx's *Capital* is as follows: "The wealth of societies in which the capitalist mode of production prevails appears as an 'immense collection of commodities'" (Marx 1867: 125). A commodity is a good that is exchanged in a certain amount for a certain amount of another good (in most cases, money). Marx (1867) formulates this relation as follows: x amount of commodity $A = y$ amount of commodity B. In capitalism, labor power and means of production are bought as commodities on markets by capitalists and used as production factors. Labor creates new products in the production process by using its labor power with the help of the means of production. The new products according to Marx contain unpaid labor time (surplus value) that is transformed into profit by selling a commodity. As a result, the initially invested sum of money capital is increased. Commodities have a use value, and thus they satisfy human needs, while commodification reduces such values to exchange values. The exchange value dominates over the use value of a commodity. Dallas Symthe's notion of the audience commodity means that consumers are no longer just the buyers of commodities but are themselves sold as commodities to advertising clients. In other words, they are transformed into exchange values. Prosumers also have a price tag, where advertisers have to pay to obtain access to a certain number of people.

Due to the permanent activity of the recipients and their status as prosumers, we can say that in the case of the internet the audience commodity is a prosumer commodity. This category does not signify a democratization of the media toward a participatory or democratic system but the total commodification of human creativity. During much of the time that users spend online, they produce profit for large corporations like Google, News Corp. (which owns MySpace), or Yahoo! (which owns Flickr). Advertisements on the internet are frequently personalized; this is made possible by surveillance, storing, and assessing user activities with the help of computers and databases. This is another difference from TV and radio, which provide less individualized content and advertisements due to their more centralized structure. But one can also observe a certain shift in the area of traditional mass media, as in the cases of pay-per-view, tele-votes, talk shows, and call-in TV and radio shows. In the case of the internet, the commodification of audience participation is easier to achieve than with other mass media.

The importance of the prosumer commodity and extractive power as principles of the contemporary web is evidenced by the continuing absolute and relative rise of internet advertising revenues. In 2008, internet advertising was the third-largest advertising market in the United States and the United Kingdom. Internet advertising revenues were only exceeded in these two countries by newspapers and TV advertising (Internet Advertising Bureau (IAB) 2009: 14; Ofcom 2009: 36). Worldwide, advertising spending on Facebook was US$605 million in 2010, which was an increase of 39 percent in comparison to 2009 (Adweek 2009).

The constant real-time surveillance of prosumers is also achieved through the proliferation of privacy statements that guarantee that personalized advertising can be operated on web platforms. Indeed, users hardly have any choice as to whether or not to agree with such policies if they want to interact with others and make use of the technical advantages Web 2.0/3.0 poses. Privacy statements are, in other words, totalitarian mechanisms that are, out of necessity, not democratically controlled by the users but under the exclusive control of corporations.

Facebook, for example, automatically uses targeted advertising. There is no way to opt out.

> We allow advertisers to choose the characteristics of users who will see their advertisements and we may use any of the non-personally identifiable attributes we have collected (including information you may have decided not to show to other users, such as your birth year or other sensitive personal information or preferences) to select the appropriate audience for those advertisements. For example, we might use your interest in soccer to show you ads for soccer equipment, but we do not tell the soccer equipment company who you are. [...] We occasionally pair advertisements we serve with relevant information we have about you and your friends to make advertisements more interesting and more tailored to you and your friends. For example, if you connect with your favorite band's page, we may display your name and profile photo next to an advertisement for that page that is displayed to your friends. (Facebook 2010)

Also, MySpace allows targeted personalized advertising that is automatically activated. Users can opt out, but doing so is very difficult. There is no menu setting in the privacy options that allows people to do so, only a link in the privacy policy that users have to follow in order to opt out. As its statement declares,

MySpace may use cookies and similar tools to customize the content and advertising you receive based on the Profile Information you have provided. Profile Information you provide in structured profile fields or questions (multiple choice questions like "Marital Status," "Education," and "Children") ("Structured Profile Information"), information you add to open-ended profile fields and questions (essay questions like "About Me," "Interests" and "Movies") ("Non-Structured Profile Information") and other non-PII about you may also be used to customize the online ads you encounter to those we believe are aligned with your interests. (Facebook 2010)

Conclusion

The social theories of Durkheim, Weber, Tönnies, and Marx make it possible to distinguish between three modes of sociality that can be applied to the realm of the web. Web 1.0 is a networked digital system of cognition, Web 2.0 a networked digital system of communication, and Web 3.0, a networked digital system of cooperation. Based on this distinction, one finds that in the past 10 years the world wide web has continuously remained primarily a web of cognition, although sites that support communication and cooperation have become more important.

Empirical analysis shows that corporate interests dominate the contemporary web. In participatory democracy theory, economic democracy is a central element of participation, and capitalist ownership structures are considered as undemocratic and, thus, nonparticipatory. This allows me to conclude that claims about the contemporary internet and the web as spaces of sociality, cooperation, and a "new economy" are uncritical and ideological. They celebrate capitalism and the capitalist character of the internet but wrap these realities in new rhetoric, thereby constituting a form of false consciousness.

Viable alternatives to celebratory web theories are critical theories of the web that are based on Karl Marx's notions of class, exploitation, and surplus value. A central mechanism for capital accumulation on the web is the surveillance of personal user data and activities. The access to these data or the analyzed data are sold to advertising clients that the right to use these data in order to present targeted advertising to the users. Contemporary internet users are to a certain extent content producers, so-called produsers or prosumers. Nonetheless, they are exploited by capital and produce surplus value because their activities are sold as commodities. They constitute an internet produsage commodity that is at the heart of class formation, exploitation, and surplus value production on the internet.

My suggestion that the contemporary internet and the contemporary world wide web are predominantly corporate spaces of capital accumulation is meant as a corrective to techno-optimistic approaches that claim that the internet has become a participatory system. My approach should not be misread as a techno-pessimistic nihilism that declares that there are no positive potentials in the internet. The internet is a dialectical space consisting of positive and negative potentials, potentials for dominative competition and for cooperation that contradict each other (for a detailed discussion of this hypothesis, see Fuchs 2008). The internet acts as critical medium that enables information, coordination, communication, and cooperation of protest movements (Fuchs 2008). It has the potential to act as a critical alternative medium for progressive social movements, as examples such as Indymedia show (Fuchs 2010a; Sandoval and Fuchs 2009). The internet is both a social medium and a space of accumulation. The extension of internet sociality toward more communication and cooperation today serves primarily corporate purposes, however. Corporations commodify and exploit sociality, that is, communication, production, and cooperation on the internet. At the same time, internet cooperation, as, for example, expressed by the free sharing of data on the internet with the help of file-sharing platforms, points toward a noncapitalist economy in which goods are not exchanged but available for free (Fuchs 2008). Cognition, communication, and cooperation on the internet, thus, have a contradictory character: They are commodified but at the same time advance the socialization and cooperation of labor that undercuts and tends to threaten corporate interests.

But the dialectic of the internet is asymmetric. Visibility is a central resource on the internet. Information can be produced easily, cheaply, and fastly, but the more important aspect of information on the internet is how many users become aware of this information and make use of it in meaningful and critical ways. Dominant actors such as corporations, political parties, or governments control a vast amount of resources (money, influence, reputation, power, etc.) that gives them advantages over ordinary citizens and protest movements. It is much easier for them to accumulate and maintain visibility on the internet. Everyone can produce and diffuse information relatively easily because the internet is a global, decentralized, many-to-many and one-to-many communication system, but not all information obtains the same attention. Amidst an ocean of information, the problem is how to draw other users' attention to information. So, for example, Indymedia, the most popular alternative online news platform, is only ranked Number 4,147 in the list of the world's most accessed websites, whereas BBC Online is ranked Number 44, CNN Online, Number 52, *The New York Times Online*, Number 115, *Spiegel Online*, Number 152, *Bildzeitung Online*, Number 246, or Fox News Online, Number 250 (alexa.com, top 1,000,000,000 sites, August 2, 2009). This shows that there is a stratified online attention economy in which the trademarks of powerful media actors work as potent symbols that help these organizations' online portals to accumulate attention.

In short, as with the material world, resources, and hence visibility, on the internet are asymmetrically distributed. Protest, critique, and participation are therefore mere potentials on the internet. Citizens and movements have to struggle in order to attain a more participatory web and a more participatory society. These struggles will not continue on their own accord, and they are currently subsumed under the dominance of capital and State. The asymmetric dialectic of the internet can only be exploded through class struggles that question the dominative and corporate character of the internet. The emergence of a participatory web is only a nonrealized potential. Its attainment is possible but not certain.

Notes

1   The research presented in this chapter was conducted as part of the project "Social Networking Sites in the Surveillance Society," funded by the Austrian Science Fund (FWF): Project Number P 22445-G17. Project coordination: Christian Fuchs.

2   Data: Google US Securities and Exchange Commission (SEC) Filing Proxy Statements 2008. Number of worldwide internet users: 1,596,270,108 (internetworldstats.com, August 14, 2009); 3-month average number of worldwide Google users (alexa.com, August 14, 2009): 32.671 percent of worldwide internet users (520 million users); 3-month average number of worldwide YouTube users (alexa.com, August 14, 2009): 18.983 percent (303 million users); 3-month average number of worldwide Blogger/Blogspot users (alexa.com, August 14, 2009): 8.869 percent (142 million users).

3   At the time when the analysis was conducted (August 2009), Twitter had relatively short terms of use. However, in September 2009, the terms were changed so that targeted advertising and the *de facto* ownership and selling of user data by Twitter became possible. Twitter's terms of use thereby became very similar to the ones by other commercial, profit-oriented Web 2.0 platform companies.

PART FOUR

Communication, Conventions, and "Crises"

10

Running on Empty?

The uncertain financial futures of public service media in the contemporary media policy environment

Peter A. Thompson
University of Wellington

This chapter provides an overview and analysis of public service media (PSM) in the context of the digital multimedia environment. Media convergence on a technical level and the proliferation of new distribution platforms have accentuated the fragmentation of audiences and revenue streams and brought formerly discrete markets into increasingly direct competition with each other (particularly in respect to online content). At the same time, the near-global ramifications of the credit crunch have driven many economies into recession and restricted advertising expenditures (Advertising Standards Authority (ASA) 2009; Benady 2009). Taken together, these trends have intensified competition for revenue among commercial media and accentuated the critical scrutiny of PSM institutions and funding mechanisms. The chapter argues that the political right and commercial media interests have sought to circumscribe the market spaces in which public service operators are able to compete for audiences and, in some cases, directly sought to delegitimate their public revenue streams. These challenges to the continued legitimation of public funding mechanisms for public service broadcasters/media providers will be explored through case studies of public service broadcasters/media providers in the United Kingdom and New Zealand. Although these are very different countries, notably in respect to the size of their respective populations and media markets, both underwent extended periods of neoliberal macroeconomic reform during the 1980s and 1990s followed by a decade of "third-way" policy responses. Since the "credit crunch," both have reverted to free-market approaches under new center-right administrations. In this respect, the political-economic structures and recent policy trajectories in the United Kingdom and New Zealand exhibit similarities. However, these cases also demonstrate that understanding the way macro-political-economic pressures are articulated into specific policy outcomes requires detailed examination of specific institutional arrangements, and the cases of the United Kingdom and New Zealand are exemplary in this regard.

Theorizing contemporary PSM

The majority of countries in the OECD have some kind of PSM provisions supported by some form of noncommercial revenue streams (see Thompson 2005; Iosifidis 2007). These capitalist economies also underwent significant shifts in macroeconomic policy paradigm toward neoliberalism/monetarism during the 1980s and 1990s. This has entailed an intensification of pressure on governments to scale back public spending and State involvement in the economy in order to accommodate the imperatives of the financial and industry sectors. This has continued despite the resurgence of "third-way" governments because social democratic initiatives have been circumscribed within the policy space that remains after market imperatives have been accommodated (Thompson 2000; Comrie and Fountaine 2005; Williams 2007). Public broadcasting policy has inevitably been embroiled in policy tensions stemming from these shifts because the media sector is both a driver of economic growth and a vital facilitator of cultural and democratic functions.

There has been a wide range of scholarship on the shaping of media policy across a range of national contexts (see e.g. Bardoel and d'Haenans 2008; Hoynes 2003; Iosifidis 2007; Jakubowicz 2006; Moe 2008; Syvertsen 2003; Van den Bulck 2008). On a broad level of approximation, these studies point to a policy trajectory away from traditional public service toward the neoliberal, market-driven paradigm. Public service models have certainly been challenged by market liberalization, the expansion of commercial competition, and the proliferation of new media platforms. However, the specific regulatory, financial, and institutional arrangements that have emerged from the accommodation of market imperatives have also varied across national contexts and have generally stopped short of wholesale withdrawal of State intervention in the media sector. Indeed, governments continue to provide subsidies to public service providers, as the 1997 Amsterdam Protocol permits them to do, but only insofar as they are proportionate to specific PSM functions and do not inhibit commercial market activity. The European Commission's "classic" 1989 *Television without Frontiers* (TVWF) has been updated and renewed by the 2007 *Audiovisual Media Services* (AMS) directives (see Williams 2007; European Commission 2009). Overall, the importance of public service has been reasserted, albeit without inhibiting commercial media development.

There is an obvious tension between the assumption that new media technologies and the proliferation of services have rendered traditional public service broadcaster/broadcasting (PSB) provisions redundant and the reassertion of the continuing need for comprehensive PSM provisions across new platforms. However, the more significant policy discourses are those that ostensibly acknowledge the need for PSB but seek to quarantine its functions to traditional broadcasting or services that are not otherwise commercially viable (see Jakubowicz 2006). As will become apparent, in some cases, the political right and private media operators may well support the continuation of public revenue streams while arguing that these should be used to support the commercial media sector.

Neo-Marxist accounts of how capital accumulation imperatives seek to colonize lifeworld spaces remains important in highlighting how political-economic macrostructures shape the arenas in which media ecologies are formed. However, these macrostructures can be articulated in different ways through the interplay of evolving institutional interests within a particular arena of activity (see Hindess 1989; Flew 2006, Van den Bulck 2008). Media systems, therefore, cannot be understood solely in terms of mechanistic responses to structural imperatives such as profit maximization. It is also the case that ostensibly similar political-economic forces may be manifested in different ways across different contexts, national or otherwise. Pearce (2000) warns that institutionalist analysis of media systems can sometimes overstate the instrumentality of agents. However, the recognition that regulatory and financial conditions are not simple determinants of institutional behavior need not imply that they exert no constraint on the channels and modalities of action available to institutional agents in a given context. The recognition that mythologies and discursive forms shape policy debates and contests of legitimation is not an alternative to political-economic analysis but a central component of it (e.g. see Born 2003, 2004; Mosco 2004; see also Chapters 11 and 12 in this book).

Indeed, policy discourses on public broadcasting funding mechanisms play a significant role in structuring what forms of public service provisions and revenue streams are politically available and sustainable. Lobbying by private commercial media and criticism from the political right has often targeted PSM funding systems in an attempt to foreclose policy alternatives that do not align with their interests. Such macro-policy frameworks may nevertheless play out differently across different national/institutional contexts. The UK and New Zealand cases are by no means atypical here, but the way PSM funding policies have played out in response to ostensibly similar political-economic pressure makes for an interesting comparison.

PSM in the UK context

The UK broadcasting system is often cited as an exemplar of PSM provision. In the predigital era, the BBC's central role in the broadcasting ecology was supported by Channel 4's complementary remit as well as the generic public service obligations incurred by private commercial television broadcasters as a condition of their operating license and allocation of spectrum. The BBC's domestic services remain fully funded through the hypothecated license fee, providing public revenue of approximately £3,600 million per year. The BBC has also been a key player in the development of free-to-air terrestrial digital services on the Freeview platform and has developed a range of online services. However, the scope of the BBC's services and the scale of its funding have been subject to increasing scrutiny by governments, commercial rivals, and (since 2003) the new integrated regulatory body, Ofcom. In 2007, the BBC Trust replaced the former board of governors. The trust plays a role in approving higher level fiscal decisions and ensuring the BBC's accountability to its Charter through public value tests and service licenses that set out the scope of BBC functions. However, it has been criticized for being more sensitive to external pressures than the former governing board (see e.g. Fisk 2009).

The BBC's continuing receipt of the hypothecated license fee (currently confirmed up to 2016) has been increasingly viewed with envy and resentment by the private media sector. Commercial operators have struggled to sustain margins in a digital multimedia market, particularly given that the ITV operators continue to shoulder public service obligations (see Williams 2007; Collins 2008; Christophers 2010). There has also been recognition in government and in Ofcom that a well-endowed BBC and the faltering fortunes of the commercial ITV companies (and Channel 5) offer a pretext for relieving the latter from some or all of their public service obligations and/or "top-slicing" the license fee and redirecting a proportion toward offsetting the opportunity costs associated with these functions. Meanwhile, other private commercial operators have argued that the BBC's expansion into digital and online services has inhibited commercial investment and development.

This was exemplified by the 2009 MacTaggart lecture given by the CEO of News Corporation (Europe), James Murdoch, in which he alleged that the BBC, Channel 4, and Ofcom are unaccountable and condemned "the dampening effect of a massive state-funded intervention which reduces the scope for program investment and commissioning from independent production companies by private broadcasters" (Murdoch 2009). He also criticized the BBC's expansion of services into new digital platforms, arguing that "rather than concentrating on areas where the market is not delivering, the BBC seeks to compete head-on for audiences with commercial providers to try and shore up support—or more accurately dampen opposition—to a compulsory licence fee." Moreover, Murdoch claimed that "the expansion of state-sponsored journalism is a threat to the plurality and independence of news provision, which are so important for our democracy." In his eyes, the BBC's extensive online content restricts commercial operators' ability to charge for content.

Murdoch's criticisms reflect institutional self-interest. They also characterize the rhetoric being deployed against PSM and State involvement in the media sector. Although the BBC's director general, Mark Thompson (2010b), has rejected Murdoch's claims, the argument that the scale and scope of BBC services have a detrimental impact on the UK media market has nevertheless gained ideological traction within industry and policy forums prioritizing economic growth in new media markets (see Cox 2004; Elstein, Cox, Donohue,

Graham, and Metzger 2004; the Digital Britain report (BIS/DCMS 2009); also Grade, as cited in the *Guardian* 2010).

Ofcom's approach to media policy is significant here. As Williams (2007) suggests, Ofcom's establishment and approach to governance reflect the New Labour predilection for pursuing social-cultural policies through market mechanisms. Williams also points to increasingly proximate linkages between regulator, industry, and government, which can align to promote or inhibit particular policy ideas. Such alignments are consistent with Flew's (2006) arguments about policy activism by nongovernment agents and Collins' (2008) contention that Ofcom's "regulatory discretion" has effectively outsourced some areas of broadcast regulation to industry stakeholders (see also Graham 2005). Ofcom's broad regulatory function is complicated by a technically complex and rapidly evolving digital media sector, which makes it difficult to anticipate every eventuality requiring governance decisions. Regulations, therefore, require adaptation in response to unfolding scenarios, increasing the need for stakeholder consultation to avoid policy being implemented unfairly or inconsistently. In turn, this provides a vector through which the discourses of industry stakeholders can potentially influence regulators and increases the risk of bureaucratic capture if regulators or government come to depend on industry support for policy legitimacy. As Van Cuilenburg and McQuail (2003) observe, "The specific content of government policies reflects the deal made in the particular time and place and the balance of power and advantage between government and industry." Although contingent and subject to contestation, such "deals" or "policy settlements" (Flew 2006) serve to demarcate the parameters of legitimate policy intervention.

The recent policy negotiations concerning the BBC license fee need to be understood in the context of the above processes. As Graham (2005), Smith and Steemers (2007), and Collins (2008) have all noted, there has been increasing pressure on government and Ofcom from the private/commercial media sector for a reduction in their public service obligations and/or to rein in the BBC's scope of functions and level of funding. This is not limited to the BBC's traditional broadcasting rivals. The British Internet Publishers Alliance has also vigorously argued that the BBC's online presence inhibits commercial investment in services. As Smith and Steemers observe, "In positioning itself as a content provider whose content will be available on demand on myriad future platforms, the Corporation is impinging on what commercial operators believe is their future route to profitability" (Smith and Steemers 2007: 52).

Although Ofcom emphasizes the continuing importance of the BBC, it has not been unsympathetic to the view that shifts in audience composition, revenue streams, and the commercial value chain are increasing the opportunity costs of public service provision, particularly for the ITV broadcasters. Christophers (2010) has pointed out that the five main terrestrial free-to-air television channels slipped from a 95 percent audience share in the 1990s to 70 percent in 2006. Although the continuing value of mass audiences offsets the decline in commercial revenue available to the mainstream commercial media, the distribution of advertiser money (already tightened by recession) across a wider range of platforms has lowered profits and increased the opportunity costs of public service provision. Ofcom's 2009 report on public service noted a decline in PSM investment across almost all the major television operators, *including the BBC*. Freedman (2008) points out that, even if one accepts that commercial media are facing intensified competition, there is no clear evidence that the BBC's operations "crowd out" commercial operators. Indeed, as Davies (2005) argues, the decline of ITV's audience share and revenue base is because of the expansion of BSkyB, rather than the BBC, whose license fee as a proportion of the overall revenue in the broadcasting/media sector has actually declined.

Although Ofcom is sympathetic to calls to release private sector media operators from public service obligations, it is also cognizant of the benefits of maintaining a plurality of platforms and providers making a contribution to the overall public service provisions (particularly in regard to regional news, current affairs, factual/educational content, and children's programs). The media ecology would certainly be weakened were it to evolve in such a way as to leave the BBC as the monolithic public service operator while any such responsibilities among the private commercial media were allowed to atrophy. As Graham (2005) observes, Ofcom is inclined to regard plurality and competition as desirable policy ends in their own right and has actively explored the possibility of "top-slicing" the license fee and redistributing a proportion to support other broadcasters' PSM obligations[1] (Graham 2005; Freedman 2008).

The UK government's 2006 White Paper on the BBC (Department of Culture, Media and Sport (DCMS) 2006) confirmed the continuation of the license fee arrangement up to 2016. It explicitly acknowledges the significance of PSM, but it also redefined the scope and normative underpinnings of the corporation's services and license fee. In line with the TVWF and AMS directives, the BBC is required to specify its range of services with regard to market impacts to justify its receipt of public funds. The White Paper also confirms the BBC's obligation to maintain a minimum 25 percent content quota commissioned from the independent production sector. Since 2007, this has been augmented by the BBC's development of the Window of Creative Competition (WOCC[2]), which aims to commission a further 25 percent over and above the statutory quota.

The 2006 White Paper also tasked the BBC with driving digital development and promoting digital take-up among the public to enable digital switchover. Freedman (2008) argues that this will divert £600 million of the license fee and extend the political role of the BBC into delivering government policy outcomes. Nevertheless, this role was invited by the BBC in its license fee negotiations with the government and Ofcom. Indeed, the BBC's lead role in

Freeview was also understood by the BBC management as insulation from any shift away from the license fee to a subscription model because the technical standards were not suited for adaptation to pay TV (see Born 2004; Smith and Steemers 2007). This nevertheless underlines the normative shift in the basis upon which the license fee is legitimated between government, Ofcom, and industry. The implicit premise of the White Paper's support for the BBC's continued existence is its subsidy of the commercial broadcasting sector. As Freedman (2008: 169) surmises, such a policy framework is likely to "enshrine the corporation in market logic."

Ofcom has emphasized the need to support key content genres and had encouraged the BBC to form collaborative partnerships with other operators (involving the sharing of production facilities) to help sustain regional content (particularly news). In March 2009, the BBC signed an MOU with the ITV network to share news production facilities, ostensibly conferring up £120 million total value on its commercial rival. However, ITV chair Michael Grade (2009) has questioned the viability of the logistical restrictions and suggested that the £120 million value notionally allocated to regional news was exaggerated to dilute demands for top-slicing (cited in Holmwood 2009b). BBC director general Mark Thompson has publicly challenged Ofcom's "ideological" drive to top-slice the license fee, although Ofcom CEO Ed Richards rejects such allegations (cited in Holmwood 2009a).

The government's 2009 Digital Britain report (BIS/DCMS 2009), meanwhile, acknowledged that the BBC's partnerships are a positive development but suggested these measures may not be sufficient to compensate for intensifying commercial pressures. Given the reluctance of government to develop new funding mechanisms, the report argued that the license fee may need to be utilized differently. It endorsed top-slicing to provide a contestable fund independent of the BBC's editorial influence, arguing that "It is clear that funding could achieve substantially more per pound of input in the hands of new operators using new media than to sustain a legacy broadcast network and studios for regional news built in and for the days of surplus in the system" (BIS/DCMS 2009:142).

This is a contentious claim. The notion that a taxpayer pound invested in new commercial digital media services will provide greater public value than a pound invested in the BBC's commissioning of independent content under WOCC presupposes that public value includes economic expansion of the private media sector. This overlooks the relative inefficiency entailed by private operators' need to pay returns to shareholders that cannot be reinvested in production. Public subsidy of commercial PSM provision, therefore, entails an opportunity cost to the taxpayer.

The Digital Britain report (BIS/DCMS 2009) correctly points out that there is, in effect, already a precedent for redirecting some of the license fee to functions/actors external to the BBC, notably in regard to the funds being devoted to digital switchover. The independent production quota and WOCC commissions, and the BBC's planned partnerships with the commercial sector might arguably be regarded as a precedent to "top-slicing." In some respects, then, the redistribution of the license fee is already underway *within* the current hypothecated system, and what the BBC is fighting to retain is its degree of allocative control over this proportion of funds. Indeed, the recent growth in financial market interest in the independent production sector (Christophers 2010) reflects the recognition of opportunities to extract surplus value from commercial ventures subsidized by public revenue streams.

In October 2010, the new coalition government's Comprehensive Spending Review (CSR) announced sweeping cuts to spending across several public sectors, including broadcasting. Although the BBC persuaded the government to drop a proposal obliging free service provision to over-75s (at an annual cost of £556 million), the license fee has been frozen until 2016 and significant new financial obligations have been imposed, diverting part of the license fee to non-BBC services and government policy initiatives (Hewlett 2010). The *Financial Times* (2010) notes that these include an additional US$230 million subsidy of digital switchover costs for poor people by 2012, a £530 million subsidy of rural broadband expansion by 2016, and an ongoing responsibility for funding the BBC World Service[3] and the BBC Monitoring Service (costing £300 million per year) as well as the Welsh Language Service, S4C (costing £102 million per year). Although budget cuts will reduce the notional cost to the BBC to £340 million, the decision potentially constitutes an effective 16 percent reduction in the BBC's real spending power. Mark Thompson has suggested that the decision retains the BBC's independence and prevents it from becoming just another "arm of the welfare state" (quoted in Hewlett 2010). This seems disingenuous, however, because the CSR policy decisions effectively rescind the license fee's hypothecated status and subject it to arbitrary revisions just like any other State departmental budget.[4]

Despite the consequences of the CSR, the emergent media policy trajectory does not follow the standard neoliberal predilection for removing State interventions (see Jakubowicz 2006). Rather, the continued provision of PSM is legitimated within the nexus of government, regulators, and industry, but the normative premise underpinning State intervention has shifted away from serving the public interest toward subsidizing other areas of government policy and economic growth in the private media sector.

PSM in the New Zealand context

The neoliberal macroeconomic reforms New Zealand underwent from the mid-1980s onward went further than in most European countries (see Kelsey 1993; Jesson 1999). An abbreviated background on the impact this had on the broadcasting sector is needed to contextualize contemporary developments. Up to 1988, the main public broadcaster was BCNZ, which encompassed Television New Zealand (TVNZ) and Radio New Zealand (RNZ). BCNZ received a hypothecated public license fee supplemented by commercial advertising. Although private commercial competition in radio had been formally permitted since the 1970s, TVNZ remained a State monopoly. In 1988, BCNZ was split and RNZ and TVNZ became separate State-owned enterprises. As state-owned enterprises (SOEs), their primary statutory function was to operate as businesses and return dividends to the Crown.

The 1989 Broadcasting Act introduced commercial competition into the television sector for the first time in the form of TV3. The Broadcasting Commission (NZ On Air) was set up to fund proposals for local audiovisual content, and the license fee revenue was diverted to this function (although this was abolished in favor of a direct appropriation in 1999). NZ On Air set up a contestable fund for which both local broadcasters and independent producers were eligible, with the majority of this money being directed toward television programming (NZ$34 million in 1989 and NZ$91 million in 2009; NZ On Air 1990, 2009). However, the contestable fund requires the agreement of a national television network to screen the content, which means that the broadcasters can effectively veto applications where the opportunity costs of screening are deemed unattractive. Coupled with NZ On Air's decision to focus its limited funds on underprovided genres (including drama and children's content but excluding news and current affairs), this meant that the contestable funding mechanism never addressed a full range of PSM objectives. Indeed, it remained vulnerable to the commercial pressures for which it was intended to compensate (see Thompson 2000, 2004; Cocker 2005; Bardoel and d'Haenans 2008). Insofar as NZ On Air's establishment recognized the potential for market failure, the contestability principle was a concession to the neoliberal concern to ensure that State intervention avoided market distortion.

The 1990s saw further deregulation with the removal of restrictions on foreign media investments and key free-trade agreements with Australia (Closer Economic Relations (CER)), and the international GATS deal, which included agreements on audiovisual goods and services. Apart from basic competition laws overseen by the Commerce Commission and content standards overseen by the Broadcasting Standards Authority (BSA), there are very few limitations on advertising or cross-media ownership. The domestic media sector was, therefore, left open to international competition and media ownership, and the free-trade agreements effectively precluded the introduction of local content quotas. This paved the way for overseas corporate ownership of the majority of domestic media and, notably, the establishment of Sky Network Television, the satellite subscription television provider that is now the largest broadcasting operator in New Zealand. By the end of the 1990s, the National-led government was planning to privatize TVNZ, but the 1999 election saw a new Labour government come to power espousing a "third-way" approach that promised to redress the neoliberal excesses of the preceding 15 years. In contrast to the UK situation, the challenge was not primarily to defend the public service *status quo* from erosion but to regenerate it in a heavily liberalized and commercialized media market.

The New Labour approach to broadcasting came under challenge from the private media sector and the political right almost from its inception. It explicitly recognized the market failures of a heavily liberalized commercial media sector, but its third-way approach led to difficulties reconciling public service and commercial media imperatives. Reregulation focused primarily on the State broadcasters, leaving the commercial operators largely alone (see Thompson 2000; Comrie and Fountaine 2006). Policy tensions emerged between the Ministry for Culture and Heritage (MCH), the Treasury, and the Ministry for Economic Development (MED), which all had rather different priorities for the sector, and these were further complicated by the shifting interests of various broadcasting actors. The centerpiece of Labour's broadcasting reforms was the 2003 restructuring of TVNZ as a Crown Company with a dual remit comprising of a wide-ranging public service Charter and a continuing expectation of commercial dividends. This was accompanied by a government commitment to provide a modest direct subsidy to TVNZ (up to NZ$15 million per year, representing less than 5 percent of its operational expenses). Importantly, the range of public service functions covered by the Charter extended beyond the local content genres subsidized by NZ On Air, and this was made explicit in MCH advice on the Charter funding to the Minister (MCH 2002; Thompson 2004).

The move to implement even this modest level of direct funding was opposed by several institutional stakeholders. Because TVNZ remained dependent on commercial revenue (90 percent including both Charter money and content commissioned through NZ On Air), it continued to compete directly for substitutable audience share and advertising revenue. Consequently, its private commercial rivals understandably regarded the direct Charter subsidy as constituting market distortion because, unlike the NZ On Air contestable fund, they were ineligible to apply for a share. Mediaworks (the operator of TV3 and C4 as well as a range of radio stations, currently owned by Ironbridge Capital) was particularly aggrieved. As its (then) CEO Brent Impey argued, "Do we really believe the Charter was meant to provide an unfair advantage so the state broadcaster can take local programming from other broadcasters? ... [TVNZ] seems more interested in beating the competition instead of adding to the fabric of New Zealand" (Impey 2003). Meanwhile, the independent production sector lobby was concerned about the direct funding for the Charter because they considered this a revenue stream that would be retained for TVNZ in-house productions rather than made available to external bids. NZ On Air was also privately concerned about the Charter appropriation because they regarded direct broadcaster funding as an important policy shift away from their own contestable fund model and hence a threat to their institutional status, not least because TVNZ was lobbying to have its contestable fund redirected to Charter functions on the pretext that it was the only television operator with such obligations. As Thompson (2004, 2007) has pointed out, despite TVNZ's appeals to the government for a discontinuation of its commercial dividend obligations, the dual remit meant that TVNZ was literally being given money through the MCH only for the Treasury to claim it back, leaving it with a net subsidy that was actually *negative*!

It is interesting to note that while these political tensions were unfolding, the legitimacy of two other public sector broadcasters was left largely unquestioned. RNZ's direct subsidy (administered by NZ On Air and at over NZ$30 million, twice the level of the TVNZ Charter subsidy) was not (then) perceived to be distorting the market because RNZ did not compete for substitutable audience share and commercial revenue.[5] Meanwhile, the Maori Television Service (established in 2003) receives funding from both the Ministry for Maori Affairs Te Mangai Paho (the Maori equivalent of NZ On Air), each worth approximately NZ$16–17 million per annum. Although MTS does carry a small amount of advertising, this represents less than 5 percent of its revenue (almost the inverse of the TVNZ ratio). However, because MTS's primary function is the promotion of Te Reo (the indigenous language), it is likewise not generally regarded as competing for substitutable audience share and revenue.

Meanwhile, the challenges to the legitimacy of TVNZ's public service provisions have continued in regard to digital television. Interestingly, its self-proclaimed mission of "inspiring on every screen" and extending its services online (and via cell phone) through program catch-up services (TVNZ Ondemand [sic]) has proven to be remarkably uncontroversial in contrast with the concerns surrounding the BBC's expansion of services. However, TVNZ's lead role in the development of the NZ version of the digital Freeview platform has not escaped controversy. Freeview (NZ) is essentially identical to the UK version, and it operates on both DTS and DTT. Its development involved a consortium of free-to-air broadcasters, including TVNZ, MTS, RNZ, and Mediaworks.[6] The government regarded Freeview as an important initiative to encourage household take-up of digital reception technology in preparation for the (still unspecified) digital switchover. To this end, it agreed to invest NZ$25 million in supporting the technical infrastructure developments and provided free spectrum licenses to operators. However, there was political disagreement behind the government's decision to allocate NZ$79 million over 6 years to fund its two new commercial-free digital channels, TVNZ 6 and TVNZ 7,[7] and help drive the uptake of Freeview.

Despite the fact that this funding largely comprised the drip-fed return of a special NZ$70 million dividend TVNZ had paid to the Treasury as part of a

2006 capital restructuring exercise, different ministerial imperatives threatened to derail the initiative. As Thompson (2007) points out, the MCH supported the subsidy because the commercial-free TVNZ 6 and 7 would enable the development of distinctive schedules to enhance Charter provisions (although the funding streams were to be kept separate). The MED also supported the subsidy, but this was premised on an independent report showing that an early analog switch off by 2015 would help stimulate the digital media sector—a development estimated to represent over NZ$200 million in economic growth. The Treasury, however, initially refused to approve the funding, arguing that it did not regard the investment as good (public) value for money (see Office of the Minister of Broadcasting 2006). High-level cabinet negotiations and recognition that the TVNZ dividend would decline were it obliged to subsidize both channels in their entirety from its commercial revenue eventually pushed the decision in TVNZ's favor. This reveals the complex institutional tensions between different Ministerial interests and indicates the differing contextual rationales underpinning the legitimation of PSM arrangements.

Nevertheless, when the funding decision was announced, it was immediately criticized by Mediaworks, which complained that the subsidy constituted market distortion. Brent Impey suggested TVNZ's funding represented "the use of taxpayer funding to subsidize a failing commercial business—it essentially amounts to a bail-out" (Impey 2006), while Rick Friesen, the head of TV, argued that they would have been willing to provide a service comparable to TVNZ 6 and 7 had they been permitted to bid for it (Friesen 2007). These arguments are significant because they represent a shift in the normative assumptions underpinning the legitimation of PSM provisions in the private commercial sector. Mediaworks' criticism was aimed at commercial-free PSM services on a platform that was still very limited in audience uptake and would not be competing for substitutable audience share or advertising revenue. This suggests an increasing sense of entitlement, implicitly assuming that *any and all* PSM funding distorts the market unless it is made contestable. Interestingly, it is the contestability rather than the actual allocation that appears to be the point of contention (TVNZ is not criticized for being the end beneficiary of the lion's share of the NZ On Air funding).

By the end of 2008, TVNZ's Charter and public funding arrangements had been roundly criticized by the government, the opposition, and its commercial rivals. This largely reflected the complex dual PSM/commercial remit and a level of funding disproportionately small compared with the expectations the Charter's scope engendered (see Thompson 2004; Comrie and Fountaine 2005; Lealand 2008). However, TVNZ was also complicit in undermining its own position because of a lack of transparency over the way it was using the funding. In 2008, a new National-led government was elected. It moved quickly to redirect the NZ$15 million Charter funding (which had never been hypothecated in the 2003 TVNZ Act) to NZ On Air, establishing a second contestable "Platinum Fund" to enable commissioning of more specific PSB-type content (NZ On Air 2010). This was welcomed by NZ On Air as well as the independent production sector and TVNZ's commercial rivals. The minister of broadcasting has argued that in the digital broadcasting environment, there is no need for a dedicated PSM provider so long as high-quality content is made available (Media 7, 2009). The new fund, however, remains subject to many of the structural limitations of the local content fund in that proposals require an agreement to broadcast and cannot ensure content decision are insulated from the imperatives of commercial scheduling.

Another recent development has been the commercial radio sector's challenges to RNZ's requests for additional public funding to maintain its services. The government informed RNZ that its funding was to be frozen and would need to deliver more operational efficiency to meet its budget restriction, citing the economic downturn as necessitating austerity. However, RNZ cited an independent report by KPMG/MCH (2007) that concluded that RNZ was already highly efficient in its budgeting and was actually chronically underfunded. Mediaworks' Brent Impey commented that it was "galling" and "outrageous" for a public broadcaster to ask for additional funding while its commercial rivals were suffering declining incomes in a tight economic environment and suggested that public sector media ought to have their funding cut by 15–20 percent to level the playing field with the commercial sector (quoted in Drinnan 2009). Interestingly, these objections are aimed at a heretofore noncontentious public revenue stream that funds a dedicated public broadcaster not competing for substitutable audience or revenue. Indeed, Impey even argued that PSM ought to be *penalized* to help compensate the private sector for the downturn in commercial revenues. Thus, the private media sector is responding to shifts in the commercial value chain by claiming a natural right to priority access to any and all audiences and revenue streams: Public service must stand aside to accommodate the imperative of private capital accumulation.

Meanwhile, the TVNZ Charter has been scheduled for abolition in 2010, but the amendment bill does not return TVNZ to SOE status and retains some generic PSB requirements, including universal service and content range and quality (Thompson 2010a). Meanwhile, the government has indicated that it wishes to retain TVNZ 6 and/or 7 in some form but has thus far been unwilling to commit to funding them. If they move to a commercial funding base, the distinctive character of their schedules will be eroded. It appears that the government does not wish to publicly abandon PSM commitments altogether but remains unwilling to provide adequate funding. The abolition of the TVNZ Charter represents a serious dilution of PSM functions. However, in contrast to the EU scenarios where the evolution of PSM is quarantined by increasingly specific definitions of legitimate functions (Jakubowicz 2006), the NZ strategy involves circumscription of PSM through strategic ambiguity, leaving TVNZ accountable to nothing except the government's transitory policy priorities.

The National government's predilection for a market-driven approach to broadcasting is nevertheless becoming clear in other ways. The government's decision to abandon a major planned review of regulations for digital broadcasting and content appears to reflect an active aversion to investigating policy issues that might demand regulatory intervention in the market (Thompson 2009). Meanwhile, TVNZ was encouraged to abandon its long-standing refusal to allow TVNZ 6 and 7 to be carried on Sky's platform. Moreover, TVNZ's recent decision to launch its new archived content channel "Heartland" exclusively on Sky's platform effectively means that half the households in New Zealand will be disenfranchised from their own televisual heritage unless they subscribe to a foreign pay-TV provider. As John Fellett, CEO of Sky TV, succinctly commented, "This vault of content which includes some of New Zealand's most beloved shows is the biggest untapped resource since the Maui oil fields" (Sky TV 2010). TVNZ will profit from the venture, but this move clearly involves the transformation of a public good into a private one.

Conclusions

The United Kingdom and New Zealand cases are distinctive, but they also exhibit some interesting similarities in recent media policy trajectories. These cannot be assumed to be a direct consequence of macro-political-economic conditions, however. The outcomes of these conditions are manifested through the specific institutional responses they motivate within the respective media ecologies of both countries. Table 10.1 identifies some of the divergences and convergences that emerge from the analysis undertaken in this chapter.

The struggles over the BBC license fee and TVNZ's Charter and digital channel funding are both indicative of moves by the private media sector to gain access to public revenue streams and/or to prevent PSM providers from enjoying privileged access to them. In both national cases, private sector lobbyists have deployed neoliberal market discourses framing PSM provisions as an infringement on the commercial sector's presumed entitlement to prioritized access to any and all audiences and revenues, and sought to curb PSM providers' role in the evolving media landscape. Neoliberal discourses conflate the development of digital media platforms and services with public service functions but may legitimate State support for PSM if this is "platform-neutral" and not restricted to public sector institutions. Political actors within government and State sector institutions, in turn, are also increasingly driven by economic priorities and thus often appear to regard the commodification of new media spaces as beneficial to economic growth. The result is both the BBC and TVNZ find themselves ever more tightly squeezed by the private commercial media operators *and* government. Despite research in both the United Kingdom and New Zealand showing that audiences value PSM provisions as citizens even

Table 10.1 Common and distinctive elements of the UK and NZ media ecologies

	UK case	NZ case
Political economic/ policy conditions	Both underwent extended periods of neoliberal macroeconomic reforms followed by extended periods of third-way policy revisions, with a recent return to governments with neoliberal priorities	
Shape of media ecology	Mixed model but with public service obligations as default, including private free-to-air broadcasters	Highly commercialized model, including State-owned enterprises with public service obligations as the exception
	Both media ecologies have suffered from the economic downturn coupled with increasing competition for ratings and revenue from other platforms. Also, the expansion of a dominant pay-TV provider has intensified market pressure on free-to-air operators (excepting the BBC and RNZ) and increased opportunity costs of PSM provision	
Regulatory arrangements	Integrated media regulator (Ofcom) with responsibility for both public service and commercial/economic functions. Increasing pressure to accommodate demands of private media operators to dilute PSM obligations	*Laissez faire* model with Commerce Commission to oversee free-market competition and Broadcasting Standards Authority (BSA) to regulate content standards. TVNZ Charter to be abolished. Planned review of media regulatory provisions canceled, although free-to-air operators concerned about market share of pay-TV provider
New media issues	BBC's extension into online services is challenged by commercial operators and is subjected to European Commission (EC) regulations on public service provisions	TVNZ's commercial extension into digital platforms and online services regarded as unproblematic by commercial sector
	Expansion of digital media services are conflated with public service functions in neoliberal policy discourses and used to legitimate "platform-neutral" funding provisions that include private sector	

(Continued)

Table 10.1 Continued

	UK case	NZ case
Public service media funding issues	BBC's license fee subject to challenges from both commercial operators and other government/regulator priorities, coupled with EC demands for specified proportional PSM funding	Contestable funding mechanisms for local content and Maori TV are legitimated. Noncontestable PSM funding mechanisms excluding private sector are opposed by commercial operators
	BBC's license fee retained but hypothecated status compromised by obligations to support digital/broadband policy, S4C, and private media sector	TVNZ's direct funding rescinded and made contestable under new New Zealand On Air (NZOA) fund. TVNZ 6 & 7's future remains uncertain after Charter
	Both cases are indicative of a normative shift toward legitimating State funding for public service media on the basis of broader economic policy functions and the eligibility of private sector media as beneficiaries of such measures	

when their consumer preferences are different (Human Capital/BBC 2004; Synovate/MCH 2007), civic voices are often subordinated to the discourses promoted by vested political-economic interests, including the commercial media operators.

The recognition of shifts in the commercial value chain and fragmentation of audience share and revenues do not mean that private sector media cannot be reasonably expected to sustain public service obligations or that public revenue streams should be cannibalized in order to subsidize commercial operators. The proliferation of channels and platforms and the tendency toward audience fragmentation do not directly translate into lost revenue due to the increased premium that advertisers place on any medium capable of delivering a mass audience (Christophers 2010). Nevertheless, the inevitable intensification of competition across providers and platforms does squeeze operational margins, with contradictory consequences for policy. On the one hand, these pressures are cited by the private media sector to legitimate appeals for increased access to public revenue streams (through either contestability or diversions of funds from top-slicing previously hypothecated license fees). As Syvertsen succinctly observes, "the idea is that unless broadcasting companies are reimbursed in some way, they cannot be expected to provide the level of diversity and quality that society expects of them" (Syvertsen 2003: 164). On the other hand, however, it is also becoming apparent that there is likely to be declining efficiency in giving taxpayer dollars to private commercial operators to pursue public service aims, particularly since for-profit media must always deliver a surplus to shareholders that cannot be allocated to programming. This requires relatively higher levels of subsidy to render public service production/scheduling viable and offset their propensity toward market failure.

The recent return to power of center-right governments in both the United Kingdom and New Zealand suggests that the default policy trajectory is likely to continue toward a dismantling of PSM provisions and a diversion of public revenue streams toward subsidizing private media operators. However, the interplay of different institutions as they negotiate regulatory and fiscal conditions can shape political-economic outcomes. The scope of policy options available to governments is subject to contestation, and the deployment of policy frames and discourses to (de)legitimate PSM provisions suggests the current trajectory can be challenged. However, that does not mean such efforts will be effective. Private media corporations lobbying for further curbs on public service provisions have so far engaged effectively with policy-makers and helped form the political channels of action that give them access to public sector revenues and audiences, while PSM are left running on empty.

Notes

1 Ofcom gave consideration to the creation of a contestable fund to support independent PSB content production (rather like the NZ On Air contestable fund), but as Graham (2005) notes, it recognized a potential problem in ensuring adequate distribution in a multimedia environment. It then promoted the notion of a public service publisher (PSP) that would provide a vertically integrated commissioner/distributor (which is similar in principle to the original Channel 4 arrangement prior to it becoming directly funded through its own commercial advertising).

2 In effect, the WOCC is a kind of contestable funding system within the BBC itself that allows proposals from both in-house and independent producers to "ensure that the best ideas are commissioned for our audiences irrespective of who makes the programs" and "ensure a level playing field between all suppliers" (BBC Commissioning, no date; see also Christophers 2010).

3 The BBC World Service has heretofore been funded through the Foreign Office. More recently, even the interim "grant-in-aid" provided by the Foreign Office up to 2014 has itself been cut as a CSR measure, necessitating the closure of several of the BBC's foreign-language services (see Thompson 2011).

4 Hewlett (2010) points out that the BBC's willingness to sign up for additional financial responsibilities (such as contributing to digital switchover) as part of the previous round of license fee discussions set a dangerous precedent, which the coalition government has fully exploited. In effect, this opened the door to further compromises in regard to the license fee's hypothecated status.

5   RNZ National deals primarily with news, current affairs, and other factual content, while RNZ Concert is the classical music station. The audience demographic is, therefore, unlikely to be interested in the typical commercial radio focus on popular music and low-brow, talk-back shows, meaning that they do not represent a zero-sum loss to the commercial market.

6   Prime TV was originally part of this group but withdrew in 2006 when it was acquired by Sky—to which Freeview is both a technical and commercial rival.

7   TVNZ 6 carries children's content during daytime, family content in the late afternoon/early evening, and arts, drama, and documentary later in the evening. TVNZ 7 carries news, current affairs, and sports.

11

Mediation, Financialization, and the Global Financial Crisis

An inverted political economy perspective

Aeron Davis

University of London

Introduction

This chapter looks at two distinct but related phenomena: the expansion of financial and business news, and the growth of financialization in Anglo-Saxon-style, free-market economies. Both of these postwar trends have been documented in different scholarly fields. The questions are how, if at all, are these developments related and, what, if any, have been the possible consequences of this relationship?

The chapter adopts what I elsewhere call an *inverted political economy of communication framework* (Davis 2007). This critical approach still assumes power originates, is played out, and recorded in material forms. However, it chooses to reverse the traditional, critical media political economy line, which explores how powerful groups and institutions, and political and economic factors shape media content and public understanding in a top-down way. Instead, it takes those sites of power, elite actors and processes, operating at the tops or centers of political and economic power, and then asks the following: What is the part played by media and culture in the activities of those actors and in the evolution of those processes?

Employing this perspective, the chapter focuses on the communicative and cultural mechanisms that link established economic and political elites to processes of financialization. The key argument is that the significance of financial media has lain in its ability to disseminate a series of discourses, narratives, and myths, about finance itself, to *financial and associated stakeholder elites*. A combination of such general discourses and more specific narratives have supported a series of high-level policy and investment decisions that, over time, have aided the growth of financialization and its dangerous creations. Ultimately, these trends have both destabilized the financial sector and sucked the resources of States and ordinary individuals into financial markets. The mechanisms and consequences of these long-term developments became painfully apparent as the financial system began to collapse in 2007 and a global recession resulted.

The chapter focuses on developments in the United States and the United Kingdom. These two countries both have overinflated financial centers, produce extensive financial news media and trading information, promote a particular brand of global, finance-led capitalism, and have suffered strongly from the recent financial crises. The chapter has four sections. The first charts the parallel, postwar growths of finance, financialization, and financial media. The second discusses how such developments are related. It makes the case that the focus of this relationship should be on *financial and associated stakeholder elites* and the *elite discourse networks* that link them. The third details larger financial market discourses and narratives and their impact on financial and associated elites. The fourth looks more closely at the recent market crises in internet company shares, property, banking, and financial products, and speculates further on the role of financial media in those.

The rise of financialization and the rise of financial media

Banking and financial centers have always been key components of large-scale capitalist societies. Over time they have come to provide vital functions for the state, corporations, and the general public. From governments balancing their books and controlling the money supply to corporations raising investment capital, to retail banking for ordinary citizens, they have a central role to play in capitalist democracies.

However, in recent decades, things have changed. A process of financialization has taken place. The term "financialization" has varying definitions. In its broader descriptions (see e.g. Philips 2006; Palley 2007), financial sectors have come to play a more dominant part relative to the economy as a whole, swallowed up and come to control significantly larger amounts of capital than either governments or nonfinancial corporations, and have been increasingly influential in government policy-making with regard to social, economic, and industrial policy. Thus, where once financial institutions made profits from servicing the financial needs of their economy and society, now they have become large-scale entities that increasingly influence the very workings of those economies and societies.

So, for example, in 2007, the gross domestic product (GDP) of the United Kingdom was estimated to be £1.24 trillion (IMF 2008), and the total managed annual expenditure of the UK government was £587 billion. However, in that same year, members of the UK-based Investment Management Association controlled £3.4 trillion worth of funds (IMA (Investment Management

Association) 2007). Also, in 2007, US$3 trillion worth of currency was traded on international exchanges daily (Steger 2009: 49), and the international banking system operated funds of US$512 trillion or 10 times the GDP value of the entire world economy (Cable 2009: 30, 146). Under such circumstances, the financial sector has outgrown the economies and states they once served. According to pre-2007 critical accounts (e.g. Strange 1986, 1998; Dore 2000; Soderberg, Menz, and Cerny 2005; Zorn, Dobbin, Dierkes, and Kwok 2005; Froud, Johal, Leaver, and Williams 2006), the processes of financialization have, by virtue of this power, contributed to a number of worrying political and economic developments. These include a decline in the power of democratically elected governments to manage their economies, being a driving force of neoliberal economic policy from antiunion legislation to deregulation, a spur to global trading imbalances, the crude imposition of IMF/"Washington Consensus" economic policies on developing economies, the destruction and/or drastic reshaping of traditional industries and the erosion of welfare systems in developed economies, a source of unstable currency and commodity values, and a cause of economic instability, bubbles, and crashes. In post-2007 accounts (e.g. Krugman 2008; Bootle 2009; Cable 2009; Elliott and Atkinson 2009; United Nations Centre for Trade and Development (UNCTAD) 2009), the financial crisis and world recession that has followed are directly tied to an out-of-control financial and banking system, led by a particularly "Anglo-Saxon" model of finance-led capitalism.

A parallel but distinct development has been the rise of financial media. Business and financial news has been circulating, in the press and newsletters, since the establishment of financial centers, largely in the eighteenth and nineteenth centuries (see Parsons 1989). For many, such forms of news expanded substantially in advanced economies after the Second World War and then, again, from the late 1970s onward (see Curran 1978; Newman 1984; Berkman and Kitch 1986; Davis 2002; Kjaer 2010). A mixture of interest from a wealthier public, and a strong rise in financial advertising, spurred this expansion. Financial advertising tripled in the period 1975–83 (Newman 1984: 221). By the late 1980s, Jones (1987) and Tunstall (1996) were concluding that the financial press had become the leading news sector in the United Kingdom's serious press. Similar expansions were noted in the US press and in broadcasting and specialist media in both countries (Tumber 1993; Shiller 2001; Cassidy 2002). Most recently, online financial news, information feeds, blogs, and other sites have also proliferated (Knorr-Cetina and Bruegger 2002; Sassen 2005; Davis 2006).

Clearly, financialization and financial media have had parallel upward trajectories. The question is how intertwined and codependent have these developments been? Of more central concern to this chapter, how has the growth of financial media contributed to the growth and shape of Anglo-Saxon-style, financialized capitalist economies? Has it had a central role to play in the most recent bubbles and crashes as well as the evolution of an unstable and unequal financial system?

Explaining the relationship between financialization and financial media

For mainstream economists and liberal/middle-ground media scholars, financial media has had little significant influence. In standard market models and classical economics, media is virtually irrelevant. The same is true of financial market theory, as is generally relayed in subject text books (e.g. Reilley and Brown 2000; Bodie, Kane, and Marcus 2003). The efficient markets hypothesis (EMH, see Fama 1970), which has dominated finance theory and practice in the postwar period, relies on notions of individual rationality and market equilibrium. Prices and equilibrium are reached by the absorption of all market-relevant information by large numbers of rational, self-serving individuals competing to buy and sell. Markets may be affected temporarily by irrational individuals or externals such as media, but ultimately always find their rational equilibrium. Although, it should be noted, with some irony, that many in high finance were happy to blame the media, at least initially, when the financial system began collapsing, domino-like, in 2008. Liberal, reflectionist accounts in media scholarship also present media as having a minimal role in events, society, and economy. Media reporting, including that in finance and business, reflects rather than influences society. In specific accounts of the rise of financial and business news (Gavin 2007; Kjaer 2010; Tambini 2010), it has developed a relatively balanced, autonomous reporting style that responds to the requirements of a more affluent general public. The failure to spot recent market crashes (2000, 2007) or fraudulent companies (Enron, Worldcom) is more to do with the natural limits of reporting practice, rather than any systemic bias or ideological leaning.

Outside mainstream economics, a mix of economic historians, behavioral and left-wing economists and practitioners, have shown rather more skepticism about classical economics and financial market theory (Keynes 1936; Shiller 1989, 2001; Soros 1994; Kindleberger 2000; Krugman 2008; Bootle 2009; Akerlof and Shiller 2009). Each of these accounts focuses on market instabilities and externalities and the irrational behavior (animal spirits) of individuals and groups. In some of these, media have, on occasion, played a significant role in fueling herd behavior, bubbles, and crashes (Shiller 1989, 2001; Cassidy 2002). Critical economists have been joined by critical media scholars. They argue that there are structural and ideological biases deeply ingrained in media reporting and that these favor capitalism and the corporate classes who benefit from them.

This has been the case in relation to media reporting of industrial relationships, economic policy, and high finance (Jenson 1987; Philo 1995; Rampton and Stauber 2002; Dinan and Miller 2007). Certainly, many ordinary people have been encouraged to put their life savings into the purchase of internet stocks at the peak of the dot-com bubble or to buy overvalued homes they could not afford in the long term (subprime mortgages) (see Shiller 2001; Cassidy 2002; Cable 2009).

Arguably, although both perspectives offer useful insights, neither deals adequately with the financialization–financial media relationship. The classical economics/reflectionist media perspective fails to engage with the realities of human behavior, or external social and economic influences, in its abstract modeling of markets and media. As Soros states (1994: 11), financial market theory "is a theoretical construct of great elegance that resembles natural science but does not resemble reality." Similarly, media are never simply a neutral reflection of society that play a minimal part in social relations.

However, the second critical position rather overplays the weight and influence of media when it comes to financial matters, financialization, and the general public. First, the day-to-day direct impact of the financial media on finance is likely to be limited. The size of the media industries is tiny when set next to those of many industrial and financial sectors. As with all professional occupations in society, those in the financial world rely relatively little on information they pick up from the "amateur" observers working in the media. They have access to a plethora of specialists, information sources, and key players. Second, whatever the intentions of journalists, their ability to investigate or criticize the financial center is limited. Financial reporting, compared to other areas of journalism, is far more dependent on business advertising than general consumer sales and subscriptions. Business and finance are also highly complex topics that most journalists struggle to understand and keep up with (see Davis 2002; Doyle 2006; Tambini 2010). Third, public understanding of, and participation in, financial affairs is also relatively limited. One survey (Tunstall 1996: 217) recorded that only 6 percent of readers of *The Sun*, *The Daily Mail*, and *The Times* in the United Kingdom chose to read "personal finance" sections, and only 4 percent looked at the "business and companies" sections. Goddard, Corner, Gavin, and Richardson (1998) found that public understanding of economic matters was very weak. According to one report (London Stock Exchange 1996), when share ownership was nearing its peak in the United Kingdom, only 3 percent of individual shareholders were active traders, and only 6 percent had ever attended a company annual general meeting (AGM). Thus, to suggest that financial media have had a significant impact on the growth and shape of financialization or on public understanding seems rather far-fetched. To argue that financial media had a starring role in the recent financial market bubbles and crashes of recent decades seems almost absurd.

However, I would argue that financial media has played a significant supportive, rather than primary, role. Its most important influence has been something less obvious, rational, or technically sophisticated. Its impact has lain in its ability to build and perpetuate certain discourses, narratives, and myths among financial and related stakeholder elite groups. Its power has been ideological and cultural, at the elite rather than public level. This is because the discourses, ideologies, and decision-making about the economy, corporate practices, and financial regulation have been decided largely by small elite groups and networks. These activities, in turn, have been aided by a mixture of mainstream financial media and more exclusive forms of communication.

Looking just at financial media, it is financial and corporate elites who are the main advertisers, sources, and consumers of financial and business news (although not on all aspects of the economy, see Gavin 2007). Indeed, several studies (Parsons 1989; Herman 1982; Hutton 1996; Bennett, Pickard, Iozzi, Schroeder, Lagos, and Caswell 2004; Davis 2007; Durham 2007; Corcoran and Fahy 2009) have noted that such media coverage, in effect, revolves around economic elites in dialog and conflict with each other, all to the exclusion of the general public. In Parson's (1989: 2) historical account of the financial press, Keynes, Galbraith, Samuelson, and Friedman have all made their impact on policy-makers through their frequent, public interventions in the financial media. At different times, the financial press have come to "constitute a significant medium through which economic ideas and opinions are legitimated ... a unique interpreter, less of mass opinion than of the views and values of a more limited and narrower elite" (Parson 1989: 2).

In effect, most financial and corporate reporting is produced by and for elites operating in these linked spheres. Yes, many economic and industrial issues do hit the headlines from time to time. However, on a day-to-day basis, the activities and decision-making of financial and corporate elites go largely unnoticed and often unreported. So do the weighty discussions of economic policy of governments, regulatory bodies, and international financial institutions such as the IMF, World Bank, and WTO. If, therefore, financial media has influenced financial and business activities, and contributed to the growth of financialization, it is likely to be among elites. Before exploring this issue, it is worth first clarifying what specific elites and financial media are being referred to.

In terms of elites, the following discussion focuses on financial and *associated stakeholder elites*—those with some form of stake in financialization. Financial elites are those who work at the higher levels of financial and banking institutions, in investment and retail banks, in fund management, as brokers and other intermediaries. Associated stakeholder elites are those in the corporate, political, and regulatory/bureaucratic communities, at both the national and international levels. They relate to financial elites by virtue of a set of dependencies, management and regulatory responsibilities. It would be a mistake to assume these elites act together and with identical goals and objectives. In fact, there are many points of tension on policy matters and in relationships and dependencies between these overlapping elite networks as well as within them. Each of these networks also makes use of overlapping but distinct forms of media and communication, be it mass media, specialist publications, or electronic exchanges and forums. At the same time, it is important to note that such elites also share important goals, discourses, and media and information sources. In various ways, they have all come to rely on the growth and success of financialization. This combination of a shared interest in financialization but divergent goals, knowledge bases, and information sources is very significant, as explained in the next section.

The relevant mainstream financial media being considered are a select group of financial publications and business channels. These include the *Financial Times, The Wall Street Journal, International Herald Tribune, The Economist, Time, Newsweek* as well as the financial programs and reporting of BBC World, CNN (CNNI/CNNfn), CNBC, News Corporation, and Bloomberg. As several studies have noted (Kantola 2006, 2009; Davis 2007; Durham 2007; Chalaby 2009; Corcoran and Fahy 2009), these media are widely consumed in all of these overlapping elite networks. Their reporting and commentaries are taken very seriously by both financial and associated stakeholder elites, if only because of the awareness that they are widely consumed among fellow and rival elites. They thus make up an important communicative architecture that supports and links such networks. In theory, such communicative structures are also likely to generate and sustain a variety of discourses, cultures, narratives, and practices.

Therefore, I would suggest that the most important contribution of financial media to financialization has been its provision of cultural discursive networks through which financial and related elites communicate—on both a conscious and an unconscious level. Such an apparatus has played a supportive role in developing a number of key discourses in general support of financialization and neoliberal, free-market economics and particular narratives justifying irrational/unstable trends in regulation and investment.

The creation of financial market discourses and narratives

One such discourse presents the financial centers of the City of London and Wall Street as key engines of growth and prosperity for the United Kingdom and United States, respectively. In today's globalized world, where countries are developing specialist labor markets, the United Kingdom and United States excel in the business of finance. In recent decades, the financial sectors of both nations have grown immensely, bringing employment, large tax revenues, and impressive balance of trade surpluses with other countries. In the United States, in 2007, although the financial sector made up only 8 percent of the economy, it was responsible for 40 percent of domestic corporate profits (Bootle 2009: 113).

In the United Kingdom, at the turn of the twenty-first century, the City employed an estimated 300,000 people, had recorded an average growth of 7 percent per year for 25 years, and a consistent annual overseas trade surplus in the tens of billions (Golding 2004: 10). According to Hutton (1996), Elliot and Atkinson (2009), and Cable (2009), this faith in the UK financial center has been clear across government and financial regulatory services. As Cable puts it (2009: 26), "After the decline of much of Britain's manufacturing industry, the City emerged as a national success story … an image of buccaneering, innovative entrepreneurship … Governments were seduced by this narrative." It is also assumed that these profits have then filtered through to the rest of the population, encouraging a sense of financial democracy, greater home ownership, and general prosperity (the "trickle-down effect" of wealth creation and dispersion in the United States). Recent assessments of the UK financial services industry, by Wigley (2008) and Bischoff and Darling (2009), very much repeat and concur with this line of argument, despite the very real costs and problems that have surfaced since 2007 (see CRESC 2009).

A second discourse relates to financial market theory and the EMH (see above). As many critics now point out, EMH-influenced thinking has provided the rational and directive parameters for deregulation of the financial markets since the early 1980s (Pratten 1993; Davis 2007; Akerlof and Shiller 2009; Bootle 2009). In regulatory terms, its credo is, eliminate outside (government or other) interference and markets will always look after themselves. The financial markets have thus become self-managing, almost mythical-like entities that, it is assumed, will always overcome human fallibilities. Such beliefs were regularly recorded in interviews and surveys of fund managers and other participants in London's financial markets (Lazar 1990; Davis 2007). In each case, there was a general expectation that the market, if not always correct in the short term, would be so in the long term.

Third, and related to EMH thinking, there has been a tendency to assume all nonfinancial markets (e.g. industrial, labor) operate best if working like liberated financial markets. Several authors record such thinking among the United Kingdom's financial elite networks (Hill 1990; Lazar 1990; Hutton 1996; Boswell and Peters 1997; Davis 2007). Anything that hinders markets, such as collectivism, strong unions, and greater state intervention, through taxation, regulation, or redistribution, is deemed a hindrance. In contrast, privatization, competition, deregulation, and lower taxes are deemed positive for markets. Consequently, City support for free-market parties, such as the Conservatives or Republicans, is particularly high. In the 1997 General Election, in the face of Labour's landslide victory, 69 percent voted Conservative and only 7 percent voted Labour (MORI 1997). In 2004, some 41 percent of UK fund managers supported the reelection of George Bush, and only 9 percent supported John Kerry (Merrill Lynch 2004). Such thinking and market assumptions are regularly relayed in the financial press (Davis 2000a; Doyle

2006; Kantola 2006). Doyle's (2006: 446) study of financial reporting, in the wake of the Enron scandal, found that "several" financial journalists interviewed "readily acknowledged that passivity in relation to pro-market ideologies is fairly characteristic of the sector."

A fourth discourse revolves around globalization, free trade, and the general freeing up of international markets. This discourse regularly supports the interests of international (often Western-based) financial institutions and investors over national governments and democratic processes. Durham's (2007) analysis of the *Financial Times*'s (*FT*) coverage of the Thai currency crisis in 1997 produced "a consistent ideological position" that elevated IMF accounts and demands over those of the Thai government (see Krugman's 2008 critique). Similarly, Kantola's (2006) analysis of *FT* content reveals that its coverage of some 32 elections between 2000 and 2005 repeatedly backed candidates who supported pro-market reforms and was critical of democracies, publics, and leaders who did not (see also Kantola 2009). Likewise, Bennett *et al.*'s (2004) study of the reporting of the World Economic Forum at Davos found that the dominant reporting frames strongly promoted the interests and policy positions of such financial elites over those of citizens and activists.

Financial media not only has played a part in the creation and circulation of financial and free-market discourses generally but also has had a significant role in the generation and sustenance of a series of specific market narratives. These have helped spur and justify a lighter regulatory regime and several irrational market movements and investment bubbles in recent decades. Such narratives have supported financial elite actions and persuaded associated stakeholder elites (as well as ordinary citizens) that such activities were safe and, also, to buy directly into these bubbles (see accounts in Kindleberger 2000; Shiller 2001; Krugman 2008; Akerlof and Shiller 2009). From the mystique of the Nobel-prize-winning economists who ran Long-Term Capital Management to the mythologies surrounding the Asian tiger economies, stories have accompanied "rational" actor participation. In each case, such stories and myths have been widely repeated and circulated in the financial media.

One key, recurring narrative that has supported the various bubbles in internet stocks, property, and financial products, since the early 1990s, has been that of the "new economy." Financial and associated stakeholder elites as well as the financial media have frequently referred to "the new-era economy," "the creative" or "knowledge-based economy," and the "end of the traditional business cycle." This narrative is tied to "an era of permanently low inflation and low interest rates," "globalization," the rise of the "service sector," and the "taming of unions and labour inflexibility" (see Shiller 2001; Cassidy 2002; Turner 2008; Krugman 2008). As trading values have become increasingly disconnected from real asset values and historical measures, elements of "the new economy" have been used to justify these discrepancies. For several observers, such narratives have been uncritically relayed and magnified by elements of the financial press and broadcasting. For Cassidy (2002) and Shiller (2001), *The Wall Street Journal*, the new financial news channels (CNBC, CNNfn, Bloomberg), as well as certain websites and specialist financial journals all fed the earlier dot-com boom and reinforced the rhetoric of "new economy." Cable (2009) is similarly critical of the media's portrayal of the property market, as a safe "one-way bet" perpetuated by ever-increasing demand in the new, low-inflation economy of the past decade.

The financial media have not created these mythical discourses and narratives. But they have endlessly circulated them, rarely subjected them to critical scrutiny, and frequently presented them as unquestionable realities. They have spread them to financial insider and outsider stakeholder elites. They have ensured that critics have been marginalized and policy choices limited to those that fit with an ideologically narrow interpretive framework.

Bubbles, ponzi schemes, and crashes: virtual discourses and financial realities

As stated, financial media cannot be held particularly responsible either for the dangerous deregulation of financial markets since the 1980s or for the extreme market bubbles and crashes that have followed. However, it has aided and abetted the creation and circulation of a number of discourses and narratives that have underwritten such developments. These, in effect, have made highly irrational market developments appear quite rational. The consequences have been felt far beyond financial markets and their elite participants. In each case, a series of giant ponzi schemes or chain letters have been facilitated through financial centers. These have centered on internet stocks, property, and financial market products. In each case, large amounts of public and individual money have been sucked into these markets. This has allowed financial elite insiders, at the top of these schemes, to profit and then leave, while outsider stakeholder elites and the public have been left with the losses and debts. As the dust clears, it is becoming apparent that the price of sustaining the financial and banking sectors has been a huge rise in personal and government debt and the destabilization of governments and public institutions.

In the case of the hi-tech bubble of the 1990s, and its collapse in 2000, the part played by creative narratives and fairy-tale accounting is now evident (see accounts in Shiller 2001; Cassidy 2002; Golding 2004; Davis, 2007). From the mid-1990s, stock markets began to boom, driven by the new telecommunication and internet industries. The Telecommunications, Media, Technology (TMT) boom, or dot-com bubble, was talked up by entrepreneurs, financial market participants, and journalists. However, these new industries did not have a trading history, often had no assets, produced no profits or dividends, and therefore, could not be valued by usual accounting measures. So, instead, stockbrokers, analysts, investors, and companies came up with their own means of evaluation that ignored conventional forms of valuation and historical trading patterns. The stock markets exploded. From 1995 to 2000, the New York Dow Jones more than tripled in value—from below 3,500 points to just under 12,000. The London Stock Market went from just over 3,000 points to almost 7,000 points. The value of stock markets as a whole became entirely detached from long-term, traditional, real-world measures. Prices, relative to company earnings (P/E ratios), tripled in that period and were rather more out of alignment than during the previous record set in 1929, just before the Wall Street Crash (see Smithers and Wright 2000; Shiller 2001). Individual internet company stocks rose dramatically. In 1998 alone, Yahoo!'s value was up 584 percent, Amazon's, 970 percent, and America Online, 593 percent. Priceline.com, an online company for selling excess airline capacity, was worth US$150 billion or more than the entire airline industry (figures in Cassidy 2002: 8, 169). Ultimately, in the collapse that began in 2000, both the US and UK stock markets lost over half their value. Many TMT companies became worthless. Crucially, financial coverage failed to adequately question such developments and, in some cases, actively promoted the "new economy" narrative that underpinned them (Shiller 2001; Cassidy 2002; Davis 2007).

The responses of governments and central banks were neither fundamental regulatory reform of the sector nor the enablement of a proper market correction in stock markets. Instead, markets, financial and other, were boosted by low interest rates and other fiscal stimuli, leading to further bubbles. Most obvious among these were the wildly overinflated property markets, including that of the highly risky "subprime" mortgage market in the United States. Once again, by various historical measures, the value of property departed from "real economy" norms quite considerably. From 1995 to 2007, house prices doubled in relation to average earnings, from four and a half to nine times that of earnings. The buy-to-let market went from 1 to 10 percent of the market in a decade (Cable 2009: 14–16). In the United States, rent returns in relation to property values (price/rent ratios) dropped considerably (Krugman 2008: 145). Many buyers, with minimal finance and capacity, were encouraged to join the market with great short-term deals that contained long-term costs they did not understand. Thus, Northern Rock, the first UK bank to fall in September 2007, had been offering 125 percent mortgages at five or six times personal incomes, when three times had been the average.

What made the property and stock market bubbles far more dangerous was what had been happening in the financial and banking communities: deregulation and bubbles in financial products. Financial deregulation had allowed a greater proportion of bank financing to take place outside of the normal regulated banking sector—the "shadow banking sector." By the time of the collapse, more money was being raised and circulated in this sector then through normal, regulated and protected, conventional means. According to Cable (2009: 34), the derivatives market, one such area, rose in value over a decade, from US$15 trillion, to US$600 trillion or 10 times the total world output. On the basis of these enormous, mythical totals of capital, banks, hedge funds, and private equity companies were able to raise and invest funds far in excess of their capital assets. By the time Northern Rock collapsed, it had assets of £1.5 billion and loans worth over £100 billion, most of which were borrowed from overinflated international money markets (Elliott and Atkinson 2009: 52).

Financial deregulation had also enabled the growth of a multiplicity of complex financial products that were promoted as a means of spreading financial risk and bringing stability but, instead, created more dangerous bubbles. It is through such forms of financial engineering that subprime mortgages could be packaged up into mortgage-backed securities and then further complicated and spliced, using collateralized debt obligations, to hide the risks. This resulted in lots of these packages being given AAA risk ratings by credit rating agencies such as Moody's, Finch, and others. This encouraged normally cautious institutions, such as pension funds, and ordinary banks to buy them. In effect, not only were mortgages sold to the poorest and least educated in society, but they were then repackaged up and sold on in complex packages to elite investors and lenders around the world. When interest rates went up, and subprime mortgage owners began to default in droves, the complex pack of cards and IOUs began to unravel and fall apart. Financial elites, as well as ordinary borrowers, had all bought into the accompanying narratives about property, low interest rates, booming economy, stable financial markets, low risks, and so on.

In 2010, we are still trying to gauge all the consequences of the collapse that followed. First, literally hundreds of banks and related financial institutions have gone under worldwide. Second, private finance debt has been transferred to public debt as large institutions, deemed "too big to fail" (e.g. Freddie Mac, Fannie Mae, AIG, RBoS, Lloyds-TSB, HBoS, Fortis, Dexia, BNP-Paribas, IKB, UBS, Wachovia, Washington Mutual), have effectively been partially or entirely nationalized, at a cost of trillions of dollars of public money worldwide. In relation to the United Kingdom, by 2009, the cost of the bank bailout was £289 billion and rising (CRESC 2009: 6–7). The United Kingdom's external debt rose from £34 billion in 1997 to £319 billion in 2007 or 22.5 percent of GDP. Two years later, after the bank bailouts and fiscal stimulus packages, it had reached 66.5 percent of GDP (Turner 2008: 26, 71). Formerly wealthy countries, such as Iceland and Greece, have become effectively bankrupted and others, such as Spain and Portugal, are struggling under their debts. Third, personal debt has risen considerably and many households have been left in negative equity. During this bubble period, in the United Kingdom, total private debt rose from £570 billion in 1997 to £1,511 billion in 2007. In the United States, it rose from US$5,547 billion in 1997 to US$14,374 billion in 2007.

Cable (2009: 130) estimated that 20–30 percent had been knocked off the value of property in the United States, and United Kingdom by 2009. In the United States, by 2008, 12 million households were in negative equity (Krugman 2008: 189). Fourth, pension funds have been devastated and welfare state systems are being severely cut back in order to balance national accounts. Fifth, unemployment has grown considerably and poverty levels are rising.

Many financial elite actors have lost their jobs and/or seen their incomes reduced. However, their salaries, bonuses, redundancy payoffs, and pension schemes, gathered over the good years, have left them very much in the black. This has led many critics to compare what has happened over the past three decades generally, and through these market bubbles, to a series of "giant chain letters" or "naturally occurring ponzi schemes" (Shiller 2001; Krugman 2008; Elliott and Atkinson 2009). In these, financial elite insiders have been the beneficiaries, and stakeholder elites (in governments, central banks, etc.) and the public (through pension funds, property, and savings) have taken on the losses and debts.

As several economists and City practitioners have pointed out (Soros 1994; Shiller 2001; Krugman 2008; Elliott and Atkinson 2009; Akerlof and Shiller 2009; Bootle 2009), much of what has happened has been built on a series of myths, narratives, and discourses, all without sound foundations. Financial news coverage, with a few notable exceptions, failed to question the specific narratives and larger discourses that were used to justify an increasingly risky and unbalanced financial system (Tett 2009; Starkman 2009; Marron 2010; Chakravartty and Schiller 2010). According to UNCTAD (2009: 21) "market fundamentalist ideology" has enabled a state of affairs whereby "Financial markets in many advanced economies have come to function like giant casinos, where the house almost always wins (or gets bailed out) and everybody else loses." For Bootle, a respected member of the financial elite of London for over 30 years, a lot of the crisis, pure and simple, must be put down to the ideology of the financial markets themselves

the *ideas* that underlay the disaster: the idea that markets know best; the idea that the markets are "efficient"; the idea that there was no good reason to be concerned about the level and structure of pay in banking; the idea that bubbles cannot exist; the idea that in economic matters, human beings are always "rational" … if you ever questioned, never mind disputed, these ideas, you were regarded as a complete no-no. (2009: 21–2).

Conclusion

As stated, it would be a mistake to simply see financial media as a major contributor to financialization and its Frankenstein-like creations. It would also be a mistake to assume that the media have the power to impose dominant financial ideologies on the masses, turning the population into unequivocal cheerleaders of capitalism. However, that does not mean that the specialized financial media, or the mainstream media more generally, has had a neutral or negligible role either. Rather, as argued here, financial media has had a significant, supportive function in the development of financialization via its influence within elite discourse networks. This has helped persuade financial and associated stakeholder elites, as to the validity of financial market discourses, narratives, and investment myths. These have become reified through financial media and other communication fora, producing unassailable ideologies of free and financial market logic. These have enabled such markets to grow, become dangerously autonomous and corrupt, to impose crude market thinking on a range of social policy processes, and to suck in public funds and private savings into unstable market bubbles. This has left government accounts, pension funds, and individual savings in high levels of debt and national polities and welfare state programs teetering on the brink.

12

The Wizards of Oz

Peering behind the curtain on the relationship between central banks and the business media

Marc-André Pigeon
Carleton University

It is perhaps one of the best-known scenes in the history of movies. Toto, Dorothy's famous white cairn terrier, looks behind a curtain and exposes the Wizard of Oz as nothing more than an ordinary man using buttons and levers to animate a booming voice emanating from a disembodied head in order to project authority and convince others of his imminent powers. While some (Littlefield 1964; Sanders 1991) have interpreted *The Wizard of Oz* as a parable about the nineteenth-century debate between advocates of the gold standard (eastern US bankers) and the silver standard (mid-western populists), this scene could, from a modern vantage point, be more usefully interpreted as a powerful and enduring parable about the nature of power projected by central bankers and their handmaidens, the business media. Like the Wizard of Oz, modern-day central bank practitioners push and pull figurative buttons and levers that also animate a disembodied discourse carried by an all-too-compliant business media. This discourse booms with the authority and power to convince an inattentive, overlabored, and understandably ill-informed public of the central bank's imminent power over all manner of economic outcome. There are very good reasons to believe, however, that modern monetary policy largely is ineffective in its stated objective, namely, regulating the generalized rate of price increases (inflation) using short-term, interest rate targets.

That is not to say that the *discourse* of modern central banking is ineffective. Until the global financial crisis of 2008 and 2009, central banks were *singularly* successful in using discursive techniques to achieve two less-known objectives. First, central bank discourse around inflation targets shielded from view a more potent and *democratic* source of control over economic outcomes, namely, the tools of fiscal policy. Second, central bank discourse obscured the institution's active role in backstopping the financial sector and its ability to "innovate" financial products that we now know jeopardized the stability of the global economy. For these reasons, I want to suggest that modern-day central bank communications practices are cornerstones in the ongoing development of *financialization*, which, following Boyer, I define as a situation where "all the elements of final demand bear the consequences of the dominance of finance" (Boyer 2000).

To suggest, however, that the media have some power to propagate beliefs or, at a minimum, to dampen or distill questions that might challenge existing belief structures brings to the fore important theoretical questions about the assumed nature of the audience, the interplay between the media and modern communications practices by institutions such as central banks, and in the case of this work, the power of language and metaphors in particular to influence elite opinion about an important policy issue. While it is beyond the scope of this chapter to delve too deeply into these questions, it is useful to briefly sketch some of the theoretical perspectives that underpin this work. First, this work assumes, following Abercrombie, Hill, and Turner (1980) and others who work in the elite-indexing tradition (Bennett 1990; Bennett, Pickard, Iozzi, Schroeder, Lagos, and Caswell 2004; Davis 2000a, b, 2003; Deacon and Golding 1994; Edelman 1988), that the media's agenda-setting effects, at least for questions such as monetary policy, are for the most part localized at the elite level, a strata of society that I define roughly as the community of individuals who tend to have above-average incomes and have an active interest in policy matters and by virtue of this active interest may be considered opinion leaders in their social circles and sometimes beyond. Second, this work reviews evidence for what Fairclough (1995) calls the "technologization of discourse," a term used to describe the increasingly strategic, self-conscious, and formal structures that govern institutional and political communications with the news media and which leverage structural features of the news business, such as the ever-present search for "information subsidies" (easy and cheap content for news holes) and the increasingly strenuous time constraints that govern news production in late modernity. Third, this work builds on a growing body of critical discourse analysis work by researchers who study metaphors and their power to shape opinion, particularly among an elite class. Fairclough (1995), for example, argues that dominant metaphors construct domains "in a way which helps to marginalize other constructions from the perspective of oppositional groups," while Koller, quoting Kress, another important critical discourse theorists, writes that "metaphorical activity occurs at sites of difference, in struggles over power, ... whenever an attempt is made to assimilate an event into one ideological system rather than another" (2004: 28).

The evidence reviewed here suggests that the media's use of strongly metaphoric language to translate the arcane language of monetary policy has been and remains a key moment in helping inflation targeting gain and retain its stranglehold on the imagination of those elite who devote intellectual resources to thinking about monetary policy. In so doing, inflation targeting has passed into conventional opinion, a taken-for-granted state of nonreflection that gives those who hold the levers of power a free hand to effect policy in a direction that, were it subject to serious scrutiny, might meet with disapproval from the electorate.

A short history of the communications revolution in central banking in Canada

For most of their history, central bankers have been content to operate largely outside of public scrutiny. Like a poker player trying to bluff an opponent, it was widely believed in the postwar period that central bank policy effectiveness would be undermined if people correctly anticipated monetary policy actions. Silence was the order of the day. Press releases were few. Speeches were far between. Central bank actions were a back-page newspaper story, if they were a story at all. In this chapter, we consider the transition from this kind of secretive or defensive communications regimes to more modern-day strategic communications strategies by looking at the Bank of Canada (henceforth, "the Bank"), one of the world's first central banks to explicitly adopt inflation targeting and the related communications practices that are viewed as a necessary complement to this policy objective. That said, it is important to stress that the broad trend from secrecy to openness documented here for the Bank also holds, albeit in less advanced form, at central banks in other developed countries, including the European Central Bank (ECB), the Bank of England, and the US Federal Reserve (Blinder, Goodhart, Hildebrand, Lipton, and Wyplosz 2001; Winkler 2002).

At the Bank, the culture of noncommunication had deep roots in its history and legitimate concerns about ensuring that outsiders were unable to profit from privileged access to information about a forthcoming Bank's decision over interest rates, capital controls, or any other central bank policy tool. In 1939, for example, the Bank put in place controls on the flow of money into and out of the country under tremendous secrecy, something that is almost unimaginable today. Similarly, in 1958, the government's decision to refinance a large amount of Victory Loans issued during Second World War was done under extreme secrecy, with the Bank at one point summoning bondholder representatives, locking them in a room, and only then revealing the purpose of the meeting. According to Babad and Mulroney (1995: 103), this was "typical" Bank of Canada behavior, "secret in every aspect." In later years, the Bank's public temerity could be attributed to a hangover effect from what has become known as "the Coyne affair," a politically messy episode in the Bank's history (1960–1) that led to the resignation of the then governor James Coyne after the government grew weary of the Bank's high interest rate monetary policy and Coyne's very public rebuke of the government over its taxation, deficit spending, and national debt policies.

In retrospect, the Bank's penchant for secrecy or noncommunication seems exaggerated. In June 1970, for example, Canada abandoned its fixed exchange rate regime (backed, importantly, by gold reserves held in the United States), an early sign that the Bretton Woods agreement was about to unravel. This policy shift warranted only the briefest of mentions in the Bank's annual report. As Charles Freedman, a former deputy governor at the Bank noted in an interview (2006), "John Crow (a former Bank of Canada Governor) commented in a speech at one point about the fact that when we went to a flexible exchange rate, you had to go to page 9 in the annual report before you'd see a reference to it. There didn't seem to be any recognition of the fact that it changed the way monetary policy worked."

The historical bias toward secrecy—and the eventual embrace of modern communication practices—can be depicted by looking at the number of speeches per year by Bank of Canada officials (Figure 12.1). In the 1960s and early 1970s, Bank of Canada governor Louis Rasminsky made an average of 2.2 speeches a year to groups outside of parliament. Under governor Gerald Bouey, the average number of speeches increased marginally to 2.6. With the appointment of John Crow in 1987, the average more than doubled to 6.4 speeches a year, setting a precedent for Gordon Thiessen, who delivered an average of 6.7 speeches a year during his term from 1994 through to 2000. Former governor David Dodge delivered an average of 17.4 speeches a year over his tenure, more than 2.5 times the output of Thiessen. Current governor Mark Carney has delivered an average of 13.5 speeches a year since taking over in 2007 but given more free reign to his deputy governors to make up for the speech gap between him and his predecessor, David Dodge.

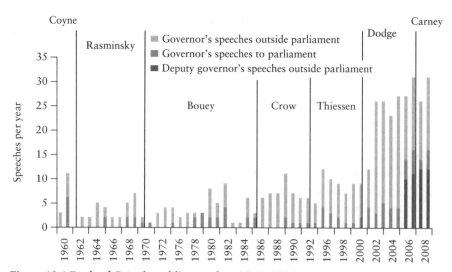

Figure 12.1 Bank of Canada public speeches, 1960–2009

This increase in communicative, for-public-consumption speech making is reflected elsewhere in what Ericson, Baranek, and Chan (1989) would call the Bank's "front-region" activities,[1] including a surge in the number and nature of press release commentary, in the introduction of regular monetary policy reports and updates, in the adoption of eight fixed interest rate policy announcement dates a year, in the use of media-lockups, in the revised content and layout of flagship publications such as the annual report, in the breadth and depth of the Bank's website, and finally, in the creation of "day schools" for journalists who want a better "understanding" of the Bank and its functioning (Pigeon 2008).

Crucially, most of these changes began with, and were integral to, the Bank's eventual and unilateral adoption of what began as a vague "price stability" objective in the late 1980s and its formal adoption of explicit inflation targets in 1991. Since then, the Bank—like most other modern-day central banks in the developed world (Goodfriend 2007)—has had one overriding objective, namely, to achieve a targeted rate of inflation (2 percent since 1995) as measured by the consumer price index (CPI) in the belief that other traditional macroeconomic policy considerations such as economic growth and employment are best served by this singular goal.

The link between inflation targeting as a formal policy objective and communications may not be obvious, so a brief explanation is warranted. From the Bank's perspective, its outward communication practices help condition public expectations—via the business media—about *future* inflation. Since the Bank believes current inflation is at least in part a function of inflationary expectations,[2] the Bank's ability to achieve its 2 percent inflation target hinges on its ability to influence these expectations, much like the Wizard of Oz tried to create desired outcomes through the power of suggestion. This communications perspective is built into the very core of the Bank's mandate—it, along with the Department of Finance, chose the CPI as its policy focus for the simple reason that it "communicated" the general idea of inflation. As Laidler and Robson (2004: 116–7), two high-profile commentators, note,

> a strong case exists for using a price index based on gross domestic product (GDP), which would encompass the prices of all goods and services produced in Canada but such an index has a number of drawbacks: it is harder to measure, can be highly sensitive to variations in commodity prices and Canada's terms of trade, appears with a long time lag, is subject to revisions, *and is not well understood by the general public*. (italics added)

While the communication revolution at the Bank is of relatively recent vintage and, as indicated earlier, integral to its inflation-targeting policy regime, the Bank has been much more consistent historically in its willingness to publicly warn against the risks of deficit spending as a practice that could, in the Bank's view, undermine the effectiveness of monetary policy. This long history can be traced back to the aforementioned Coyne affair, through to the 1980s when the central bank in its rare public pronouncements (mostly its annual report) dropped hints about the supposed inflationary and "crowding out"[3] effects of government spending, through to a more vigorous push of the "deficits are simply bad" message in the 1990s that coincided with the federal government's own vigorous promotion of this view.

The central bank is hardly alone in its concern about deficits—Canada's public space and, indeed, most public spaces in most developed countries, has long been dominated by a brigade of anti-deficit, anti-fiscal policy media pundits, think tanks, and other institutions. The Bank's weight in this debate, however, is noteworthy because most anti-deficit advocates predicate their case against the use of deficit spending on the presumed ability of the central bank to shoulder the counter-cyclical macroeconomic policy burden. That is, the bank lowers interest rates when inflation falls *below* its 2 percent target because this is interpreted as a sign of excessively weak economic growth. Symmetrically, it *increases* interest rates when inflation exceeds 2 percent because this is interpreted as a sign of overly strong economic growth. The result is a "just right" policy approach that bypasses the political process and leaves no room for fiscal policy.

From the Bank's perspective, the past 20 or so years of low inflation in Canada (and elsewhere) is proof that a sound communication strategy can manage inflation expectations and keep inflation tame. From a critical perspective, this same evidence can be interpreted as a testament to the Bank's communicative ability to depoliticize the practice of monetary policy and, in so doing, handcuff the political and economic case for using fiscal policy as a macroeconomic stabilization tool.

The media's role

As suggested in the introduction, the Bank's ability to achieve its communications objectives hinges on an accommodating business media since these media play a crucial role in shaping elite opinion with respect to important economic issues such as monetary policy.[4] Until the widespread adoption of the internet, there was almost no other way for the Bank to get its message across to this audience other than by speaking directly to the political and financial community. To explore the relationship between the Bank, the news media, and what I have called the elite, I looked at the quantum, bias, and rhetorical features of 30 years of monetary policy news coverage in *The Globe and Mail*, a newspaper owned by Canadian media conglomerate CTVglobemedia that bills itself as "Canada's National Newspaper" and that in 2009 had an average daily paid circulation of 315,000 (Canadian Newspaper Association (CAN) 2009), making it the largest daily newspaper in Canada. I chose to focus on the *Globe and Mail* content for two reasons. First, in part due to its large circulation, *The Globe* is *the* opinion leader among Canadian newspapers and, by extension, the broadcast media. Soroka (2002), for example, finds that *The Globe* "is a significant predictor of other newspapers' emphasis on three issues: debt and deficit, inflation and taxes," all of which are relevant to this study. Second, over the past 30 or so years, *The Globe*, quite consciously and notwithstanding its claim to being Canada's national newspaper, has reduced or eliminated circulation to rural areas and lower income parts of major urban centers while concentrating newspaper boxes in areas frequented by higher income individuals. Throughout, *The Globe*'s editorial stance has largely reflected the views of this increasingly elite readership by projecting ideas and arguments that the newspaper itself characterizes as "socially liberal and fiscally conservative,"[5] a tidy summary of the dominant political culture in all of Canada's major political parties.

I chose newspapers as my analytical focal point for two reasons. First, newspapers provide the raw material that informs morning, afternoon, and evening newscasts on radio, television (Ericson *et al.* 1989: 180), and increasingly, the internet. Second, newspapers are the preferred medium for politicians seeking detailed and sustained coverage of an issue, reflecting a "media hierarchy" whereby "newspapers (are) for major ongoing issues, television for ongoing images, and radio as a residual medium" (Ericson *et al.* 1989: 236). In my work, I used an open-source software package called *Yoshikoder*,[6] which treats words as "data points" that can be counted and analyzed numerically to produce statistics and time trends. To obtain my newspaper sample, I used Factiva, a *Dow Jones & Co.* database that offers a sophisticated search engine, generous downloading privileges, and full-text coverage extending back to the paper's first electronic edition of November 14, 1977. I chose a set of keywords that attempts to walk a fine line in the inherent trade-off between the quality of the sample (efficiency) and sample size. The search pattern is indicated in the note attached to Figure 12.2.

To get a sense of the shape and size of *The Globe*'s increasingly elite audience, we can construct a statistical profile of the "average" reader from a regular *Report on Business* section of the newspaper called "Financial Facelift," which *The Globe* has published since May 1999. The column is part of the "personal finance" or "news-you-can-use" output discussed by prominent business journalist Jeffrey Madrick (2001) in some of his work: Each column profiles a reader facing some financial challenge and includes a detailed accounting of their financial situation. Table 12.1 outlines some of the key demographic and financial variables derived by entering financial data from 176 columns over a period stretching from 1999 through to April 2006 into a Microsoft Access database developed for this research. It shows that demographically *The Globe*'s readership is roughly comparable to average and median data for Canada as a whole. Financially and occupationally, however, the average of *The Globe*'s reader earning is roughly double (in average and median income terms) what the average Canadian earns. From a balance-sheet perspective, the gap is even greater, with these representative *Globe* readers reporting net worth 2.5 times the Canadian average.

Figure 12.2 Frequency of the *Globe and Mail* coverage of monetary policy matters, 1978–2006
Note: Search performed in the Factiva database using the following search string: RST = GLOB, "monetary policy," "Bank of Canada," "interest rate," and "Gerald Bouey" or "John Crow" or "Gordon Thiessen" or "David Dodge".

Quantity evidence

Figure 12.2 shows the result of my effort to quantify the ebb and flow of *The Globe*'s monetary policy coverage. The evidence fits the historical record remarkably well, giving us some confidence in our sampling procedure and suggesting that until the early 1990s, *The Globe*'s agenda was set largely by real-world events, elite infighting, and the paper's own agenda; afterward, *The Globe* followed the Bank lead, with coverage ebbing and flowing according to the Bank's carefully managed "front-region" communication efforts.

Figure 12.2 shows, for example, a sharp increase in the number of monetary policy items from 1979 through to 1982, a period in which the Bank, following the US Federal Reserve, helped drive domestic mortgage rates to near 20 percent and thousands took to the streets in protest of the resulting economic carnage. *The Globe*'s monetary policy coverage subsequently subsided, spiking briefly in 1985 with the collapse of the Northland Bank of Canada and Canadian Commercial Bank. Coverage increased again beginning in 1988, a year after Crow took over as governor and indicated his intent to direct monetary policy toward the aforementioned price stability objective. Coverage peaked in 1990, as the Bank's price stability target increasingly became the source of elite infighting, with provincial premiers, elements of the business community, labor, and even some former academic supporters lining up against its ill-defined policy agenda.

In 1991, monetary policy news coverage fell sharply as the Bank, with the Department of Finance's support, adopted an inflation-targeting regime that aimed to reduce inflation to 2 percent by 1995. In Figure 12.2, we can almost

Table 12.1 Profile of targeted *Globe and Mail* audience based on data compiled from Financial Facelift column, May 1999 to April 2006

	Financial Facelift data	National data
Demographic profile		
Average age	41.0	39.0
Median age	40.0	39.5
Gender		
Male	46%	49%
Female	54%	51%
Married/couple	75%	71%
Income		
Average income (before taxes)	Can$117,828	Can$68,880
Median income	Can$108,704	Can$56,640
Average expenses	Can$68,691	Can$66,857
Median expenses	Can$63,804	NA
Balance sheet		
Average assets	Can$597,420	Can$237,200
Median assets	Can$462,750	Can$136,600
Average liabilities	Can$136,590	Can$55,200
Median liabilities	Can$110,400	Can$29,000
Average net worth	Can$460,830	Can$182,000
Median net worth	Can$279,000	Can$81,000

1 Financial Facelift data collected from 176 columns beginning in 1999 through to April 2006. Data were entered into a proprietary Microsoft Access database that yielded the tabulations in this table.
2 The Financial Facelift columns mostly profile married or otherwise engaged couples (the 176 columns surveyed profiled 306 individuals). The data presented here reflect the total number of individuals profiled (i.e. 306). The average-age data, for example, represent the average age of *all* individuals profiled in the column.

Sources: Demographic data: Statistics Canada 2006a; average income data: Statistics Canada 2006b,c; balance sheet data: Statistics Canada 2001.

"see" a tentative elite consensus begin to form around this time. With the exceptions of 1993 and 1998, the search pattern shows *The Globe*'s coverage leveling off at about 50 items per year for the rest of the decade. Finally, we see a spike in the number of items beginning in 2001, a period that coincided with four major events that speak of the Bank's increasingly sophisticated communications practices. First, an experienced senior bureaucrat named David Dodge took over as governor and dramatically increased the volume of public presentations. Second, the Bank renewed its inflation-targeting regime for a 5-year period. Third, the Bank was called upon to react to the financial and economic consequences of 9/11 and engage in a great deal of outreach to the media and, through them, the public. Fourth, 2001 was the first full year of fixed policy announcement dates, a move designed to focus media attention on events in Canada by reducing speculation about the Bank's perceived tendency of responding to changes in US monetary policy rather than charting an independent course worthy of a sovereign nation.

Quality or voice evidence

Using the sample depicted in Figure 12.3, we also can measure the extent to which different voices were used as sources in *The Globe*'s coverage of fiscal and monetary policy matters. In critical theory and critical discourse analysis, analysts are urged to attend to voices that are represented and *how* they are represented. For the purposes of this research, monetary policy news sources were grouped into two main categories, namely, "Bay Street"[7] (financial sector commentators) and "Main Street" (commentators representing small- and medium-sized businesses plus manufacturing), with Bay Street *generally* supporting the Bank, even in its pursuit of such an ill-defined concept as "price stability," and "Main Street" *generally* critical of the Bank's pursuit of low inflation and price stability but rarely offering a compelling theoretically based alternative.[8] Above all, Main Street simply wanted the pain of high interest rates to stop. We also can identify a third type of source I have called "Heterodox" because they offered a theoretically grounded critical alternative to the "monetarist" views of Bay Street and the pragmatic concerns of Main Street.

Using these categorizations, we find Bay Street was the dominant source by a wide margin, although the split was more even than found in similar research conducted for fiscal policy (Pigeon 2008). Figure 12.3 shows that *The Globe* cited Bay Street sources more frequently than Main Street and Heterodox sources

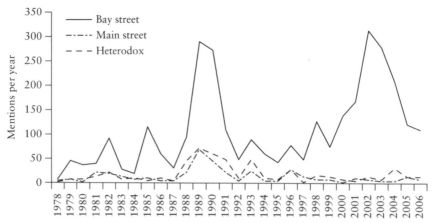

Figure 12.3 Bay Street versus Main Street and Heterodox views in monetary policy discourse—mentions by category, 1978–2006

but that the gaps in mentions were relatively small over the period through to 1997. It also shows a rather strong correlation between the incidence of Bay Street citations and Main Street plus Heterodox citations from about 1987, which is when John Crow became governor at the Bank and the number of citations for all categories spikes higher, through to 1996 and 1997, when economist Pierre Fortin used his position as head of the Canadian Economics Association to argue (unsuccessfully) for a more inflation-tolerant view at the Bank.

In the late 1990s and especially after 2000, Figure 12.3 also shows a sharp increase in Bay Street citations, which I believe speaks to the depoliticization of monetary policy as a discretionary policy tool thanks to the Bank's embrace of strategic communication practices. By this point, alternative critical voices had been sidelined while "within-consensus" voices (those who supported inflation targeting as proposed) had plenty to talk about given the Asian financial crisis in 1997–8, debates about whether to adopt the US dollar in the 1999 and 2000 period, the move to fixed announcement dates in late 2000, David Dodge's appointment as governor in 2001, and Canadian dollar gyrations from 2001 through to today.

Finally, this analysis squares with the agenda-setting data presented a moment ago. The Bank's explicit and unrelenting pursuit of an ill-defined price stability target beginning in 1987, relatively primitive communication practices, and Crow's acerbic personality helped make inflation more of an issue than it otherwise might have been, a contention supported by the dissensus among elites over the "price stability" target and the corresponding increase in media attention. In the early going, the Bank was simply a "bad" communicator in the sense that its utterances or lack thereof created rather than dissipated negative media attention. The 1991 inflation-targeting regimes, combined with a fortuitous drop in inflation, almost immediately stitched together a tentative consensus, which was briefly challenged in 1993 when the Liberal Party failed to reappoint Crow as governor. Thiessen's clear fealty to the inflation-targeting regime combined with a laid-back personality and a focused communications effort put the inflation-targeting consensus on a firmer footing. The seemingly sharp and somewhat permanent increase in coverage beginning in 2001 was due in part to the force of governor Dodge's personality, his considerable communicative abilities, and in part to the permissiveness of "within-consensus" debates.

Rhetorical evidence

Metaphors are potentially powerful rhetorical tools because of their ability to reveal, conceal, and color our interpretations. For cognitive theorists, they map features from a "source domain" to a "target domain." The more concrete and culturally embedded the source domain and the greater its role in early childhood development, the greater the potential power of the metaphor to shape our world view. From this, we can infer that the power of a metaphor is a function of the quality of the metaphor (concreteness, imageability, early childhood role) and its quantity (frequency of exposure). I will address first the question of quality. By carefully reading through my sample of the *Globe* monetary policy coverage, I identified four main categories of monetary policy metaphors:

1 *Monetary policy is war*—This class of metaphor calls on the Bank to *target, combat, fight, battle,* and *defend* against inflation, which is perceived as an *entrenched enemy* and a *threat* that must be *tackled, defeated, beaten, vanquished,* and *resisted* using interest rates as an *arsenal, weapon,* and *unguided missile* despite the potential for *casualties* and a *body count.* Fortunately, the Bank was *victorious* in its *campaign* against inflation in the early 1990s, leaving more room to *maneuver* in the years to come. Koller (2004) suggests that war metaphors are common in business news and serve to build cohesion among a predominantly male audience. The use of war metaphors in monetary policy discourse plays another complimentary role, however, because they also minimize attention to the casualties of the war on inflation, namely, workers who bear the brunt of layoffs caused by rising interest rates. In short, the "monetary policy is war" metaphors work roughly the way Gramm (1996) suggests they do in his study of dominant economic metaphors, namely, as apologetics for those who make decisions—such as central bankers—with important distributional consequences.

2 *Inflation is a siren's song*—This class of metaphor calls on the Bank to resist the sirens' song by *staying the course* despite the entrancing allure of inflation as extolled by the Bank's critics in the manufacturing, labor union, academic, and political classes. The Bank must *show resolve* and turn a *blind eye* to its victims. It must demonstrate *perseverance, determination, steadfastness, firmness* while being *tough, strict,* and *tightfisted* with its control over the money supply. It must not *waver* or *let up* in its efforts to *restrict* the money supply. The Bank must do all this lest it, like the fabled sailors in the allegory, be lead (and lead others) to its demise. This class of metaphor has strong ties to the "monetary policy is war" metaphors because the Bank's job can be likened to that of a general who must set aside feelings for the daily tragedies of war while keeping a firm and steady eye on the larger strategic, long-run picture.

3 *Monetary variables are liquids*—In this class of metaphor, the Bank increases the money supply by *injecting liquidity* into the market; inflation is *wrung* or *squeezed* out of the economy; inflation can

evaporate; exchange rates *float* in the international market; interest rates and the exchange rate can *dive, plunge,* or *drift*, all because of the sudden movement of animal spirits (another popular economic metaphor); and interest rates can *shore up* or *dampen* the economy and/or inflation. For the most part, these metaphors are utilitarian, employed frequently in academic and popular discourses. The depoliticization effects of these metaphors only really occur when writers use them in a disciplinary context. Thus, the governor of the Bank is likened to a *pilot* said to be at the *helm* of the Bank, which is characterized as a *ship* that must *stay the course* with its price stability and inflation-targeting objectives. The resulting impression is of a Bank that is more or less *in control* and understands the tendency of markets to create *stormy seas* of liquidity that *slosh* around the global economy. Crucially, the Bank achieves its policy objectives by *anchoring* expectations—where animal spirits express themselves—to its inflation target, a metaphor that speaks explicitly of the Bank's communicative function and that can be loosely translated as follows: "the Bank's job is to persuade everyone that it exercises the control that it claims it does."

4 *Inflation is a disease*—This category of monetary policy metaphors works on two levels. First, like "monetary policy is war," it attributes a "bad" to inflation. Disease is *contagious, dirty,* and *deadly*. Second, "inflation is like a disease" metaphors tap into the traditional view of medicine and doctors as demigods who symbolize the steady progress of history, science, and knowledge. Thus, inflation is a *disease* that is *contracted* by the Canadian economy, which in turn is often characterized as a *sick patient convalescing* from inflation *fever*. The Bank is a doctor who knowledgeably *administers doses* of interest rate policy that are like *medicine* and *tourniquets*.

Quantitatively, I was able to roughly gauge the impact of these metaphors by associating a set of unique keywords to each category and then counting word frequencies. The results of this exercise are encouraging, supporting the conclusion that the metaphoric language of monetary policy is strongly discouraging of critical thinking. Figure 12.4 puts the use of metaphoric activity in the context of the total news corpus (for a given year). Strikingly, it reveals a long-term stability in the relative use of all the major metaphor categories except the "siren song" class. The stability and weight of "war" metaphors are especially intriguing, suggesting that this class of metaphor is a permanent feature of the monetary policy discourse in Canada. With some exceptions, the "disease" and "liquid" metaphors are similarly stable through time, again suggestive of their deeply embedded (but less pervasive) nature in the discourse. The "siren song" metaphors by contrast trend lower through time, a fact that is probably attributable to (a) the absence of dramatic interest

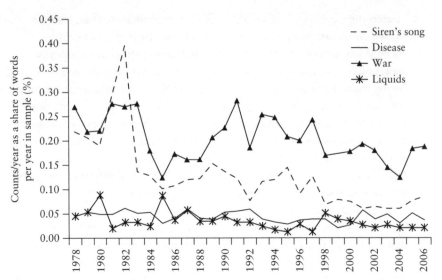

Figure 12.4 Major metaphor categories for monetary policy, counts/year as a fraction of words in sample, 1978–2006

rate events like those of the early 1990s, (b) relatively stable inflation, and (c) the absence of divisive leadership exemplified by John Crow.

In sum, the monetary policy discourse draws heavily on two well-known categories of metaphors frequently discussed in the cognitive literature, namely, metaphors built around restraint ("siren song" metaphors) and violence ("war" metaphors). "Disease" and "liquid" metaphors are probably less grounded in the sense that, for the most part, they do not bear on our early childhood development to the same universal extent or in the same manner.

Conclusion

The evidence suggests that the Bank has been effective in convincing the policy community and the public that it has the ability to control inflation. It has done so through a purposeful strategy that integrates communications considerations into the *heart* of its policy-making process, choosing the CPI as its policy target on purely communicative grounds. The media have given this strategy effect, taking the technical language of monetary policy and, drawing on Bay Street sources, translated it with metaphors that suggest the Bank's masterly control over an inflation nemesis.

Remarkably, this communications endeavor has been achieved against the backdrop of an academic debate over whether in fact central banks have had *anything* to do with the global trend toward low inflation since the early 1990s, a debate well known in the back regions of central banking (Angeriz and Arestis

2006) but rarely voiced in front-region interactions with the news media. In my research, I interviewed a very senior Bank official (since retired) who, in a moment of candor, told me, for example, that "it's a very real historical issue as to how much of the success that we attribute to inflation targeting is really attributable to changes in the structure of global trade, the reduction in the cost of global communications, and so on" (Confidential interview August 4, 2006, Ottawa). More remarkably perhaps, the author has had several discussions with senior Statistics Canada personnel who confirm what many suspect, namely, that the CPI is a deeply flawed measure of inflation (Statistics Canada is responsible for this tabulation). Given the Bank's questionable influence over such a flawed measure, a case can be made that central bank talk serves two deeper purposes beyond "anchoring" inflation expectations.

First, the Bank's communication efforts insulate it from much critical scrutiny in an area where it *does* play a vital role, namely, in the traditional central bank role of backstopping the financial system (Goodhart 1988), which since the early 1980s has been consolidating within Canadian borders while expanding abroad. The situation is paralleled in most other developed countries that have undergone financial "big bangs," that is the regulatory effacement of barriers between insurance, banking, investment banks, and trusts into one-size-fits-all, super-sized financial institutions that "innovate" financial products and adopt increasingly levered positions characteristic of financialization and the lead up to the 2008–9 financial crisis. The Bank's complicity in this process was vividly illustrated in the spring of 2008 when it sponsored changes to the Bank of Canada Act that gave it the power to purchase *any* security of its choosing for whatever purpose it deemed necessary to protect the integrity of Canada's financial system and to do so without making public anything about the transaction. This purely communicative policy change did away with the previous requirement of notifying the public whenever the Bank purchased securities not explicitly enumerated in the Bank of Canada Act, a requirement viewed by the Bank as akin to yelling "fire" in a crowded theater because these types of purchases would tend to happen only in times of extreme financial stress. This little-noted and largely misunderstood legislative change occurred even as the Bank continued to trumpet the "openness" and "accountability" built into its adherence to easy-to-monitor inflation targets.

Second, the modern central bank's communications efforts are also an exercise in distraction in the sense that they take our eye away from where the real and enduring power over economic outcomes is to be found—in our democratically elected institutions and their power to affect change through spending and taxation. If central banks are assumed to have near-perfect control over inflation outcomes and if this in turn means that central banks necessarily adopt counter-cyclical (symmetric) policy stances, then there is really no need for the politicians to get their hands messy with fiscal policy.

The 2008–9 crisis briefly exposed the hollowness of the assumptions underpinning this view, but despite the sudden pragmatic reembrace of fiscal policy, few have called for a permanent return to activist fiscal policy. Instead, most worry about the "destabilizing" effects of rising government deficits and debt ("sovereign default risk") and the "inflationary-effects" of central bank policy interventions because of all the "money sloshing" around in the banking system. In short, the narrative is shaping up as one where the central bank must once again discipline the Canadian economy by vanquishing any hint of inflation while scolding sovereign governments about their fiscal policies.

This attempt to reimpose what is essentially the inflation-targeting discourse of the past 20 years is particularly distressing because it coincides with a growing community of economic scholars (Mitchell 2008; Wray 1998) who persuasively argue that the limits of fiscal policy are, for the most part, self-imposed. While the rationale for this argument is too detailed to address here, the nub of the argument rests on recognizing the full implications of abandoning the same gold standard regime that may have been the genesis of Frank L. Baum's *The Wonderful Wizard of Oz* and whose abandonment arguably kick-started the communications revolution in central banking:[9] In a non-gold standard world such as ours, sovereign governments create money *ex nihilo* every time they spend. They are no more limited in this capacity than a scorekeeper in a football game—only self-imposed rules define the limits of our score keeping, much like poor self-image limited the development of the characters in *The Wizard of Oz*. The media, unfortunately, have not seen fit to peer behind the curtain and discuss this new, persuasive, research. Rather, they have actively constructed and propagated a deception based on the purported folly of fiscal policy and the sanctity of monetary mechanisms. In so doing, this discourse prevents people from recognizing that much of the power to wrestle control over economic outcomes lies in having the heart, the mind, and the courage to see true and through the forces of monetary mystification.

Notes

1   "Front-region" refers to the intersection of government, bureaucratic, and media discourses, the "public sphere" if you will; bureaucrats and governments typically try to impose some "enclosure" on internal discourse, to fence it in and allow only a well-defined narrative to be exposed in front-region activities 4.

2   For example, unions typically base their wage demands on expected inflation to avoid a loss in real income for their members. If union and employers are reasonably certain that the Bank can deliver on its 2 percent inflation target, then wage increase will tend to settle around this figure, potentially creating a self-fulfilling prophecy such that the general rate of price change (influenced greatly by wage settlements) is on target at 2 percent.

3   "Crowding out" refers to the theory that the government borrowing displaces private-sector borrowing by "using up" a supposedly limited pool of savings.

4   As I argue elsewhere (Pigeon 2008), television, radio, and the general news section of newspapers played an important—albeit second order—role in spreading elite views about monetary policy (crystallized through, and by, the business media) to the general nonelite public. The general public's views, in turn, were measured (and fed back to the elite) using the technology of public-opinion polling that, following Lewis (2001), I argue acted largely as a barometer of the degree to which elite views—carried through these more general interest media—were becoming the instinctual—rather than elaborated—response to monetary policy (and fiscal policy) questions.

5   Personal communication with Warren Clement, a long-time editorial writer at *The Globe and Mail*.

6   For information on this software package and related theoretical work, visit the Yoshikoder homepage at http://www.yoshikoder.wordpress.com/.

7   "Bay Street" is Canada's version of "Wall Street." In other words, this downtown Toronto street represents the hub of Canada's financial sector.

8   In a 2007 column, *National Post* editor Terence Corcoran (2007) echoed this view, noting that Canada's "now sacrosanct inflation targets" were not always popular among business leaders. Corcoran quotes Catherine Swift, head of the Canadian Federation of Independent Business (CFIB), as praising Dodge upon his retirement for taking "the punch bowl away just as the party was getting good and everybody was starting to have a good time" (a common metaphor used to describe inflation-targeting monetary policy) and contrasts this quotation with what she had said in the early 1990s, when she accused Crow of instituting a policy that "guaranteed that domestic business will be crippled" and noted that "when you kill an economy, one of the things you kill is inflation."

9   In Pigeon (2008), I note that the Bank's first serious attempts to engage with the public occurred around the time of the collapse of the Bretton Woods agreement.

Bibliography

Abercrombie, N., Hill, S., & Turner, B. (1980), *The Dominant Ideology Thesis*, London: George Allen & Unwin Ltd.

Abondance (2002), "Transcript du chat avec Matt Cutts et Stephanie Kerebel." Available at http://chat.abondance.com/google.html [accessed March 24, 2011].

Advertising Standards Authority (ADS) (2009), "New Zealand Advertising Industry Turnover, December." Available at http://www.asa.co.nz/industry_turnover/media_turnover_with_explanatory_notes_2010%20final%20.pdf [accessed April 6, 2011].

Adweek (2009), "Facebook to Surpass MySpace in Ad Revenue." Available at http://www.adweek.com/aw/content_display/data-center/research/e3i9759cd94a98520c084225bab62a588b4 [accessed March 24, 2011].

Ahrens, F. (2010, February 24), "Washington Post Newspaper Earns Profit in 4Q," *The Washington Post*. Available at http://www.washingtonpost.com/wp-dyn/content/article/2010/02/24/AR2010022401924.html [accessed April 6, 2011].

Ahrens, F. & Klein, A. (2003, August 12), "Parent Firm May Drop AOL from Its Name: Officials Are Debating a Change to Time Warner," *The Washington Post*, p. E1.

Akerlof, G. & Shiller, R. (2009), *Animal Spirits: How Human Psychology Drives the Economy, and Why It Matters for Global Capitalism*, Princeton, NJ: Princeton University Press.

Aksoy, A. & Robins, K. (1992), "Hollywood for the 21st Century: Global Competition for Critical Mass in Image Markets," *Cambridge Journal of Economics*, 16(1): 1–22.

Albarran, A. (1996), *Media Economics: Understanding Markets, Industries and Concepts*, Ames, IO: Iowa State University Press.

Albarran, A. (2010), *The Media Economy*, New York: Routledge.

Albarran, A.B. & Gormly, R.K. (2004), "Strategic Response or Strategic Blunder? An Examination of AOL Time Warner and Vivendi Universal," in R.G. Picard (ed.), *Strategic Responses to Media Market Changes* (pp. 35–45), JIBS Research Reports Series, no 2004–2, Jönköping, Sweden: Jönköping International Business School.

Albarran, A. & Dimmick, J. (1996), "Concentration and Economies of Multiformity in the Communication Industries," *Journal of Media Economics*, 9(4): 41–50.

Albarran, A. & Dimmick, J. (2006), "Concentration and Economies of Multiformity in the Communication Industries," in G. Doyle (ed.), *The Economics of the Mass Media* (pp. 268–77), Cheltenham, UK: Edward Elgar.

Albarran, A. & Mierzejewska, B. (2004), "Media Concentration in the U.S. and European Union: A Comparative Analysis." Paper presented at the 6th World Media Economics Conference—Centre d'études sur les médias and Journal of Media Economics, HEC Montréal, Canada, May 12–15.

Alexa.com (2010), "Top Sites by Country." Available at http://www.alexa.com/topsites/countries [accessed March 24, 2011].

Almiron, N. (2010), *Journalism in Crisis: Corporate Media and Financialization*, Cresskill, NJ: Hampton.

Amin, A. (2002), "Spatialities of Globalization," *Environment and Planning A*, 34: 385–99.

Ammori, M. (2010), *TV Competition Nowhere: How the Cable Industry Is Colluding to Kill Online TV*, Washington, DC: Free Press. Available at http://www.freepress.net/files/TV-Nowhere.pdf [accessed March 24, 2011].

Andrejevic, M. (2007), "Surveillance in the Digital Enclosure," *The Communication Review*, 10: 295–317.

Angeriz, A. & Arestis, P. (2006), "Has Inflation Targeting had Any Impact on Inflation?" *Journal of Post Keynesian Economics*, 28(4): 559–71.

Apple Inc. (2008), "Submission of Apple Inc. to Broadcasting Notice of Public Hearing CRTC 2008–11, Canadian Broadcasting in New Media." Available at http://support.crtc.gc.ca/applicant/docs.aspx?pn_ph_no=2008-11&call_id=74489 &lang=E&defaultName=Apple%20Inc.&replyonly=&addtInfo=&addtCmmt=&f nlSub= [accessed September 20, 2010].

Arango, T. (2007, December 24), "A New Ear for Time Warner," *International Herald Tribune*, p. 10.

Arango, T. (2010, January 10), "How the AOL–Time Warner Merger Went So Wrong," *The New York Times*. Available at http://www.nytimes.com/2010/01/11/ business/media/11merger.html [accessed August 2, 2010].

Arrington, M. (2008), "Technorati to Launch Blogger Advertising Network." Available at http://techcrunch.com/2008/02/29/technorati-to-launch-blogger-advertising-network/ [accessed March 24, 2011].

Arsenault, A. & Castells, M. (2008a), "Switching Power: Rupert Murdoch and the Global Business of Media Politics: A Sociological Analysis," *International Sociology*, 23(4): 488–513.

Arsenault, A. & Castells, M. (2008b), "The Structure and Dynamics of Global Multi-Media Business Networks," *International Journal of Communication*, 1: 707–48.

Atkinson, R.D. (2010), "Network Policy and Economic Doctrines." Paper presented at the Telecommunications Policy Research Conference, Arlington, VA, October 1–3.

Auer, M. (2007), "Is Bigger Really Better? TV and Radio Ownership Policy Under Review," *Policy Options*, 28(8): 78–83. Available at http://www.irpp.org/po/ archive/sep07/auer.pdf [accessed September 20, 2010].

Auerbach, P. (1988), *Competition: The Economics of Industrial Change*, Oxford: Blackwell.

Babad, M. & Mulroney, C. (1995), *Where the Buck Stops*, Toronto: Stoddart.

Babe, R.E. (1995), *Communications and the Transformation of Economics*, Boulder, CO: Westview.

Bagdikian, B. (1983), *The Media Monopoly*, Boston, MA: Beacon.

Bagdikian, B. (1986), *El Monopolio de los Medios de Difusión*, México: Fondo de Cultura Económica.

Bagdikian, B. (2004), *The New Media Monopoly* (6th ed.), Boston, MA: Beacon Press.

Baidu, Inc. (2010), *Annual Report*, Beijing, PRC: Baidu. Available at http://phx. corporate-ir.net/External.File?item=UGFyZW50SUQ9Mzg3OTIzfENoaWxkSUQ9 MzkyNDAwfFR5cGU9MQ==&t=1 [accessed March 24, 2011].

Baker, C.E. (2007), *Media Concentration and Democracy*, New York: Cambridge University.

Baldwin, T.F., McVoy, D.S., & Steinfield, C. (1996), *Convergence: Integrating Media, Information, and Communication*, Thousand Oaks, CA: Sage Publications.

Bank of Canada (2009), "Financial System Review." Available at http://www. bankofcanada.ca/en/fsr/index.html [accessed September 20, 2010].

Bar, F. & Sandvig, C. (2008), "US Communication Policy after Convergence," *Media, Culture & Society*, 30(4): 531–50.

Baran, P.A. & Sweezy, P.M. (1966), *Monopoly Capital*, New York: Monthly Review Press.

Bardoel, J. & d'Haenans, L. (2008), "Reinventing Public Service Broadcasting in Europe: Prospects, Promises and Problems," *Media, Culture & Society*, 30(3): 337–55.

Barfe, L. (2003), *Where Have All the Good Times Gone? The Rise and Fall of the Music Industry*, London: Atlantic Books.

Batt, R.S., Christopherson, S., Rightor, N., & Van Jaarsveld, D. (2001), *Networking, Work Patterns and Workforce Policies for the New Media Industry*, Washington, DC: Economic Policy Institute.

BBC Commissioning (no date), "WOCC—Window of Creative Competition." Available at http://www.bbc.co.uk/commissioning/tv/network/wocc.shtml [accessed April 4, 2010].

BCE (2001), "Annual Report." Available at http://www.bce.ca/en/investors/financialperformance/annualreporting/archives/bce/index.php#a2003 [accessed September 20, 2010].

BCE (2003), "Annual Report." Available at http://www.bce.ca/en/investors/financialperformance/annualreporting/archives/bce/index.php#a2003 [accessed September 20, 2010].

BCE (2007), "Annual Report." Available at http://www.bce.ca/en/investors/financialperformance/annualreporting/archives/bce/index.php#2007 [accessed September 20 2010].

Becerra, M. & Mastrini, G. (2009), *Los Dueños de la Palabra*, Buenos Aires: Prometeo.

Bell, D. (1973), *The Coming of Post-Industrial Society*, New York: Basic Books.

Benady, D. (2009, March 24), "Biggest Brands: Top 100 UK Advertisers 2009," *Marketing Magazine*. Available at http://www.marketingmagazine.co.uk/news/893106/Marketings-Top-100-UK-advertisers-2009/ [accessed February 23, 2010].

Benkler, Y. (2003), "Freedom in the Commons: Towards a Political Economy of Information," *Duke Law Journal*, 52(6): 1245–76.

Benkler, Y. (2006), *The Wealth of Networks: How Social Production Transforms Markets and Freedom*, New Haven, CN: Yale University Press.

Benkler, Y. (2010), "Correspondence: A New Era of Corruption?" *The New Republic*. Available at http://www.tnr.com/print/article/correspondence-new-era-corruption [accessed March 24, 2011].

Benkler, Y., Faris, R., Gasser, U., Miyakawa, L., & Schultze, S. (2010), *Next Generation Connectivity: A Review of Broadband Internet Transitions and Policy from Around the World*, Cambridge, MA: Berkman Center for Internet & Society. Available at http://cyber.law.harvard.edu/publications/2010/Next_Generation_Connectivity [accessed March 24, 2011].

Bennett, L.W. (1990), "Toward a Theory of Press-State Relations in the United States," *Journal of Communication*, 40(2): 103–25.

Bennett, L.W., Pickard, V.W., Iozzi, D.P., Schroeder, C.L., Lagos, T., & Caswell, C.E. (2004), "Managing the Public Sphere: Journalistic Construction of the Great Globalization Debate," *Journal of Communication*, 54(3), 437–55.

Berkman, R. & Kitch, W. (1986), *Politics in the Media Age*, New York: McGraw-Hill Book Company.

Bielby, D.D. & Harrington, C.L. (2008), *Global TV: Exporting Television and Culture in the World Market*, New York: New York University Press.

Bielby, W. & Bielby, D. (1992), "Cumulative Disadvantage in an Unstructured Labor Market," *Work and Occupations*, 19: 366–89.

Bielby, W. & Bielby, D. (1996), "Women and Men in Film: Gender Inequality Among Writers in a Culture Industry," *Gender and Society*, 10(3): 248–70.

Bielby, W. & Bielby, D. (2003), "Controlling Prime-Time: Organizational Concentration and Network Television Programming Strategies," *Journal of Broadcasting and Electronic Media*, 47(4): 573–96.

BIS/DCMS (2009), "Digital Britain: Final Report (The Carter Report)." Available at http://webarchive.nationalarchives.gov.uk/+/http://www.culture.gov.uk/images/publications/digitalbritain-finalreport-jun09.pdf [accessed January 12, 2010].

Bischoff, W. & Darling, A. (2009), *UK International Financial Services—The Future: A Report from UK Based Financial Service Leaders to the Government*, London: HM Treasury.

Blinder, A., Goodhart, C., Hildebrand, P., Lipton, D., & Wyplosz, C. (20201), *How Do Central Banks Talk?* Geneva, Switzerland: International Center for Monetary and Banking Studies.

Bloomberg (2010), *Bloomberg Professional*, New York: Bloomberg.

Bodie, Z., Kane, A., & Marcus, A. (2003), *Essentials of Investment* (5th ed.), London: McGraw Hill.

Bootle, R. (2009), *The Trouble with Markets: Saving Capitalism from Itself*, London: Nicholas Brealey Publishing.

Born, G. (2003), "Strategy, Positioning and Projection in Digital Television: Channel Four and the Commercialization of Public Service Broadcasting in the UK," *Media, Culture & Society*, 25(6): 773–99.

Born, G. (2004), *Uncertain Vision: Birt, Dyke and the Reinvention of the BBC*, London: Secker & Warburk.

Boswell, J. & Peters, J. (1997), *Capitalism in Contention—Business Leaders and Political Economy in Modern Britain*, Cambridge: Cambridge University Press.

Bouquillion, P. (2008), *Les industries de la culture et de la communication. Les stratégies du capitalisme*, Paris: Presses Universitaires de Grenoble.

Boyd-Barrett, O. (2006), "Cyberspace, Globalization and Empire," *Global Media and Communication*, 2(1): 21–41.

Boyer, R. (2000), "Is a Finance-Led Growth Regime a Viable Alternative to Fordism? A Preliminary Analysis," *Economy and Society*, 29(1): 111–45.

Boyle, J. (1996), *Shamans, Software and Spleens*, Cambridge, MA: Harvard University.

Braman, S. (2010), "The Interpenetration of Technical and Legal Decision-Making for the Internet," *Information, Communication & Society*, 13(3): 309–24.

Brenner, R. (2002), *The Boom and the Bubble*, New York: Verso.

Bruns, A. (2008), *Blogs, Wikipedia, Second Life, and Beyond: From Production to Produsage*, New York: Peter Lang.

Business Insights (2009a), *Key Trends in Converged Communications*, London: Global Business Insights.

Business Insights (2009b), *The Videogame Market Outlook: Evolving Business Models, Key Players, New Challenges and the Future Outlook*, London: Global Business Insights.

Bustamante, E. (1999), *La televisión económica. Financiación, estrategias, mercados*, Barcelona: Gedisa.

Bustamante, E. (2004), "Cultural Industries in the Digital Age," *Media, Culture & Society*, 26(6): 803–20.

Bustamante, E. & Miguel, J.C. (2005), "Los grupos de comunicación iberoamericanos a la hora de la convergencia," *DIA-LOGOS*, 72, Lima: FELAFACS.

Cable, V. (2009), *The Storm: The World Economic Crisis and What It Means*, London: Atlantic Books.

Calabrese, A. & Sparks, C. (2004), *Toward a Political Economy of Culture*, New York: Rowman & Littlefield.

Caldwell, J. (2008), *Production Culture*, Durnham, NC: Duke University.

Calhoun, C. (1992), "The Infrastructure of Modernity," in H. Haferkamp & N.J. Smelser (eds), *Social Change and Modernity* (pp. 88–114), Berkeley, CA: University of California Press.

Canada, Standing Senate Committee on Transport and Communications (2006), *Final Report on the Canadian News Media*. Ottawa: Government of Canada. Available at www.parl.gc.ca/39/1/parlbus/commbus/senate/com-e/tran-e/rep-e/repfinjun06vol1-e.pdf [accessed April 5, 2011].

Canadian Broadcasting Corporation (CBC)/Media Technology Monitor (MTM) (2009), *Personal TV: Anytime, Anywhere—English Market*, Ottawa, ON: CBC/MTM.

Canadian Film and Television Production Association (CFTPA) (2010), *Profile 2009: An Economic Report on the Canadian Film and Television Production Industry*, Ottawa, ON: Canadian Film and Television Production Association & Association des Producteurs de Films et de Télévision du Québec, with the Department of Canadian Heritage. Available at http://www.cftpa.ca/newsroom/pdf/profile/profile2009-en.pdf [accessed September 20, 2010].

Canadian Newspaper Association (CNA) (2009), *Daily Newspaper Paid Circulation Data, 2009*, Toronto: Canadian Newspaper Association.

Canadian Newspaper Association (CNA) (2010), "Ownership." Available at http://www.cna-acj.ca/en/about-newspapers/ownership/ownership [accessed September 20, 2010].

Canadian Radio-television and Telecommunications Commission (CRTC) (2002), "Status of Competition in Canadian Telecommunications Markets; Deployment/Accessibility of Advanced Telecommunications Infrastructure and Services." Available at http://www.crtc.gc.ca/eng/publications/reports/PolicyMonitoring/2002/gic2002.pdf [accessed September 20, 2010].

Canadian Radio-television and Telecommunications Commission (CRTC) (2004), "Broadcasting Policy Monitoring Report." Available at http://www.crtc.gc.ca/eng/publications/reports/PolicyMonitoring/2004/bpmr2004.pdf [accessed September 20, 2010].

Canadian Radio-television and Telecommunications Commission (CRTC) (2006), "Bell Globemedia Inc., on Behalf of Its Licensed Subsidiaries Change in Effective Control." Available at www.crtc.gc.ca/eng/archive/2006/db2006-309.htm [accessed September 20, 2010].

Canadian Radio-television and Telecommunications Commission (CRTC) (2007), "Broadcasting Decision CRTC 2007–429: Transfer of Effective Control of Alliance Atlantis Broadcasting Inc.'s Broadcasting Companies to CanWest MediaWorks Inc." Available at www.crtc.gc.ca/eng/archive/2007/db2007-429.htm [accessed September 20, 2010].

Canadian Radio-television and Telecommunications Commission (CRTC) (2008), "Broadcasting Public Notice CRTC 2008–4: Diversity of Voices." Available at www.crtc.gc.ca/eng/archive/2008/pb2008-4.pdf [accessed September 20, 2010].

Canadian Radio-television and Telecommunications Commission (CRTC) (2009a), "Communications Monitoring Report." Available at http://www.crtc.gc.ca/eng/publications/reports/policymonitoring/2009/2009MonitoringReportFinalEn.pdf [accessed March 25, 2011].

Canadian Radio-television and Telecommunications Commission (CRTC) (2009b), "Pay Television, Pay-per-View, Video-on-Demand and Specialty Services: Statistical and Financial Summaries, 2005–2009." Available at http://www.crtc.gc.ca/eng/publications/reports/BrAnalysis/psp2009/psp2009.htm [accessed September 20, 2010].

Canadian Radio-television and Telecommunications Commission (CRTC) (2009c), "Broadcasting Order CRTC 2009 452: Reference to the Federal Court of Appeal—Applicability of the Broadcasting Act to Internet Service Providers." Available at http://www.crtc.gc.ca/eng/archive/2009/2009-452.htm [accessed September 20, 2010].

Canadian Radio-television and Telecommunications Commission (CRTC) (2009d), "Telecom Regulatory Policy CRTC 2009–657: Review of the Internet Traffic Management Practices of Internet Service Providers." Available at http://www.crtc.gc.ca/eng/archive/2009/2009-657.htm [accessed September 20, 2010].

Canadian Radio-television and Telecommunications Commission (CRTC) (2010), "Broadcasting Regulatory Policy 2010–167: A Group-Based Approach to the Licensing of Private Television Services." Available at http://www.crtc.gc.ca/eng/archive/2010/2010-167.htm [accessed September 20, 2010].

Canwest (2009), "Annual Report." Available at http://replay.waybackmachine.org/20100104144907/http://canwestglobal.com/investors/investor_documents/F09/q4/CGCC_AR_Q4_2009_FINAL.pdf [accessed April 7, 2011].

Carveth, R. (2004), "The Economics of Online Media," in A. Alexander, J. Owers, R. Carveth, C.A. Hollifield, & A.N. Greco (eds), *Media Economics: Theory and Practice* (pp. 265–83, 3rd ed.), Mahwah, NJ: Lawrence Erlbaum Associates.

Cassidy, J. (2002), *Dot.Con: The Greatest Story Ever Told*, London: Penguin/Allen Lane.

Castells, M. (1996), *The Rise of the Network Society*, Malden, MA: Blackwell.

Castells, M. (2000), "Toward a Sociology of the Network Society," *Contemporary Sociology*, 29(5): 693–9.

Castells, M. (2001), *The Internet Galaxy*, New York: Oxford University Press.

Castells, M. (2009), *Communication Power*, New York: Oxford University Press.

Caves, R. (2000), *Creative Industries: Contracts between Art and Commerce*, Cambridge, MA: Harvard University Press.

Chakravarty, P. & Schiller, D. (2010), "Neoliberal Newspeak and Digital Capitalism in Crisis," *International Journal of Communication*, 4: 670–92.

Chalaby, J. (2009), *Transnational Television in Europe: Reconfiguring Global Communications Networks*, London: IB Tauris.

Chambers, T. & Howard, H. (2005), "The Economics of Media Consolidation," in A.B. Albarran, S.M. Chan-Olmsted, & M. Wirth (eds), *Handbook of Media Management and Economics* (pp. 363–86), Mahwah, NJ: Lawrence Erbaum.

"Changing the Channel" (2010, May 29), *The Economist*, 395(8684): 1–14.

Chan-Olmsted, S. (1998), "Mergers, Acquisitions, and Convergence: The Strategic Alliance of Broadcasting, Cable Television, and Telephone Services," *Journal of Media Economics*, 11(3): 33–46.

Chase, K. (2008), "Moving Hollywood Abroad, Divided Labor Markets and the New Politics of Trade in Services," *International Organization*, 62(4): 653–87.

Christophers, B. (2010), "Television's Power Relations in the Transition to Digital—the Case of the United Kingdom," *Television & New Media*, 9(3): 239–57.

Christopherson, S. (1996), "Flexibility and Adaptation in Industrial Relations: The Exceptional Case of the U.S. Media Industries," in L. Gray & R. Seeber (eds), *Under the Stars: Essays on Labor Relations in Arts and Entertainment*, Ithaca: Cornell University Press.

Christopherson, S. (2002), "Project Work in Context: Regulatory Change and the New Geography of the Media," *Environment and Planning*, 34: 2003–5.

Christopherson, S. (2006), "Behind the Scenes: How Transnational Firms Are Constructing a New International Division of Media Labor," *Geoforum*, 37(5): 739–51.

Christopherson, S. (2008), "Beyond the Self-expressive Creative Worker, an Industry Perspective on Entertainment Media," *Theory, Culture and Society*, 25(7–8): 73–95.

Christopherson, S. & Rightor, N. (2010), "The Creative Economy as 'Big Business': Evaluating State Strategies to Lure Film Makers" (special issue on "The Creative Economy and Economic Development"), *Journal of Planning Education and Research*, 29(3): 336–52.

Christopherson, S. & Storper, M. (1986), "The City as Studio, the World as Backlot: The Impact of Vertical Disintegration on the Location of the Motion Picture Industry," *Society and Space*, 4: 305–20.

Christopherson, S. & Storper, M. (1989), "The Effects of Flexible Specialization on Industrial Politics and the Labour Market," *Industrial and Labour Relations Review*, 42(3): 331–47.

Christopherson, S., Figueroa, M., Gray, L.S., Parrott, J., Richardson, D., & Rightor, N. (2006), "New York's Big Picture: Assessing New York's Position in Film, Television and Commercial Production. A Report to the New York Film, Television and Commercial Initiative." Available at http://www.ilr.cornell.edu/wied/industry/arts/projects.html [accessed March 25, 2011].

"Clear Channel Sells TV Assets to Providence Equity" (2007). *The Boston Globe*. Available at http://www.boston.com/business/globe/articles/2007/04/23/clear_channel_sells_tv_assets_to_providence_equity/ [accessed March 25, 2011]

CNN/Money (2004, 18 February), "Comcast Bids for Disney." CNN news scripts.

Coase, R. (1937), "The Nature of the Firm," *Economica*, 4: 386–405.

Cocker, A. (2005), "New Zealand On Air: A Broadcasting Public Policy Model?" *Political Science*, 57(2): 43–54.

Collins, R. (2008), "Hierarchy to Homeostasis? Hierarchy, Markets and Networks in UK Media and Communications Governance," *Media, Culture & Society*, 30(3): 295–317.

Collins, R., Garnham, N., & Locksley, G. (1988), *The Economics of Television: The UK Case*, London: Sage Publications.

Comcast (1999), "Comcast Press Release." Available at http://www.comcast.com [accessed April 20, 2010].

Comcast Cablevision v. Broward County (2000), No. 99-6934-VIV. United States District Court, Southern District of Florida.

Communications Energy Paperworkers Union of Canada (CEP) (2007), "Intervention re: Broadcasting Notice of Public Hearing CRTC 2007–11." Available at http://support.crtc.gc.ca/applicant/applicant.aspx?pn_ph_no=2007-11&lang=E [accessed September 20, 2010].

Compaine, B. (2001), "The Myths of Encroaching Global Media Ownership." *Open Democracy*. Available at http://www.opendemocracy.net/media-globalmediaownership/article_87.jsp [accessed March 25, 2011].

Compaine, B. (2005), *The Media Monopoly Myth*, New York: New Millenium Research Council.

Comrie, M. & Fountaine, S. (2005), "Retrieving Public Service Broadcasting: Treading a Fine Line at TVNZ," *Media, Culture & Society*, 27(1): 101–18.

Comrie, M. & Fountaine, S. (2006), "Back to the Future in New Zealand: Can a 'Third Way' Compromise Reinvigorate Public Service Broadcasting?" in C. Nissen (ed.), *Making a Difference: Public Service Broadcasting in the European Media Landscape*, Eastleigh: John Libbey.

comScore (2009), "Canada Digital Year in Review: Canada." Available at http://
comscore.com/Press_Events/Presentations_Whitepapers/2010/2009_Canada_
Digital_Year_in_Review/(language)/eng-US [accessed September 20, 2010].

comScore (2010a), "Data Passport—First Half 2010." Available at http://www.
comscore.com/Press_Events/Presentations_Whitepapers/2010/The_comScore_
Data_Passport_-_First_Half_2010/(language)/eng-US [accessed April 6, 2011].

comScore (2010b), "Data Passport—Second Half 2010." Available at http://www.
comscore.com/Press_Events/Presentations_Whitepapers/2010/comScore_Data_
Passport_-_Second_Half_2010/(language)/eng-US [accessed April 6, 2011].

comScore (2010c), "comScore Reports Global Search Market Growth of 46 Percent in
2009." Available at http://www.comscore.com/Press_Events/Press_Releases/2010/1/
Global_Search_Market_Grows_46_Percent_in_2009 [accessed January 29, 2010].

Cooper, M.N. (2009), "The Case Against Media Consolidation: Evidence on
Concentration, Localism and Diversity. Donald McGannon Media Research Center,
Fordham University." Available at http://fordham.bepress.com/cgi/viewcontent.cgi?
article=1000&context=mcgannon_research [accessed April 6, 2011].

Corcoran, F. & Fahy, D. (2009), "Exploring the European Elite Sphere: The Role of
the *Financial Times*," *Journalism Studies*, 10(1): 100–13.

Corcoran, T. (2007, December 12), "Jury Still Out on Dodge," *National Post*, p. FP19.

Correa, F.R. (2000), "Interview with Google's Sergey Brin." Available at http://www.
linuxjournal.com/article/4196 [accessed September 1, 2010].

Cowhey, P.F. & Aronson, J.D. (2009), *Transforming Global Information and
Communication Markets: The Political Economy of Innovation*, Cambridge, MA:
MIT Press.

Cox, B. (2004), *Free for All? Public Service Television in the Digital Age*, London:
Demos.

Crain, M. (2009), "The Rise of Private Equity Media Ownership in the United States:
A Public Interest Perspective," *International Journal of Communication*, 3: 208–39.

CRESC (2009), *An Alternative Report on UK Banking Reform: A Public Interest
Report from CRESC*, Manchester: Centre for Research on Socio-Cultural Change.

Crotty, J. (2005), "The Neoliberal Paradox: The Impact of Destructive Product Market
Competition and 'Modern' Financial Markets on Nonfinancial Corporation
Performance in the Neoliberal Era," in G.A. Epstein (ed.), *Financialization and the
World Economy* (pp. 77–110), Northampton, MA: Edward Elgar Publishing.

Crotty, J., Epstein, G., & Kelly, P. (1998), "Multinational Corporations in the
Neo-Liberal Regime," in D. Baker, G. Epstein, & R. Pollin (eds), *Globalization and
Progressive Economic Policy* (pp. 117–43), Cambridge: Cambridge
University Press.

Curran, J. (1978), "Advertising and the Press," in J. Curran (ed.), *The British Press: A
Manifesto* (pp. 229-67), London: MacMillan.

Curran, J. & Seaton, J. (2003), *Power without Responsibility: The Press, Broadcasting,
and New Media in Britain* (6th ed.), London: Routledge.

Curtin, M. (2005), "Murdoch's Dilemma, or 'What's the Price of TV in China?'"
Media, Culture & Society, 27(2): 155–75.

Curtin, M. (2007), *Playing to the World's Biggest Audience: The Globalization of
Chinese Film and TV*, Berkeley, CA: University of California Press.

Curtin, M. (2009), "Thinking Globally: From Media Imperialism to Media Capital,"
in J. Holt & A. Perren (eds), *Media Industries: History, Theory, and Method* (pp.
108–19), Malden, MA: Wiley-Blackwell.

Curwen, P. (2008), "A Settled Structure for the TMT Sector Remains a Mirage in
2006/7," *Info*, 10(2): 3–23.

Dahlgren, P. (1995), *Television and the Public Sphere*, London: Sage Publications.

Darnton, R. (2009), "Google and the New Digital Future," *New York Review of Books*, 106(20): 82–4.

Davies, G. (2005), "The BBC and Public Value," in D. Helm, D. Green, M. Oliver, S. Terrington, A. Graham, B. Robinson *et al.* (eds), *Can the Market Deliver? Funding Public Service Television in the Digital Age* (pp. 129–50), Eastleigh: John Libbey.

Davis, A. (2000a), "Public Relations, Business News and the Reproduction of Corporate Elite Power," *Journalism*, 1(3): 282–304.

Davis, A. (2000b), "Public Relations, News Production and Changing Patterns of Source Access in the British National Media," *Media, Culture & Society*, 22(1): 39–59.

Davis, A. (2002), *Public Relations Democracy: Public Relations, Politics and the Mass Media in Britain*, Manchester: Manchester University Press.

Davis, A. (2003), "Whither Mass Media and Power? Evidence for a Critical Elite Theory Alternative," *Media, Culture & Society*, 25: 669–90.

Davis, A. (2006), "Media Effects and the Question of the Rational Audience: Lessons from the Financial Markets," *Media, Culture & Society*, 28(4): 603–25.

Davis, A. (2007), *The Mediation of Power: A Critical Introduction*, London: Routledge.

Davis, N. (2009), *Flat Earth News*, London: Vintage.

Day, P. (2000), *Voice and Vision: A History of Broadcasting in New Zealand* (Vol. 2). Auckland: Auckland University Press/Broadcasting History Trust.

Deacon, D. & Golding, P. (1994), *Taxation and Representation: The Media, Political Communication and the Poll Tax*, London: John Libbey & Co. Ltd.

Demers, D. & Merskin, D. (2000), "Corporate News Structure and the Managerial Revolution," *Journal of Media Economics*, 13(2): 103–21.

Dennis, E. (2003), "Prospects for a Big Idea—Is There a Future for Convergence," *The International Journal of Media Management*, 5(1): 7–11.

Department of Commerce (2009), *Survey of Current Business*. Washington, DC: Department of Commerce.

Department of Culture, Media & Sports (DCMS) (2006), *White Paper: A Public Service for All—The BBC in the Digital Age*, London: HMSO. Available at http://webarchive.nationalarchives.gov.uk/+/http://www.bbccharterreview.org.uk/have_your_say/white_paper/bbc_whitepaper_march06.pdf [accessed May 31, 2010].

Desai, M.A. (2009), "The Decentering of the Global Firm," *World Economy*, 32: 1271–90.

Deuze, M. (2007), *Media Work*, Malden, MA: Polity Press.

Devlin, A. (1996), "Michael Mauldin on Lycos." Available at http://www.annonline.com/interviews/960923/ [accessed September 2010].

Dicken, P. (2003), *Global Shift: Reshaping the Global Economic Map in the 21st Century* (5th ed.), London: Sage Publications.

Diebert, R., Palfrey, J., Rohozinski, R., & Zittrain, J. (eds) (2010), *Access Controlled: The Shaping of Power, Rights, and Rule in Cyberspace*, Boston, MA: MIT.

Dimmick, J. (2006), "Media Competition and Levels of Analysis," in A. Albarran, S. Chan-Olmsted, & M. Wirth (eds), *Handbook of Media Management and Economics* (pp. 345–62), Mahwah, NJ: Lawrence Erlbaum Associates.

Dinan, W. & Miller, D. (2007), *Thinker, Faker, Spinner, Spy: Corporate PR and the Assault on Democracy*, London: Pluto.

Dobuzinskis, A. (2010). "Global Movie Box Office Nears $30 Billion in 2009." *TalkTalk*. Available at https://www.talktalk.co.uk/entertainment/news/reuters/2010/03/10/global-movie-box-office-nears-30-billion-in-2009.html [accessed March 24, 2011].

Dobuzinski, A. (2010), "Yahoo News." Available at http://in.news.yahoo.com/137/20100311/371/tbs-global-movie-box-office-nears-30-bil.html [accessed September 2010].

Dore, R. (2000), *Stock Market Capitalism: Welfare Capitalism: Japan and Germany versus the Anglo-Saxons*, Oxford: Oxford University Press.

Dover, B. (2008), *Rupert's Adventures in China: How Murdoch Lost a Fortune and Found a Wife*, Sydney: Viking.

Doyle, G. (2002a), *Media Ownership*, London: Sage Publications.

Doyle, G. (2002b), *Understanding Media Economics*, London: Sage Publications.

Doyle, G. (2006), "Financial News Journalism: A Post-Enron Analysis of Approaches Towards Economic and Financial News Production in the UK," *Journalism: Theory, Practice and Criticism*, 7(4): 433–52.

Doyle, G. & Frith, S. (2004), "Researching Media Management and Media Economics." Paper presented at the 6th World Media Economics Conference—Centre d'études sur les médias and *Journal of Media Economics*, HEC Montréal, Canada, May 12–15.

Doyle, J. (2008), "Stones Gather Dollars: 1989–2008," *Pop History Dig*. Available at http://www.pophistorydig.com/?tag=rolling-stones-steel-wheels-tour [accessed February 28, 2010].

Drinnan, J. (2009), "'Poor' RNZ Cops One from the Privates," *New Zealand Herald*. Available at http://www.nzherald.co.nz/business/news/article.cfm?c_id=3&objectid=10595054&pnum=0 [accessed September 5, 2009].

duGay, P. (1996), *Consumption and Identity at Work*, London: Sage Publications.

Duménil, G. & Lévy, D. (2005), "Costs and Benefits of Neoliberalism: A Class Analysis," in G.A. Epstein (ed.), *Financialization and the World Economy* (pp. 17–45), Northampton, MA: Edward Elgar Publishing.

Dunbar, J. (2008), "Networks of Influence: The Political Power of the Communications Industry," in R.E. Rice (ed.), *Media Ownership* (pp. 243–67), Cresskill, NJ: Hampton Press.

Dunning, J. (2001), *Global Capitalism at Bay?* London: Routledge.

Durham, F. (2007), "Framing the State in Globalization: *The Financial Times'* Coverage of the 1997 Thai Currency Crisis," *Critical Studies in Media Communication*, 24(1): 57–76.

Durkheim. E. (1982), *Rules of Sociological Method*, New York: Free Press.

Dyer-Witheford, N. (1999), *Cyber-Marx*, Chicago, IL: University of Illinois.

Eatwell, J. (1982), "Competition," in I. Bradley & M. Howard (eds), *Classical and Marxian Political Economy: Essays in Memory of Ronald Meek* (pp. 203–28), London: Macmillan.

Edelman, M. (1988), *Constructing the Political Spectacle*, Chicago: University of Chicago Press.

Elliott, L. & Atkinson, D. (2009), *The Gods that Failed: How the Financial Elite Have Gambled Away Our Futures*, London: Vintage.

Elstein, D., Cox, D., Donohue, B., Graham, D., & Metzger, G. (2004), *Beyond the Charter: The BBC after 2006, Report of the Broadcasting Policy Group (for the Conservative Party)*, London: Premium Publishing.

Epstein, E.J. (2010), *The Hollywood Economist*. Brooklyn, NY: Melville House Publishing.

Ericson, R.V., Baranek, P.M., & Chan, J.B.L. (1989), *Negotiating Control*, Toronto: University of Toronto Press.

Ernst, D. & Kim, L.S. (2002), "Global Production Networks, Knowledge Diffusion, and Local Capability Formation," *Research Policy*, 31: 1417–29.

EUMap (2008), *Television Across Europe: Regulations, Policy, & Independence*, Budapest: Open Society Initiative/EU Monitoring Advocacy Program.

European Commission (2009), "History of TVWF—the Television without Frontiers Directive." Available at http://ec.europa.eu/avpolicy/reg/history/historytvwf/index_en.htm [accessed March 30, 2010).

European Commission (2010), *A Digital Agenda for Europe*. Brussels: EC. Available at http://eur-lex.europa.eu/LexUriServ/LexUriServ.do?uri=COM:2010:0245:FIN:EN:PDF [accessed March 26, 2011].

Experien Hitwise Canada (2010), "Main Data Centre: Top 20 Sites & Engines." Available at http://www.hitwise.com/ca/datacenter/main/dashboard-10557.html [accessed September 20, 2010].

Experien Hitwise (2010), "Main Data Centre, Top 20 Social Networking Websites." Available at http://www.hitwise.com/us/datacenter/main/dashboard-10133.html [accessed September 20, 2010].

Facebook (2010), "Privacy Policy." Available at http://www.facebook.com/#!/policy.php [accessed March 28, 2011].

Fairclough, N. (1995), *Critical Discourse Analysis: The Critical Study of Language*, London, New York: Longman.

Fama, E. (1970), "Efficient Capital Markets: A Review of Theory and Empirical Work," *Journal of Finance*, 25(2): 383–417.

Fama, E. (1980), "Agency Problems and the Theory of the Firm," *Journal of Political Economy*, 88(2): 288–307.

Federal Communications Commission (2000), *Report on International Telecommunications Markets*. Washington, DC: FCC. Available at http://hraunfoss.fcc.gov/edocs_public/attachmatch/DA-01-117A1.pdf [accessed March 26, 2011].

Financial Times (2010, October 19), "Osborne Confirms £340m Cut in BBC Spending." Available at http://www.ft.com/cms/s/0/240a1ab8-db4c-11df-ae99-00144feabdc0,s01=1.html#axzz1ETMLvIyI [accessed February 16, 2011].

Fine, J. & Elkin, T. (2002), "AOL Time Warner Does Great Selling Job—to Itself: Media Conglomerate Is Its Own Top Ad Customer." Available at https://adage.com/abstract.php?article_id=34023 [accessed March 4, 2010, requires subscription for full-text access].

Fisk, R. (2009, April 16), "How Can You Trust the Cowardly BBC?" *The Independent*. Available at http://www.independent.co.uk/opinion/commentators/fisk/robert-fisk-how-can-you-trust-the-cowardly-bbc-1669281.html [accessed February 16, 2011].

Fitzgerald, S. (forthcoming), *Corporations and Cultural Industries*, New York: Rowman & Littlefield.

Flew, T. (2006), "The Social Contract and Beyond in Broadcast Media Policy," *Television & New Media*, 7(3): 282–305.

Flew, T. (2007), *Understanding Global Media*, New York: Palgrave Macmillan.

Flew, T. (2011), *The Creative Industries, Culture and Policy*, London: Sage Publications.

Flew, T. & Gilmour, C. (2003), "A Tale of Two Synergies: An Institutional Analysis of the Expansionary Strategies of News Corporation and AOL–Time Warner." Paper presented to Australia and New Zealand Communication Association (ANZCA03): Designing Communication for Diversity, Brisbane, July 9–11. Available at http://eprints.qut.edu.au/195/ [accessed February 27, 2010].

Florida, R. (2002), *The Rise of the Creative Class*, New York: Basic Books.

Fortune (2005, July 25), "World's Largest Corporations," *Fortune*, 152(2): 119–39.

Fortune 500 (2008, May 5), "The Fortune 500 Ranked within Industries," *Fortune*, 157(9): F49–50.

Foster, J.B. (2000), "Monopoly Capital at the Turn of the Millennium," *Monthly Review*, 51(11): 1–17.

Foster, J.B. & Magdoff, F. (2009), *The Great Financial Crisis: Causes and Consequences*. New York: Monthly Review Press.

Foster, J.B. & McChesney, R.W. (2009), "Monopoly-Finance Capital and the Paradox of Accumulation," *Monthly Review*, 61(5): 1–20.

Fox, E. (1990), *Días de Baile: el Fracaso de la Reforma de la Televisión de América Latina*, México DF: FELAFACS-WACC.

Fox, E. & Waisbord, S. (eds) (2002), *Latin Politics, Global Media*, Austin: University of Texas.

FPInformart (2010), *FP Historical Reports (by Company)*, Proprietary Electronic Database, Toronto: Postmedia.

Frean, A. (2010, April 10), "The Miramax Brothers Tell Disney: Let Us Buy It Back," *The Times*, 33.

Freedman, C. (2006, July 4), Interview, Ottawa.

Freedman, D. (2008), *The Politics of Media Policy*, Cambridge: Polity Press.

Freeman, C. & Louca, F. (2001), *As Time Goes By: From Industrial Revolutions to the Information Revolution*, Oxford: Oxford University.

Frieden, R.M. (2008), "Lies, Damn Lies and Statistics: Developing a Clearer Assessment." Available at http://works.bepress.com/robert_frieden/11 [accessed March 26, 2011].

Friedman, J. (2010, May 4), "Twitter, Facebook Soar as Myspace Sags in US Market Share," *The Next Web*. Available at http://thenextweb.com/us/2010/05/04/twitter-facebook-soar-myspace-sags-market-share/ [accessed August 2, 2010].

Friesen, R. (2007), Comments Made during the "Free to a Good Home" Discussion Panel at the New Broadcasting Futures: Out of the Box Conference, Wellington, New Zealand, August 27.

Frobel, F., Heinrichs, J., & Kreye, O. (1980), *The New International Division of Labour*, Cambridge: Cambridge University Press.

Froud, J., Johal, S., Leaver, A., & Williams, K. (2006), *Financialization and Strategy: Narrative and Numbers*, London: Routledge.

Fuchs, C. (2008), *Internet and Society: Social Theory in the Information Age*, New York: Routledge.

Fuchs, C. (2010a), "Alternative Media as Critical Media," *European Journal of Social Theory*, 13(2): 173–92.

Garnham, N. (1990), *Capitalism and Communication: Global Culture and the Economics of Information*, London: Sage Publications.

Garnham, N. (2000), *Emancipation, the Media, and Modernity*, New York: Oxford University Press.

Garnham, N. (2005), "From Cultural to Creative Industries," *International Journal of Cultural Policy*, 11(1): 15–29.

Gavin, N. (2007), *Press and Television in British Politics: Media, Money and Mediated Democracy*, Houndsmill, Basingstoke: Palgrave Macmillan.

General Electric (2009), *Annual Report*. Fairfield, CT: Author. Available at http://www.ge.com/ar2008/pdf/ge_ar_2008.pdf [accessed April 6, 2011].

Gilder, G. (1994), *Life after Television*, New York: W.W. Norton.

Goddard, P., Corner, J., Gavin, N., & Richardson, K. (1998), "Economic News and the Dynamics of Public Understanding," in N. Gavin (ed.), *The Economy, Media and Public Knowledge* (pp. 1–18), Leicester: Leicester University Press.

Golding, T. (2004), *The City: Inside the Great Expectations Machine* (2nd ed.), London: FT/Prentice Hall.

Goldman, E. (2007), "AFP v Google Settles." Available at http://blog.ericgoldman.org/archives/2007/04/afp_v_google_se.htm [accessed September 22, 2010].

Goldsmith, B. & O'Regan, T. (2003), *Cinema Cities, Media Cities: The Contemporary International Studio Complex*, Sydney: Australian Film Commission.

Goldstein, K. (2007), *Measuring Media: Ownership and Diversity*. Revised report prepared for Canwest Mediaworks Inc., submitted to the CRTC's Diversity of Voices hearings.

Goldstein, K. (2009), "Remarks." Paper presented at Ink and Beyond: Conference of the Canadian Newspaper Association, Montréal, QC, May 21.

Goodfriend, M. (2007), "How the World Achieved Consensus on Monetary Policy," *Journal of Economic Perspectives*, 21(4): 47–68.

Goodhart, C. (1988), *The Evolution of Central Banks*, London: The MIT Press.

Google Inc. (2009), "Reply Comments in Response to Broadcasting Notice of Public Hearing CRTC 2008–11." Available at http://support.crtc.gc.ca/applicant/docs.aspx?pn_ph_no=2008-11&call_id=74398&lang=E&defaultName=Google%20Inc.&replyonly=&addtInfo=&addtCmmt=&fnlSub= [accessed September 20, 2010].

Grade, M. (2009), "Speech to the Institute of Economic Affairs." Available at http://www.itvplc.com/media/speeches/michael_grade_speech_to_the_institute_of_economic_affairs/ [accessed April 12, 2010].

Graham, A. (2005), "It's the Ecology, Stupid," in D. Helm, D. Green, M. Oliver, S. Terrington, A. Graham, B. Robinson *et al.* (eds), *Can the Market Deliver? Funding Public Service Television in the Digital Age* (pp. 78–100), Eastleigh: John Libbey.

Gramm, W.S. (1996), "Economic Metaphors: Ideology, Rhetoric, and Theory," in J.S. Mio & A.N. Katz (eds), *Metaphor: Implications and Applications*, Mahwah, NJ: Lawrence Erlbaum Associates Inc.

Grant, P. (2008), "Reinventing the Cultural Tool Kit." Paper presentation at the Canadian Film and Television Production Association "Prime Time in Ottawa" Conference, Ottawa, ON, February 22.

"The Great Telecoms Crash" (2002, July 18), *The Economist*, 364(8282): 9.

Greenwald, B., Knee, J., & Seave, A. (2009, October), "The Moguls New Clothes." *The Atlantic*. Available at http://www.theatlantic.com/magazine/archive/2009/10/the-moguls-8217-new-clothes/7664/ [accessed March 26, 2011].

Grehan, M. (2006), "Google's Matt Cutts: The Big Interview—Parts One and Two." Available at http://www.clickz.com/clickz/column/1714909/googles-matt-cutts-the-big-interview [accessed April 6, 2011].

Grimmelman, J. (2007), "The Structure of Search Engine Law." Available at http://ssrn.com/abstract=979568 [accessed March 26, 2011].

Grossberg, L. (2006), "Does Cultural Studies Have Futures (or What's the Matter with New York?)," *Cultural Studies*, 20(1): 1–32.

Guardian (2010, 29 August), "Michael Grade: BBC Too Big." Comments from "On the Sofa," Edinburgh International Television Festival. Available at http://www.guardian.co.uk/media/2010/aug/29/michael-grade-bbc-too-big [accessed August 29, 2010].

Hallin, D.C. & Mancini, P. (2004), *Comparing Media Systems: Three Models of Media and Politics*, Cambridge: Cambridge University Press.

Handel, J. (2010, April 7), "A New Entertainment Union—and a Possible Name," *The Huffington Post*. Available at http://www.huffingtonpost.com/jonathan-handel/a-new-entertainment-union_b_529136.html [accessed August 12, 2010].

Hardt, M. & Negri, A. (2004), *Multitude*, New York: Penguin.

Hartley, J. (2009), "From the Consciousness Industry to the Creative Industries," in J. Holt & A. Perren (eds), *Media Industries: History, Theory, and Method* (pp. 231–44), Malden, MA: Wiley-Blackwell.

Hayek, F. (1945), "The Use of Knowledge in Society," *American Economic Review*, 35(4): 519–30.

Held, D. (1996), *Models of Democracy*, Cambridge: Polity Press.

Henderson, J., Dicken, P., Hess, M., Coe, N., & Yeung, H.W.C. (2002), "Global Production Networks and the Analysis of Economic Development," *Review of International Political Economy*, 9(3): 436–64.

Henry, D. (2002, October 14), "Mergers and Aggravations: Why Most Big Deals Don't Pay Off," *Business Week*, 60–70.

Herman, E. (1982), "The Institutionalisation of Bias in Economics," 4(3): 275–92.

Herman, E. & McChesney, R.W. (1997), *The Global Media*, London: Cassell.

Hesmondhalgh, D. (2002), *The Cultural Industries*, London: Sage Publications.

Hesmondhalgh, D. (2007), *The Cultural Industries* (2nd ed.), London: Sage Publications.

Hesmondhalgh, D. (2009a), "Politics, Theory and Method in Media Industries Research," in J. Holt & A. Perren (eds), *Media Industries: History, Theory, and Method* (pp. 245–55), Malden, MA: Wiley-Blackwell.

Hesmondhalgh, D. (2009b), "The Digitalization of Music," in A.C. Pratt & P. Jeffcutt (eds), *Creativity, Innovation and the Cultural Economy* (pp. 57–73), London: Routledge.

Hewlett, S. (2010, October 25), "CSR Deal Has Serious Implications for BBC's Independence," *Guardian.co.uk Organgrinder Blog*. Available at http://www.guardian.co.uk/media/organgrinder/2010/oct/25/csr-bbc-independence-steve-hewlett [accessed February 16, 2011].

High, J. (2001), "Split Personality: A Brief History of Competition in Economic Theory," in J. High (ed.), *Competition* (pp. xiii–xlv), Cheltenham, UK: Edward Elgar.

Hill, L. (2004), Can Media Artists Survive Media Consolidation? *The Journal of the Caucus of Television Producers, Writers and Directors*, XXII: 17–21.

Hill, S. (1990), "Britain: The Dominant Ideology Thesis after a Decade," in A. Abercrombie, S. Hill, & B. Turner (eds), *Dominant Ideologies* (pp. 1–37), London: Unwin Hyman Ltd.

Hindess, B. (1989), *Political Choice and Social Structure—An Analysis of Actors, Interests, and Rationality*, Cheltenham: Edward Elgar.

Hofkirchner, W. (2008), "How to Achieve a Unified Theory of Information," in J. Díaz Nafría & F. Salto Alemany (eds), *Qué es Información?, Actas al Primer Encuentro Internacional de Expertos en Teorías de la Información, Un Enfoque Interdisciplinar* (pp. 503–21), Léon: Universidad de León.

Hogan, M. (1977), *Informal Entente*, London: University of Missouri.

Holmwood, L. (2009a, June 30), "Ofcom Chief Exec Hits Back at BBC Director General's Top-Slicing Claims," *Guardian*. Available at http://www.guardian.co.uk/media/2009/jun/30/ofcom-bbc-thompson-richards [accessed April 12, 2010].

Holmwood, L. (2009b, June 30), "ITV Chief Casts Doubt on News Partnership with BBC," *Guardian*. Available at http://www.guardian.co.uk/media/2009/jun/30/grade-doubts-itv-bbc-tieup [accessed April 12, 2010].

Holson, L. & Sorkin, A.R. (2004, February 17), "Disney Board Rejects Bid from Comcast as Too Low," *The New York Times*. Available at http://query.nytimes.com/gst/fullpage.html?res=9F04E1DA143DF934A25751C0A9629C8B63 [accessed April 12, 2011].

Holt, J. & Perren, A. (eds) (2009), *Media Industries: History, Theory, and Method*, Malden, MA: Wiley-Blackwell.

Hope, W. (2010), "Time, Communication, and Financial Collapse," *International Journal of Communication*, 4: 649–69.

Horwitz, R. (2005), "On Media Concentration and the Diversity Question," *The Information Society*, 21: 181–204.

Hoskins, C., McFayden, S., & Finn, A. (2004), *Media Economics: Applying Economics to New and Traditional Media*, London: Sage Publications.

Hoynes, W. (2003), "Branding Public Service: The 'New PBS' and the Privatization of Public Television," *Television & New Media*, 4(2): 117–30.

Huang, J.S. & Heider, D. (2008), "Media Convergence: A Case Study of a Cable News Station," *The International Journal on Media Management*, 9(3): 105–15.

Human Capital/BBC (2004), *Measuring the Value of the BBC—A Report by the BBC and Human Capital*, London: BBC.

Hutton, W. (1996), *The State We're In*, London: Vintage.

IBISWorld (2009), *Global Wireless Telecommunications Carriers*, IBIS World Industry Report I5111-GL, Los Angeles, CA: IBISWorld.

IBISWorld (2010a), *Global Advertising*, IBIS World Industry Report. L6731-GL, Los Angeles, CA: IBISWorld.

IBISWorld (2010b), *Global Music Production and Distribution*, IBIS World Industry Report Q8712-GL, Los Angeles, CA: IBISWorld.

IDATE (2009), *DigiWorld Yearbook 2009*, Montpellier, France: IDATE.

IMF (2008), Available at http://www.imf.org [accessed March 26, 2011].

Impey, B. (2003), "Commentary from 'New Zealand Broadcasters Respond and Floor Discussion'," Paper presented at the A New Future for Public Broadcasting Conference, Wellington, November 20–21. Available at http://www.newfuture.govt.nz/index.html [accessed December 10, 2004].

Impey, B. (2006, November 15), Quoted comments in "Repeats Star in TVNZ's New Look," *NZ Herald*, p. A1.

International Federation of Phonographic Industries (IFPI) (2010), "Digital Music Report." Available at http://www.ifpi.org/content/library/DMR2010.pdf [accessed March 26, 2011].

International Telecommunications Union (ITU) (2010), *World Telecommunication/ICT Development Report 2010*, Geneva, Switzerland: ITU.

International Telecommunications Union/United Nations Centre for Trade and Development (ITU/UNCTAD) (2007), *World Information Society Report: Beyond WSIS*, Geneva, Switzerland: ITU.

Internet Advertising Bureau (2009), *Internet Advertising Revenue Report, 2008*, New York: PriceWaterhouseCooper. Available at http://www.iab.net/media/file/IAB_PwC_2008_full_year.pdf [accessed October, 2010].

Internet Advertising Bureau Canada (2009), "2009 Actual & 2010 Estimated Canadian Online Advertising Revenue Survey." Available at http://www.iabcanada.com/wp-content/uploads/2010/11/IABCda_2009Act2010Budg_CdnOnlineAdRev080910_Eng.pdf [accessed April 6, 2011].

Internet World Stats (2010), "International Usage Statistics: The Internet Big Picture." Available at http://internetworldstats.com/stats.htm [accessed March 26, 2011].

Investment Management Association (IMA) (2007), *Survey of Members*, London: IMA.

Iosifidis, P. (2007), "Public Television in Small European Countries: Challenges and Strategies," *International Journal of Media and Cultural Politics*, 3(1): 65–87.

Ip, B. (2008), "Technological, Content, and Market Convergence in the Games Industry," *Games and Culture*, 3(2): 199–224.

Jakubowicz, K. (2006), "Public Service Broadcasting: The Beginning of the End or a New Beginning in the 21st Century?" Paper presentation at the RIPE 2006 conference on Public Service Broadcasting in the Multimedia Environment: Programmes and Platforms. Available at http://yle.fi/ripe/Keynotes/Jakubowicz_KeynotePaper.pdf [accessed March 24, 2010].

Jenkins, H. (2006a), *Convergence Culture: Where Old and New Media Collide*, New York: New York University Press.

Jenkins, H. (2006b), *Fans, Bloggers, and Gamers*, New York: New York University.

Jenson, K. (1987), "News as Ideology: Economic Statistics and Political Ritual in Television Network News," *Journal of Communication Studies*, 37(4): 8–27.

Jesson, B. (1999), *Only Their Purpose Is Mad—The Money Men Take Over New Zealand*, Palmerston North: Dunmore Press.

Jessop, B. (2008), *State Power*, Malden, MA: Polity.

Jin, D.Y. (2007), "Transformation of the World Television System under Neoliberal Globalization, 1983–2003," *Television and New Media*, 8(3): 179–96.

Jin, D.Y. (2008), "Neoliberal Restructuring of the Global Communication System: Mergers and Acquisitions," *Media, Culture & Society*, 30(3): 357–73.

Jones, N. (1987), *The Media and Industrial Relations: The Changing Relationship*, Warwick Papers in Industrial Relations, No. 18, Warwick University.

Jubak, J. (2002, October 16), "Mergers and Acquisitions Made in the 1990s because of Supposed Synergies Are Beginning to Fall Apart in This Decade," CNBC Show: Business Center, CNBC News Transcripts.

Kantola, A. (2006), "On the Dark Side of Democracy: The Global Imaginary of Financial Journalism," in B. Cammaerts & N. Carpentier (eds), *Reclaiming the Media: Communication, Rights and Democratic Media Roles* (pp. 192–216), Bristol: Intellect.

Kantola, A. (2009), "The Disciplined Imaginary: The Nation Rejuvenated for the Global Condition," in A. Roosvall & I. Salovaara-Moring (eds), *Communicating the Nation* (pp. 230–51), Stockholm: Nordicom.

Keane, M. (2006), "Once Were Peripheral: Creating Media Capacity in East Asia," *Media, Culture & Society*, 28(6): 833–55.

Kelsey, J. (1993), *Rolling Back the State: Privatisation of Power in Aotearoa/New Zealand*, Wellington: Bridget Williams Books.

Keynes, J. (1936), *The General Theory of Employment, Interest and Money*, London: Macmillan.

Kindleberger, C. (2000), *Manias, Panics and Crashes* (4th ed.), New York: John Wiley and Sons Ltd.

Kiss, J. (2008), "Times Online and the Case of the Site Link Spammer." Available at http://www.guardian.co.uk/media/pda/2008/jan/31/timesonlineandthecaseoft [accessed September 22, 2010].

Kjaer, P. (2010), "Expansion and Autonomy: The Rise of the Business Press," in L. Chouliaraki & M. Morsing (eds), *Media, Organisation and Identity* (pp. 70–89), Houndsmill, Basingstoke: Palgrave Macmillan.

Klemming, L. & Sondag, J. (2008, May 22), "Time Warner Spinning Off Cable Unit; Push by Investors; Media Giant to Get $9. 25B Dividends." *Bloomberg News*.

Knorr-Cetina, K. & Bruegger, U. (2002), "Global Microstructures: The Virtual Societies of Financial Markets," *American Journal of Sociology*, 107(4): 905–50.

Koller, V. (2004), *Metaphor and Gender in Business Media Discourse: A Critical Cognitive Study*, New York: Palgrave MacMillan.

KPMG/MCH (2007), *Radio New Zealand: Baseline Review*, New Zealand: NZ Ministry for Culture & Heritage, November.

Krugman, P. (2008), *The Return of Depression Economics and the Crisis of 2008*, London: Penguin Books.

Lacroix, J.G. & Tremblay, G. (1997), "The 'Information Society' and Cultural Industries Theory," *Current Sociology*, 45(4): 1–162.

Laidler, D.E.W. & Robson, W.B.P. (2004), *Two Percent Solution: Canadian Monetary Policy Since 1991*, Toronto: C.D. Howe Institute.

Lash, S. & Urry, J. (1994), *Economies of Signs and Space*, London: Sage Publications.

Latour, B. (2005), *Reassembling the Social: An Introduction to Actor-Network-Theory*, New York: Oxford.

Lazar, D. (1990), *Markets and Ideology in the City of London*, Basingstoke: Macmillan.

Lealand, G. (2008), "Broadcasting and Public Policy in New Zealand," in D. Ward (ed.), *Television and Public Policy: Change and Continuity in an Era of Global Liberalization* (pp. 149–61), New York: Lawrence Erlbaum Associates.

Lessig, L. (1999), *Code and Other Laws of Cyberspace*, New York: Basic Books.

Lessig, L. (2000), "Foreword to Symposium on Cyberspace and Privacy," *Stanford Law Review*, 52(5): 987–1003.

Lessig, L. (2004), *The Future of Ideas*, New York: Random House.

Lewis, J. (2001), *Constructing Public Opinion*, New York: Columbia University Press.

Liberty Media (2008), "Company Overview-History." Available at http://replay. waybackmachine.org/20090210180915/http://libertymedia.com/overview/history. htm [accessed April 6, 2011].

Littlefield, H.M. (1964), "The Wizard of Oz: Parable on Populism," *American Quarterly*, 16(1): 47–58.

London Stock Exchange (1996), *Report on the Committee on Private Share Ownership*, London: LSE.

Los Angeles County Economic Development Corporation (LAEDC) (2010), *Entertainment & the Media in Los Angeles*, Los Angeles: LAEDC.

Lukács, G. (1971), *History and Class Consciousness: Studies in Marxist Dialectics*, Cambridge, MA: MIT Press.

MacDonald, A. (2010), Down the Rabbit Hole: "The Madness of State Film Incentives as a 'Solution' to Runaway Production." Working Paper. Available at http://works. bepress.com/adrian_mcdonald/ [accessed July 31, 2010].

Macpherson, C.B. (1973), *Democratic Theory*, Oxford: Oxford University.

Madrick, J. (2001), *The Business Media and the New Economy*, Cambridge, MA: Joan Shorenstein Center.

Magarrey, P. (2006, October 10), "The Little Paper that Shrank," *Ryerson Review of Journalism*. Available at http://journalism.ryerson.ca/m4045/ [accessed September 20, 2010].

"Magic Restored" (2008, April 17), *The Economist*, 387(8576): 73–4.

Maich, S. (2005, May 16), "Better Off Without You," *Maclean's*, 118(20): 33.

Mansell, R. (2010), "Power, Interest and the Knowledge Economy." Paper presented at the International Association of Media and Communication Researchers Conference, Braga, Portugal, July 18–22.

Marcuse, H. (1964), *One-Dimensional Man: Studies in the Ideology of Advanced Industrial Society*, Boston: Beacon.

Markusen, A., Gilmore, S., Johnson, A., Levi, T., & Martinez, A. (2006), *Crossover: How Artists Build Careers across Commercial, Nonprofit and Community Work*, Minneapolis, MN: Project on Regional and Industrial Economics, University of Minnesota.

Marotte, B. (2000, November 25), "Videotron CEO Resigns Post," *The Globe and Mail*, p. B3.

Marron, M.B., Sarabia-Panol, Z., Sison, M.D., Rao, S., & Niekamp, R. (2010), "The Scorecard on Reporting of the Global Financial Crisis," *Journalism Studies*, 11(2): 27–83.

Marx, K. (1867), *Capital: Volume I*, London: Penguin.

Marx, K. & Engels, F. (1846/1970), *The German Ideology*, New York: International Publishers.

Mastrini, G. & Becerra, M. (2001), "Cincuenta años de concentración de medios en América Latina: del patriarcado artesanal a la valorización en escala," in F. Quirós & F. Sierra (eds), *Crítica de la Economía Política de la Comunicación y la Cultura* (pp. 179–208), Sevilla: Comunicación Social.

Mastrini, G. & Becerra, M. (2006), *Periodistas y Magnates. Estructura y Concentración de las Industrias Culturales en América Latina*, Buenos Aires: Prometeo.

McChesney, R.W. (1998), "The Political Economy of Global Communication," in R.W. McChesney, E.M. Wood, & J.B. Foster (eds), *Capitalism and the Information Age* (pp. 1–26), New York: Monthly Review Press.

McChesney, R.W. (1999), *Rich Media, Poor Democracy*, Urbana, IL: University of Illinois Press.

McChesney, R.W. (2000), "The Political Economy of Communication and the Future of the Field," *Media, Culture & Society*, 22(1): 109–16.

McChesney, R.W. (2001), "Global Media, Neoliberalism, and Imperialism," *Monthly Review*, 52(10): 1–19.

McChesney, R.W. (2004), *The Problem of the Media*, New York: Monthly Review Press.

McChesney, R.W. (2008), *The Political Economy of Media: Enduring Issues, Emerging Dilemmas*, New York: Monthly Review Press.

McChesney, R.W. & Nichols, J. (2010), *The Death and Life of American Journalism*. Philadelphia, PA: Nation Books.

McChesney, R.W. & Schiller, D. (2003), *The Political Economy of International Communications: Foundations for the Emerging Global Debate about Media Ownership and Regulation*, United Nations Research Institute for Social Development, Technology, Business and Society, Programme Paper No. 11, Geneva, Switzerland: UNRISD.

McClintock, P. (2005, May 2), "Clear Channel Doing the Splits," *Daily Variety*, p. 1.

McDonald, P. & Wasko, J. (eds) (2008), *The Contemporary Hollywood Film Industry*, Oxford: Blackwell.

McFadden, D. (1997), "Antitrust and Communications: Changes after the Telecommunications Act of 1996," *Federal Communications Law Journal*, 49(2): 457–72.

McKercher, C. & Mosco, V. (eds) (2008), *Knowledge Workers in the Information Society*, Lanham, MD: Lexington Books.

McNulty, P. (1967), "A Note on the History of Perfect Competition," *Journal of Political Economy*, 75(4): 395–9.

McQueen, T. (2003), "Dramatic Choices: A Report on Canadian English-Language Drama." Available at http://www.crtc.gc.ca/eng/publications/reports/drama/drama2.pdf [accessed September 20, 2010].

McRobbie, A. (2002), "Clubs to Companies: Notes on the Decline of Political Culture in Speeded Up Creative Worlds," *Cultural Studies*, 16(4): 516–31.

Media 7 (2009, March18), "Broadcasting Funding Debate," *TVNZ* 7.

"Media Companies' High Spirits" (2010, February 27), *The Economist*, 8671: 67.

Meisel, J.B. & Sullivan, T.S. (2000), "Portals: The New Media Companies," *Info—The Journal of Policy, Regulation and Strategy for Telecommunications*, 2(5): 477–86.

Melody, W. (1987), "Information: An Emerging Dimension of Institutional Analysis," *Journal of Economic Issues*, 21(3): 1313–39.

Melody, W. (2007a), "Cultivating Knowledge for Knowledge Societies at the Intersections of Economic and Cultural Analysis," *International Journal of Communication*, 1: 70–8.

Melody, W. (2007b), "Can Short-Term Cash Flow 'Investor Value' Incentives Satisfy Long-Term Diversified Public Policy Objectives?" Paper presented at the Columbia Institute for Tele-Information (CITI) Conference "Private Equity Acquisitions in Media and Telecom," Columbia University, New York, September 28.

Menger, P. (1999), "Artistic Labor Markets and Careers," *Annual Review of Sociology*, 25: 541–74.

Merrill Lynch (2004), *Global Fund Manager Survey*, London: Merrill Lynch.

Microsoft (2009), "Press Release: Microsoft Opens Windows to African Language Speakers," Available at http://dev.absol.co.za/publisher_crn/pebble. asp?relid=5683&t=45 [accessed April 6, 2011].

Middleton, C. & Givens, J. (2010), "Open Access Broadband Networks in Australia, Canada, New Zealand and Singapore." Paper presented at the Telecommunications Policy Research Conference, Arlington, VA, October 1–3.

Miège, B. (1989), *The Capitalization of Cultural Production*, New York: International General.

Miège, B. (2000), *Les Industries du Contenu face à l'ordre Informationnel* [Content Industries in the Information Order], Grenoble: Presses Universitaires de Grenoble.

Miège, B. (2007a), *La société Conquise par la Communication: les Tic entre Innovation Technique et Ancrage Social* [Society Conquered by Communications: The Positioning of ICTs between Technological Innovation and Social Roots], Grenoble: Presses Universitaires de Grenoble.

Miège, B. (2007b), "Nouvelles Considérations et Propositions Méthodologiques sur les Mutations en cours dans les Industries Culturelles et Informationnelles" [New Considerations and Methodological Concerns Regarding Current Mutations in the Cultural and Informational Industries], in P. Bouquillion & Y. Combès (eds), *Les Industries de la Culture et de la Communication en Mutation* (pp. 228–50), Paris: L'Harmattan.

Miège, B. (2011a), "The Cultural Industry Theory: Reconsiderations, Persistent Specificities and Adapting Modalities to Contemporary Issues," in J. Wasko, G. Murdock, & H. Sousa (eds), *Blackwell Handbook of Political Economy of Communication*, Malden, MA: Blackwell.

Miège, B. (2011b), "Les Mutations en cours des Industries Culturelles et Informationnelles (Suite)" [Current Mutations in the Cultural and Informational Industries (Revised)], in P. Bouquillion & Y. Combès (eds), *La Diversité culturelle*, Paris: L'Harmattan.

Miguel de Bustos, J.C. (1993), *Los Grupos Multimedia: Estructuras y Strategias en los Medios Europeos*, Barcelona: Bosch.

Milberg, W. & Winkler, D. (2010), Financialisation and the Dynamics of Off-Shoring in the USA, *Cambridge Journal of Economics*, 34(2): 275–93.

Mill, J.S. (1859), *On Liberty*, Boston: St. Martin.

Miller, P.H. (2007), "An Overview of the Canadian Program Rights Market, 2007." Available at http://www.crtc.gc.ca/eng/publications/reports/miller07.htm#n97b [accessed September 20, 2010].

Miller, T. (2009), "Television Is Finished, Television Is Done, Television Is Over." Inaugural Attallah Lecture, Carleton University School of Journalism and Communication and the Communication Graduate Caucus, Ottawa, Canada, March 18.

Miller, T., Govil, N., McMurria, J., & Maxwell, R. (2001), *Global Hollywood*, London: British Film Institute.

Miller, T., Govil, N., McMurria, J., Wang, T., & Maxwell, R. (2005), *Global Hollywood II*, London: British Film Institute.

Milton, J. (1644), *Areopagitica, and, of education*, Oxford: Clarendon Press.

Ministry for Culture and Heritage (MCH) (2002), "Ministerial Briefings 2002—Arts Culture and Leisure." Appendix VI: TVNZ.

Mitchell, W. (2008), *Full Employment Abandoned: Shifting Sands and Policy Failures*, Cheltenham, UK: Edward Elgar.

Moe, H. (2008), "Public Service Media Online? Regulating Public Broadcasters' Internet Services—A Comparative Analysis," *Television & New Media*, 9(3): 220–38.

Moran, A. & Keane, M.A. (2006), "Cultural Power in International TV Format Markets," *Continuum: Journal of Media & Cultural Studies*, 20(1): 71–86.

MORI (1997), *Captains of Industry Polls*, London: MORI.

Mosco, V. (1996), *The Political Economy of Communication: Rethinking and Renewal*, London: Sage Publications.

Mosco, V. (2004), *The Digital Sublime: Myth, Power, and Cyberspace*, Cambridge, MA: MIT Press.

Mosco, V. (2009a), *The Political Economy of Communication* (2nd ed.), London: Sage Publications.

Mosco, V. (2009b), "Working Knowledge: Why Labour Matters for Information Studies," *Canadian Journal of Information & Library Sciences*, 33(3/4): 193–214.

Motion Picture Association of America (MPAA) (2010), "Theatrical Market Statistics 2009." Available at http://www.mpaa.org/Resources/091af5d6-faf7-4f58-9a8e-405466c1c5e5.pdf [accessed March 29, 2011].

Mueller, M. (1999), "Digital Convergence and Its Consequences," *Javnost—the Public*, 6(3): 11–28.

Murdoch, J. (2009), "The Absence of Trust." The 2009 MacTaggart Lecture, Edinburgh International Television Festival, August 28. Available at http://image.guardian.co.uk/sys-files/Media/documents/2009/08/28/JamesMurdochMacTaggartLecture.pdf [accessed October 15, 2009].

Murdock, G. (1990), "Redrawing the Map of the Communications Industries: Concentration and Ownership in the Era of Privatization," in M. Ferguson (ed.), *Public Communication: The New Imperatives*, London: Sage Publications.

Murdock, G. (1993), "Communications and the Constitution of Modernity," *Media, Culture & Society*, 15(4): 521–39.

Murdock, G. (2006), "Notes from the Number One Country: Herbert Schiller on Culture, Commerce, and American Power," *International Journal of Cultural Policy*, 12(2): 209–27.

Murdock, G. & Golding, P. (2005), "Culture, Communications and Political Economy," in J. Curran & M. Gurevitch (eds), *Mass Media and Society* (pp. 60–83, 4th ed.), London: Hodder Education.

Murray, S. (2005), "Brand Loyalties: Rethinking Content within Global Corporate Media," *Media, Culture & Society*, 27(3): 415–35.

Nakashima, R. & Liedtke, M. (2010, August 11), "Netflix Boosts Library with Hollywood Deal," *The Globe and Mail*, p. B10.

Napoli, P. (1999), "Deconstructing the Diversity Principle," *Journal of Communication*, 49(4): 7–34.

Naspers (2010), "Annual Report." Available at http://www.naspers.com/downloads/ar/2010/naspers_ar2010.pdf [accessed March 24, 2011].

Neff, G., Wissinger, E., & Zukin, S. (2005), "Entrepreneurial Labor among Cultural Producers: 'Cool' Jobs in 'Hot' Industries," *Social Semiotics*, 15(3): 307–34.

Negroponte, N. (1995), *Being Digital*, New York: Knopf.

Newman, K. (1984), *Financial Marketing and Communications*, London: Holt, Rinehart and Winston.

"Newspaper Group Call to Block BBC iPhone Apps" (2010), http://news.bbc.co.uk/2/hi/technology/8522441.stm [accessed April 6, 2011].

Nichols, J. & McChesney, R.W. (2009, March 18), "The Death and Life of Great American Newspapers," *The Nation*. Available at http://www.thenation.com/article/death-and-life-great-american-newspapers [accessed September 20, 2010].

Niles, R. (2010), "Student Journalists Need to Learn SEO More Than They Need AP Style. Available at http://www.ojr.org/ojr/people/robert/201004/1843/ [accessed September 22, 2010].

Noam, E. (2001), *Interconnecting the Network of Networks*, Cambridge, MA: MIT Press.

Noam, E. (2006), "How to Measure Media Concentration," Available at http://www.ft.com/cms/s/2/da30bf5e-fa9d-11d8-9a71-00000e2511c8.html#axzz1HxsVb4c5 [accessed March 29, 2011].

Noam, E. (2008), "Are the American Media Becoming More Concentrated?," in R.E. Rice (ed.), *Media Ownership: Research and Regulation* (pp. 145–58), Cresskill, NJ: Hampton Press.

Noam, E. (2009), *Media Ownership and Concentration in America*, Oxford: Oxford University Press.

Noll, M. (2003), "The Myth of Convergence," *The International Journal of Media Management*, 5(1): 12–13.

Nordicity (2007), "Study of Broadband Exhibition of Television Programming in Canada and the U.S." Available at http://www.nordicity.com/reports/BNPH%20 2007-10%20-%20Nordicity%20Report%20for%20BEX.ppt [accessed September 20, 2010].

NZ On Air (1990), *NZ On Air Annual Report 1989–90*, Auckland: NZ On Air.

NZ On Air (2009), "NZ On Air Annual Report 2009." Available at http://www.nzonair.govt.nz/media/37891/ar%2008-09.pdf [accessed March 12, 2010].

NZ On Air (2010), "The Platinum Television Fund." Available at http://www.nzonair.govt.nz/media/45998/platinum%20fund%20criteria%202010-2011.pdf [accessed March 12, 2010].

OECD (Organisation for Economic Co-operation and Development) (2007a), "Participative Web: User-Created Content." Available at http://www.oecd.org/dataoecd/57/14/38393115.pdf [accessed March 29, 2011].

OECD (2007b), *OECD Communications Outlook 2007*, Paris: OECD.

OECD (2008), "OECD Information Technology Outlook 2008." Available at http://puck.sourceoecd.org/vl=14775418/cl=35/nw=1/rpsv/ij/oecdthemes/99980134/v2008n16/s1/p1l [accessed March 29, 2011].

OECD (2009), *OECD Communications Outlook 2009*, Paris: OECD.

OECD (2010), "The Evolution of News and the Internet." Available at http://www.oecd.org/dataoecd/30/24/45559596.pdf [accessed March 29, 2011].

Ofcom (2009), *The Communications Market Report 2009*, London: Ofcom. Available at http://stakeholders.ofcom.org.uk/binaries/research/cmr/cmr09.pdf [accessed March 29, 2011].

Ofcom (2010), *The Communications Market Report 2010*, London: Ofcom. Available at http://stakeholders.ofcom.org.uk/binaries/research/cmr/753567/CMR_2010_FINAL.pdf [accessed March 29, 2011].

Office of the Minister of Broadcasting (2006), "Digital Television: TVNZ Digital Services Proposal." Digital Television Cabinet Paper #5. Available at http://www.mch.govt.nz/publications/digital-tv/Digital%20Television%20TVNZ%20Digital%20Telvision%20Services%20Proposal.pdf [accessed February 2, 2007].

Olsen, S. (2001, June 7), "Ballmer: Would Not Launch MSNBC Again." *CNET News*. Available at http://news.cnet.com/Ballmer-Would-not-launch-MSNBC-again/2100-1023_3-268073.html [accessed September 20, 2010].

O'Reilly, T. (2005), "Web 2.0: Compact Definition." Available at http://radar.oreilly.com/archives/2005/10/web_20_compact_definition.html [accessed September 15, 2009].

Palley, T. (2007), *Financialization: What It Is and Why It Matters*, Political Economy Research Institute Working Paper 153, Amherst, MA: University of Massachusetts Amherst.

Papandrea, F. (2010), "Australia Search Engines, 2001–2010." Data prepared for the International Media Concentration Research Project, Columbia University Institute for Tele-Information. Available at http://internationalmedia.pbworks.com/ [accessed October 2010].

Parsons, W. (1989), *The Power of the Financial Press: Journalism and Economic Opinion in Britain and America*, London: Edward Elgar.

Pateman, C. (1970), *Participation and Democratic Theory*, Cambridge: Cambridge University.

Paterson, C. (2005), "News Agency Dominance in International News on the Internet," in D. Skinner, J. Compton, & M. Gasher (eds), *Converging Media, Diverging Politics: A Political Economy of News in the United States and Canada* (pp. 145–64), Lanham, MD: Rowman & Littlefield.

Pauwels, C. & Loisen, J. (2003), "The WTO and the Audiovisual Sector: Economic Free Trade vs. Cultural Horse Trading," *European Journal of Communication*, 18(3): 281–313.

Pearce, M. (2000), "Perspectives of Australian Broadcasting Policy," *Continuum: Journal of Media & Cultural Studies*, 14(3): 367–82.

Perrons, D. (2003), "The New Economy and Work-Life Balance: Conceptual Explorations and a Case Study of New Media," *Gender, Work & Organization*, 10(1): 65–93.

Peters, J.D. (2004), "The 'Marketplace of Ideas': A History of the Concept," in A. Calabrese & C. Sparks (eds), *Toward a Political Economy of Culture* (pp. 65–82), Boulder, CO: Rowman & Littlefield.

Philips, K. (2006), *American Theocracy: The Peril and Politics of Radical Religion, Oil and Borrowed Money in the 21st Century*, New York: Penguin.

Phillips, K. (2009), *Bad Money: Reckless Finance, Failed Politics, and the Global Crisis of American Capitalism*, New York: Penguin.

Philo, G. (ed.) (1995), *Glasgow Media Group Reader, Vol. 2: Industry, Economy, War and Politics*, London: Routledge.

Picard, R. (1989), *Media Economics*, Thousand Oaks: Sage Publications.

Picard, R. (2002), *The Economics and Financing of Media Companies*, New York: Fordham University Press.

Picard, R. (2009), "Tremors, Structural Damage and Some Casualties, but No Cataclysm," Paper presented to the U.S. Federal Trade Commission workshop "From Town Crier to Bloggers: How Will Journalism Survive the Internet Age?" Washington, DC, December 1–2.

Pigeon, M.-A. (2008), "Conflict, Consensus, Convention: The Depoliticization of Canada's Macroeconomic Discourse," School of Journalism and Communication, Carleton University, October.

Polanyi, K. (1944/1957), *The Great Transformation*, Boston: Beacon.

Pool, I. (1990), *Technologies without Boundaries*, Boston, MA: Harvard University.

Porter, M. (1980), *Competitive Strategy*, New York: Free Press.

Possebon, S. (2007), "O mercado Das Comunicacoes—Um Retrato Ate 2006," in M. Ramos & S. dos Santos (eds), *Políticas de Comunicacao*, San Pablo: Paulus.

Potts, J. & Cunningham, S. (2008), "Four Models of the Creative Industries," *International Journal of Cultural Policy*, 14(3): 233–47.

Pratt, A.C. (2009), "The Creative and Cultural Economy and the Recession," *Geoforum*, 40(1): 495–6.

Pratt, A.C. & Jeffcutt, J. (eds) (2009), *Creativity, Innovation and the Cultural Economy*, London: Routledge.

Pratten, C. (1993), "The Stock Market," Occasional Paper 59, Cambridge: Cambridge University Press.

PriceWaterhouseCooper (PWC) (2008), *Global Media and Entertainment Outlook*, New York: PWC.

PriceWaterhouseCoopers (PWC) (2000–2010), *Global Entertainment and Media Outlook, 2010–14*, New York: PWC.

Project for Excellence in Journalism (PEJ) (2009), "The State of the News Media, 2009." Available at http://www.stateofthenewsmedia.org/2009/ [accessed March 29, 2011].

Project for Excellence in Journalism (PEJ) (2010), "The State of the News Media, 2010." Available at http://www.stateofthenewsmedia.org/2010/ [accessed March 29, 2011].

Quantcast (2010), "Quantcast US Site Ranking." Available at http:\\www.quantcast.com [accessed July 1, 2010].

Quantcast (2011), "Quantcast Web Usage Statistics February 3, 2011." Available at http://www.quantcast.com [accessed February 3, 2011].

Québec Commission des Relations du Travail (2008), "Décision: Syndicat canadien de la fonction publique, section locale 2808 (employés de bureau), et Syndicat canadien de la fonction publique, section locale 1450 (journalistes, photographes, statisticiens et préposés aux archives-transmissions du Journal de Québec), v. Le Journal de Québec, une division de Corporation Sun Média, et Dominic Salgado, Frédéric Perreault, Bernard Plante, Geneviève Riel-Roberge, Marc-André Boivin, Charles Bolduc, Mathieu Bruckmuller, Yann Perron, Geneviève Larivière, Jancimon Reid, Reine-May Crescence, Hubert Lapointe, Dominique Lavoie, Mélanie Tremblay, Antoine Leclair, Pierre Gauthier et Nathalie Bissonnette." Available at http://www.crt.gouv.qc.ca/decisions/2008/2008QCCRT0534.pdf [accessed September 20, 2010].

Quebecor Inc (2009, January 24), "*Journal de Montréal* Locks Out Employees." Available at http://www.marketwire.com/press-release/Journal-de-Montreal-Locks-Out-Employees-941279.htm [accessed September 20, 2010].

Rampton, S. & Stauber, J. (2002), *Trust Us, We're Experts: How Industry Manipulates Science and Gambles Away Your Future*, Los Angeles: Jeremy P. Tarcher.

Rantisi, N. (2004), "The Designer in the City and the City in the Designer," in D. Power & A. Scott (eds), *Cultural Industries and the Production of Culture* (pp. 91–109), New York: Routledge.

Raphael, C. (1997), "Political Economy of Reali-TV," *Jump Cut: A Review of Contemporary Media*, 41: 102–9.

Reilly, F. & Brown, K. (2000), *Investment Analysis and Portfolio Management* (6th ed.), Fort Worth, TX: Dryden Press.

Rice, R.E. (ed.) (2008), *Media Ownership: Research and Regulation*, Cresskill, NJ: Hampton Press.

Rugman, A. & Brewer, T. (eds) (2003), *The Oxford Handbook of International Business*, Oxford: Oxford University Press.

Samuelson, P. (2010), "Google Book Search Settlement as Copyright Reform." Paper presented at the Telecommunications Policy Research Conference, Arlington, VA, October 1–3.

Sanders, M. (1991), "Setting the Standards on the Road to Oz," *The Numismatist*, July, pp. 1042–50.

Sandoval, G. (2010a, September 29), "Fight for Senate Anti-Piracy Bill Rages." Available at http://news.cnet.com/8301-31001_3-20018091-261.html?tag=nl.e703 [accessed March 29, 2011].

Sandoval, G. (2010b, June 29), "Netflix Delights Studios with Big Checks." Available at http://news.cnet.com/8301-31001_3-20012024-261.html [accessed March 29, 2011].

Sandoval, M. & Fuchs, C. (2009), "Towards a Critical Theory of Alternative Media," *Telematics and Informatics*, 27(2): 141–50.

Sassen, S. (2005), "The Embeddedness of Electronic Markets: The Case of the Global Capital Markets," in K. Knorr-Cetina & A. Preda (eds), *The Sociology of Financial Markets* (pp. 17–37), Oxford: Oxford University Press.

Sayer, A. (2001), "For a Critical Cultural Political Economy," *Antipode*, 33(4): 687–708.

Schatz, T. (2008), "The Studio System and Conglomerate Hollywood," in P. McDonald & J. Wasko (eds), *The Contemporary Hollywood Film Industry* (pp. 13–42), Oxford: Blackwell Publishing.

Scherer, E. (2010), "Context Is King." *AFP-MediaWatch*, 7: 4–14. Available at http://mediawatch.afp.com/public/AFP-MediaWatch_Automne-Hiver-2009-2010.pdf [accessed March 29, 2011].

Schiller, D. (1996), *Theorizing Communication: A History*, New York: Oxford University Press.

Schiller, D. (1999a), *Digital Capitalism: Networking the Global Market System*, Cambridge, MA: The MIT Press.

Schiller, D. (1999b), Deep Impact: The Web and the Changing Media Economy, *Info—The Journal of Policy, Regulation and Strategy for Telecommunications*, 1(1): 35–51.

Schiller, D. (2007), *How to Think about Information*, Urbana: University of Illinois Press.

Schultz, J. (1994), "Media Convergence and the Fourth Estate," in J. Schultz (ed.), *Not Just Another Business: Journalists, Citizens and the Media* (pp. 15–34), Sydney: Pluto Press.

Schumpeter, J.A. (1943/1996), *Capitalism, Socialism, and Democracy*, London: Routledge.

Schumpeter, J.A. (1950), *Capitalism, Socialism and Democracy* (3rd ed.), New York: Harper.

Schwartz, B. (2009), "Hitwise: Facebook (Sort of) More Visited than Google on Christmas." Available at http://searchengineland.com/hitwise-facebook-more-visited-than-google-on-christmas-32554 [accessed March 29, 2011].

Scott, A. (2004), "The Other Hollywood: The Organizational and Geographic Bases of Television-Program Production," *Media, Culture & Society*, 26(2): 183–205.

Screen Actors Guild (2006), "Entertainment Industry Groups Testify at FCC Hearing." Available at http://www.sag.org/content/entertainment-industry-groups-testify-at-fcc-public-hearing [accessed March 29, 2011].

Screen Actors Guild (2007), "Casting Data Report, 2007–8." Available at http://www.sag.org/files/sag/documents/2007-2008_CastingDataReports.pdf [accessed March 29, 2011].

Sherman, J. (2006, January 9), "CBS Corp. in the Fish Bowl; Industry Watching for How Net Evolves." *Television Week*, p. 17.

Shiffman, D. (2008), *The Age of Engage*, Ladera Ranch, CA: Hunt Street.

Shiller, R. (1989), *Market Volatility*, Cambridge, MA: MIT Press.

Shiller, R. (2001), *Irrational Exuberance*, New Jersey: Princeton University Press.

Shirky, C. (2003), "Power Laws, Weblogs, and Inequality." Available at http://www.shirky.com/writings/powerlaw_weblog.html [accessed March 29, 2011].

Shirky, C. (2008), *Here Comes Everybody*, London: Penguin.

Sinclair, J. (1999), *Latin American Television*, New York: Oxford.

Singh, J.P. (2002), "Information Technologies and the Changing Scope of Global Power and Governance," in J.N. Rosenau & J.P. Singh (eds.), *Information Technologies and Global Politics: The Changing Scope of Power and Governance* (pp. 1–38), Albany: State University of New York Press.

Sky TV (2010), "New Channel to Launch on Sky," Media Release, March 5. Available at http://www.skytv.co.nz/Default.aspx?tabid=202&art_id=31346 [accessed March 5, 2010].

Smith, P. & Steemers, J. (2007), "BBC to the Rescue! Digital Switchover and the Reinvention of Public Service Broadcasting in Britain," *Javnost—the Public*, 14(1): 39–56.

Smithers, A. & Wright, A. (2000), *Valuing Wall Street: Protecting Wealth in Turbulent Markets*, New York: McGraw Hill.

Smythe, D.W. (1981/2006), "On the Audience Commodity and Its Work," in M.G. Durham & D.M. Kellner (eds), *Media and Cultural Studies* (pp. 230–56), Malden, MA: Blackwell.

Soderberg, S., Menz, G., & Cerny, G. (eds) (2005), *Internalizing Globalization: The Rise of Neo-Liberalism and the Decline of National Varieties of Capitalism*, Houndsmill, Basingstoke: Palgrave Macmillan.

Soderlund, W.C. & Hildebrandt, K. (2005), *Canadian Newspaper Ownership in the Era of Convergence: Rediscovering Social Responsibility*, Edmonton, AB: University of Alberta Press.

Soroka, S.N. (2002), *Agenda-Setting Dynamics in Canada*, Vancouver: University of British Columbia Press.

Soros, G. (1994), *The Alchemy of Finance: Reading the Mind of the Market* (2nd ed.), London: John Wiley and Sons.

Standard & Poor's (2010), *Global Industry Surveys, Media: Europe*, New York: Standard & Poor's.

Starkman, D. (2009, May 1), "Power Problem," *Columbia Journalism Review*, pp. 24–30.

Starr, P. (2009, March 4), "Goodbye to the Age of Newspapers (Hello to a New Era of Corruption)," *The New Republic*. Available at http://www.tnr.com/article/goodbye-the-age-newspapers-hello-new-era-corruption?page=0,4 [accessed March 29, 2011].

Statistics Canada (2001), *The Assets and Debts of Canadians: An Overview of the Results of the Survey of Financial Security*, Ottawa, ON: Statistics Canada.

Statistics Canada (2006a), *2006 Census*, Ottawa, ON: Statistics Canada.

Statistics Canada (2006b), *Average Household Expenditures, 2006*, Ottawa, ON: Statistics Canada.

Statistics Canada (2006c), *Average Market Income by Economic Family Types, 2001–2005*, Ottawa, ON: Statistics Canada.

Statistics Canada (2007), *Television Broadcasting Industry, by North American Industry Classification System (NAICS), Annual (Dollars unless Otherwise Noted)*. CANSIM, Table 357-0001, Ottawa, ON: Statistics Canada. Available at http://cansim2.statcan.gc.ca/cgi-win/cnsmcgi.exe?Lang=E&RootDir=CII/& ResultTemplate=CII/CII___&Array_Pick=1&ArrayId=3570001 [accessed March 29, 2011].

Statistics Canada (2008), *Dwelling Characteristics and Household Equipment by Income Quintile for Canada, 2008*. Cat. No. 62F0042XDB, Ottawa, ON: Statistics Canada. Available at http://www.statcan.gc.ca/bsolc/olc-cel/olc-cel?lang=eng&catno=62F0042X [accessed March 29, 2011].

Statistics Canada (2009), "Spending Patterns in Canada, 2008." Available at http://www.statcan.gc.ca/pub/62-202-x/62-202-x2007000-eng.htm [accessed September 20, 2010].

Statistics Canada (2010a), *Financial and Taxation Statistics for Enterprises, 2008*. Cat. No. 61-219-X, Ottawa, ON: Statistics Canada. Available at http://www.statcan.gc.ca/pub/61-219-x/61-219-x2008000-eng.pdf [accessed September 20, 2010].

Statistics Canada (2010b), *Capital and Repair Expenditures: Industry Sector 51, Information and Cultural Industries, Annual (Dollars) (Broadcasting and Telecommunications) (2001–2009)*, CANSIM, Table 029-0013. Ottawa, ON: Statistics Canada. Available at http://cansim2.statcan.gc.ca/cgi-win/cnsmcgi.exe?Lang=E&RootDir=CII/&ResultTemplate=CII/CII___&Array_Pick=1&ArrayId=0290013 [accessed September 20, 2010].

Statistics Canada (2010c), *Capital and Repair Expenditures on Construction and Machinery and Equipment, by Industry, Canada, Actual Data, Annual (Dollars) (Broadcasting and Telephone (1984–1993)*. CANSIM, Table 029-0033. Ottawa, ON: Statistics Canada. Available at http://cansim2.statcan.gc.ca/cgi-win/cnsmcgi.exe?Lang=E&RootDir=CII/&ResultTemplate=CII/CII___&Array_Pick=1&ArrayId=0290033 [accessed September 20, 2010].

Steger, M. (2003), *Globalization: A Very Short Introduction*, Oxford: Oxford University Press.

Steger, M. (2009), *Globalization: A Very Short Introduction* (2nd ed.), Oxford: Oxford University Press.

Storper, M. (1993), "Flexible Specialisation in Hollywood: A Response to Aksoy and Robins," *Cambridge Journal of Economics*, 17(4): 479–84.

Storper, M. (1997), *The Regional World*, London: Guildford.

Storper, M. (2000), "Geography and Knowledge Flows: An Industrial Geographer's Perspective," in J. Dunning (ed.), *Regions, Globalization and the Knowledge-Based Economy* (pp. 42–62), Oxford: Oxford University Press.

Storper, M. & Christopherson, S. (1984), "Flexible Specialization and Regional Agglomerations: The Case of the U.S. Motion Picture Industry," *Annals of the Association of American Geographers*, 77(1): 104–17.

Strange, S. (1986), *Casino Capitalism*, Oxford: Blackwell.

Strange, S. (1998), *Mad Money: When Markets Outgrow Governments*, Ann Arbor: University of Michigan Press.

Straubhaar, J. (2008), *World Television: From Global to Local*, Los Angeles: Sage Publications.

Sunstein, C.R. (2007), *Republic.Com 2.0*, Princeton, NJ: Princeton University Press.

Swedberg, R. (2005), "The Economic Sociology of Capitalism," in V. Nee & R. Swedberg (eds), *The Economic Sociology of Capitalism* (pp. 3–40), Princeton, NJ: Princeton University.

Sweezy, P.M. (1968), *The Theory of Capitalist Development*, New York: Monthly Review Press.

Synovate/MCH (2007), "'New Zealanders' Perceptions of the Importance and Contribution of Public Broadcasting," Research report prepared for the Ministry for Culture and Heritage, June. Available at http://www.cultureandheritage.govt.nz/publications/PublicBroadcastingOutcomesResearchReport22Aug07.pdf [accessed February 12, 2008].

Syvertsen, T. (2003), "Challenges to Public Television in the Era of Convergence and Commercialisation, *Television & New Media*, 4(2): 155–75.

Tambini, D. (2010), "What Are Financial Journalists For?" *Journalism Studies*, 11(2): 158–74.

Tapscott, D. & Williams, A.D. (2006), *Wikinomics: How Mass Collaboration Changes Everything*, London: Penguin.

Tartakoff, J. (2010), "The (Short) History of Twitter's Plans to Make Money." Available at http://www.guardian.co.uk/media/pda/2010/mar/29/twitter-making-money [accessed March 29, 2011].

Teather, D. (2005, March 18), "Analysis: Viacom Signals the End of the Road for Media Juggernauts," *Guardian*, p. 23.

Teer-Tomaselli, R., Wasserman, H., & de Beer, A.S. (2007), South Africa as a Regional Media Power, in D.K. Thussu (ed.), *Media on the Move: Global Flow and Contra-Flow* (pp. 153–64), London: Routledge.

Terranova, T. (2004), *Network Culture: Politics for the Information Age*, London: Pluto.

Tett, G. (2009), *Fools Gold: How Unrestrained Greed Corrupted a Dream, Shattered Global Markets and Unleashed a Catastrophe*, London: Free Press.

Thelwall, M. & Hasler, L. (2006), "Blog Search Engines," *Online Information Review*, 31(4): 467–79.

Thierer, A. (2005), *Media Myths: Making Sense of the Debate Over Media Ownership*, Washington DC: Progress & Freedom foundation.

Thierer, A. & Eskelsen, G. (2008), *Media Metrics: The True State of the Modern Media Marketplace*, Washington, DC: The Progress and Freedom Foundation. Available at http://www.pff.org/mediametrics [accessed March 29, 2011].

Thompson, P.A. (2000), "A Road to Nowhere?—Broadcasting and the 'third way' in New Zealand," *Communication Journal of New Zealand*, 1(1): 20–58.

Thompson, P.A. (2004), "Unto God or Unto Caesar? Television after the TVNZ Charter," *Communication Journal of New Zealand*, 5(2): 60–91.

Thompson, P.A. (2005), "Mechanisms for Setting Broadcasting Funding Levels in OECD Countries." Report commissioned by Te Manatu Taonga/New Zealand Ministry for Culture and Heritage. Available at http://www.mch.govt.nz/publications/broadcast-funding/MCH-OECD-Funding-Report.pdf [accessed September 2010].

Thompson, P.A. (2007), "From the Digital Sublime to the Ridiculous? TVNZ's New Digital Services and the Future of Public Television in New Zealand," *Communication Journal of New Zealand: (Special Edition on Broadcasting Histories, Digital Futures)*, 8(1): 43–62.

Thompson, P.A. (2009), "Move Along Folks—Nothing to See Here: How National's Broadcasting Policy Cover-Up Favours Sky," Foreign Control Watchdog #121, August, CAFCA. Available at http://www.converge.org.nz/watchdog/21/04.htm [accessed March 29, 2011].

Thompson, P.A. (2010a), "Amending What Doesn't Need a-Fixing? Who Picks up the Tab for the Government's TVNZ Bill?" *Take #58. The SDGNZ film and television quarterly*, Autumn, 9–10.

Thompson, M. (2010b), "MacTaggart Lecture, 2010, Edinburgh International Television Festival." *Guardian*, August, 27. Available at http://www.guardian.co.uk/media/2010/aug/27/mark-thompson-mactaggart-full-text [accessed August 27, 2010].

Thomson Financial (2009), *Custom Analysis of Mergers and Acquisitions in Telecommunications, Media and Entertainment Sectors in Canada, 1984-2008*, Toronto: Author.

Throsby, D. (2001), *Economics and Culture*, Cambridge: Cambridge University Press.

Throsby, D. (2008), "Modelling the Cultural Industries," *International Journal of Cultural Policy*, 14(3): 217–32.

Thussu, D.K. (2006), *International Communication: Change and Continuity* (2nd ed.), London: Arnold.

Thussu, D.K. (2007), "The 'Murdochization' of News? The Case of Star TV in India," *Media, Culture & Society*, 29(4): 593–611.

The Times (2003, September 19), "Time Warner Drops AOL," p. B27.

Time Warner (2009), *Annual Report*. New York: Time Warner. Available at http://phx. corporate-ir.net/External.File?item=UGFyZW50SUQ9MzkxNTR8Q2hpbGRJRD0 tMXxUeXBlPTM=&t=1 [accessed March 29, 2011].

Time Warner Cable (2008, May 21), "Time Warner and Time Warner Cable agree to separation," Press release.

Tinic, S. (2005), *On Location: Canada's Television Industry in a Global Market*, Toronto: University of Toronto Press.

Toffler, A. (1980), *The Third Wave*, New York: Bantam.

Tomlinson, J. (2007), "Cultural Globalization," in G. Ritzer (ed.), *The Blackwell Companion to Globalization* (pp. 352–66), Malden, MA: Blackwell.

Tönnies, F. (1988), *Community & Society*, New Brunswick, NJ: Transaction Books.

Toughill, K. (2009, March 19), "CTV: Operating Profits and Job Losses." *The Canadian Journalism Project (J-Source.ca)*. Available at http://www.j-source.ca/ english_new/detail.php?id=3533 [accessed September 20, 2010].

Transport Canada (2003), *Restrictions on Foreign Ownership in Canada—TP 14500E*, Ottawa, ON: Transport Canada.

Trejo Delarbre, R. (2010), "Muchos Medios en Pocas Manos: Concentración Televisiva y Democracia en América Latina," *Intercom, Revista Brasileira de Ciencias da Comunicacao*, 33(1):17–51.

Tumber, H. (1993), "'Selling Scandal': Business and the Media," *Media, Culture & Society*, 15(3): 345–61.

Tunstall, J. (1996), *Newspaper Power: The National Press in Britain*, Oxford: Oxford University Press.

Tunstall, J. (2008), *The Media Were American: U.S. Mass Media in Decline*, Oxford: Oxford University Press.

Turner, G. (2008), *The Credit Crunch: Housing Bubbles, Globalisation and the Worldwide Economic Crisis*, London: Pluto Press.

TVNZ (2003), "The TVNZ Charter." Available at http://www.tvnz.co.nz/tvnz_ detail/0,2406,111535-244-257,00.html [accessed June 6, 2003].

United Kingdom (2010), *Digital Economy Act 2010, c.24*, London: UK Statute Law Database. Available at http://www.statutelaw.gov.uk/content. aspx?activeTextDocId=3699621 [accessed March 29, 2011].

United Kingdom, House of Lords, Select Committee on Communications (2008), *The Ownership of the News*, Vol. 1, London: Stationary Office. Available at http://www.publications.parliament.uk/pa/ld200708/ldselect/ldcomuni/122/122i. pdf [accessed March 29, 2011].

United Nations Centre for Trade and Development (2009). *The Global Economic Crisis: Systemic Failures and Multilateral Remedies, UNCTAD/GDS/2009/1*, New York/Geneva: United Nations Conference on Trade and Development.

United States, Bureau of Labor Statistics (2002, 2006, 2008), *Quarterly Census of Employment Wages*, Washington, DC: BLS. Available at http://www.bls.gov/cew/ [accessed March 29, 2011].

United States, Department of Commerce, Bureau of the Census (2002), *Non-Employer Statistics*, Washington, DC: DOC. Available at http://www.census.gov/econ/ nonemployer/index.html [accessed March 29, 2011].

United States, Department of Commerce, Bureau of the Census (2006), *Non-Employer Statistics*, Washington, DC: DOC. Available at http://www.census.gov/econ/ nonemployer/index.html [accessed March 29, 2011].

"Update 1—Big US Newspaper Publisher Exits Bankruptcy" (2010, March 19), *Reuters*. Available at http://reuters.com/assets/print?aid=USN1917418020100319 [accessed March 29, 2011].

Ursell, G. (2000), "Television Production: Issues of Exploitation, Commodification and Subjectivity in UK Television Labor Markets," *Media, Culture & Society*, 22(6): 805–25.

Ursell, G. (2003), "Creating Value and Valuing Creation in Contemporary UK Television: Or 'Dumbing Down' the Workforce," *Journalism Studies*, 4(1): 31–46.

Vaidhyanathan, S. (2004), *The Anarchist in the Library*, New York: Basic.

Van Couvering, E. (2008), "The History of the Internet Search Engine: Navigational Media and the Traffic Commodity," in A. Spink & M. Zimmer (eds), *Web Search: Multidisciplinary Perspectives* (pp. 177–206), Berlin: Springer.

Van Cuilenburg, J. & McQuail, D. (2003), "Media Policy Paradigm Shifts—Towards a New Communications Policy Paradigm," *European Journal of Communication*, 18(2): 181–207.

Van den Bulck, H. (2008), "Can PSB Stake Its Claim in a Media World of Digital Convergence?—The Case of the Flemish PSB Management Contract Renewal from an International Perspective," *Convergence: The International Journal of Research into New Media Technologies*, 14(3): 335–49.

Van der Wurff, R. & Van Cuilenburg, J. (2001), "Impact of Moderate and Ruinous Competition on Diversity: The Dutch Television Market," *Journal of Media Economics*, 14(4): 213–29.

Venturelli, S. (2005), "Culture and the Creative Economy in the Information Age," in J. Hartley (ed.), *Creative Industries* (pp. 391–8), Oxford: Blackwell.

Verrier, R. (2010), "L.A. County's Entertainment Sector Posts Big Losses in 2009," *Los Angeles Times*. Available at http://latimesblogs.latimes.com/ entertainmentnewsbuzz/2010/01 [accessed February 20, 2010].

Viacom (2008), "About Viacom." Available at http://www.viacom.com/aboutviacom/ Pages/default.aspx [accessed March 29, 2011].

Viacom International, et al. v. YouTube, Inc., YouTube LLC, and Google, Inc. (2010). United States District Court, Southern District of New York. Available at http:// graphics8.nytimes.com/packages/pdf/business/20100623-google-decision.pdf [accessed March 29, 2011].

Vivanco Martínez, Á. (2007), "Concentración de Medios en las Sociedades Democráticas: ¿peligro Para la Libertad de Expresión o Condición de Subsistencia?" en *Diálogo político3*, Buenos Aires: Fundación Konrad Adenauer.

Warner, W.B. (2008), "Networking and Broadcasting in Crisis: Or How Do We Own Computable Culture?" in R.E. Rice (ed.), *Media Ownership: Research and Regulation* (pp. 77–102). Cresskill, NJ: Hampton Press.

Wasko, J. (2001), *Understanding Disney*, Cambridge: Polity Press.

Wasko, J. (2004a), Show Me the Money: Challenging Hollywood Economics, in A. Calabrese & C. Sparks (eds), *Toward a Political Economy of Culture* (pp. 131–50), Boulder, CO: Rowman & Littlefield.

Wasko, J. (2004b), *How Hollywood Works*, London: Sage Publications.

Waterman, D. (2000), "CBS-Viacom and the Effects of Media Mergers: An Economic Perspective," *Federal Communication Law Journal*, 52(3): 531–50.

Watkins, M. (2008) "Strange Bedfellows at BCE: Ontario Teachers and U.S. Private Equity Funds," in M. Moll & L.R. Shade (eds), *For $ale to the Highest Bidder: Telecom Policy in Canada* (pp. 55–60), Ottawa: Canadian Centre for Policy Alternatives.

Weber, M. (1968), *Economy and Society: An Outline of Interpretive Sociology*, New York: Bedminster.

Wee, G. (2007a, December 28), "New CEO May Dismantle Time Warner; AOL, Magazine and Cable Units Could Be Sold," *Financial Post*, p. F11.

Wee, G. (2007b, October 16), "Time to Cut 2,000 Jobs at AOL: Turns Focus to Ads," *Financial Post*, p. F16.

White, J. (2008), "Keeping Canadian Culture: Why Canadians Need Self-Determination of Our Telecom Industry," in M. Moll & L.R. Shade (eds), *For $ale to the Highest Bidder: Telecom Policy in Canada* (pp. 37–54). Ottawa: Canadian Centre for Policy Alternatives.

Wigley, B. (2008) *London: Winning in a Changing World*, London: Merrill Lynch Europe Ltd.

Wikipedia (2010), "Wikipedia: About." Available at http://en.wikipedia.org/wiki/Wikipedia:About [accessed March 29, 2011].

Williams, G. (2007), "From Isolation to Consensus: The UK's Role in the Revision Process of the Television without Frontiers Directive," *Westminster Papers in Communication and Culture*, 4(3): 26–45.

Winkler, B. (2002), "Which Kind of Transparency? On the Need for Effective Communication in Monetary Policy-Making," *IFO-Studien*, 48(3): 401–27.

Winseck, D. (2008), "The State of Media Ownership and Media Markets: Competition or Concentration and Why Should We Care?" *Sociology Compass*, 2(1): 34–47.

Winseck, D. & Pike, R. (2007), *Communication and Empire: Media, Markets, and Globalization, 1860–1930*, Durham, NC: Duke University Press.

Wirtz, B.W. (2001). "Reconfiguration of Value Chains in Converging Media and Communications Markets," *Long Range Planning*, 34(4): 489–506.

Wray, R. (1998), *Understanding Modern Money*, Northampton, MA: Edward Elgar Publishing.

Wyatt. E. (2009, July 26), "Television Fledgling Keeps It Real," *The New York Times*. Section: Arts & Leisure, pp. 1, 7.

Yoo, C. (2008), "Network Neutrality, Consumers, and Innovation," *University of Chicago Legal Forum*, 25: 179–262.

Zallo, R. (1992), *El Mercado de la Cultura: Estructura Económica y Política de la Comunicación*, Donostia: Gakoa.

Zamaria, C. & Fletcher, F. (2008), *Canada Online! Internet, Media and Emerging Technologies: Uses, Attitudes, Trends and International Comparisons, Year Two Report, 2007*, Toronto, ON: Canadian Internet Project. Available at http://www.ciponline.ca/en/docs/2008/CIP07_CANADA_ONLINE-REPORT-FINAL%20.pdf [accessed September 20, 2010].

ZenithOptimedia (2010), *Advertising Expenditure Forecasts July 2010*, London: ZenithOptimedia.

Zimmer, M. (2008), "The Externalities of Search 2.0: The Emerging Privacy Threats When the Drive for the Perfect Search Engine Meets Web 2.0," *First Monday*, 13(3).

Žižek, S. (1994), *Mapping Ideology*, London: Verso.

Zook, M.A. (2005), *The Geography of the Internet Industry*, Oxford: Blackwell.

Zorn, D., Dobbin, F., Dierkes, J., & Kwok, M. (2005), "Managing Investors: How Financial Markets Reshaped the American Firm," in K. Knorr-Cetina & A. Preda, (eds), *The Sociology of Financial Markets* (pp. 269–89), Oxford: Oxford University Press.

Index